Only at Comic-Con

Only at Comic-Con

· ·

Hollywood, Fans, and the Limits of Exclusivity

ERIN HANNA

Rutgers University Press

New Brunswick, Camden, and Newark, New Jersey, and London

Library of Congress Cataloging-in-Publication Data

Names: Hanna, Erin, 1980– author.
Title: Only at Comic-Con : Hollywood, fans, and the limits of exclusivity /
    Erin Hanna.
Description: New Brunswick : Rutgers University Press, 2019. | Includes
    bibliographical references and index.
Identifiers: LCCN 2019009182 | ISBN 9780813594712 (cloth : alk. paper) |
    ISBN 9780813594705 (pbk. : alk. paper)
Subjects: LCSH: San Diego Comic-Con. | Comic book fans. | Comic books,
    strips, etc.—Marketing. | Motion pictures and comic books. | Fandom—United States. |
    Popular culture—United States.
Classification: LCC PN6714 .H36 2019 | DDC 741.5/973—dc23
LC record available at https://lccn.loc.gov/2019009182

A British Cataloging-in-Publication record for this book is available from the British Library.

♾ The paper used in this publication meets the requirements of the American National
Standard for Information Sciences—Permanence of Paper for Printed Library Materials,
ANSI Z39.48-1992.

www.rutgersuniversitypress.org

Manufactured in the United States of America

For the family I lost, the family I found,
and the family who has always been there

Contents

Only at Comic-Con

Introduction

●●●●●●●●●●●●●●●●●●●●●●

The San Diego Comic-Con
and the Limits of Exclusivity

> Nerds have never been more important
> for Hollywood.
> —Marc Graser, *Variety*, 2008

In December 2017, a federal jury ruled in favor of the San Diego Comic-Con in a trademark infringement suit against Dan Farr Productions, organizers of the Salt Lake Comic Con.[1] Both the plaintiff and the defendant were large comic conventions claiming to bring a broad cross section of popular culture fans together with promotion and professional guests from the media industries.[2] At the heart of this legal battle, which began in 2014, were the words "comic con," and who was allowed to claim them. San Diego Comic Convention, the nonprofit corporation that runs the San Diego Comic-Con (Comic-Con for short), had been using the phrase since its first convention in 1970, and in 2005, the organization trademarked the hyphenated "Comic-Con," along with their logo (which included the words "comic con" without a hyphen).[3] In its 2014 filing, San Diego Comic Convention asserted its ownership of the name Comic-Con, along with other non-hyphenated iterations of the phrase, arguing that because of its "extensive

1

and continuous" use of these marks in the promotion of its event and brand, they had become "valuable assets" that were "representative of the quality events and services" that the San Diego Comic-Con provided and symbolic of the convention's "goodwill and positive industry reputation."[4] But the defendants and organizers of the Salt Lake Comic Con, Dan Farr and Bryan Brandenburg, argued that although the capitalized, hyphenated "Comic-Con" may be the property of the San Diego Comic-Con, the non-hyphenated phrase "comic con" was a generic term that had long been used to describe fan conventions around the country and should be fair game.[5]

Their argument was a compelling one. Though the history of the San Diego Comic-Con dates back to 1970, when the event attracted 300 attendees and was known as San Diego's Golden State Comic-Con, the first convention to use some iteration of "comic con" in its title was 1964's New York Comicon.[6] Following that event, a handful of regional comic book conventions in the 1960s also used the phrase prior to the founding of the San Diego Comic-Con.[7] Not only that, but the usage of the word "con" to describe fan conventions dates back even earlier, to at least 1940, when the Chicago Science Fiction Convention went by the name Chicon.[8] The judge deemed this evidence insufficient, and the jury was only allowed to hear about the San Diego Comic-Con's use of the term dating back to its founding in 1970.[9] So in making their case, the defendants instead presented evidence of over a hundred other conventions in the United States—such as the New York Comic Con, Amazing Arizona Comic Con, Tampa Bay Comic Con, and Seattle's Emerald City Comic Con—all of which used "comic con" in their name.[10] They also highlighted a slew of media coverage that used the phrase "comic con" as a more generic reference to these and other conventions around the country.[11] And yet the San Diego Comic-Con was still able to convince the jury that the phrase "comic con" belonged to them, even if they had not vigorously enforced their trademark in the past. In addition to their nearly fifty-year history using the term, they cited a survey in which 80 percent of consumers identified Comic-Con as a brand name associated with the San Diego convention, rather than a generic category of fan events.[12] They were also able to dig up some damning emails in which one of the Salt Lake organizers, Bryan Brandenburg, referenced "hijacking the Comic-Con brand."[13] Despite this last bit of evidence to the contrary, the jury found that Brandenburg and Farr had not intentionally infringed on San Diego Comic Convention and awarded the organization twenty thousand dollars, just a tiny fraction of the twelve million dollars in damages it had originally requested. In August 2018, the plaintiff won a more decisive victory in the case when, after a series of appeals, the judge issued a permanent injunction preventing the Salt Lake convention from using any version of the Comic-Con trademark and ordered that the defendants pay four million dollars in legal fees to San Diego Comic Convention.[14] In upholding the Comic-Con trademark, these rulings set the stage for licensing agreements between the San Diego Comic-Con and other conventions around the country (as was the case with Portland's Rose City Comic Con) and, most likely, continued legal battles.[15] They also provided evidence of something I frequently explain when talking about my research: Comic-Con is not the same as "comic con." And this is a book about Comic-Con.[16]

I decided to open *Only at Comic-Con* with this court case for two reasons. First, because it captures some of the (understandable) confusion surrounding Comic-Con's place in what has become, in recent years, an increasingly crowded field of popular culture conventions. In 2016, the *Wall Street Journal* published an article called "The Rise of the Cons," which commented on an explosion of fan conventions catering to a wide array of tastes—from fitness buffs to beer drinkers. "In an effort to capitalize on recent growth," the article read, "international event-planning firms have been buying up mom-and-pop cons, starting new events and diving into unexplored markets. ShowClix, a platform for live-event organizers, tallied 519 major pop-culture fan gatherings in the U.S. last year, up from 469 in 2014," and "comic cons" were reported to be "the beating heart of this empire."[17] The increased visibility of comic conventions—in cities and towns around the country and in articles like this one—means that while many people are familiar with these events, or even the San Diego Comic-Con, in particular, there is often a great deal of confusion about where one ends and the other begins. For example, one year, as I was traveling from Portland to San Diego, an airport shuttle bus driver told me that he had been attending "Comic-Con" since the early 1990s but stopped going because it had gotten too big. Though he clearly had years of experience as a fan and convention-goer, in describing his experiences at "Comic-Con," he cited at least three different conventions, none of which were located in San Diego or affiliated with the San Diego Comic-Con in any way. This conflation of Comic-Con with "comic cons" even happens in coverage of the event. For example, in 2017, I excitedly dug into a *Rolling Stone* article about the founding of the San Diego Comic-Con only to discover that the author had incorrectly identified the New York Comic Con, which is run by the global media events firm, ReedPop, as one of Comic-Con's numerous "outposts."[18] While, as Rob Salkowitz notes, "the idea that a term in common use like 'comic con' can be trademarked and controlled by a single large organization does not sit well in a culture where fans consider themselves co-owners of content and brands that cater to their interests," Comic-Con's concern that their brand is being diluted or confused with unaffiliated conventions is not completely unfounded.[19]

Salkowitz's observations about the conflict between the corporate and cultural ownership of a term like "comic con" is indicative of the contradictions arising under what Henry Jenkins calls "convergence culture," where consumers participate alongside industries in the production and circulation of culture.[20] While this labor might yield a kind of affective ownership or sense of a communal popular culture, the underlying structures of institutional power, as this book argues, remain largely unchanged. Depending on how the term circulates and who uses it, "comic con" can feel like it belongs to everyone, despite a push to make it the legal property of a single organization. For this reason, the Comic-Con lawsuit also provides an entry point to a concept that is central to this book: exclusivity. The term "comic con" the defense argued, was a generic one, but Comic-Con organizers, in defending their trademark, seemed to suggest that the popularity of their event was at least partly responsible for popularity of the term. They had made Comic-Con a viable brand, one that they now owned. So as the term grew increasingly popular—and profitable—so did its value as an exclusive trademark. When you think about it, the idea that something can become more exclusive even as it becomes increasingly generic, seems a bit contradictory. But this contradiction is indicative of how exclusivity functions as a cultural construct that relies on the power to produce, enforce, or negotiate limits. This same contradiction is evident in discourses about fans, Comic-Con, and Hollywood, where popularity, mainstreaming, and growth somehow manage to simultaneously inflate and dilute the event's exclusivity. Hollywood, this book argues, engages with audiences through a system of exchange built upon both the construction of exclusivity and its subsequent undoing: Media fans are said to constitute an exclusive audience of influencers, but *everyone* is (or should be) a fan of something; the content presented at Comic-Con is exclusive, but stories about it are meant to be shared widely. *Only at Comic-Con* makes sense of these contradictions by thinking about the material and ideological boundaries that I call the limits of exclusivity. The remainder of this introduction follows these two threads, providing further context surrounding Comic-Con as an object of study by situating it in a landscape of fan conventions that has exploded in recent years and elaborating on the limits of exclusivity, a theory that grows out of Comic-Con's place at the intersections of fandom and the media industries. Similarly, this book draws on both fan and media industries research to interrogate industry power and fan labor at the San Diego Comic-Con.

Why Comic-Con?

When I first attended Comic-Con in 2009, I was a graduate student at the University of Michigan embarking on the first research trip of my career. I took the trip because I wanted to witness what I had been hearing about for several years: the massive proliferation of Hollywood promotion at the convention. At the time, I knew I wanted to do research that examined media industries and fans, but when I boarded the plane to San Diego, I did not know that I would devote so many years of my life to thinking about Comic-Con. On the last day of the convention, I walked up an outdoor staircase to the second floor of the San Diego Convention Center to snap a picture of the crowds (figure I.1). As I watched people flowing in and out of the convention center, I thought about all the celebrities, previews, give-aways, and other exclusive promotions I had encountered over four days at the convention. I traveled to Los Angeles for the first time during this same research trip, but the San Diego Comic-Con brought me closer to Hollywood than I had ever felt in my life. In that moment, I realized that the answers to so many of my questions about how the ever increasing discourses about the power and influence of fan culture could possibly square with the economic and cultural heft of an industry like Hollywood were right there, only at Comic-Con.

The research for this book draws on a combination of participant-observation, discourse analysis, and historiography. In researching this book, I attended the San Diego Comic-Con seven times over a period of ten years; analyzed decades of popular and trade discourse about the event; traveled to the San Diego History Center and Michigan State University archives to examine old programs, documents, and letters; and amassed my own archive of Comic-Con and comic convention ephemera dating back to the mid-1960s. I drew on research in critical political economy, media industry studies, fan studies, and comic studies. Together, these methods and

FIGURE I.1 San Diego Comic-Con, 2009. (Photo by the author.)

theories provided me with the tools I needed to tell a story about Comic-Con that helps to explain not only the event but also its historical context and cultural impact. And yet, painting a complete picture of the San Diego Comic-Con experience is still complicated. As a pop culture convention that is covered extensively in the press, many have at least heard of it. Some may have seen references to Comic-Con on shows like *The Big Bang Theory* (CBS, 2007–2019) or *Entourage* (HBO, 2004–2011); followed Conan O'Brien's annual pilgrimage for his TBS talk show, *Conan* (2010–); watched coverage on cable channels like SyFy, HBO, and AMC; or seen highlights and interviews with celebrities on shows like *Entertainment Tonight* (CBS, 1981–), *Access Hollywood* (NBC, 1996–), *Good Morning America* (ABC, 1975–), or *The Today Show* (NBC, 1952–). Others may have read about Comic-Con in industry trades like *Variety* and the *Hollywood Reporter*; stumbled upon articles in the *New York Times*, *Los Angeles Times*, the *Washington Post*; or even read about Comic-Con in the pages of their local paper. Many more will have seen content about the convention online—on entertainment news sites, corporate websites, and, of course, on social media.

Despite this wide-ranging media coverage, scholarly examinations of the San Diego Comic-Con are few and far between. Most frequently, Comic-Con is invoked in comic, fan, and media industries scholarship to provide context for broader cultural and historical phenomena.[21] Other scholars, such as Anne Gilbert and Lincoln Geraghty, have provided more sustained analyses of the convention in the context of fan/producer relationships and the affective significance of consumption and collecting, respectively.[22] Finally, Ben Bolling and Matthew J. Smith's *It Happens at Comic-Con* (2014), collects essays written by former students of Smith's Comic-Con Field Study Program, providing evidence of the array of ethnographic research opportunities that Comic-Con affords.[23] Outside of cinema and media studies, Rob Salkowitz's *Comic-Con and the Business of Popular Culture* (2012) uses the convention as an entry point into his discussion of the place of comics in the media industries, while the San Diego Comic-Con's own coffee table book *Comic-Con: 40 Years of Artists, Fans, and Friends* (2009) presents a visual and written overview of the convention's history.[24] All of this writing provides crucial context and raises important questions about Comic-Con's significance to comics and fan cultures, media industries, and fan and media interactions. As the first scholarly monograph on the topic, *Only at Comic-Con* expands on this research to provide an understanding of both the historical and contemporary impact of the San Diego Comic-Con, particularly as it relates to questions of exclusivity, fan labor, and Hollywood's promotional presence at the event.

It is important to note, however, that while popular and academic discourses—this book included—may provide snapshots of the convention, there is no single Comic-Con experience. Instead, attendees can curate their own experience of the event, choosing four days of activities from over two thousand hours of programming, which includes close to one thousand panels—many of which feature industry professionals—devoted to comics, film, television, toys, games, and other niches of popular culture and fandom; over five hundred screenings, including an anime program and an independent film festival; the academic Comic Arts Conference; over one thousand retailers and exhibitors in the over 460,000-square-foot Exhibit Hall; and the increasing number of offsite activities and events called activations, sponsored by advertisers as wide ranging as Amazon, Warner Brothers Home Video, Nintendo, Mac Cosmetics, and HGTV.[25] As writer and longtime Comic-Con attendee Mark Evanier put it, "Everyone has a very different Comic-Con. You have to roll your own."[26] Because attendees have such expansive interests, from comics to cosplay, television to tabletop games, and because of the huge scope of the convention itself, it is impossible to produce an account of Comic-Con that accurately represents the entire range of experiences available. And yet, this is precisely what gets worked and reworked in discourses about the event, which attempt to capture something about the Comic-Con experience for readers or viewers, the vast majority of whom have never attended.

Coverage aimed at such audiences frequently highlights cosplay, for example, creating a kind of monolithic idea about what it means to participate in the event.[27] This might also explain why almost everyone I meet asks me if I dress up in costume when I attend Comic-Con to conduct field research (I don't). Cosplay, of course, is one of many practices associated with fan conventions, and though it is a burgeoning area of fan studies research, it is not a central focus in this book.[28] Indeed, grappling with the scope of this project has been one of the challenges of researching something that appears, from the outside, to be a relatively contained object of study. However, to borrow a phrase from another doctor (one cited much more frequently than I), the Comic-Con experience—both historical and contemporary—is most definitely "bigger on the inside."[29] In the same way that Comic-Con's increased size and scope have made the convention a "roll your own" kind of experience, I hope the gaps and absences in this book will be identified and filled in different ways by different readers and writers, continuing a conversation that is as dynamic and varied as the convention itself.[30] As a scholar whose work sits at the intersection of media industries and fan studies research, my contribution is to examine another common tendency in Comic-Con coverage, which is to connect the event (and fan culture) to the media industries, and Hollywood, in particular.[31] In doing so, however, I also try to capture aspects of the Comic-Con experience that may be less familiar to readers—its historical roots in comic fandom, the significance of waiting in line, the organization and programming of promotional content, and the role of retail in the convention space—especially because most people don't attend Comic-Con, but experience it by consuming coverage of the event. To most people, Comic-Con exists only as a concept, a discursive construct pieced together through articles, images, and footage. And this is exactly what makes studying it so important. Indeed, this book argues that because the vast majority of media consumers will *never* attend Comic-Con, the discourses that emerge from the event are crucial nodes of research, as they produce a kind of Comic-Con imaginary that works to define and shape not just cultural ideas about Comic-Con but the Comic-Con experience itself.

Another way to capture the Comic-Con experience is by thinking about its place among the hundreds of other conventions across the globe. But, as the Salt Lake Comic Con lawsuit suggests, this relationship is complicated too. The San Diego Comic-Con is one of the largest conventions in North America, with over 130,000 attendees each year. Comic-Con first broke the 100,000 mark back in 2005—the same year organizers trademarked the phrase "Comic-Con"—making it the largest North American comic convention at that time and the first to exceed 100,000 attendees. In 2006, that number shot up to 123,000, and attendance has hovered around 130,000 ever since, having been capped based on the size of the San Diego Convention Center.[32] Today, numerous comic conventions attract close to or over 100,000 attendees, like Seattle's Emerald City Comic Con, the Denver Comic Con, Toronto's Fan Expo Canada, the Salt Lake Comic Con (which changed its name to FanX Salt Lake Comic Convention after the lawsuit) and the New York Comic Con, which reportedly surpassed Comic-Con in 2014, attracting 151,000.[33] The biggest comic conventions, however, reside outside of North America. Japan's Comiket (Comics Market) is held twice a year and attracts over 550,000 attendees, while Lucca Comics and Games Festival in Italy has recorded attendance numbers of over 250,000, making it the largest comic convention in the European market.[34] These high attendance numbers are evidence of the increased popularity of comic conventions in the twenty-first century, but they may not be the best indicator of an individual convention's scale or impact, according to Comic-Con's chief communication and strategy officer, David Glanzer. In a 2016 interview, he stated that Comic-Con "stopped issuing press releases for attendance at our events because conventions count attendees any number of different ways. We are comfortable saying that our attendance is well in excess of 135,000 individual attendees. If we counted our people the way some other events count, we would have in excess of 320,000."[35] Not only that, but such numbers only capture what's happening *inside* the convention center, leaving out the reported 200,000 people without Comic-Con tickets who flood downtown San Diego during Comic-Con to participate in offsite events and marketing activations that don't require a badge.[36]

The similarities between the San Diego Comic-Con and these other conventions extend beyond questions of scale, however. While specific content may vary from year to year and event to event, most North American comic conventions are structurally similar.[37] As Matthew Smith put it, a comic convention is "one-part trade show, with industry leaders debuting and promoting many of their upcoming releases. It is also one-part swap meet, where vendors sell everything from vintage comics and artwork to the latest videos and exclusive toys. It is one-part meet and greet, where creators and fans can interact through autograph signings and panel presentations. It is also one-part floor show, where people go to see and be seen, with some decked out in elaborate costuming."[38] These events share something else in common too. They include a huge array of media and popular culture products beyond comics, making the phrase "comic con" somewhat of a misnomer these days. Conventions using this phrase are largely assumed to be multigenre conventions, aligning them with events like Atlanta's Dragon Con, which was founded in 1987 and, as organizers describe, "combine[s] fandoms and genres into a single convention."[39] But as chapter 1 of this book demonstrates, the San Diego Comic-Con relied on this kind of multigenre framework from the very beginning. The phrase "comic con," then, has also become somewhat interchangeable with other terms, like fan convention or pop culture convention. So what makes Comic-Con unique? And, more importantly, what makes Comic-Con worthy of academic study? This book is called *Only at Comic-Con*, after all.

First and foremost, Comic-Con's history and longevity make it a standout among competing conventions—in North America at least.[40] While it was not the first comic convention and the jury is out on whether it still qualifies as the largest, Comic-Con is the longest-running comic book convention in North America, marking its fiftieth anniversary in 2019. The convention's history spans massive changes in the media landscape since 1970, including the rise of the Hollywood blockbuster, television's multi-channel and post-network eras, the increased deregulation and conglomeration of the media industries, the digital revolution, and the rise of social media, to name just a few. While Italy's Lucca Comics and Games Festival, founded in 1966, and Japan's Comiket, founded in 1975, have similarly rich histories that promise to illuminate much about their particular national contexts as well as the transnational reach of fan culture, most of Comic-Con's North American challengers emerged in the twenty-first century.[41] We might characterize these more recent conventions as *responding to* the notion that fans were becoming an increasingly lucrative cultural niche, while, as I discuss in the next section of this introduction, the San Diego Comic-Con was frequently cited as *evidence of* these arguments.

Comic-Con is also unique because of its nonprofit status. While there are other comic conventions presented by nonprofits, like the Denver Comic Con, most large comic conventions are owned by for-profit companies, many of which run events in cities across North America and, in some cases, the world.[42] For example, ReedPop, an offshoot of the UK-based trade show company Reed Exhibitions, owns both the Emerald City and New York Comic Cons, along with nearly forty other conventions around the world.[43] In fact, the economic heft and oftentimes global reach of these event companies might help to explain why the San Diego Comic-Con's lawsuit targeted Salt Lake Comic Con, amid a crowded field of conventions ostensibly infringing on their trademark. While Dan Farr productions provoked Comic-Con's ire by employing marketing practices that may have been designed to conflate the San Diego and Salt Lake events, it is also a relatively small company in comparison to a corporate subsidiary like ReedPop, which stayed conspicuously silent during the three-year legal entanglement.[44]

Comic-Con's incorporation as a nonprofit has an interesting and slightly dubious origin story. When Comic-Con's founder, Shel Dorf, was trying to recruit special guests, he convinced author Ray Bradbury to wave his usual five-thousand-dollar speaking engagement fee and attend the very first Comic-Con free of charge by telling him that Comic-Con was "a non-profit group to advance the art form."[45] The convention continued to operate in this capacity unofficially until 1975, when San Diego Comic Convention actually incorporated as a nonprofit. Its goals, according to the articles of incorporation, were "(1) to promote the historical and educational appreciation of the artistic media as it relates to comics, science fiction, and related art forms, and (2) to organize, promote, sponsor, hold and conduct an annual 'comic convention' which will be a forum for the historical and educational appreciation of comics and related art forms."[46] Comic-Con's nonprofit status allows the convention organizers to frame the event around an ethos of education, service, and community that often seems at odds with the massive (and massively lucrative) event the convention has become.[47] The introduction to *Comic-Con: 40 Years of Artists, Writers, Fans & Friends*, asserts that "over the four decades of the event, one thing has remained the same at Comic-Con: The convention is an event run by fans."[48] Given Comic-Con's ongoing reliance on volunteer labor for everything from co-ordination to crowd control, this seems relatively accurate. However, as modern criticisms

of Comic-Con suggest, a fan event small enough to be concocted and organized by a small group, consisting primarily of teenagers, and a convention
that necessitates a paid board of directors, are two very different entities.
In 1970, Comic-Con's bank account topped out at $16.80, while the organ-
ization's 2015 tax return documented a total of $28,080,797 in net assets.[49]
The same year, Comic-Con also reported 3,400 volunteers and forty-
nine paid employees, including a board of directors with salaries ranging
from $6,996 to $208,894 for workweeks from two to sixty hours long.[50] As
a nonprofit, Comic-Con is barred from capitalizing on this labor in the
same way as for profit operations like ReedPop, but if Comic-Con is truly
an "event run by fans" the amount of money flowing in and out of the convention is evidence that fan labor has the ability to yield substantial economic gains.[51]

Because Comic-Con's nonprofit status makes it exempt from state and
federal taxes, those critical of the convention argue that the influx of money
to this nonprofit is now primarily expended to produce a convention in support of publicity for massive corporate entities in the media industries.[52] In
combating these critiques, Comic-Con organizers generally lean on the
event's educational goals. As David Glanzer put it "We have a mission to
bring comics and related popular art to a wider audience. . . . So while people
see images in the media of many attendees dressed in costume, or big booths
on the exhibit floor, there are also two floors of meeting space that are used
for panels, workshops and programs that highlight areas of art that the public may not be generally aware [sic]."[53] However, as I have argued, the convention's exclusivity and its contemporary popularity are built on those
things that the wider audience *does* see. While Glanzer's statement suggests that those attending the convention may go seeking an inside glimpse
at Marvel's Cinematic Universe and leave having discovered underground
comix, for example, the mediation of the Comic-Con experience—which
is what the majority of consumers encounter and where most of the arguments about the event's exclusivity take root—doesn't enable that same kind
of discovery.

Glanzer's defense of Comic-Con's nonprofit status relies largely on the
content presented at Comic-Con; however, in the 1990s and 2000s, San
Diego Comic Convention also brought two San Francisco area conventions
into the fold. The nonprofit took the reins of APE: The Alternative Press
Expo, from 1995 to 2014 and, in 2002, took over the fifteen-year-old Won-

derCon because it was "right in line with Comic-Con's mission statement."[54] More recently, Comic-Con announced plans to build a permanent museum in San Diego's Balboa Park that would "capture the excitement and magic of Comic-Con in a year-round attraction."[55] While these affiliated events and sites are evidence that Comic-Con's mission extends beyond this single event, they do not address the conflict at the heart of these critiques, which draws attention to how, as the San Diego Comic-Con has grown and expanded over the years, its status as an intermediary between media audiences and media industries has become increasingly problematic. This tension surrounding Hollywood's presence at the event is at the center of *Only at Comic-Con*.

The Limits of Exclusivity: Comic-Con, Hollywood, and Geek Chic

In 2003, *Spider-Man* (Sam Raimi, 2002) producer Avi Arad reportedly told a Comic-Con audience, "I have to congratulate you all because you are the first community ever to manage to bring Hollywood to them."[56] Luckily, San Diego's proximity to Los Angeles meant that for Hollywood it was a relatively short trip. In fact, it was probably a short trip for most of the people in the room at that time. Comic-Con has always drawn fans from around North America and the world, but for a large contingent of attendees who live in San Diego or the Southern California region attending Comic-Con isn't just fun, it's also convenient. The same is true for Hollywood, who, as I discuss in chapter 1 of this book, dabbled in promotion at Comic-Con as early as the 1970s. However, it wasn't until the turn of the twenty-first century that discourses about Comic-Con, fans, and Hollywood began intersecting with greater frequency outside the convention center. In 1997, the *Hollywood Reporter* ran an item titled "San Diego Comic Con Draws Hit Hungry Hollywood." While the story focused primarily on Hollywood's growing interest in Comic-Con as a place to obtain the rights to comic books for film or television adaptations, it also noted the industry's burgeoning marketing presence, citing the promotional appearances of actors David Hasselhoff, Tia Carrere, and director Paul Verhoven.[57] Although the history of Hollywood promotion at Comic-Con begins well before 1997, this article represents one of the earlier mentions of Comic-Con in the trades, suggesting that the event was gaining a higher profile in Hollywood at the time. That same year, Comic-Con organizers published a press release highlighting its "increased media attention," which seemed to cultivate—as much as comment on—Comic-Con's newfound "national exposure."[58] By 2001, DreamWorks, Fox, Warner Brothers, Sony, and New Line were all promoting their films at the convention, and *Daily Variety* noted that Exhibit Hall displays by "DreamWorks and the Sci-Fi Channel rival[ed] those of comicbook giants Marvel and DC."[59]

In 2002, *Hollywood Reporter* ran another article, which suggested that Comic-Con was "a key destination for Hollywood movie marketers looking to reach a burgeoning target demographic . . . few other events," it went on, "attract such a captive audience of hardcore pop-culture fanatics from throughout the nation. Realizing that a presentation at Comic-Con can generate excitement about a property that travels beyond the convention hall and around the globe over the Internet, Hollywood studios are flocking to the show with bigger and more lavish presentations, panels and promotions."[60] And in 2004, *Variety* cited Hollywood's presence at Comic-Con—"nearly every major studio showed clips and flew in a bevy of stars from upcoming genre pics"—as central evidence that "fandom has become fashionable."[61] This discourse about the influence of Comic-Con and its fans extended beyond the industry trades, with *USA Today* and CNN.com also reporting on Hollywood's presence at Comic-Con that year.[62] As the CNN article acknowledged, "the convention has always been a powerful marketing tool," but this coverage was indicative of a broader discursive shift that linked Comic-Con's promotional power to the rising power of nerds, geeks, and fans, both as a demographic of consumers whose taste in film had become increasingly connected to popular blockbuster filmmaking and as producers of early buzz and publicity.[63] While the press captured this notion in a range of different ways, a 2004 *Variety* cover encapsulated the phenomenon in two words that highlighted how the exclusivity of the event and its attendees were elevated through the exclusivity of Hollywood promotion: "geek chic" (figure I.2).[64]

As I describe in chapter 3, Hollywood's increased visibility at Comic-Con was further solidified in 2004, when organizers added a new space called Hall H, a large programming room specifically set aside for Hollywood promotion. At the same time, superhero, science fiction, and fantasy franchises like *Spider-Man*, *Star Wars*, and *Lord of the Rings* were topping the box office, a trend that continued and amplified into the 2010s.[65] While

H'wood corrals nerd herd...

By PETER BART

GEEK SALAD: *Hollywood courted geeks as Jude Law, far left; Keanu Reeves, center; and Stan Lee, bottom right, met fans at Comic-Con.*

The annual carnival at Comic-Con reminds us that, while Internet geeks don't yet rule the world, they sure scare the hell out of Hollywood. Anyone surveying the promotional frenzy at the San Diego gathering last week would conclude that the major studios spend almost as much time worrying about their geek constituencies as they do prepping for their confreres at ShoWest.

A panoply of screenings, pitches and product placements were mobilized to demonstrate to the assorted Webbers, comicbook crazies and random gamesters that the latest studio product is so cool it's practically cryogenic. Stars like Keanu Reeves and Jude Law were recruited to pitch their wares.

The sprawling convention has become, in fact, an industrial trade show masking as a fan show.

Sure, the denim-clad geeksters are eager to trade gossip on the latest failed test screenings or troubled trailers, but the studio reps are there to build excitement for their wannabe tentpoles and product accoutrements.

All of which serves as a bittersweet reminder of that brief moment when the Internet emerged as a great democratizing force in the movie business. Appropriately or not, the "The Blair Witch Project" was the abiding symbol of that moment — that movie seemed like it fell out of some futuristic time capsule.

Here was a blockbuster that was neither the product of a Hollywood promotion nor a creation of effete film critics. It was the People's Movie. The fans not only discovered it, *Turn to page 5*

'Net nerds meet fantasy faves of yesteryear p.16

GEEK CHIC

... but 'Netsters wary of showbiz wooing

By BEN FRITZ

The term "geek" used to be an insult. "Now 'geek' is a badge of honor," says Kerry Conran, director of Paramount's upcoming "Sky Captain and the World of Tomorrow."

Conran is a self-confessed geek who has crossed the bridge to become a Hollywood director.

Putting a fanboy in charge of a $70 million movie with 2,100 CGI shots is just one sign of how Hollywood's going geek and geek is going Hollywood. (For example, the hottest guy on Fox's "The O.C." is a Comic-Con attendee.)

As fandom has become fashionable, Hollywood has targeted and wooed geeks. But the mating dance online and in person isn't an easy one.

When the Internet boomed in the late '90s, it was touted as a vehicle for democracy: Everyone would get an equal voice. Instead, it's morphing into a marketing tool.

That makes Hollywood nervous because fan sites are among the few outlets it can't control — even though it is certainly trying.

While fans love the attention (and the exclusive content it brings), it's making them anxious: Geeks pride themselves on being maverick outcasts and are wary about becoming mainstream.

The July 22-25 Comic-Con Intl. in San Diego, which drew more than 75,000 attendees, was emblematic of the growing tension. A cavernous new 6,500-seat hall was filled for Hollywood presentations. With the "Lord of the Rings" trilogy's $2.9 billion global box *Turn to page 41*

FIGURE I.2 *Variety*'s geek chic cover story (August 2–8, 2004).

Hollywood's production of blockbusters, franchises, and adaptations was nothing new, Tino Balio suggests that in the 2000s, as conglomerates grew increasingly conservative and studios decreased in-house production, tentpoles that were "instantly recognizable and exploitable across all platforms and all divisions of the company" became a key strategy in Hollywood's economic "flight to safety."[66] While this conservative strategy suggests an investment in mainstream audiences, rather than a niche demographic of moviegoers, coverage of Comic-Con largely distilled these economic decisions into statements like, "nerds have never been more important to Hollywood."[67]

As Hollywood's presence at Comic-Con gained increased media attention, the event's popularity seemed to be both fueled by and fueling exclusivity. Attendance numbers rose steadily and—as I discuss in chapter 2— demand for tickets increased significantly, particularly when the event shifted to online sales in 2006 and again to a lottery system in 2014. By 2018 Comic-Con's economic impact on the region was estimated at more than $147 million, over $70 million more than any other event the San Diego Convention Center hosted that year.[68] While, as *Only at Comic-Con* demonstrates, the actual reasons for this growth are complicated and far from organic, there is no doubt that the media hype surrounding Hollywood promotion at Comic-Con fueled its notoriety. David Glanzer, who was serving as Comic-Con's director of marketing at the time, put it quite clearly and succinctly, in fact: "Hollywood and the studios have an ability to market their presence at the show more than others."[69] To put it another way, the proliferation of discourses that surround Hollywood promotion, fans, and Comic-Con are the direct result, not just of Hollywood's cultural and economic power but also of the inability of other individuals, industries, organizations, and communities to compete.

This is one of the many reasons, I argue, that discourses about Hollywood, fans, and Comic-Con often hinge on exclusivity. They identify Comic-Con as an exclusive media event in order to suggest that fans are an exclusive demographic of tastemakers. And the evidence they present—that celebrities and film studios are flocking to Comic-Con—highlights the exclusivity of Hollywood as a powerful media institution. Not only that, but the event itself is steeped in the idea of exclusive experiences. Collectors can purchase "exclusive" merchandise, companies give away "exclusive" swag, studios screen "exclusive" footage and throw "exclusive" parties, and attendees who manage to (literally) win the lottery and buy Comic-Con tickets or wait in line for hours or days have "exclusive" access to all of it.[70] In these cases, exclusivity points to the presence of something specific—an event, an item, an audience, an industry. But it is important to remember that exclusivity is not actually defined by presences at all, but by the power to produce absences. The word "exclusive," after all, is semantically rooted in exclusion.

This means that for something to be considered exclusive, access must also be limited in some way. As Pierre Bourdieu suggests, limits work to organize our understanding of our social world, but in internalizing these limits we also tend to forget they exist.[71] For this reason, it is important to think about the *limits of exclusivity*: the power of limits, the power to set limits, and how these limits ultimately mask and naturalize the power imbalances that allow them to function in the first place. Exclusivity is also a significant driver of value, meaning that controlling and limiting access are frequently deployed as promotional strategies.[72] Thus the limits of exclusivity, which manifest around the event space, attendees, and the industry, work to situate Comic-Con as a site of media industry promotion. But even more important, *Only at Comic-Con* argues, are the ways in which Hollywood is able to shape, adjust, expand, and overcome these limits, ultimately maintaining its power as a hegemonic media institution—even in a space that seems to celebrate the cultural impact of fandom.

As I have already discussed, Comic-Con is one of many large fan conventions in the world, but there is an exclusive aura surrounding the event that exceeds its status as just another convention. That aura of exclusivity has been cultivated both by Comic-Con organizers, seeking to brand the event, and through Hollywood's use of the space as a promotional launch pad, which has a tendency to overshadow other facets of the convention. Comic-Con is also confined to a specific space (San Diego) and time (summer, usually July) each year, which means the exclusivity of the experience is also rooted in spatiotemporal limits. For this reason, Comic-Con aligns with Nick Couldry's description of "media rituals" as "actions organized around key media related categories and boundaries, whose performance reinforces, indeed helps legitimate, the underlying 'value' expressed in the idea that the media is our access point to our social center."[73] *Media Rituals: A Critical Approach* (2003) builds on Couldry's earlier work in *The Place of Media Power* (2000), where he argues that the physical spaces where audiences encounter and interact with the media industries reveal much about how these institutions maintain and normalize their significant cultural and economic power.[74] While both books help to explain why Comic-Con—a site that brings fans and industry together—manages to reinforce the power of the media industries even as it celebrates fans, Couldry's theorization of media rituals, in particular, captures how the limits of exclusivity get negotiated in the interplay between media coverage of the event and the event itself.

Comic-Con's exclusivity is heightened because of its material limits. It only happens once a year, and the convention center, hotels, and the city of San Diego can only accommodate so many people. For this reason, not everyone who wants to go to Comic-Con can get in—the cost of tickets is increasingly prohibitive, and even if you can afford tickets, not everyone can afford the time it takes to actually attend. And if these factors don't present barriers to access, potential attendees must still contend with the fact that only a small percentage of them will actually be able to purchase Comic-Con tickets. In 2014, for example, an estimated 900,000 people participated in the event's online ticket sales.[75] For those without Comic-Con tickets, media coverage, social media, and sanctioned and covert live streams are all readily available points of access to the convention, but the mediated content that emerges and circulates most widely is usually connected to media industry promotion.[76] So while these promotional discourses overcome the limits of exclusivity to spread beyond the convention center, the reason that they are worth spreading or paying attention to at all seems to be rooted in the idea that Comic-Con is an exclusive experience.[77] There is still something special about *being there*.

To understand this aspect of the event and its relationship to industry promotion, it is useful to consider what Joseph B. Pine II and James H. Gilmore call the "experience economy." In order to increase profits, Pine and Gilmore argue, companies should (and do) shift their focus away from merely selling commodities, goods, or services to selling experiences instead.[78] For example, a store might charge one dollar for a regular cup of coffee, but with the right kind of experience and ambiance, the price could double or triple.[79] As I discuss throughout this book, the exclusivity of the Comic-Con experience is frequently invoked in discourses about how that experience is valued. In Comic-Con's early years, this meant unprecedented access to comics industry professionals and hard-to-find comic books and collectables. Today, Comic-Con's Exhibit Hall, where vendors sell exclusive merchandise, offers the most direct translation of Pine and Gilmore's experience economy in a retail context.[80] Indeed, the best Comic-Con exclusive I ever encountered was called Exclusive Man and consisted of an empty action figure package—I paid five dollars for it (figure I.3). I loved Exclusive Man because its satire was built on the idea that while companies in the Exhibit Hall were selling material goods, they were really profiting on the intangible idea and experience of exclusivity. Hollywood promotion at Comic-Con is similarly steeped in this interplay between the materiality of the experience and

FIGURE I.3 Exclusive Man, manufactured by Applehead Factory. (Photo by the author.)

the immateriality of affect. While fans consuming Hollywood promotion at Comic-Con are largely operating in ideological frameworks of cultural capital, when Hollywood appears at the convention, it is seeking economic gains.[81] For this reason, it is crucial to note that what Pine and Gilmore are really talking about when they describe an economy built on selling experiences, is the production of what Marx described as surplus value, which allows companies to profit on unpaid labor time.[82] In the manufacture and sale of commodities, goods, and services, this surplus value comes from the labor of workers, hired to extract, manufacture, or deliver the product. But in the experience economy, as Pine and Gilmore describe it, value is "created within each customer," and surplus value, it seems, is directly tied to the affective labor of those participating in the experience.[83] If the "inaccessibility" of products and experiences is, as Mark Jancovich puts it in his discussion of cult movie fandom, "one of the pleasures of the scene," not only does this contribute to the production of value in Comic-Con's experience economy but it also suggests something about the individuals who attend the event.[84]

Comic-Con attendees are often marked as an exclusive group; first, for overcoming economic, spatial, and temporal limits to actually attend and, second, through their resulting identification—in industrial and popular discourses—as "tastemakers" and "influencers."[85] As Henry Jenkins et al. suggest, however, what began as a "push for exclusivity" at Comic-Con "has given rise to a push for publicity."[86] In other words, if identifying Comic-Con fans as exclusive meant *excluding* the average media consumer, the industry sought to overcome the limits of this exclusivity by blurring the lines between production and consumption and extracting value from Comic-Con fans both as signifiers of idealized consumers *and* producers of free publicity.[87] For this reason, it is worth turning back to the discourses linking Comic-Con, Hollywood, and the rise of geek chic, which defined exclusivity by connecting taste and fan labor while simultaneously overcoming the limits of exclusivity to construct a discursive notion of fandom that enveloped much of mainstream popular culture.

As an articulation of taste we might think about how geek chic, as Bourdieu put it, "classifies and it classifies the classifier."[88] In other words, discourses about taste tell us something about a particular group, but in the process they also tell us something about the interests and ideologies that created that category in the first place. What Jonathan Gray, Cornel Sandvoss, and C. Lee Harrington describe as "the first wave" or the "'fandom is beautiful' phase" of fan studies drew heavily on Bourdieu's work on taste and cultural capital in order to signal the importance of studying fans both because of the *kind* of culture they consume and because of what they *do* with that culture.[89] This scholarship, the authors argue, did little to dismantle the binary between production and consumption, but rather reconfigured it by suggesting that "consumers not producers called the shots."[90] Early fan studies scholarship certainly provides more nuance and complexity than the discourses about geek chic that began circulating in the popular and trade press some ten years later, but it takes a remarkably similar rhetorical approach, which is to link taste and productivity to elevate a particular mode of media consumption as exclusive. With geek chic, however, fan tastes and practices weren't just unique and worthy of intellectual attention, they were also cool.

But, as Christine Quail's "hip/square dialectic" model suggests, recuperating geek and fan culture by refashioning it as "cool," usually does very little to disrupt the status quo.[91] In 2006, for example, the *Hollywood Reporter* suggested that when "hundreds of filmmakers and marketers from the studios and agencies make the trek to San Diego for Comic-Con International, it's as if Hollywood's high school-like hierarchy is being stood on its head" and went on to say that Comic-Con "has grown far beyond its science fiction and comic book roots to become a place where the entertainment industry comes to market its wares."[92] While the first quote hinged on the idea that until recently, fans were definitively uncool and outside the mainstream, the second explained this reversal by suggesting that Comic-Con and its fans had become *more* mainstream thanks to Hollywood's presence there.[93] A key feature of these discourses, then, was to suggest that fans had become an elite and exclusive demographic, even as they constructed a notion of fan culture so broad that it became increasingly difficult to distinguish from the so-called mainstream.[94] If, as the *Today Show* reminded its viewers in 2012, "Comic-Con is all about the kind of characters and storylines that powered seven of last year's top ten movies," did this mean everyone who watched these films was a fan?

Of course not *everyone* is a fan. But by asserting that fans were the new arbiters of taste who were recognized, appreciated, and even feared by the Hollywood elite, geek chic discourses seemed to suggest that becoming a fan might not be such a bad idea.[95] And being a fan—in Hollywood's terms—was primarily a matter of spending your time and, more importantly, spending your money.[96] As John Hegeman, the head of international marketing for Lionsgate put it, "This isn't a demographic. It's a psychological profile. Age has nothing to do with it. Gender has nothing to do with it. They're fans."[97] Of course, intersecting categories of identity like gender, age, class, race, and sexual orientation have *everything* to do with fan culture.[98] Instead, what Hegeman seems to be describing is an industry ethos that—much like practices of colorblind casting that Kristen Warner describes—advances an ideology of universality and "maintain[s] an idealistic but myopic view of the world based upon normative (white) assumptions."[99] *Only at Comic-Con* engages primarily with notions of fandom that are "socially constructed by media industries," homogenizing fans into what Philip Napoli calls an "institutionalized audience."[100] At first glance, such discourses seem to be presenting an inclusive image of fan culture in which everyone can participate. But what they actually do, as work by scholars like Rebecca Wanzo, Kristen Warner, Suzanne Scott, Kristina Busse, and Mel Stanfill demonstrate, is allow the limits of exclusivity to operate in covert ways that reify hegemonic ideas about fan culture as straight, white, cisgender, and/or male.[101]

This was crystalized for me when I attended *Entertainment Weekly*'s annual "Women Who Kick Ass" Comic-Con panel in 2013 and watched actresses Michelle Q, Danai Gurira, Tatiana Maslany, Michelle Rodriguez, and Katee Sackhoff discuss, with incredible rigor, candor, and critical thought, the state of women in the industry, representation in the media, and specific problems facing women of color, anticipating the increased visibility of such topics in the wake of the 2016 U.S. election and 2017's #MeToo movement. As the panel concluded, a white, male attendee a few rows up from me retitled the panel in a coarse, dismissive shout: "women who talk too much." Evidently, even this single hour on a day of programs that included high-profile film reveals like DC's *Batman v Superman: Dawn of Justice* and Marvel's *Avengers: Age of Ultron* was more than he could take. Capturing what Derek Johnson describes as "the politics of cultural loss in which some fans perceive threats to their consumer sovereignty and privilege from the potential improvement of service to other consumers," this incident suggests that there is a fundamental divergence between the homogeneous fan culture articulated through the phrase "geek chic" and the kinds of "toxic fan practices" that have become increasingly visible since the mid-2010s.[102] If the "Women Who Kick Ass" panel revealed (or even anticipated) a burgeoning progressive streak in popular culture, the hostile response of this single loud voice, which carried across a crowd of thousands, similarly captured how easily a regressive backlash, however marginal, can force its way into the discourse. I could actually see the man shout out in front of me, but the outburst traveled much farther, even making its way into media coverage of the panel.[103] Hollywood's economic investment in the *idea* of fandom and its tendency to "play all sides of the struggles between different fandoms," as Johnson puts it, can have the same effect, amplifying and legitimizing even the most toxic response to progressive politics by "absorbing it into franchise strategy rather than being disrupted by it."[104]

While it might be easy to dismiss this single unruly voice, the sentiment behind the backlash also manifested in less obvious ways, like the consistent hum of conversations coming from audience members who chose to tune out the discussion, or the mass exodus of attendees who took the hour-long panel as an opportunity to use the restroom or visit the concession stand, even the casual observation by the man sitting next to me, that Comic-Con programmers must have scheduled this panel to clear out the room between the Warner Brothers and Marvel Studios presentations. There might only be one person in a room of 6,500 who was bold enough to proclaim out loud his belief that women—and especially women of color—who talk about their experiences are "women who talk too much." But there were many more who engaged with this panel *as if* this were true. I tell this story to gesture to the fact that there are plenty of good reasons to think about the limits of exclusivity and how they work to conceal underlying power imbalances, many of which extend beyond this book's focus on media industry promotion and fan labor. While *Only at Comic-Con* does not take the recent explosion of discourse surrounding toxic attitudes, misogyny, racism, and hate in fandom as its central focus, I hope that providing a broad theorization of exclusivity as something that is constructed and amplified by the power of the media industries helps to explain how the industry's simultaneous appeals to exclusivity (and, therefore, exclusion) and universality, contributes to the production and circulation of discourses that are, at best, contradictory and, at worst, an impediment to genuine inclusion, even if and when the industry and culture appear to be shifting in more progressive directions.

One reason for this disconnect is that geek chic discourses are not reflecting an audience so much as they are identifying what Derek Johnson calls an "audience function" by deploying "discursively imagined audiences" to reinforce long-standing industrial hierarchies and "grant meaning and value to the creative practice and identity of authors."[105] And in the discourses

about geek chic, the function of this imagined audience of fans is to reinforce the cultural and economic power of the media industries. The result
is that this homogenized notion of fandom is ultimately reconstituted under
an umbrella of exclusivity that is tethered to the same kinds of insider discourses that we frequently see surrounding laborers in the media industries.[106] For example, when another 2006 article invoked the idea of fans as
tastemakers to declare that at Comic-Con "geeks decide what's cool," it also
suggested that, "Comic-Con and its 100,000-plus attendees have become
some of the biggest, most vital cogs in the Hollywood promotion
machines."[107] This example is just one of a slew of similar statements emerging from Comic-Con that position fans as what John Caldwell calls
"producer-generated-users" by suggesting that fan consumption and productivity are valuable *because* they generate or work in concert with industry
promotion.[108] The end result is that discourses about the exclusivity of
Comic-Con fans ultimately rest on and reinforce the industry's cultural and
economic power, but this power also allows the tastes and activities associated with Comic-Con and its fans to be understood as exclusive and increasingly popular in the same breath. This conflation of the popular with the
exclusive is precisely what Kristina Busse described when she said, "with geek
chic, the general culture has embraced certain levels of geekiness just as
audience engagement and convergence culture have made fans more
acceptable."[109] Of course, as Busse points out, such discourses also belie the
underlying gendered hierarchies that continue to permeate fan culture.[110]

The fact that Busse places geek chic in the context of convergence culture is particularly significant because Henry Jenkins's 2006 book grows out
of the same discursive thrust, both theorizing and advancing an iteration of
media culture where, as he puts it, "rather than talking about media producers and consumers as occupying separate roles, we might now see them
as participants who interact with each other according to a new set of rules
that none of us fully understand."[111] When it comes to Hollywood's cultivation of Comic-Con's geek chic, however, we can see these rules come into
focus—popular understandings of fandom grow increasingly broad, caus-
ing moments of rupture like the one described earlier, even as the range of
possible fan activities are circumscribed by their utility to the industry. It's
especially significant to note, then, that *Convergence Culture* is not a book
about fans, in the strictest sense. Rather, as Jenkins puts it, the book shows
how "entrenched institutions are taking their models from grassroots fan
communities, and reinventing themselves for an era of media convergence

and collective intelligence," suggesting that fan culture was and is increasingly appealing to the media industries as a model of heightened consumer engagement in the digital era.[112] For Hollywood, "learning to speak geek" wasn't just about recognizing and normalizing fan tastes that aligned with their products, it also meant finding ways to overcome the limits of exclusivity and reach a much larger audience by making fandom work for them—literally.[113] In the words of Lisa Gregorian, a VP of marketing for Warner Brothers, "word of mouth is now one individual impacting a couple hundred individuals who can impact thousands. Social networking has allowed us to empower one fan to impact thousands of potential viewers."[114]

As Gregorian's comment suggests, the activities at the center of convergence culture might also be understood as what Tiziana Terranova calls "free labor . . . the moment where this knowledgeable consumption of culture is translated into productive activities that are pleasurably embraced and at the same time often shamelessly exploited."[115] In fact, I can't think of a more apt description for the kinds of activities happening at Comic-Con. As labor becomes a central question in studies of media industries and fan cultures, examining how exclusivity, industry power, and fan labor function at Comic-Con may be one way to start untangling the increasingly complex relationship between media industries and their audiences at a time when production and consumption both seem to fall under the category of work.[116] Usually, these interactions are mediated and expedited through social networks like Twitter, Instagram, and Facebook or online shopping and streaming interfaces like Amazon and Netflix that encourage us to share key details about our tastes and buying habits. All of these interactions are framed as a collaborative project to make the media more responsive, more interactive, more pleasurable—better. As television critic Maureen Ryan put it, drawing parallels between the physical space of Comic-Con and the virtual spaces of social media, "Twitter is successful because it, like Comic-Con, levels the playing field. Attendees may not walk away from Comic-Con having had a personal conversation with the creative folks behind 'Lost' or 'The Twilight Saga: New Moon.' But attendees of those hot-ticket panels will walk away knowing that those well-paid creative folk care about what the fans think."[117] Comic-Con, as this quote suggests, has largely been defined by the ways in which fans and industry are converging. But the aura of exclusivity surrounding Comic-Con—and Hollywood—also sets them apart.

This book traverses a range of spaces and times where fans and industry converge, even as the limits of exclusivity ensure their separation in order to reinforce Hollywood's cultural and economic hegemony. Chapter 1, "Origin Stories," traces the early history of the San Diego Comic-Con, beginning with its roots in what has been described as the "golden age" of comic fandom during the 1960s. As the geek chic discourses described earlier suggest, Comic-Con's history is often invoked in narratives of growth that culminate in Hollywood's recognition and elevation of the event and its fans. But Hollywood is also frequently cited in criticism that Comic-Con has sold out or lost something as it moved away from its roots in comic books and grew increasingly enmeshed in film and television promotion. Countering these narratives, I argue that throughout its history, Comic-Con has always blurred the lines between fan and professional labor and cultivated an environment that promoted comics alongside film, television, and other media. Not only does this chapter historicize the notion of exclusivity surrounding the San Diego Comic-Con, it also illustrates how seamlessly Hollywood promotion was able to slide into and capitalize on that same framework.

If chapter 1 examines the historical continuity of exclusivity at Comic-Con, chapter 2, "The Liminality of the Line and the Place of Fans at Comic-Con," focuses on a more recent expression of exclusivity that has become a formative part of the Comic-Con experience: waiting in line. At Comic-Con, waiting in line evokes both material and ideological limits. It suggests a separation of inside and outside, both in the literal sense of gaining entry and as a signifier of the insider status of the event and its attendees. But the line itself is a liminal space, neither inside nor outside. For that reason, I argue, it functions as a metaphor for the place of fans who, in their interactions with industry promotion at Comic-Con, find themselves straddling the line between production and consumption. Outside of Comic-Con, waiting in line is somewhat quotidian activity that might be thought of in much the same way as media consumption, as something one does with their "free" time. But the prominence and proliferation of lines at Comic-Con, I argue, make the *work* of being a consumer significantly more visible.

Comic-Con attendees wait in line for all kinds of experiences, but one of the most prominent is attending panels in the 6,500-seat Hall H, which is known for its high-profile Hollywood promotions. Chapter 3, "Manufacturing Hall H Hysteria," moves from the place of fans in line to the place of Hollywood in the convention center. This chapter complicates and critiques the idea of "Hall H hysteria," a phrase used in the trades to signal both the enthusiasm and the unruliness of fans at Comic-Con. In doing so, I provide a detailed account of my experience attending a day of panels in Hall

H to demonstrate how the exclusivity of Hollywood promotion at Comic-Con is carefully constructed and in need of constant maintenance. Throughout this account, I integrate evidence from media coverage of the panels in order to argue that while the promotions in Hall H emphasize an organic and unpredictable experience of *being there*, this exclusivity is intended to propel promotion well beyond the walls of the convention center.

Finally, chapter 4, "Ret(ail)con" returns to the history of the San Diego Comic-Con and its connection to comics culture in order to explore one final space where audiences and industry come together at the convention, even as the power structures that divide them are firmly reinforced: the Exhibit Hall. This chapter decenters production as a site of meaning in order to examine the role of retail and consumption in this space over the history of the convention, from its early designation as the Dealers' Room to its gradual shift into the Exhibit Hall of today. Just as Comic-Con's early history blurred the lines between fan and industry labor, this space long positioned consumerism and retail transactions as exclusive experiences because of the scarcity of comic retailers in the 1960s and '70s. However, with the introduction of a comics trade show in the 1980s and the influx of film and television exhibitors and their licensees in the 1990s and 2000s, this exclusivity grew increasingly intertwined with trade show–style promotion and reconfigured consumption as a pathway to insider access. As this trajectory demonstrates, the industry's mode of engagement with fans at Comic-Con isn't just about finding new ways to extract value by engaging them as tastemakers and promotional laborers, it also means ensuring they remain what has long been the most reliable and profitable kind of audience: consumers. And if, as the conclusion to this book suggests, the industry is increasingly treating *all* audiences like Comic-Con fans, understanding and deconstructing the ways that Hollywood deploys the limits of exclusivity to make consumption *feel* special isn't just important, it's necessary.

For this reason, *Only at Comic-Con* follows both from recent calls to incorporate audiences into media industries research and the increased interest in media industries arising in fan studies.[118] But its inception also grows out of the work of scholars like Dallas Smythe and Eileen Meehan, who made a case for viewing audiences as part of the political economy of the media industries.[119] So while recent debates about the relationship between critical political economy and media industry studies suggest what Meehan and Janet Wasko describe as a "critical crossroads," cultural and economic approaches to media industries and fans are not incompatible.[120] Henry

Jenkins describes convergence culture as something that "occurs in the brains of individual consumers," while Smythe's work provides a critical complement, suggesting that "much of the *work* that audience power does for advertisers takes place in the heads of audience members" (my emphasis).[121] In examining how media industries and audiences converge, then, it is crucial to also consider how they diverge. And these top-down and bottom-up approaches might just meet in the middle, at Comic-Con. The underlying power that enables Hollywood to simultaneously construct and overcome the limits of exclusivity at Comic-Con, even as attendees are bound to those limits, I argue, is a key way to acknowledge what keeps the industry and fans separate as well as what brings them together.

1

Origin Stories

• • • • • • • • • • • • • • • • • • • •

Comic-Con and the Future
of All Media

> This is the future, not just of comics,
> but of all media. Movie studios are going
> to come to this convention every year to
> see what's new.
> —Jack Kirby, 1971

Morgan Spurlock's 2011 documentary, *Comic-Con Episode IV: A Fan's Hope*, begins with a visual primer in Comic-Con history, signaled by the click and whirl of an old slide projector. A mock slide show titled "1970 San Diego" flips through a series of black and white photographs: a handmade, stenciled sign reading, "Comics Convention Registration"; shoppers browsing in the dealers' room; artist Russ Manning, posing with his sketch of Tarzan; a collector rifling through a box of comics; aficionados enjoying an art display; a table of six panelists addressing a room full of attendees; and comic artist Don Newton and his son posing in matching Superman costumes

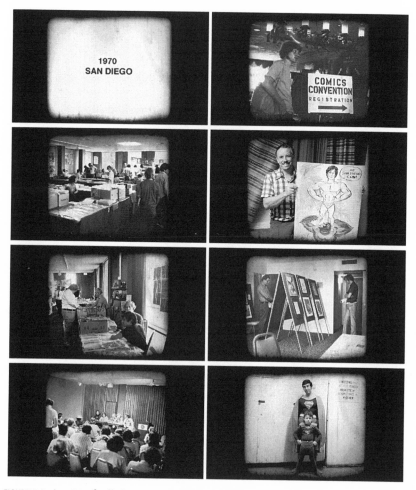

FIGURE 1.1 A series of still photos mimic a slide-show presentation about Comic-Con's early history in the opening sequence of *Comic-Con Episode IV: A Fan's Hope* (Spurlock 2011).

(figure 1.1). Accompanying the slide show is an audio recording of a Channel 39 news segment with the event's founder, Shel Dorf.[1]

ANNOUNCER: The first annual Golden State Comic-Con gets underway this weekend at the U.S. Grant Hotel. Artist Shel Dorf says that he hopes to make this event an annual thing.

NATALIE BEST: Will this be open to the public?

DORF: Ah . . . yes. This is a chance for the amateur fan and amateur writer to really meet with the professionals and find the magic secret of how it's done.[2]

FIGURE 1.2 Footage of fans entering Comic-Con 2010, featured in the opening sequence of *Comic-Con Episode IV: A Fan's Hope* (Spurlock, 2011).

When asked about the size of the gathering, Dorf optimistically speculates that attendance at the 1970 convention could hit five hundred.[3] At that moment, the film cuts from the antiquated, black and white slide show to colorful moving images filmed at Comic-Con in 2010. As the opening credits roll, we see slow motion and accelerated glimpses of fans—many in costume—pouring into the convention hall, all accompanied by a swelling and downright heroic score (figure 1.2). In the space of one and a half minutes, Spurlock manages to spin a compelling yarn evoking the same epic scope we've come to expect from superhero stories, be they on multiplex screens or in the pages of comic books. And, like any good superhero myth, this one provides an origin story of an underdog, imbued with almost otherworldly powers, who is reborn as an unstoppable force. That force, the film suggests, resides in the power, ambition, and resilience of fandom.

Clearly, a narrative in which fans—and their tastes and cultural practices—rise from the margins to become a cultural force is a powerful myth. It is one that gets repeated again and again as Hollywood uses venues like Comic-Con to propel its vision for fan culture—and its utility to the industry—into the mainstream. Given that the exclusivity of fans as a powerful demographic of tastemakers is frequently identified as a contemporary phenomenon, deterministically tied to a narrative of digital democracy, it is not surprising that this pre-credits sequence of *Comic-Con*

Episode IV represents the bulk of the eighty-eight-minute film's overt discussion of history. Add to that the fact that none of the slide show's seven images were actually taken at the first Comic-Con in 1970 and it becomes clear that in this film, like so many other celebratory discourses about the power and influence of fandom, constructing a compelling narrative of growth and acceptance takes precedence over historical accuracy and precision.[4] In such narratives, the fates of pop culture fans and the media industries seem deeply and unproblematically intertwined, propelling each other forward in utopic symbiosis. They also point to the ways in which the exclusivity of Comic-Con was defined and redefined in the process. While Comic-Con's early years provided an exclusive space for fans and professionals to come together in celebration of comics and the popular arts, the Comic-Con of the twenty-first century redefines exclusivity as the product of insider access to the media industries and their marketing blitzkrieg.

What these narratives frequently omit, however, is the later ambivalence, even downright dissatisfaction, with the event, particularly on the part of comic fans and professionals, who often complain that the object of their fandom has been marginalized as a result of Hollywood's presence. Some of this frustration makes its way into Spurlock's largely celebratory film by way of longtime comics dealer Chuck Rozanski.[5] In the film, we find him struggling just to break even at Comic-Con. For Rozanski, the crux of Comic-Con's problem is the steady disappearance of comics, and more importantly, comics buyers, from the event: "Even though they have comic in the name of the event, very little of the convention anymore is actually comics. . . . we can't use the loading docks anymore cause frickin' Lucasfilm owns the loading docks. You know, that kind of pisses you off. It really does. Because it's our house." But despite his struggles to turn a profit at a convention that seems to have left him behind, as the film ends, he proclaims that instead of heaven, "I wanna die and go to Comic-Con."

This ambivalence occasionally crops up in the press too. For example, writing for *Variety* in 2008, TV critic Brian Lowry described his experiences at Comic-Con in the mid-'70s—"Comic-Con was truly about comic books, and the only stars one was likely to see there were the artists and writers who created them"—and lamented its growth as Hollywood discovered the convention's promotional possibilities.[6] In 2013, the *Atlantic* published an article titled "How the Nerds Lost Comic-Con," which echoed Lowry's sentiments, claiming that as Hollywood promotion at the event propelled it into the mainstream, longtime comic book fans found themselves frozen out—unable to get tickets, or inconvenienced by the massive crowds.[7]

I have also heard fans express these concerns at Comic-Con's annual "Talk Back" panel, which provides an open forum for attendees to give feedback on the event. A 2011 exchange between a longtime attendee and Comic-Con's president at the time, John Rogers, neatly encapsulates the tension between comics and Hollywood at the event.[8] The attendee began by saying they had been going to Comic-Con "since back when it was a comic book convention, 1981." Rogers, who usually remained quite stoic during these sessions, quietly making notes as the flow of complaints and suggestions flew at him, interrupted to argue that comics were still central to the convention. When the attendee suggested that the majority of people were there to see film and television content, Rogers replied, "What we like to say is that we're celebrating the popular arts which, of course, would include film and television." The attendee interrupted, "We used to celebrate the unpopular ones." Rogers went on to suggest that Comic-Con itself had helped to push comics into the mainstream: "one of the things we've always done is brought people in who are fans of a movie, like a Batman movie, and gotten them exposed to other comic books on the floor and other comic book items through programming."[9] Not surprisingly, Rogers's arguments echoed Comic-Con's mission statement by placing the emphasis on comics and implying that the presence of film and television was a way to further increase awareness of the comic arts: "Comic-Con International: San Diego is a nonprofit educational corporation dedicated to creating awareness of, and appreciation for, comics and related popular art forms, primarily through the presentation of conventions and events that celebrate the historic and ongoing contribution of comics to art and culture."[10] The limits of exclusivity are clearly at play here as the fan's complaints and Rogers's response negotiate the push and pull desire to legitimate and promote comics as a popular art form, while still keeping them exclusive to a small group of fans. Even in arguing for the place of comics in mainstream popular culture, Comic-Con organizers deploy the exclusivity of comic books in order to disavow their commodity status.

Nowhere is this ambivalence more pronounced than in Shel Dorf's reaction to the event's success. In a 2006 interview he said, "We had no idea it would get this big . . . to me, it's just become an ordeal. I don't know of any way to make it smaller, though, I guess in some ways it's become too much of a success."[11] Dorf passed away in November 2009, four months after Comic-Con celebrated its fortieth anniversary. Having been hospitalized for quite some time, he was unable to take part in the celebrations, but his friend, Mark Evanier, said Dorf would have been unlikely to attend regardless: "He didn't like how big the one he started had become, didn't like how top movie stars were eclipsing top comic creators."[12]

Dorf made this sentiment clear in numerous letters to Comic-Con organizers and friends over the years, where he would fluctuate between warm nostalgia and pride for what he had helped to create and contempt for what it had become.[13] Having ended his "active participation" in 1984, Dorf remained a voice on the sidelines, attending the convention and sending occasional letters to members of the Comic-Con committee, including clippings from articles and old programs.[14] But relations soured as he grew more and more alienated from the committee, evidenced by a letter he wrote to the board of directors in 1994, asking that they remove his founder credit from all future Comic-Con publications. He explained, "the con has changed so much from the friendly little fannish effort I started that I do not feel a kinship to it any longer."[15] Ultimately, Dorf regretted and retracted this request, but tensions lingered, as evidenced by his 1999 letter to Comic-Con's president, John Rogers, accepting an invitation to join Comic-Con's thirtieth anniversary celebration. Dorf wrote, "I now know that I will always feel a parental closeness to the con. Those first establishing five years were tougher than anyone could imagine. . . . As a parent, I have been critical of different directions the thing took. But I did neglect to constantly say, 'good work.' My praise far exceeded my criticism. I hope we can reconcile past differences and move on."[16]

By all accounts, Dorf's ongoing ambivalence was the product of the particularities of his personality paired with Comic-Con's extreme growth and change in the years after he retired.[17] His frustrations seemed to increase as the event grew larger and as the Comic-Con committee itself became more self-sustaining and financially solvent.[18] But while Dorf was troubled by Comic-Con's growth in his later years, this was not always the case. As president of Comic-Con for its first fifteen years, he saw attendance increase from 300 attendees in 1970 to almost 5,500 in 1984, fulfilling Dorf's promise in 1970 that "the years to come will see us grow and San Diego will take it's [sic] rightful place in the world of fandom."[19] Dorf's response, once this dream was realized, suggests that Comic-Con, and the relationships it fosters between fandom and industry, are much more complex and fraught than they appear. At the core of these complexities is the desire to experience a reciprocal relationship with the industry—not only to express love but also to get something in return. But instead of drawing the industry into fandom's "gift economy," Dorf's reactions suggest that Comic-Con had become too embroiled in the capitalist interests of the media industries.[20] While he envisioned Comic-Con as an "exchange of love . . . between the creative artist and the audience," Dorf felt that his protégés on the Comic-Con board of directors, and the increased industry presence, which he described specifically as "Hollywood," had foregrounded business and economics over the love of the popular arts.[21] So while Comic-Con's growth over the years is a crucial part of the mythology surrounding the event, the *way* this growth occurred seems to be a frequent source of consternation.

At the heart of all of this ambivalence and frustration—from professionals, fans, and even Comic-Con's founder—are two critiques. The first is that industry interests at Comic-Con have eclipsed those of fans. This represents a key tension emerging out of convergence culture: while fan and media industry interests often converge, this has a tendency to happen only when fans work in concert with industry goals.[22] A second, and related, critique is that the role of comics has diminished at Comic-Con as Hollywood moved in to the event. As the Talk Back example suggests, this complaint grows out of the tension between comics' commodity status and their position as a marginalized art form. As I describe in this chapter, early fans and Comic-Con organizers came together, in large part, to legitimize comics and argue for their importance in popular culture. But in the same way that the industry tends to celebrate only those fan practices that adhere to its capitalist goals, comic books have been increasingly legitimated in economic, rather than cultural, terms—as intellectual property to be bought, sold, and owned by large media conglomerates.

This chapter argues that in order to make sense of Comic-Con's growth and contemporary popularity, it is necessary to understand its history. In doing so, I explore how Comic-Con's roots in comic fandom, its founding, and the practices established in the convention's early years laid groundwork for the future, blurring the lines between fan and professional labor and cultivating an environment that promoted comics alongside film, television, and other media. From a contemporary vantage point, Comic-Con's connection to Hollywood appears closely aligned with Patricia Ventura's description of neoliberal culture, which "impels us to extend the market, its technologies, approaches, and mindsets into all spheres of human life, to move the ideology of consumer choice to the center of individual existence, and to look to ourselves rather than larger social-welfare structures or society as the source of our success or blame for our failure—indeed, to define 'success' and 'failure' in market terms."[23] But, as this chapter demonstrates, the historical and cultural frameworks that enabled such ideologies to be enacted at and through the San Diego Comic-Con also predate the rise of neoliberalism as a prominent political and cultural discourse.[24] Take for example, famed comic book artist Jack Kirby's 1971 proclamation that Comic-Con was "the future, not just of comics, but of all media. Movie studios are going to come to this convention every year to see what's new."[25] Kirby's words position recognition from Hollywood as a measure of growth, imagining a future where Comic-Con's exclusivity as a media event grows out of its relevance—not to fans, but to the media industries. Though it may seem deeply prophetic now, this statement, made one year after Comic-Con's inception, is even more valuable for the evidence it provides about the convention's history: Comic-Con was primed, from the very beginning, to be a comfortable place not just for fans but also for Hollywood.

Double Fans and Industry Alter Egos

Though Comic-Con was founded in 1970, its roots reside in the consolidation of comic book fandom that started ten years earlier with the establishment of what Paul Lopes describes as "an organized social network of fans."[26] The choice of the phrase "social network" is an interesting one given the significant roles digital social networks now play in fan cultures. But before platforms like Facebook, Twitter, and Tumblr existed, there were letter columns, fanzines, fan clubs, and conventions. While scholars often emphasize the way that the digital economy has altered the relationship between producers and consumers, both by yielding a more affective and influential audience and by producing conditions under which this audience's labor is exploited for capitalist gain, the early history of comics fandom and subsequent founding of Comic-Con suggests that in some cultural spheres, key attributes of convergence culture and neoliberal ideologies have long been in place.[27] There are undoubtedly differences, especially in terms of scale, participation, and sheer profit, but the Comic-Con of the twenty-first century, with its exclusive environment where fans and professionals come together to celebrate and promote popular culture across media, cannot be separated from the event's history and its place in the history of comics fandom.

Though comics existed in the form of newspaper strips beginning in the 1890s, and as books by the mid-1930s, fans of the medium didn't find one another right away.[28] As a truly mass medium that told stories in a broad cross-section of genres, the early audience for comic strips and books was somewhat diffuse and amorphous.[29] At the beginning of the 1950s, some readers attempted to mobilize around EC comics, producer of titles like *Tales from the Crypt* (1950–1955) and *Weird Science* (1950–1953). Fans published a number of short-lived fanzines, but when they realized that the bulk of EC readers fell between the ages of 9 and 13, they gravitated, instead, toward what seemed to be a more mature fandom surrounding science fiction literature.[30] EC also joined a number of other publishers in promoting their own official fan club, the "Fan-Addict Club," beginning in 1952. However, this effort stalled as the moral panic inflamed by the 1954 U.S. Senate Subcommittee to Investigate Juvenile Delinquency and Fredric Wertham's *Seduction of the Innocent* (1954) led to the establishment of the Comics Code Authority in 1954, and wiped out EC comics in 1955.[31]

Science fiction fandom, on the other hand, was three decades old by the time comics fans came together in the early 1960s. It grew out of letters published in the back pages of *Amazing Stories* in the 1920s, developed into stand-alone science fiction fanzines in the early 1930s, and flourished at the first World Science Fiction Convention in 1939.[32] As evidenced by the migration of EC fans to science fiction fandom in the 1950s, many future members of comics fandom were already active in this community.[33] Such individuals, known as "double fans," helped to draw comics into science fiction fandom, and vice versa.[34] In 1960, Pat and Dick Lupoff's science fiction fanzine, *Xero*, included a popular column on comics titled, "All in Color for a Dime," and the success of this column inspired science fiction fans Maggie Curtis and Don Thompson to produce their fanzine, *Comic Art*, in 1961.[35] Curtis and Thompson picked up on the Lupoffs' call for the formation of a "general comics fandom" by impressing upon readers that their publication, though likely to be read primarily by their friends in science fiction fandom, was geared specifically toward comic art.[36] However, they defined the term somewhat broadly: "Comic art, for our purposes, covers a wide field. Besides comic books and comic strips, it includes movie and TV cartoons, gag and sport and political cartoons and the Big and Better Little Books of years ago.

Subject matter ranges from horror and adventure to satire and gentle humor."[37] Reading Curtis and Thompson's definition of comic art, it is hard not to think of Comic-Con's mission statement, authored many years later, which similarly laid the groundwork for an approach to comic fandom that encompassed "the popular arts," more generally.[38]

In the process of defining and legitimating comics as an art form, scholars have made the important case for medium specificity, focusing on what makes the form unique.[39] However, the ties between science fiction and comics fandom paired with relatively broad definitions of what constituted comic content suggest that these early fan tastes did not necessarily operate within the same medium-specific constraints. Indeed, these early comics fans exhibited precisely the kind of "migratory behavior" that Henry Jenkins describes as a signature feature of convergence culture.[40] But, as Shawna Kidman argues, the comics industry, too, has long promoted this same migratory ethos through "licensing and other synergistic business practices that placed their characters at the center of interactive and multimedia corporate strategies."[41] This makes understanding the fan and industry relationship especially complicated, as it is difficult to honor the early contributions of comic and science fiction fans without simultaneously critiquing the ways in which these contributions fed the capitalist machinations of the comics industry.

Indeed, the role of the industry in the establishment of comics fandom is extremely significant, especially since much of the foundational scholarship in fan studies theorizes fan cultures as arising from a place of resistance, appropriating texts rather than working in concert with the industry.[42] In the case of comics, however, it was when the industry deepened its involvement with readers that an "organized social network of fans" truly began to gel.[43] According to *Overstreet's Comic Book Price Guide*, an authoritative source in the world of comic collectors and fans, editors at the three major comics publishers—Julius Schwartz of DC, Stan Lee of Marvel, and Bill Harris of Gold Key—"were most influential in bringing comics readers into Fandom."[44] Following the same trajectory as science fiction magazines did decades earlier, these editors used their letters columns to publish and respond to feedback from readers, share the names and mailing addresses of individual fans so that they could communicate with one another, and promote amateur fanzines.[45]

In 1961, the same year that "double fans" Don Thompson and Maggie Curtis published *Comic Art*, Jerry Bails and Roy Thomas published the influential comics fanzine, *Alter Ego*.[46] This publication was the direct result of a meeting between Bails and DC editor Julius Schwartz, who also happened to be one of the founding members of science fiction fandom. Schwartz, along with Mort Weisinger, co-published *Time Traveler* in 1932, one of the earliest science fiction fanzines.[47] Soon after, the two men formed Solar Sales Service, a literary agency specializing in science fiction, and by the 1940s, both Schwartz and Weisinger were working as editors at DC Comics.[48] Bails had been corresponding with Schwartz about starting a Justice League of America newsletter and met with him in January 1961, during a visit to New York.[49] Schwartz told Bails of his experiences in science fiction fandom and introduced him to the concept of fanzines, even showing him copies of *Xero*.[50] "I dug up some fan magazines from a drawer and showed them to him," Schwartz would later recall, "His eyes popped out. He didn't realize there was a fan movement in science fiction with fan magazines. I told him they were called 'fanzines.'"[51] With this newfound knowledge, Bails used the names and addresses Schwartz had been publishing in DC's letter columns to reach out to fellow fans, publishing the first issue of *Alter Ego* a few months later.[52] Over the next ten years, comics fandom would flourish (albeit maintaining somewhat subcultural status) with over six hundred different fanzines publishing 2,720 issues that included content such as reviews, articles on comic history, indexing and pricing information for collectors, and illustrations, all while providing a forum for amateur artists and writers to publish their work.[53] These fanzines, along with letter columns in comic books, were instrumental in familiarizing readers with the names of professional artists and writers, deploying the trope of authorship to help legitimize the field and elevate the work of comics producers.[54]

While there is no doubt that Schwartz played an important role in this process, any speculation about his motivations is complicated by his intersecting identities as fan and professional, evidence of a long-standing tendency in comics culture that Benjamin Woo describes as "erasing the lines between labor and leisure."[55] Indeed, Schwartz himself once stated that, "If I played any part in encouraging the formation of comic fandom . . . it's because I was (and still am) a fan at heart."[56] So were his actions an attempt to mentor and pass the torch to a new generation of fans? Or were they a savvy business decision that would build a loyal readership and appreciation of comics history at the same time that DC was reviving their golden age superheroes?[57] The answer is most likely some combination of the two. As Kidman suggests, the relationship between fans and the comics industry at that time offered advantages to both groups, "generally in affective terms for fans and in economic terms for industry."[58] However, these gains were the result of significant work on the part of comic fans. Melissa Gregg defines this "affective labor," at the core of scholarly debates about fans and active audiences, as "human activity that does not result in a direct financial profit or exchange value, but rather produces a sense of community, esteem, and/or belonging for those who share a common interest."[59] Understood this way, the industry's economic gains might be seen as a by-product of affective fan labor, while the primary product was the formation and maintenance of the community itself. But, as Michael Hardt argues, the "subjectivities" and "sociality" produced through affective labor are also "directly exploitable by capital."[60] So coming at a time when comic sales were down and the general public saw the medium as a disposable, low cultural form consumed primarily by children, it is also important to remember that this affective labor had the overt aim of supporting and legitimating the comic arts and, by extension, ensuring the industry was successful.[61]

This was certainly the case for *Alter Ego* cofounder Jerry Bails, whose contributions to comics fandom earned him the title, "the father of comics fandom."[62] Among his many contributions was the formation of the Academy of Comic-Book Fans and Collectors (ACBFC) in 1962, which grew out of Bails's long-standing belief that comic book writers and artists deserved to be recognized and credited for their achievements.[63] The ACBFC was an attempt to bring in new fans and institutionalize comic fandom by distributing "The Alley Awards" for comic books (Schwartz's DC swept the awards in their first year).[64] The group also published a fanzine called *The Comic Reader*, endorsed best practices for selling and trading comics, encouraged community-building activities among comic fans, and engaged in industry outreach.[65] As a professor of natural science at Wayne State University, Bails's contributions to comics culture were part of his leisure time, not a professional pursuit, but this does not mean his activities were beneficial *only* to fandom. Nor does it mean that the leisure time of fans exists outside influence or interests of the industry. Rather, this kind of affective community building represents the way fandom, as a leisure activity, is both essential to the functioning of capitalism and impossible without it.[66]

Indeed, this parallel establishment of comics fandom and elevation of the comics industry made the connection between fan and professional that much stronger.[67] Fanzines provided opportunities for fans to gain exposure and, like the science fiction fans before them, some sought to parlay their amateur work into professional gigs. While Jerry Bails maintained his amateur status, despite his massive contributions to comics fandom, *Alter Ego*'s other founding editor, Roy Thomas, quickly moved from fan to professional.[68] After a weeklong stint at DC Comics in 1965, he spent over fifteen years as a writer and editor at Marvel Comics, eventually replacing Stan Lee as Marvel's editor-in-chief in 1972.[69] Marvel shared the news of Thomas's employment in a 1966 "Marvel Bullpen Bulletin": "Roy's a fan who's made it! Although employed as a school teacher in St. Louis (his subject was English!) Roy never lost his love for comic mags—Marvels, to be exact! So after a lot of correspondence back and forth, we decided it would be cheaper to hire him for the bullpen than to keep shelling out money for those air-mail stamps!"[70] This announcement seems to suggest that other than his experience as an English teacher, Thomas's primary qualifications for his new writing job at Marvel were his loyalty to the brand and his engagement as a Marvel fan (despite the fact that he had worked for DC first). This puts the announcement squarely in line with much of the communication in Marvel's "Bullpen Bulletins," a regular feature in which the editor-in-chief, Stan Lee, shared insider gossip about the company and its employees and flattered Marvel's fan base, ultimately constructing the Marvel brand around a community made up of loyal fans *and* pros.[71]

Did Thomas stop being a fan the day he walked through the doors of Marvel's head office as an employee? Yes and no. While his passion for comic books remained, he received clear instructions from Stan Lee not to disclose any Marvel plots or news, limiting his ability to participate in fanzine publishing.[72] As he transitioned from fan to pro, the nature of his labor also changed from unpaid, affective labor to paid industry work, and his success represented the promise of mobility between fan and professional identities. For this reason, I argue, we can also understand the work of early comics fans as "creative activities that hold the *promise* of social and economic capital" [my emphasis], what Brooke Erin Duffy calls "aspirational labor."[73] Kathleen Kuehn and Thomas F. Corrigan similarly argue that this kind of forward-looking "hope labor" is distinct from other kinds of free labor in that it is motivated by the promise of paid work down the road.[74]

While these theories of aspirational labor emerged in the context of the digital economy and neoliberal culture, the comic publishers of the 1960s, much like the creative industries of today, were precarious environments. Fans frequently attempted to break into the industry only to be met with disappointment, while those that did make the transition from fan to pro could be doubly exploited—both for their affective labor as fans and for their hope labor as aspiring or early-career professionals.[75] These fans-turned-pros joined comic writers and artists who were also there for the love of the game, so to speak—underpaid, overworked, and employed under work-for-hire contracts that gave their publishers the rights to the characters they created.[76] Abigail De Kosnik suggests that this move from amateur to professional status could be one way to compensate fan labor, but paid labor does not necessarily preclude exploitation.[77] In his history of American comic books, for example, Jean-Paul Gabilliet goes as far as to describe the comics industry as "one of the most retrograde publishing environments" of the 1960s, where "creators saw themselves systematically wronged as they lost their rights once they changed employers."[78] Indeed, environments of precarity, such as the comics industry in the 1960s and the digital economy of the twenty-first century, add significant complications to the prospects (and benefits) of professionalization. More often than not, the promise of a successful transition from fan to professional is a way to motivate more unpaid and underpaid labor. By the 1970s, not only had the industry hired an influx of enthusiastic fan-pros, but they also began to compete with their amateur fan base by publishing "Pro-zines" that featured the publisher-owned work of professional artists. These publications found a way to transform affective and aspirational labor into direct profit by competing with, and often undercutting, the very fanzines that had helped to launch comics fandom a decade earlier.[79]

Perhaps the best examples of the collision of affective and aspirational labor in comic fandom, however, are comic conventions. Not only do they celebrate comics and fan culture, but they also celebrate the industry; they offer a space where a community can come together, but this space is also a commercial one, where comics and collectibles can be bought, sold, traded, and promoted. The first convention to prominently feature comics was held in Detroit's Hotel Tuller on May 24, 1964, and attracted approximately seventy fans.[80] A year later, in 1965, Jerry Bails and future Comic-Con founder Shel Dorf built upon the Hotel Tuller convention to organize Detroit's first "Triple Fan Fair" from July 24 to 25, an event that combined comics, films, and fantasy, in order to appeal to the same kinds of eclectic tastes that characterized science fiction's double fans.[81] This "cross-fandom approach," however, was as much a marketing strategy to ensure high attendance numbers as it was a product of the overlapping interests between fans.[82] Of course, the affective labor of organizing such a convention and attracting a large audience was not necessarily tied to economic profit but to the promotion of comics and comic fandom itself.

The second and more well known convention, the New York Comicon, occurred two months after the Hotel Tuller convention, on July 27, 1964. Not only did the New York Comicon originate the now ubiquitous shorthand, "comic con," but it was also notable for its inclusion of a number of professional attendees, which would become a standard feature of future conventions.[83] But the participation of comics professionals at the New York Comicon didn't exactly set the stage for probing explorations of the realities of work in the industry. According to Bill Schelly's account of the event, when one fan inquired about the salary for comic writers and artists, Steve Ditko, the co-creator of Spider-Man and Doctor Strange, "declined to answer with a shake of his head."[84] Although fans seemed to be getting closer to the industry, certain boundaries between fan and professional could not be dismantled. If anything, comic conventions reified the boundaries between the industry and fans by building on the affective labor that filled letter columns and fanzines in order to amplify the exclusivity of professional artists and writers and help shore up the comics industry's burgeoning star system.[85]

Thus, as comic book fandom continued to develop into the 1970s, it became increasingly focused on content and creators' rights, but, as Kidman argues, "did not criticize the [industry's] labor practices, financial priorities, and internal power hierarchies so long as those aspects of the business remained at a far enough remove from the stories themselves."[86] This emphasis on content and authorship is key, as it sets the stage for comics to be unmoored from the print medium, expanding into a more amorphous, multimedia intellectual property. But it also takes collective labor and industry power out of the equation; the very things that most impacted Comic-Con as it developed from a grassroots fan event to an industry space.

The history of comics fandom, and of Comic-Con itself, suggests that the dual function of the convention—to elevate comics and the popular arts and to bring fans and pros together—hinges on the affective and aspirational labor of the fans who organized and attended the event. This makes these intersecting histories surprisingly resonant in the context of contemporary discourses about digital media.[87] In many ways, the birth of comic fandom and subsequent founding of Comic-Con grew out of what Henry Jenkins has described as a "collaborationist" approach on the part of the comics industry, which encouraged reader feedback and contributed to the formation of comics fandom.[88] Similarly, the synergistic nature, to borrow an industry term, of early comics fandom, meant that from the beginning, comics and other media were to be, as 1975 Comic-Con president Richard Butner put it, "interconnected...beyond disentanglement."[89] The remainder of this chapter examines how these overlaps, among fans and pros and among different media forms, were integral not only to the founding vision of Comic-Con but also to the convention's relationship to Hollywood.

A History of the ProFan(e)

Much has changed since Comic-Con was founded in 1970, but the importance of early comics fandom's collaborationist approach has always been crucial to the event. According to the official history, Comic-Con's inception sprung from "an amazing confluence of fan groups" that emerged in San Diego during the mid-'60s.[90] Two of these fan groups were the Underground Film Society and the San Diego Science Fantasy Society, and, as the names indicate, their investment in popular culture was not limited to comic books. Though the two groups comprised primarily teenaged boys, an older member of the San Diego Science Fantasy Society, Ken Krueger (himself a participant in early science fiction fandom) owned Alert Booksellers in Ocean Beach, which became a popular meeting spot.[91] In the late 1960s, these groups came together, calling themselves the "ProFanests."[92] While the reference to profanity signified devotion to secular, popular entertainment, this title also indicated the importance of fans and professionals joining together because of a mutual interest in popular culture.[93] Some members worked in publishing or retail, while others were aspiring artists and writers who published their own fanzines.[94] Over time, more fans and pros were brought into the fold, but it was not until the ProFanests met Shel Dorf and his group of comic fans that the idea for Comic-Con began to form.

Shortly after moving to San Diego in 1969, a cash-strapped Dorf decided to sell some of his comics while he looked for work and responded to a classified ad from an aspiring comics dealer named Barry Alfonso. The twelve-year-old Alfonso couldn't afford everything Dorf was selling, but directed him to a seventeen-year-old mail-order comics dealer named Richard Alf, who ran ads in the pages of Marvel comics and stored his inventory of approximately 20,000 books in his parents' garage.[95] Through Alfonso and

Alf, Dorf met two other teenaged dealers, Bob Sourk and Mike Towry. Dorf, then thirty-five, became a kind of leader to the group, and they formed the San Diego Society for Creative Fantasy.[96] According to most accounts, it was around this time that Dorf suggested the idea of holding a convention.[97] When Bob Sourk met Scott Shaw! at a local bookshop, he invited him to attend one of their meetings.[98] Over time, Shaw!'s friends from the Pro-Fanests joined in, and the two groups merged.

They organized a one-day "Minicon" in March 1970, and that event helped to raise enough funds to run the first Comic-Con for three days that summer.[99] The guest of honor at that first event was Forrest J. Ackerman. Ackerman, like Julius Schwartz, was a founding member of science fiction fandom who managed to break into the publishing industry to become the editor of the horror movie magazine, *Famous Monsters of Filmland*, and the co-creator of the comic book character, Vampirella.[100] As a fan-turned-professional who worked at the intersections of comics, film, horror, and science fiction, Ackerman fit neatly into the double fan and pro/fan frameworks that characterized early comics fandom. His appearance helped to bring in enough attendees (around 145) to make the Minicon a success and, with the help of additional financing from organizer and dealer Richard Alf, enabled organizers to put plans in motion for the first Comic-Con on July 1–3, 1970.[101]

The "confluence of fan groups" that led to the founding of Comic-Con certainly follows the template laid out in comics and science fiction double fandom.[102] Though there was a thriving fan community in San Diego in the 1950s and 1960s, most of these groups were focused on science fiction, fantasy, and film.[103] Integrating comic fandom into this preexisting community was a deliberate strategy to make Comic-Con a more successful event.[104] But these fan groups were also notable because a large number of their members, though only teenagers at the time, were or would become involved in the business of comic books and/or the creative industries.[105] Several of the original Comic-Con committee members earned money as comic dealers and used these channels to promote and finance the event.[106] Others went on to successful careers in writing, cartooning, and marketing.[107] Even Shel Dorf was able to secure more professional opportunities, including a "dream job" as a letterer for the *Steve Canyon* comic stip.[108] As the name of Shaw!'s fan club, the ProFanests, suggests, though Comic-Con was founded by a group of individuals identifying themselves as fans of comics and popular culture, they were not operating entirely outside of industrial frameworks.

Instead, many of Comic-Con's organizers either had professional aspirations or were already contributing to the comic and publishing industries in some capacity.

It is not surprising, then, that Comic-Con's programming extended the affective and aspirational labor done by early comic fandom by emphasizing the shared investments of fans and comic professionals in uplifting the medium, while also using the convention to promote the possibility of upward mobility for fans. For those with the inclination, the convention offered many opportunities to learn about and seek out work in the comic, film, and television industries. "A San Diego Comic-Con Retrospective," published in the 1979 souvenir book, emphasized two important aspects of the convention in its first ten years: It encouraged affective labor by allowing fans to "meet and play groupie" to "professional comic talent," and it promoted aspirational labor by allowing "the upcoming amateur or semiprofessional artist" to share their work and "elevate himself and his [sic] career."[109] In a letter published in the 1973 souvenir book, Dorf described how pivotal comic fandom was to the evolution of the art form: "We believe in comic fandom. It is the source (as has already been proven) of future artists, writers, and editors. The fan and the pro have a lot to offer each other. The sellers of rare material serve an even more important function—they help us fill the gaps in our collection and make available the stuff that has gone before. By studying the work of those who have laid the groundwork for the industry, we can learn to seek out new directions, and help to build and diversify the field of comics."[110] Dorf's statement demonstrates that, even in 1973, the overlaps between fans and professionals attending the event were already deeply ingrained. Not only that, but this relationship, as Dorf presents it, was also based on the performance of affective labor by fans and professionals, all in the name of advancing the comics industry. The collaborationist nature of the event, paired with organizers' broad appeals to popular culture fandom, opened the door for a more general conflation of fan and professional investments, which reverberates throughout Comic-Con's history.[111]

Programming that encouraged overlaps between fan and professional identities, as well as affective and aspirational labor, was also evident across Comic-Con's early history. Beginning in its founding year, Comic-Con included an art show to which both fans and professionals could contribute, blurring the line between amateur and professional art.[112] In 1973, Comic-Con introduced a Sunday Brunch, where fans could pay five dollars to "actually sit down at the same table with [their] favorite pro and delve into the inner workings of his (or her) mind."[113] That same year, Carmen Infantino, then the president and head publisher of DC Comics, offered "an informative talk on the production and economics of comics" but also used this talk to promote DC's upcoming titles.[114] During the presentation, DC's production manager, Sol Harrison, discussed the company's "Junior Bullpen Program," a contest for aspiring comics professionals.[115] The prize? An apprenticeship at DC Comics and the guarantee of "a basic wage."[116] By the early 1980s, Comic-Con programming had expanded to include a number of panels explicitly geared toward professionalizing amateur fans, such as, "How to Break Into TV" or "How to Break Into Comics."[117] A noticeable trend emerges from these examples: though Comic-Con celebrated the fans and industries that made up comics and popular culture, the event's programming frequently situated the relationship between fans and industry as an aspirational one; helping fans to be more like professionals and positioning fans as important and viable participants in the comic and entertainment industries. This programming encouraged aspirational labor by highlighting the potential for upward mobility and by framing work in comics and other creative industries as exclusive career paths, while using affective labor to downplay the fact that, as DC's "Junior Bullpen Program" contests suggested, what these industries were offering was often, at best, "a basic wage."

The ease with which fan identification moved between amateur and professional at Comic-Con was not accidental. Shel Dorf was explicit about his desire to close this gap between fans and pros, or at least to facilitate the interweaving of fandom and cultural production by allowing "the amateur fan and the amateur writer to really meet with the professionals and find the magic secret of how it's done."[118] He would later elaborate on his motivations for founding Comic-Con: "I decided cartoonists were the only entertainers who didn't hear the laughter and applause, so I created a public convention where the pros could meet their fans and the young hopefuls could get advice on their careers."[119] Ultimately, this sentiment suggests that Dorf saw Comic-Con as a potential service or show of respect to artists, who "didn't hear the laughter and applause," while also allowing fans to benefit from their wisdom. This altruistic goal is certainly admirable, especially in relation to the experience of many comic artists who gave up the rights to their creations through work-for-hire contracts.[120]

As Tiziana Terranova argues, it is important to remember that free labor may not always be exploitative, particularly when viewed within a historical context.[121] Much in the same way that the early days of comic fandom grew out of both affective and aspirational labor, Comic-Con was founded upon the idea of building a community of fans and pros, in which participants' unpaid labor was "willingly conceded in exchange for the pleasures of communication and exchange."[122] But, when viewed from a contemporary context, it is possible to see how these principles simultaneously blurred the lines between fan and professional and reinforced a hierarchy around those who produce culture and those who consume it. This created a situation in which the affective labor of Comic-Con's early (and young) organizers could be perceived as beneficial and empowering to fans even as it was explicitly geared toward serving artists and advancing the industry. As I discuss in the conclusion to this chapter, this dynamic has become increasingly complicated, as the industry presence at Comic-Con has shifted from individual artists to large corporations and conglomerates. However, the fact remains that the industry was always on Comic-Con's guest list.

Beyond Disentanglement

As I have argued, Comic-Con's founding years and early programming built on the history of comics fandom, resulting in an environment that cultivated an affective and aspirational connection between fans and professionals. This connection helped to carve out the space for a much more pronounced industry presence down the road, one that would extend well beyond comics publishers. But, as Comic-Con's organizers have long argued—often in an attempt to counter critiques about Hollywood's encroachment—film and television content was always a part of the event.[123] The 1973 souvenir book, for example, included a large comic art component, but it also incorporated clippings of old film advertisements, even an autographed photo of Joan Crawford.[124] In the early 1970s, Comic-Con featured several guests from film and television, including actors Kirk Alyn, Walter Koenig, and Adam West; animators Chuck Jones and Bob Clampett; and filmmakers Frank Capra and George Pal.[125] Film screenings have always been a significant part of Comic-Con too. Before the days of home video or on-demand content, Comic-Con gave attendees exclusive access to old serials like *Flash Gordon* (Frederick Stephani, 1936) or *Superman* (Spencer Gordon Bennet and Thomas Carr, 1948).[126] But the films screened at Comic-Con were not always explicitly linked to superheroes or science fiction and selections such as *Scarlet Street* (Fritz Lang, 1945), *Mr. Smith Goes to Washington* (Frank Capra, 1939), and *Oceans 11* (Lewis Mileston, 1960) also targeted a more general audience of cinephiles.[127]

Shel Dorf's involvement in 1960s comics fandom, as an organizer of the 1965 Detroit Triple Fan Fair, was crucial in establishing this multimedia "blueprint" for Comic-Con.[128] In a 1982 Q & A for Comic-Con's Souvenir Book, Dorf explained that his idea was to model Comic-Con on the Triple Fan Fair, which he described at length: "One part was a bazaar, where they would be selling all kinds of comic books and newspaper strips. A second part of it was where they would be showing old movies. And the third part was where we'd have guests from the science fiction and comics field doing live demonstrations. . . . The main objective behind all this is to create a public gathering place for people who enjoy these media—science fiction, movies and comics with the accent on comics because there had already been science-fiction conventions."[129] Dorf's description suggests that the Triple Fan Fair was an attempt to appeal to a broad cross-section of fandom, while also carving out a new space for a burgeoning community of comics fans. As I outlined earlier, the founding of Comic-Con similarly relied on the strength of preexisting, multimedial fan groups in the San Diego area in order to promote comics and build support for a comic convention. The result was an event that closely resembled Detroit's Triple Fan Fair, with a variety of programming, but with a special emphasis on comics. Nowhere is the influence of the Triple Fan Fair on Comic-Con more apparent than in the similarities between the two logos, both of which were designed by Dorf to feature comics, film, and science fiction/fantasy literature (figures 1.3 and 1.4).[130] Though both of these events were the result of a collective effort, Dorf's contributions as the chairman of one of the first comics conventions in the United States and his role as the architect of Comic-Con suggests a clear connection between the two. Comic-Con remained a somewhat insular space until the turn of the twenty-first century, but its long-standing, multimedial approach anticipated the more mainstream notion of fandom as exclusive, but expansive, that now permeates popular discourses.

When Comic-Con incorporated in 1975, not only did it institutionalize the nonprofit's support for the comic arts, but it also paired this goal with the inclusion of other media forms in its mission statement: "(1) to promote the historical and educational appreciation of *the artistic media as it relates to comics, science fiction, and related art forms*, and (2) to organize, promote, sponsor, hold and conduct an annual "comic convention" which will

FIGURE 1.3 Triple Fan Fair Logo, 1965.

FIGURE 1.4 San Diego's Golden State Comic-Con Logo, 1970.

be a forum for the historical and educational appreciation of comics and *related art forms*" (my emphasis).[131] Comic-Con's president at the time, Richard Butner, further explained their mission to be inclusive of different media and different fandoms in Comic-Con's 1975 Souvenir Book: "The San Diego Comic Convention is not concerned only with comic-art (comic books and stories). It has made films, television, science fiction, and animation permanent and important parts of its program. Why? It is simply that a fan of one field will more than likely be a fan of one or two or more of the others and, *each of these fields are interconnected with others beyond disentanglement*. To neglect any of them would be an injustice not only to the field ignored, but to its sister fields" (my emphasis).[132] The interconnectivity that Butner describes evokes some of contemporary convergence culture's defining qualities, such as the flow of narratives and audiences across media forms.[133] But it also anticipates an emerging trend in Hollywood, as the industry would spend much of the 1980s and 1990s pursuing synergy and consolidating media ownership.[134] Though Comic-Con was far too small in the 1970s to be seen as a force shaping popular culture on such a grand scale, the fact that the event resonates with more contemporary consumer and industry trends may help to explain why Hollywood promotion was able to slip in and fit so comfortably there decades later.

In fact, even in these early years, there were numerous instances of film and television promotion at the Comic-Con. For example, the March 1970 Mini-Con program tied Forrest Ackerman's appearance at the convention to his cameo in an upcoming B-horror film, *Blood of Frankenstein* (Al Adamson, 1971).[135] Several years later, in 1975, director George Pal appeared at Comic-Con to promote his film, *Doc Savage: The Man of Bronze* (1975), based on the popular pulp hero.[136] This kind of promotion was somewhat naturalized by the event's emphasis on bringing fans and professionals together, making it difficult to determine where fandom ended and industry intervention began. *Star Trek* (NBC, 1966–1969), which has long had a prominent place at the convention, stands out as one such example (figure 1.5).[137]

Star Trek was explicitly marketed to science fiction fans from the very beginning, with a preview screening presented at the September 1966 World Science Fiction Convention just a few days before the series premiered on NBC.[138] But the show was also viewed with suspicion by some literary science fiction fans who dismissed it as "science fiction for nonreaders" and, as Francesca Coppa suggests, may have also been averse to the show's active

FIGURE 1.5 The cover of the 1974 program was illustrated by Milton Caniff and featured a mash-up between *Star Trek* and his comic strip, Steve Canyon.

female fan base.[139] The result was that *Star Trek* fandom became slightly more insular as it developed, and fans of the show began to organize their own conventions in 1972, three years after it ended its run on NBC. Unlike Comic-Con in the early 1970s, however, the first *Star Trek* convention received a remarkable amount of media attention in several national publications—including advanced coverage in *Variety*. This was thanks, in large part, to the intervention of Paramount vice president Bob Newgard.[140] While attendance at the 1972 San Diego Comic-Con was over 900, the first "*Star Trek* Lives!" convention in New York that year attracted over three thousand fans.[141]

Given *Star Trek* fandom's increased prominence, it comes as no surprise that the next year, Comic-Con featured an entire program of *Star Trek* content. The event was already open to a range of media and was well positioned to respond to (and benefit from) this increased interest and publicity around *Star Trek* fandom. The program that year included special guests, D. C. Fontana, a *Star Trek* writer and the executive producer of the forthcoming *Star Trek: The Animated Series* (NBC, 1973–1975), and Walter Koenig, who played Chekov on the original series. Comic-Con 1973 also featured a *Star Trek* display room with "books, slides, photos, buttons, etc., for sale, and some stills from the animated Star Trek on view" and a sneak preview of the opening credits of the animated series set to premiere in the fall.[142]

While the inclusion of *Star Trek* programming in 1973 responded to a general thrust within fandom, the through line was clearly a promotional push for *Star Trek: The Animated Series*. This was especially evident in a letter titled "Star Trek Lives (pass it on)," written by one of the show's writers, David Gerrold, and published in the 1973 souvenir book.[143] In his letter, Gerrold attempted to mobilize the same affective labor that helped to keep *Star Trek* on NBC through 1969.[144] He asked fans to participate in a letter-writing campaign to convince the network to move the upcoming *Star Trek: The Animated Series* into prime time instead of airing it as a Saturday morning cartoon.[145] Then, drawing a direct line between affective labor and industry profit, he also encouraged fans to push for a feature film by demonstrating their willingness to spend money: "Paramount has to be convinced that even one movie would be profitable."[146]

As this example demonstrates, promotion at Comic-Con often relied on the slippage between the personal interests of individual fans (keeping or reviving their favorite TV show) and the professional interests of individual artists (keeping their job). But the more seamlessly these interests could be integrated into promotional discourses, the more they seemed positioned to have a palpable impact on the economic goals of the industries that profited from the labor and consumption of both groups. While fans writing letters were laboring affectively in the hopes that they could see more of the media they loved, for a professional like David Gerrold, who was relatively low in the corporate pecking order, rallying a letter-writing campaign was another manifestation of aspirational labor—as he knew, no doubt, that saving *Star Trek* could lead to more work. The stakes, which were decidedly different in both cases, led both groups to do unpaid promotional labor for Paramount, the owner of the *Star Trek* franchise. While the animated series lasted for only twenty-two episodes, in 1979, Paramount produced *Star Trek: The Motion Picture*, relaunching a transmedia franchise that continues to this day. In a certain sense, Comic-Con's environment in the early 1970s—a fledgling comic convention appealing to an interconnected network of fandoms, already deeply invested in the intermingling of fan and pro—made it the perfect place to dissolve the boundaries between passion and promotion.

If *Star Trek*'s promotional presence at Comic-Con grew out of the passions of a pre-existing fan base, then the early presence of *Star Wars* (George Lucas, 1977) at the convention was an industry-led promotional thrust that attempted to build a similarly passionate fan base around brand new material.[147] In fact, Lucasfilm's publicist at the time, Charles Lippincott, took inspiration from *Star Trek* fandom in promoting the film, suggesting that these fans "were the first ones to merchandise the TV show themselves, showing there was a market for that kind of thing."[148] In 1976, a year before the film was released in theaters, Lippincott ran a Comic-Con panel called "The Making of *Star Wars*," which featured a slideshow and early footage. He also set up a table in the Dealers' Room where he talked to fans and sold posters for $1.75.[149] Lippincott had traveled to the science fiction and fantasy convention Westercon to promote the film earlier that summer and was met with some incredulity from the crowd.[150] So when he visited Comic-Con, he brought along two comics industry allies with the hope that they would help to unite comics and science fiction fandom and stir up interest in the film. The first was the artist behind Marvel's six-part *Star Wars* adaptation, Howard Chaykin, and the second was its writer, early comics fan turned pro, Roy Thomas.[151] Building on overlapping fan tastes was an explicit part of Lippincott and Lucas's marketing strategy, so Comic-Con, which had already embraced a broad definition of fandom, seemed an ideal venue to promote the film.[152] According to Thomas, their presentation at Comic-Con "was possibly the *first* time a movie company had gone all out to woo hardcover SF/comics fans in advance with its product" and Lippincott has been credited with "pioneering the marketing of genre pictures to their core audiences" (original emphasis).[153] But Comic-Con attendees weren't just a potential audience for the film, they also provided valuable input. Lippincott recalled, "I had a lot of guys coming to the booth interested in merchandise, so I questioned them about things like what was the best model manufacturing company."[154] While such fan outreach is more commonly incorporated into industrial practices today, particularly through social media, the intimate environment of Comic-Con in the 1970s allowed for plenty of in-person interaction between fans and professionals. As 1971 Comic-Con dealer Lee Roberts recalled, "the co-mingling of pros and fans was much more common back then . . . the celebrity guests could comfortably browse and bargain, just like the rest of us."[155] This meant that friendly conversation with fans about their tastes, even specific details like their preferences in model manufacturers, fit easily into the convention's informal atmosphere, allowing market research and promotion to be seamlessly integrated into the event.[156]

The promotion of *Star Wars* at Comic-Con occurred at a pivotal moment in Hollywood history, as the industry transitioned to a profit model built on blockbusters and franchises beginning in the mid-1970s.[157] Integral to this strategy was the coordination of marketing and saturation booking to ensure a large turnout in the first few weeks of a film's release. A well-received film would benefit from positive word of mouth, while a poorly received film with effective marketing would minimize losses with a strong opening weekend.[158] This emphasis on maximizing ticket sales suggests that as a niche audience, fans were of less import to Hollywood than mainstream consumers, making this early outreach at Comic-Con more experimental than anything else. Similarly, the Marvel *Star Wars* comic book promoted at Comic-Con operated as an experimental transmedia paratext, with two issues published in advance of the film's theatrical release in order to build interest, and the remaining four issues published after the film premiered.[159] Despite paying for the rights, Marvel shouldered the bulk of the risk, echoing today's hierarchical, economic relationship that often situates comic books as ancillary to Hollywood content (even when blockbuster films draw on comics as source material).[160]

If, in the context of the New Hollywood of the 1970s and '80s, studios were finding ways to experiment with and profit by expanding the reach of niche content into the mainstream, they were also learning more about niche audiences. Fans could supply unpaid promotional labor—in the form of word of mouth—while their consumption patterns were a model for the ideal consumer—repeat customers who would see the film *and* buy the merchandise. Lots of it. In 1976, *Star Wars* was simply an upcoming film release that aligned closely with the same kinds of intertwined interests represented at Comic-Con: film serials, comic books, science fiction and fantasy literature. But its success at the box office signaled the beginnings of a shift. The content was mainstream, but it most certainly belonged at Comic-Con.

Other examples of early Comic-Con film previews included *Superman* (Richard Donner, 1978), *Blade Runner* (Ridley Scott, 1982), *Outlander* (Peter Hyams, 1981), and *The Right Stuff* (Philip Kaufman, 1983). The latter three films were presented by Jeff Walker, a specialist in the marketing of "genre entertainment" at conventions. Walker was hired by Warner Brothers, so the story goes, after their head of marketing was "booed off the stage" for failing to recognize the name Kal-El during a Comic-Con preview of the *Superman* film.[161] Since that time, Walker has worked as a freelance specialty publicist, helping Hollywood market their films at Comic-Con and other fan conventions.[162] In 2011, "the man who brought Hollywood to Comic-Con," as the *Los Angeles Times* described Walker, was presented with Comic-Con's Inkpot Award for "fandom services."[163] Not only had Hollywood promotion been normalized as part of the event, it was framed as a service to the fan community.

Despite the increased profile of Hollywood promotion at Comic-Con, comic art was and is still very much a part of the event. In 2013, for example, 26 percent of Comic-Con's panels were devoted to comics, as opposed to a total of 23 percent featuring film and television content.[164] This raises some questions about the popular opinion of longtime attendees: that Comic-Con ceded its convention space to other media (especially Hollywood), which pushed comics into the margins. But these critiques are less a reflection of the event's programming and have much more to do with the popularity of film and television and Hollywood's ability to dominate the headlines. For this reason, I argue that the "problem" of Hollywood's saturation of Comic-Con has been confused with, even replaced by, a more affective critique of the status of comics at the event. In other words, comic art was not pushed out by the inclusion of other kinds of media and media fans but by the *industry* presence at Comic-Con, which benefited from the affective and aspirational labor of fans and burgeoning pros. And, as this chapter illustrates, the earliest and most profound industry presence at Comic-Con was the comic book industry itself.

Conclusion: When Marvel Talks, Fans Listen

Long before Hollywood ostensibly discovered Comic-Con in the twenty-first century, the comics industry paved the way for corporate promotion and fan outreach at the convention. Comic art has always been a fixture in Comic-Con's souvenir books, which are distributed to attendees each year. From the very beginning, artists would contribute illustrations, sometimes with personalized messages to Comic-Con fans. But in 1975, the same year Comic-Con incorporated as a nonprofit, the two largest comics publishers, Marvel and DC, also began to address fans in the pages of Comic-Con's souvenir books.[165] These full-page ads featured popular superheroes welcoming fans to Comic-Con and framed the event as an opportunity for outreach. In 1980, for example, a Marvel ad showed three fans—a man, a woman, and a young boy—surrounded by Marvel heroes. It read, "When San Diego Fans Talk, Marvel Listens" (figure 1.6).[166] The Marvel ad paints a rosy picture of the relationship between the publisher and its fans, contributing to the long-standing myth that the comics industry occupies a privileged place at the convention, one grounded in affect over economics. But, as a print ad in the event's souvenir book, what it is really suggesting—and what this company and the media industries writ large have always suggested—is that when Marvel talks, they want their fans to listen.

Of course, Comic-Con and the comics industry have changed dramatically since this ad was published in 1980. Flip through the pages of recent Comic-Con programs and you will see comic art, articles about comic book history, and tributes to great comic artists and writers. Ask comic book fans why they attend Comic-Con and they will surely tell you it is about their love of comics. But walk into the convention center, walk around the streets of downtown San Diego, and the experience becomes something quite different. Film and television advertising is everywhere, from interactive

FIGURE 1.6 Marvel ad from Comic-Con Souvenir Book, 1980.

exhibits, to viral marketing, to skyscrapers adorned with massive banners. Even though Comic-Con contains the word "comic," even if, in the hearts and minds of some attendees and fans, it is a celebration of the comic arts, even if the organization's mission statement emphasizes "comics" before "related popular art forms," as a medium, comics are a tiny part of the media industries, particularly in terms of hard numbers and profit.[167]

This is due, in large part, to the significant deregulation and conglomeration that swept through the media industries in the 1980s and 1990s, which, as I explore further in chapter 4, reconfigured the economic goals of the comics industry. In 2005, Marvel Comics changed its name to Marvel Entertainment, literalizing this shift away from comics as a medium and toward their viability as intellectual property.[168] Just four years later, Disney purchased Marvel for four billion dollars, incorporating the comic company's valuable intellectual property into the massive media conglomerate.[169] Shortly after Marvel's sale to Disney, DC underwent a very similar change when, in 2009, DC Comics was renamed DC Entertainment and TimeWarner folded the company into Warner Brothers.[170] Not only are the two most prominent and prolific companies in the comics industry owned by two of the largest media conglomerates on the planet but their business model has changed dramatically. In 2012, the estimated size of the entire American and Canadian comics market was about $680 million. That same year, Disney grossed $611,075,000 domestically on a single film: Marvel's *The Avengers* (Joss Whedon, 2012).[171]

In light of these developments, not only is Shel Dorf's ambivalence about Comic-Con's success understandable, it is completely reasonable. His original goal in founding Comic-Con was to celebrate "entertainers who don't hear the applause," and organize a convention "for the public to attend, to gather and pay tribute to them."[172] In many ways, Comic-Con continues to do exactly that. Take Marvel Studios' 2012 *Iron Man 3* (Shane Black, 2013) panel, for example, which demonstrates how effective the company has been at transforming Iron Man from a moderately well-known character, present in the pages of Marvel Comics since 1963, to a lucrative intellectual property and transmedia franchise. During the presentation, Marvel president Kevin Feige was "interrupted" midsentence by the sound of Luther Vandross's "Never Too Much." The crowd of 6,500 erupted as the large screens in Comic-Con's Hall H cut to an image of Robert Downey Jr., emerging from behind the massive black curtains in the back of the hall. He grooved down the aisle, illuminated by the explosion of camera flashes and the light from an Iron Man glove on his right hand, which he repeatedly flashed at the audience and the cameras while he made his way to the stage. When Downey Jr. reached the stage he asked three questions, each one met with an increasing frenzy of cheers and applause: "How much do I love you?"; "How much do you love me?"; and "Why aren't we watching any footage yet?"[173] Occupying the Tony Stark persona, Downey Jr. did more than give fans a chance to pay tribute; he *demanded* applause.[174] But instead of direct-ing this applause to underrecognized artists, as Dorf intended, the shared economic goals of Marvel and its parent company, Disney, meant funnel-ing that recognition back toward the tried and true Hollywood star system. Today, when Marvel talks, Comic-Con fans listen. And so does everyone else.

If, as Comic-Con chairman Richard Butner suggested in 1975, a diver-sity of fan interests helped to ensure that fields like comics, film, television, science fiction, and animation were "interconnected with others beyond dis-entanglement," then the industrial emphasis on synergy and conglomera-tion over the next three decades manifested this interconnectivity, not just in the minds of Comic-Con fans but also in the economic logic through which the media industries operate.[175] Instead of being valuable as a material commodity, comics' economic value now lies in their status as intellectual property to be transformed into something else, a way to deliver branding and marketable ideas to a mass market of mainstream consumers, in addi-tion to a specialty market of comic book aficionados. Despite the clear dif-ferences between these markets, our contemporary pop culture vernacular identifies both groups as fans. This is no less true of Comic-Con, which has, in recent years, exploded in size, scale, and scope and received increased media attention as a site of film and television promotion. Though the event remains a space for comics devotees, it is also a place for families, gamers, toy collectors, film buffs, and binge-watchers as well as casual consumers and interested bystanders. But when we speak about these disparate groups, we usually call them fans too. In many ways, Comic-Con has become what Jack Kirby prophesized in 1971, "the future of all media."[176]

Even though this chapter explains how Comic-Con's history ensured it was a comfortable place for the industry, this explanation should not be mis-taken for justification or a condemnation of fans. On the contrary, this slow transformation highlights the importance of paying closer attention to the histories and agency of fans and fan groups, even as we critique the hegemonic power of Hollywood and other media industries. As Comic-Con grew in size and scope over the years, Dorf saw the intimacy and indi-viduality of the event as compromised. Its exclusivity as a small gathering of fans and professionals working together to celebrate comics and the popu-lar arts was replaced with exclusivity of a wholly other kind. As the industrial presence surrounding comics, film, and television increased and gradually converged at Comic-Con, it paved the way for a new definition of exclusivity that hinged on who has access to what industry-produced content, how, and when. In the next chapter, I examine how this exclusivity impacts the literal and figurative place of fans at Comic-Con today, as they spend countless hours in a liminal time and space between inside and outside, labor and leisure: waiting in line.

2

The Liminality of the Line
and the Place of Fans
at Comic-Con

• • • • • • • • • • • • • • • • • • • •

> Everything's a line here. That's the way
> it is.
> —Comic-Con attendee, 2011

A 2014 episode of CBS's *Big Bang Theory* (2007–2019), "The Convention Conundrum," opens with a slow pan that reveals the show's four protagonists, Howard, Sheldon, Leonard, and Raj, hunched nervously over their laptops. "T-minus 60 seconds," Howard announces solemnly. "It all comes down to this," says Raj, hands raised to his chest, almost in prayer. "I've got butterflies," stutters Leonard, to which Sheldon replies, "don't get soft on me Hofstadter! I will slap those glasses right off your face!" When their next-door neighbor, Penny, enters and asks, "What's going on?" Leonard answers, "We're about to buy tickets for Comic-Con." As soon as the online sale goes live, the men smash at keyboards, yelling the refrain familiar to anyone who has attempted to buy Comic-Con tickets in recent years: "refresh, refresh, refresh."[1]

This cold open has two punch lines: one for people who have purchased (or attempted to purchase) Comic-Con tickets—approximately 900,000 in 2014—and one for the majority of the show's estimated twenty million viewers.[2] For Comic-Con fans, the joke grows out of familiarity with the event's often frustrating online ticket sales, which sell out at an increasingly staggering rate each year.[3] For the uninitiated, the joke is rooted in the extreme gravitas with which the characters approach the online ticket sale and the reaction from Penny who, bemused and a bit mystified by the whole thing, comments, "This is a whole lotta weird before coffee." The gag exemplifies the way in which the limits of exclusivity work to unify niche and mainstream audiences in order to make *everyone* feel like a fan. Identifying with Sheldon, Leonard, Raj, and Howard evokes the pleasure of sharing an inside joke with friends or exchanging war stories. Identifying with Penny, on the other hand, is pleasurable because it comes from a place of intellectual distance. Perhaps this is why the show has been criticized for simultaneously appealing to and mocking geek and fan culture.[4] But *The Big Bang Theory*, which was one of the highest-rated sitcoms on television during its eleven year run *and* a regular presence at Comic-Con, didn't necessarily rely on dividing inside and outside. Instead, it sat somewhere in between—taking the pleasure of such inside jokes and making them widely accessible.[5] The humor derived from this scene, and its meaning, exists in that liminal space and, as I argue throughout this chapter, thinking about in-between spaces— both conceptual and literal—is key to understanding the place of fans in contemporary culture.

At the end of the opening credits sequence, we rejoin the men, still refreshing, albeit with less enthusiasm and hope. When Leonard finally makes it to the online queue, they are dismayed to find out that they are number 50,211 in line. Upon hearing that the only remaining tickets are for Sunday, the last day of Comic-Con, Sheldon declares, "Sunday's the worst, everybody's leaving, all the good panels are over, and the only T-shirts they have left are small and XXXL." When the last of the Sunday tickets disappear too, he rapidly recalibrates, "Not Sunday! I love Sunday!" The men sit in shock as the reality sinks in: they don't have tickets to Comic-Con. This "conundrum," to which the episode's title refers, highlights the importance of Comic-Con's lines—both real and virtual—as sites of meaning and power.

With the parallel explosion of industry promotion and attendance in recent years, waiting in line has become a defining part of the Comic-Con experience.[6] As one attendee succinctly put it, "Everything's a line here. That's the way it is."[7] In order to attend Comic-Con, one *must* spend time in line; depending on the length of the line and the determination of the attendee, this time can range from hours to days. Lining up is such a significant practice, in fact, that the Comic-Con Events Guide addressed it in their FAQ section between 2002 and 2012, answering the question, "What are all these lines for?" with a diverse range of possibilities: Depending on where the line is, the reasons vary. There are often long lines at the ATMs in the lobby, the Starbucks, and FedEx, each of which is quite popular. On the Upper Level, there are lines for the various Autograph sessions, Badge Pickup, popular programming events [panels], and (on Saturday) the Masquerade. In the Exhibit hall, a line could be for an individual booth event or for the concession stands."[8] The disappearance of this question in recent years demonstrates not only a tacit acceptance of lines and wait times but also an accumulation of knowledge over time; waiting is so integral and predictable that explaining the ontology of lines to Comic-Con attendees is hardly necessary. Instead, this question was replaced with a growing number of maps, rules, and procedures, which prompted organizers to introduce a supplemental forty-to fifty-page Quick Guide in addition to their already hefty Events Guide.

While this may seem excessive, the lines at Comic-Con are complicated and convoluted, even sowing confusion among convention staff and volunteers at times.[9] Attendees arriving before the convention opens must wait in a long, snaking line around the convention center to enter the event and, once inside, they will inevitably encounter even more lines for exclusive merchandise sales, giveaways, or photo ops in the Exhibit Hall or one of Comic-Con's other programming rooms (figure 2.1).[10] For example, one might line up early in the morning (or, as is increasingly common, overnight) to be among the first wave of fans to enter the convention center. This crowd is then guided up the escalators and into Sails Pavilion (figure 2.2). Here, attendees disperse in various directions. Some will join lines for programming rooms like the 4,800-seat Ballroom 20, which often houses large panels, primarily for popular television shows. This line takes attendees back outside, through a series of tents, and up and down stairs behind the convention center. Others will join one of two lines for the Exhibit Hall, which opens its doors shortly thereafter. At that time, attendees in these lines are shuttled back downstairs into the hall, and many immediately join lines for exclusive merchandise sales, free giveaways, and photo ops.[11] But many never

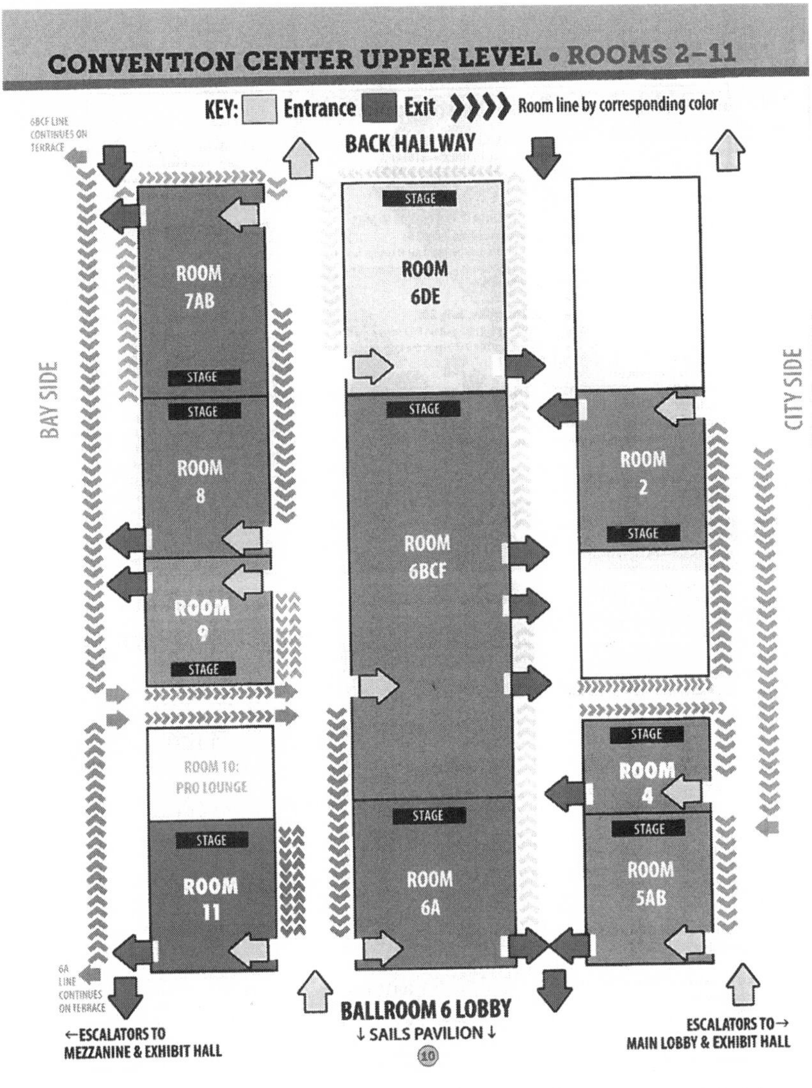

CONVENTION CENTER UPPER LEVEL • ROOMS 2–11

KEY: ▢ Entrance ▮ Exit ⟫⟫⟫ Room line by corresponding color

BACK HALLWAY

6BCF LINE
CONTINUES ON
TERRACE

BAY SIDE

CITY SIDE

ROOM
7AB

STAGE

ROOM
6DE

STAGE

STAGE

STAGE

ROOM
8

ROOM
2

STAGE

ROOM
6BCF

ROOM
9

STAGE

ROOM 10:
PRO LOUNGE

STAGE

STAGE

ROOM
4

STAGE

STAGE

ROOM
11

STAGE

ROOM
6A

ROOM
5AB

6A
LINE
CONTINUES
ON TERRACE

BALLROOM 6 LOBBY
↓ SAILS PAVILION ↓
⑩

←ESCALATORS TO
MEZZANINE & EXHIBIT HALL

ESCALATORS TO→
MAIN LOBBY & EXHIBIT HALL

FIGURE 2.1 Map of programming room lines from the Comic-Con International Quick Guide, 2017.

enter the convention center at all, opting instead to skip the general line and join the line for Hall H, Comic-Con's largest programming space and home to the convention's high-profile Hollywood panels.

Offsite marketing activations, which I discuss in the conclusion of this book, also form long lines, often well in advance. HBO's 2017 *Game of Thrones* "Winter Is Here" activation, for example, provided its own microcosm of

FIGURE 2.2 Exhibit Hall line in Sails Pavilion, 2016. (Photo by the author.)

the Comic-Con experience, complete with ever-present and repetitive queuing. Many participants lined up overnight to access the activation, which was open for limited hours each day. After what was, for some, a roughly thirteen-hour wait, participants would enter the activation and join new lines, some lasting thirty minutes or more, for a series of photo ops—like donning a costume and wielding a sword for a 360-degree video—which were tracked (along with participants' personal information) using an RFID wristband and sent out via email for future social media sharing. Participants could also partake of free samples of *Game of Thrones* beer and wine and left with a handful of giveaways that included exclusive figures manufactured by the collectable company Funko.[12] Finally, demonstrating how the grammar of lines translates to digital spaces too, *The Big Bang Theory*'s cold open reminds us that Comic-Con's reliance on waiting begins long before attendees arrive at the San Diego Convention Center. Despite the fact that, in recent years, organizers have turned to a lottery system for badge sales, their online portal still uses the structuring logic of the line as potential attendees are held in a virtual "waiting room," often for more than an hour, until they are selected at random to enter the online sales portal.

At Comic-Con, waiting in line suggests a clear divide between inside and outside, both in the literal sense of gaining entry to the event or gaining access to individual activities at the event, and as a signifier of the exclusivity of Comic-Con and its attendees. However, the line itself is also a liminal space, neither inside nor outside. As such, it functions as a metaphor for the place of fans who, particularly in their interactions with the media industries, find themselves somewhere between labor and leisure as they are rewarded for consumer activities while also producing free publicity for Hollywood.[13] In this chapter, I argue that the act of waiting in line constitutes a form of labor that produces a heightened aura of exclusivity, increased publicity, and surplus value around industry promotion at Comic-Con. While a quotidian activity like waiting in line might be viewed in much the same way as media consumption—something someone does with their free time—the prominence and proliferation of lines at Comic-Con make the *work* of being a consumer significantly more visible.

In order to understand how lines work and how fans work in line, this chapter places particular emphasis on the lines for Comic-Con's 6,500-seat Hall H. While my next chapter details what happens *inside* Hall H, this chapter argues that what happens before attendees gain entry is just as crucial. For this reason, I begin by examining Comic-Con's lines in relation to the otherwise quotidian process of waiting and queuing. Then I consider how the bodies of attendees produce and maintain the line and its power structures. The result, I argue, is an economy of waiting that informs both how attendees at Comic-Con use their time and how that expenditure of time produces value for the media industries. Finally, I conclude this chapter with a discussion of 2011's "Camp Breaking Dawn" line in order to unpack the complexities of negotiating power in the liminal space of the line.

The Liminality of the Line

Of all the fascinating things that fans and industry do to make meaning, both together and separately, why consider waiting in line at Comic-Con? On the surface, waiting in line is quite a mundane and familiar activity— you certainly don't have to go as far as Comic-Con to experience the feelings of powerlessness and aggravation as you are robbed of your time, waiting for your morning coffee or making your way through airport security. A 2012 *New York Times* article estimated that "Americans spend roughly 37 billion hours each year waiting in line."[14] "The dominant cost of waiting," the *Times* argued, "is an emotional one: stress, boredom, that nagging sensation that one's life is slipping away."[15] According to Richard Larson, an engineering professor and expert in queuing theory, it is not the length of the wait that frustrates most people, but the perception that they are wasting their time doing nothing at all.[16] But, as scholarship on everyday life suggests, these kinds of banal routines and seemingly aimless practices are particularly powerful precisely because they are so familiar or seem so inconsequential that they become almost invisible.[17] The fact that waiting in line seems, on the surface at least, to be somewhat antithetical to productivity makes it a particularly compelling process to study in the context of fan labor. The question of fan labor and its utility to the industry grows out of a long-standing interest in theorizing the productivity of fans.[18] Indeed, as Matt Hills points out, "fan studies has tended to stress fandom's 'textual productivity' and (para)textual creativity" at the expense of more commonplace consumption-based practices like waiting and binging.[19] Thus, as Joe Moran argues, revaluing consumption as a productive practice or highlighting the creativity and productivity of media consumers has also "produced a limiting notion of the everyday that values the creative and recreational over the banal and boring," either by ignoring the less interesting aspects of daily life or by reframing them in a more exciting context.[20]

Similarly, the lines at Comic-Con take a very repetitive aspect of our daily lives (waiting) and transplant it to a much more exciting context (waiting for exclusive experiences like a celebrity appearance, free giveaways, or sneak previews). The line for Comic-Con's Hall H, for example, forms many hours, even days, in advance of panels, stretches to as much as a mile and a half long, and is populated by thousands of fans with sleeping bags and folding chairs who must brave hours of direct sunlight in the afternoon or camp out on the hard concrete at night (figures 2.3 and 2.4).[21] The conditions surrounding this line demonstrate a willingness to wait in an exclusive context that exceeds what many would tolerate at the post office, supermarket, or their local coffee shop. For this reason, waiting in line at Comic-Con illustrates the importance of exclusivity in reframing the "banal and boring" as something productive and meaningful, while also linking these seemingly positive qualities to the presence of media industry promotion and products.[22] As an example of what Henri Lefebvre describes as "compulsive time," spent somewhere *between* labor and leisure, waiting in line at Comic-Con also brings the place of fans at the event, and in popular culture, more generally, into greater relief.[23]

FIGURE 2.3 Hall H line, 2016. (Photo by the author.)

FIGURE 2.4 General line for Comic-Con's Exhibit Hall and panels, 2013. (Photo by the author.)

The space of the line and the "compulsive time" of waiting evoke Victor Turner's anthropological descriptions of the liminal ritual phase where participants are "neither here nor there . . . betwixt and between."[24] While the study of ritual is, as Nick Couldry points out, "one of the most contested areas of anthropology," the concept of liminality itself remains a useful paradigm through which to theorize how the spatiotemporal aspects of a media event like Comic-Con resonate on an ideological level.[25] Couldry is one of a number of media scholars to explore ritual practices in relation to media spaces and events.[26] However, my work here is less concerned with the ritual nature of such practices and instead builds on Couldry's suggestion that we use this framework to interrogate the operation of power, more broadly.[27] What do we make of this uneasy, in-between space, which fans frequently occupy at Comic-Con?

In the line, this means a time and space of waiting, where fans are neither fully inside nor outside of the event. But this liminality also extends to the ways in which popular understandings of fandom are constructed through discourses by and about Hollywood. It is in the industry's interest to perpetuate the notion that Comic-Con fans are insiders and tastemakers who circulate buzz and publicity online, while ensuring they remain outside the industry, as consumers and unpaid laborers. As Sara Gwenllian-Jones has argued, "Fandom needs to be understood as a liminal, fetishistic and highly engaged consumer culture that is both born of and fully implicated in the cultural processes it supposedly 'resists.'"[28] While this kind of liminality is often observed in mediated contexts and virtual spaces, the liminality of the Comic-Con line is a physical manifestation of these ideological constructs, which fans negotiate as they confront different forms of power, from the rules and regulations governing the event and its lines to the hegemonic power of the media industries.[29]

Keeping Fans in Line

Among the countless lines at Comic-Con, the Hall H line stands out as the most notorious of all. Though Hall H is the largest programming room at the convention, it is equipped with only enough seats to accommodate roughly 5 percent of Comic-Con attendees.[30] In recent years, the room has hosted panels for blockbuster film franchises, such as *Twilight*, *Hunger Games*, *The Hobbit*, *X-Men*, *Star Wars*, and Marvel and DC's respective "cinematic universes" and popular television shows like *Game of Thrones* (HBO, 2011–2019) and *The Walking Dead* (AMC, 2009–). Though Hall H programming consists of numerous panels running throughout the day, Comic-Con's policy is that they do not clear any of their programming rooms at the end of panels. This means that once the room is at capacity, those still waiting in line are only admitted when the attendees inside leave and more seats become available. With long and unpredictable lines, especially for panels featuring media industry participants and promotions, many attendees plan their time at Comic-Con around this policy, lining up overnight or in the early morning hours to ensure their entry. Once inside, many remain there for the entire day of programming, even if that means sitting through hours of panels of little or no interest to them.[31] In Hall H, these practices and policies have resulted in a massive demand for seats in the room at the beginning of the day, making waiting in line feel like a near necessity.

Beginning in 2014, Comic-Con organizers introduced a wristband policy for the Hall H line, which was designed to track attendees and more accurately predict the odds of gaining entry into the room. Attendees can now line up the evening before to receive a wristband, which guarantees their access to the hall. Depending on the length of the line and the speed of the staff, the distribution process alone can last for hours, often stretching past midnight.[32] From there, attendees can immediately join the Hall H line and remain there overnight or return to their hotels and join the end of the line the next morning, no later than 7:30 A.M., at which point the wristbands effectively expire. Because the wristbands do not guarantee specific seats or sections in the room, attendees who wish to secure seats near the front of the room have to remain in line in order to do so.[33] This fact, paired with Comic-Con's policy of distributing wristbands the evening before panels in Hall H, may have further exacerbated the convention's already long lines and wait times as many people now line up for hours (or days) to receive a wristband, only to sleep overnight in a second line to secure a seat near the front of the room. In 2015, for example, the line for the *Star Wars: The Force Awakens* (J. J. Abrams, 2015) panel, scheduled for 5:30 P.M. on Friday, July 10, began to form nearly forty-eight hours in advance and had already grown to approximately five thousand people twenty-four hours before the actual presentation took place.[34] In 2009, I waited roughly three hours for a day of Hall H panels that included films like *Twilight: New Moon* (Chris Weitz, 2009), *Alice in Wonderland* (Tim Burton, 2009), and *Avatar* (James Cameron, 2009). Though many attendees were already in line by the time I joined, I was able to secure a seat in the middle of the room and made my way up to the front half of the room later in the day. In contrast, in 2013 I waited approximately six hours for a day of panels that included presentations by Marvel and Warner Brothers (DC's parent company) and sat in the very last row.

It is no wonder that the *Verge* once referred to the Hall H line as "the worst line in fandom."[35] But while the line and the Hall itself have often been a source of angst, it is also worth noting that this line is produced *by fans*, both in the sense that their bodies construct the material trajectory and hierarchies of the line and because their willingness to wait produces—or at least enhances—the perceived value of these promotions. For this reason, I argue that the process of waiting in line at Comic-Con should be understood as a kind of labor that maintains the line and its power structures, while also producing value through an economy of waiting.

The massive scale and spectacle of the crowds at Comic-Con may seem overwhelming and excessive to the uninitiated, but for those who attend regularly, dealing with a large number of people has simply become part of the event, particularly as the convention has grown over the years. Reports of attendance numbers have varied widely in recent years but usually fall somewhere between 130,000 and 170,000 people.[36] Providing an apt description, Jonah Weiland, the editor of *CBR.com* (*Comic Book Resources*), likened Comic-Con to "a city erupt[ing] inside a city."[37] A 2016 description of the crowds in the *Los Angeles Times* explained how negotiating the sheer volume of people has made attending Comic-Con increasingly difficult: "Crossing the street becomes a test of patience and proximity. Walking the clogged convention floor becomes an exercise in forced bovine impersonation. Trying to get into a panel for something like 'Game of Thrones' or DC Entertainment or Marvel Studios reveals itself to be an endurance trial concocted by the most sadistic YA author. Instead of the 'Maze Runner,' you have the Line Waiter."[38]

Indeed, the crowds have become a recurring part of discourses about Comic-Con; so much so that the spectacle overshadows the very micro-organizational tactics that this event requires to keep it running smoothly. For organizers to control the crowds, it is necessary to control how, when, and how many attendees move through the convention center. In an interview, Comic-Con's David Glanzer, touched on such crowd control strategies when he discussed, "the transformation of certain corridors of the convention center to one-way avenues for pedestrian traffic to limit bottle-necking in the meeting areas" and a "division of the team dedicated to handling lines."[39]

Because the crowds at Comic-Con have exploded in the past decade, so too have the rules by which attendees must conduct themselves. The 1991 Comic-Con Event Guide suggests that organizers wished to avoid overburdening the event's approximately fifteen thousand attendees with too many rules: "You're here to have fun. We're here to make it possible for you to have fun, not to impose rules on you."[40] By 2012, facing approximately five times the attendees, rules had been reframed as a necessary part of Comic-Con: "You're here to have fun. We're here to make it possible for you to have fun. For all that to happen, Comic-Con has a few rules that are necessary for the safety and comfort of everyone at the convention. Please comply so that you and everyone else can enjoy the convention."[41] For organizers to keep the event as orderly as possible, it became necessary to control when, how, and how many attendees moved through the lines and the spaces of the convention center.[42] But the fact that crowd control strategies are integral to the operation of any large event does not mean they are free from ideology or immune to the operation of power.

Keeping attendees "in line," is one way in which the space of Comic-Con works to control crowds. Of course, the phrase "in line" has dual meanings. The first refers to the literal act of waiting in line, while the second meaning evokes the more symbolic purpose of the line, to keep attendees orderly, calm, and compliant; transforming them into what Michel Foucault calls "docile bodies."[43] In *Discipline and Punish*, Foucault argues that the meticulous organization and structuring of space works to exercise control on the body, making individuals subject to and complicit in relationships of power.[44] Although Comic-Con seems very distant from the kind of institutionalized hubs of power that Foucault examines—prisons, hospitals, schools, workhouses—its superficial distance from these ideologically and politically loaded locales makes it an ideal place in which to seek out and critique the functioning of power. Indeed, this is precisely Foucault's point; that power can and does operate *everywhere*, often in the name of efficiency.[45] The efficiency of a line is that it produces an instantaneous hierarchy based on the order in which individuals join. Not only that, but the bodies of those in line produce a visual representation of this hierarchy. In fact, the line's very existence relies on those who wait, simultaneously producing and being subjected to the hierarchical structure of the line. In addition to the numerous barriers, tents, and even colored tape running along the floor of the convention center to mark off specific areas, the bodies of attendees themselves are significant tools in the production of the line.

While waiting to gain entry into Comic-Con's Hall H in 2012, for example, I was one of several attendees directed by line security to reposition myself in the middle of a high-traffic pedestrian and cycling path in order to mark the snaking trajectory of the line, up and down the San Diego marina. Effectively sitting in the middle of a small street, our bodies were not just in the line, but of the line, and the power dynamics were such that in order to keep our place, we dared not defy the guard's logic in using us as human roadblocks. Instead, approximately thirty minutes later, the security supervisor arrived, described our placement as being in violation of the fire marshal's rules, and directed us back to our original positions. Again, we complied. With our bodies no longer positioned to physically mark the trajectory of the line in space, our placement at a break in the line in a high-traffic area meant that we were frequently misinterpreted as the line's endpoint. Our roles rapidly changed from visual markers to de facto traffic controllers, redirecting people to the end of the line (much farther away), and even answering questions that might otherwise be directed to Comic-Con staff and security.

As this anecdote suggests, the maintenance of the line requires a mutual desire and willingness on the part of attendees and security staff to work collaboratively to keep the order. As one member of Comic-Con security told me, maintaining this kind of control is achieved primarily through keeping everyone in the line calm, comfortable, and happy. Having observed lines at Comic-Con for many years, I believe that this "automatic functioning of power" is accomplished by making attendees allies in the maintenance of the line; including them in the procedures, explaining how the line is being organized, inviting them to report line jumpers, and instilling in them a sense of trust and confidence in the actions of security and staff.[46] Comic-Con's aforementioned wristband policy, for example, was not introduced to solve the problem of long wait times or eliminate the need for lines altogether. Instead, the color-coded wristbands would allow organizers to more accurately track the size of the line, reduce instances of line cutting, and enable attendees to better anticipate their chances of gaining entry into Hall H.[47]

But the maintenance of the line also relies on the power to control information. One security guard told me in 2012 that each morning, his team met with their supervisors in order to get instructions for the day (figure 2.5). As he shared this general information about the organizational hierarchy with me, I noticed a red binder marked "line control" clutched at his side (figure 2.6). When I asked for specific information about the binder's contents, he became slightly uncomfortable and was unwilling to show or tell me exactly what was inside.[48] It is easy to imagine what documents this binder *might* have contained: maps of lines and line placement around the convention center, security policies, Comic-Con policies, fire marshal rules, and so forth. But the response to my inquiry betrayed much more. Security's mandate of maintaining control of the line by keeping crowds calm, comfortable, and happy requires strict control of information as well as space. Attendees must know just enough to trust security's actions, and to achieve this trust, security must control or have access to information that attendees do not. Ultimately, for a line to work effectively, it must be maintained in both the material and the ideological sense. While maintenance of the line is the official job of event staff and security, the bodies of attendees form the line, and their consent to the rules ultimately produces the line's hierarchical structure.[49] In this way, we can locate attendees who do the work of

FIGURE 2.5 Comic-Con staff meeting, 2012. (Photo by the author.)

FIGURE 2.6 Hall H line control binder, 2012. (Photo by the author.)

waiting in a liminal space between their roles as active agents, invested in the production and outcome of the line, and "docile bodies" whose complicity enables the line to function as an exercise of power. But what does the work of waiting really produce?

The Economy of Waiting (In Line)

In order to understand waiting in line as an economy, it is integral to consider how, as David Harvey argues, "the intersecting command of money, time, and space forms a substantial nexus of social power that we cannot afford to ignore."[50] As I have argued, the organization of bodies in space helps to construct the hierarchies and power relationships integral to the functioning and ordering of the line, but time spent waiting in line also produces different forms of value for fans and the industry. While the line itself can be most readily understood as a demarcation of space that changes over time, waiting is tied to one's time and how one chooses to use it. Marx's assertion that all economy is reducible to an "economy of time" suggests that we need to think about how time in line is valued and how that value is connected to social power.[51]

Because attendees in line at Comic-Con are trading time for experiences, it is tempting to see the act of waiting in line as part of the "shadow cultural economy" that John Fiske described as existing "outside the cultural industries" and centering on the accumulation of cultural rather than economic capital.[52] More recently, Karen Hellekson similarly characterized fandom as a "gift economy," in which value is attached to the social, rather than the economic, aspects of production and consumption.[53] However, the fan texts that Hellekson describes deliberately circumvent the exchange of money as a way to avoid lawsuits because the industry "retain[s] exclusive rights to make money from their property."[54] At Comic-Con, the time fans spend waiting is exchanged for promotional material, similarly controlled and distributed by the industry. For some, this may mean simply getting into a panel and being among the first to see exclusive footage or hear surprise announcements, but the longer one waits, the better the seat, which also means a better view of the action on stage, a closer encounter with the celebrities in attendance, and, presumably, a better overall experience. For the largest programming rooms, Hall H and Ballroom 20, this can mean the difference between watching the action unfold on stage or relying on the mediation of the massive screens positioned around the room.[55] Waiting can also lead to personal encounters with celebrities through autograph sessions and photo ops, or free swag and the purchase of collectables in the Exhibit Hall.[56] Indeed, as Suzanne Scott has suggested, Hollywood is increasingly invested in participating in this "gift economy" as a way to "regift" promotional materials to fans and mainstream audiences, alike, while also obscuring underlying economic imperatives.[57] In this way, the economies that both Fiske and Hellekson describe, though not overtly commercial, are circumscribed by the hegemony of the media industries.

The economy of waiting at Comic-Con is similarly bound to the economic imperatives of the media industries in that fans are largely rewarded with promotional content—something media consumers encounter almost every day—in an exclusive context where industry representatives can frame this content as a gift to their fans.[58] For this reason, rather than seeing fans as simply operating outside the industry, we can also think of fandom as a liminal culture that is overtly *excluded* from profiting on the institutionalized capitalist paradigms that empower media industries, while simultaneously being tapped as a source of income and unpaid labor.[59] One reason for this exclusion is that fandom is frequently situated as a leisure activity, even as these activities feed a capitalist system.[60] But, as Eileen Meehan argued in 1993, "fan work may be a labor of love, but it is still labor."[61] The way in which industry promotion extracts value from the liminal context of waiting-as-labor is closely tied to the limits of exclusivity.

The valuation of time operates in a unique way for fans at events like Comic-Con. Because the event is subject to the constraints of time and space—it only happens once a year and the demand for tickets far outpaces supply—the Comic-Con experience is elusive and, as a result, exclusive.[62] Attending Comic-Con also requires a significant investment of money. In 2018, four-day passes were priced at $231, plus an additional $45 to gain access to the event's Exhibit Hall on Preview Night. And convention-rate hotel rooms ranged from $178 to $439 per night, while many other downtown hotel rooms were priced as high as $1,429.[63] As the costs associated with attending Comic-Con suggest, the exclusivity that accompanies the event and its attendees means that for some, particularly those residing outside of Southern California, access to Comic-Con is a signifier of not just the exclusivity of particular tastes but also of exclusivity growing out of significant economic privilege. Moreover, the ability to wait in line at Comic-Con suggests a kind of bourgeois sensibility, in which having money to spend also means being able to spend time. Thus waiting in line at Comic-Con is an investment of time that builds on a parallel investment of what Pierre Bourdieu calls "disguised forms of economic capital."[64] Ultimately, this conversion of economic to cultural capital is concealed by the allure of exclusivity that surrounds both the event and the promotional content it hosts.

While this exclusivity grows out of the high demand for seats in programming rooms, promotions in the Exhibit Hall, or access to offsite events, this demand itself is a response to scarcity produced by the cost of attending, the limitations of the space, and the singularity of industry content like sneak previews, celebrity appearances, free giveaways, or exclusive merchandise for sale. For this reason, it is important to consider the relationship between waiting and the distribution of power through the production of scarcity.[65] As sociologist Barry Schwarz argues, "To be able to make a person wait is, above all, to possess the capacity to modify [their] conduct in a manner congruent with one's own interests."[66] Hollywood not only exploits the spatiotemporal limits of exclusive venues like Comic-Con, it also manufactures its own limits by curating specific content and experiences. These limits produce a sense of exclusivity at Comic-Con and inflate the value of Hollywood's products and promotions. Many of these manufactured limits are easy to locate, especially when they exploit external factors like space and time. For example, Disney promoted *Star Wars: The Force Awakens* (J. J. Abrams, 2015) through a Hall H panel with a special reel of footage that was later released online for all to see. But in addition to this widely available content, the studio also staged a live concert and fireworks display exclusively for Hall H audience members. While the concert could be filmed and shared online, the perceived value of experiencing this event in person grew out of the limits of exclusivity. As the saying goes, "you had to be there."[67]

In other cases, however, the industry's intervention in manufacturing scarcity at Comic-Con is more covert. In 2016, for example, I participated in an offsite activation promoting Warner Brothers' *Suicide Squad* (David Ayer, 2016) and cosponsored by Samsung. I spent roughly three hours in line (with the line stretching far ahead and even farther behind me), before finally entering the Hard Rock Hotel's restaurant, which was redesigned to simulate the film's Belle Reve Penitentiary. Inside were several experiences—a behind the scenes VR featurette, a bar with *Suicide Squad* branded snacks and water bottles, a temporary tattoo station, and photo ops. In addition, participants could have the message of their choice etched into keepsakes like key chains and shot glasses and could design and print custom beer cozies and T-shirts on demand. Shortly after I entered the activation, however, the printing stations began to run out of the most popular items. Shot glasses and T-shirts disappeared (and eventually so did the key chains and beer cozies), the tattoo station closed its line, and the crowd dwindled as they collected their custom printed swag and had little left to do but leave the activation (figure 2.7). Upon entering the building I was told that I was free to stay as long as I wished, so I decided to see how long that invitation would remain open. I watched as staff members brought in plates and heat lamps and restocked their supply of T-shirts, but the lines for the various stations remained closed. I leaned against the wall wondering how long it would be before someone noticed me and wondered what would happen when they did. Sure enough, after approximately twenty minutes a staff member approached and asked me to leave, telling me they needed to clear the room for a private event. When I exited the building I noticed that while the line for the activation had also been closed to the public, staff were leading VIPs and exceptionally polished (and likely professional) cosplayers dressed as characters from the film into the activation, a camera crew following close behind. Inside, I later found out, they were joined by the cast of *Suicide Squad*, who had just finished their panel in Hall H.[68] Like the formation of the line to get into the activation, the gradual wind down of the event and exodus from the space felt organic, but it was actually heavily orchestrated by the promoters, who, in controlling access to giveaways and gradually closing down stations, had pushed the limits of exclusivity so far that even those who had exchanged their time in line could not earn unmitigated access to the activation. After these participants were steered out (or in my case, asked to leave), promoters filled the space with a more exclusive group of individuals who would ultimately function as signifiers of the same crowd.

All this seems to suggest that erring on the more conservative side by limiting access, even if it means disappointing fans, feels safer for the industry—particularly when it comes to publicity at live events. But this logic doesn't quite match the PR discourses that circulate at and about Comic Con; that, as director Zack Snyder once put it, "one Comic-Con fan is worth 100 moviegoers."[69] This certainly explains the confused and frustrated reactions of many attendees at the event's annual Talk Back sessions, who struggle to understand why studios are not more invested in accommodating *everyone* who wants to see high-profile Hollywood promotions. Usually, though, this criticism is directed at Comic-Con's failure to stand up to the studios, rather

FIGURE 2.7 *Suicide Squad* Belle Reve Penitentiary activation, 2016. (Photo by the author.)

than complaining to or about the studios themselves. As one fan put it, "You have a tremendous amount of power and I think we as fans would appreciate if you use it judiciously to benefit us and not to accommodate the convenience of the studios."[70] Of course, if Hollywood promotion were truly about the over 130,000 people at the event, then it would be only logical that they try to reach as many of those individuals as possible. Instead, the scarcity of access not only guarantees a more predictable and controlled response to the promotional content at Comic-Con, it also provides the impetus for increased media coverage and motivates fans to take ownership of their exclusive experiences by sharing them outside the event. So while my own experience at the *Suicide Squad* activation was illuminating, it was not necessarily surprising when you consider the larger context of Comic-Con, where attendees often stand in as idealized signifiers of media consumers.

For these reasons, the fan experience inside exclusive and popular spaces like Comic-Con's Hall H might best be understood as an accumulation of fan cultural capital, which John Fiske, drawing on Pierre Bourdieu, describes as "the appreciation and knowledge of texts, performers and events."[71] For some attendees, this means simply getting into Hall H and being among the first (even if only by minutes or hours) to see exclusive footage or hear surprise announcements. But because Hall H is such a large space, the investment of additional time in line can also mean the difference between watching the action unfold on stage and watching the massive screens positioned around the room. The longer one waits, the better the seat, which also means a better view, a closer encounter with the celebrities in attendance, and, presumably, a more exclusive and valuable experience.

While Fiske argues that fan cultural capital is largely excluded "from official cultural capital and its convertibility . . . into economic capital," as a signifier of exclusivity, its meaning and value become much more complex, particularly as promotional discourses make the boundaries between fan culture and "official culture" increasingly porous.[72] Much in the same way that the system of capital transforms labor into surplus value, the economy of waiting at Comic-Con transforms attendees' time waiting in line into a kind of surplus promotion for Hollywood. While the promotional content presented at Comic-Con may hold a fixed economic cost, the heft of its accompanying cultural capital increases exponentially along with demand, which is most visibly signified by the line itself. The longer the wait, the more valuable and worthwhile the experience becomes. As one attendee described their Hall H experience, "Waiting five-and-a-half hours in line for that only made it more special."[73] Waiting, then, is a material practice that produces an aura of value and promises exclusivity *before* the experience has even happened. And it does so by providing visual evidence—proof in the form of hundreds, even thousands, of bodies in space—of the collective belief that the end of the line is worth waiting for. Fans' willingness to wait helps to maintain Hall H's status as an exclusive space that houses highly anticipated Hollywood content. However, Hollywood also deploys fandom as a discursive construct in much the same way outside of Comic-Con: to signify the value of their media promotions and commodities.

These power imbalances between the industry and Comic-Con attendees become quite glaring when you consider the economy of waiting as a kind of liminal context where the gift economy of fandom collides with the political economy of the media industries. Hollywood has significant tools and resources that allow them to measure and monetize the economic value of their efforts at Comic-Con. As Lisa Gregorian, chief marketing officer of Warner Bros. Television Group described, "We have a lot of monitoring and sentiment systems that we use. We preplan everything that we are going to be tracking, and then after Comic-Con is over we look at the return on our investment across all of the amplification that we've received due to being in San Diego."[74] For fans, on the other hand, "the waiting-in-line economy operates outside the public records."[75] While riding "a rocket ship made of cheers" during Zach Snyder's 2013 unveiling of *Batman v Superman* (2016) may be a personally significant experience that carries with it a degree of cultural capital, only Warner Bros. has the resources to convert this experience back into economic capital.[76] When fans in Hall H exploit their cultural capital by sharing their experiences on social media platforms, it becomes a quantifiable part of the political economy of the media industries.

"Camp Breaking Dawn"

When the film adaptation of Stephenie Meyer's popular *Twilight Saga* was first previewed at Comic-Con in 2008, a large contingent of *Twilight* fans began attending the event each year to follow the promotion of the franchise. In fact, this particular fandom is frequently invoked in lamentations about the "mainstreaming" of Comic-Con, which is often directly connected to complaints about overcrowding and lines.[77] These complaints about an influx of female fans are ideologically problematic and part of a larger collection of gendered and misogynistic discourse about *Twilight* fans.[78] Not only that, but the claim that *Twilight* "ruined" Comic-Con by inviting crowds and mainstream content is completely unfounded.[79] Hollywood's presence at Comic-Con is built into the very DNA of the event. In 1976, attendees saw production stills from *Star Wars*, in 1988, Warner Brothers tried to sell fans on Michael Keaton as *Batman*, and in 2001, the highly anticipated launch of the *Lord of the Rings* Trilogy was promoted with a behind-the-scenes featurette and a surprise appearance by actor Ian McKellen.[80] These three examples, all of which occurred before 2008, are among the top grossing films of all time; if that's not mainstream, I don't know what is. If anything, Hollywood's response to the passion, enthusiasm, and labor of fans at Comic-Con is the cause of this so-called mainstreaming because its promotions inflate the value and influence of this relatively small segment of its audience in order to create increased publicity outside the event. With this in mind, the discussion that follows brings together the spatial and ideological dimensions of the line, illustrating how the industry capitalizes on the labor of fans when it is contained in this liminal context.

On Monday, July 18, three days before the official start of the 2011 San Diego Comic-Con, a small line began to form outside the entrance to Hall H. The group of thirty fans were waiting to see Summit's panel for *Twilight Saga: Breaking Dawn—Part 1* (Bill Condon, 2011), scheduled for Thursday, July 21, at 11:15 A.M.[81] A small subset of this group had initially arrived at the San Diego Convention Center to form a line on Sunday evening, but was turned away by Comic-Con officials, who told them to leave and return the following day.[82] When the group returned and a line began to form on Monday, they were informed of a new Comic-Con policy beginning that year: fans would not be permitted to form a line for any panels until they had obtained their Comic-Con badges.[83] The group of early arrivals stood their ground, but faced continual reminders from Comic-Con staff, who told them, "You are not a line. You are not official."[84] At one point, line member Arianna Ruiz reported, she was even told, "You don't exist."[85] This last statement represents a simultaneous recognition and disavowal. As a direct address to the fans in line, it acknowledges their existence on the most basic level, as individuals who are physically present in a contentious space and therefore difficult to ignore. But the content of the statement disavows their existence on an ideological level, so that fans' failure to follow the rules and regulations that govern Comic-Con and its queuing processes is met with threats of exclusion. Such a simple assertion, with so many complex ramifications, exists in part due to the liminal time and place in which fans found themselves: forming an "unofficial" line before an event that cultivates exclusivity in order to celebrate and profit on fans, all at the same time.

In addition to these kinds of threats, there was a general sense of disorganization, confusion, and mixed messages. Although fans were told they could not stand in line, no officials ultimately intervened to stop them, exposing the tenuous nature of security's power, particularly outside the temporal parameters of the event, before they, too, become "official" in the eyes of *Twilight* fans. Further, the badge policy described to fans in line was not published on Comic-Con's website and was nowhere to be found in the 2011 Comic-Con Events Guide, which had a section clearly marked "Convention Policies."[86] As one fan suggested, this confusion was actually a motivating factor in joining the line earlier than usual: "They were told that they couldn't line up, then they were told that they could line up, so everything was kind of up in the air. So I think everybody kinda thought well, we should just get down there and get in line in case, because we don't want to miss out, you know, on the chance that we wouldn't get in or we wouldn't be up where we wanted to be, maybe."[87] So in the absence of any official acknowledgment or regulation by Comic-Con, the members of the line known as "Camp Breaking Dawn" reportedly began "self-regulating."[88] Rather than subscribe to these particular rules and risk losing their place in line, fans ignored Comic-Con staff and enforced the hierarchy of the line unofficially instead. By coming together to peacefully maintain the integrity and fairness of the line, days before it was officially policed by Comic-Con volunteers or security, fans demonstrated a willingness to enforce the rules of Comic-Con and, by extension, obey the wider cultural rules associated with standing in line and waiting one's turn, demonstrating just how internalized these power structures can become.

By the time I joined the *Breaking Dawn* line at around 8 A.M. on Thursday morning, a large number of people were in line, but well under the room's capacity of 6,500. I waited approximately three hours to enter Hall H and secured a seat halfway up the room, positioned in clear view of one of the many enormous screens displaying a video feed of the panel. The figures on stage were small but visible, and any missing nuances in the panelists' facial expressions were displayed in the medium shots onscreen. Despite the long wait time leading up to the panel, hundreds of seats sat empty behind me, even as the stars of the film were being introduced on stage.[89] As my experience suggests, waiting in line for days was not necessary to ensure entry into Hall H, or even to ensure a reasonable view of the stage. However, the fact that many fans chose to spend this additional time waiting demonstrates how significant the line can be, not only to producing value around the event but also in cultivating a sense of community and shared experience that resonates beyond this promotional context.[90] The greater the challenge, it would seem, the more personally significant the panel experience can become. This is how the work of waiting in line helps to transform the process of publicity, something that could feel quite cold and mechanical, especially in a room full of thousands of people, into a seemingly intimate and fulfilling experience. But while members of Camp Breaking Dawn most certainly got something out of the experience that transcends an economic bottom line, this does not mean such a bottom line does not exist for the industry.

Even though Comic-Con organizers would not recognize the line as "official," Summit Entertainment recognized and took full advantage of the early fan presence, effectively overriding Comic-Con's regulations and legitimating the line. The first images of the Comic-Con line to be heavily circulated and cited online were photographs sourced from fans but posted on Summit Entertainment's official *Twilight Saga* Twitter account and Facebook page on Monday, July 18.[91] The first post announced that the line had begun to form, while subsequent tweets recruited fans to share their pictures and provided updates about the status of the line.[92] On July 20, Summit's Twitter feed retweeted information from the fan site *Twilight Lexicon*, informing readers that more than 250 people had already joined the line and adding to the urgency and excitement around attending the panel.[93] In effect, this official *Twilight* Twitter feed acted as an aggregator of images and information about waiting in line for fans wishing to follow the action. More importantly, these updates drew on fan-produced content to promote the event and used the growing line to create increased buzz and excitement. In fact, as one fan noted, the photos and information about the campout that began to circulate on Twitter and Facebook motivated more and more people to join the line early.[94] In addition to this social media presence, media coverage of the line played a role in producing a sense of urgency by using the bodies of fans in line as a signifier of the value of both the waiting process and the promotional content that awaited them in Hall H. Describing her experience, Melissa Miller noted that the media coverage of Camp Breaking Dawn influenced her expectations about the crowd: "I had seen news reports of people beginning to line up for the panel as early as Monday afternoon, so I had expected there to be a TON of people, hungrily waiting for their shot to glimpse the film's stars. When I arrived to set up camp in a spot in the second row of the second tent, there were plenty of people ahead of me, sure, but a couple of hundred, tops—nowhere near the 6,500 that Hall H could accommodate."[95] While Comic-Con attendees, like Miller and myself, have the opportunity to experience the line as a discursive construct and weigh that against the reality of being there in person, those watching or reading coverage at home are left, instead, with an impression about the event that stands in for the experience, whether it is entirely accurate or not. And because of Comic-Con's exclusive status, those impressions dominate and even reshape the reality of the convention space.

For example, Summit took further advantage of the "Camp Breaking Dawn" line by staging a "surprise" meet and greet on Thursday morning before the panel. At around 6:30 A.M., five of the film's cast members appeared with a small entourage, serving muffins and coffee in *Twilight* mugs and signing autographs for the fans who had waited patiently in line—some for hours, some for days.[96] While this came as a surprise to excited fans, Summit Entertainment had already notified media outlets about this publicity stunt, and several cameras followed the actors, documenting the genuine excitement of the fans and the generosity of the performers who "rewarded fans for their patience."[97] One fan commented, "It was unbelievable that they would be here at 6:30 in the morning, I mean that's really dedication to their fans."[98] Given this enthusiasm, it seems clear that the goodwill gesture of this meet-and-greet had the desired effect. That fans were shocked and flattered by the stars' appearance on Thursday morning, however, is indicative of a massive disconnect in what is expected of fans in this liminal space between labor and leisure and what is expected of Hollywood actors. The fan's comment that the stars' early arrival was demonstrative of their dedication to their fan base illustrates very clearly the uneven power relations between celebrities and fans in line; where a twenty-minute appearance at 6:30 A.M. displays a level of dedication commensurate with, or even greater than, the dedication of fans who stood in line for as many as four days. Further, the juxtaposition of the bodies of fans who had been sleeping outside for days and the bodies of actors who had been made-up and styled in anticipation of their photo op is an uncomfortable reminder of the class and cultural inequalities that make such power relationships all the more problematic.[99]

These inequalities are even more pronounced in light of the fact that fans were not visited by the film's biggest stars, Robert Pattinson, Kristen Stewart, and Tayler Lautner, but by secondary character actors Nikki Reed, Ashley Greene, Boo Boo Stewart, Elizabeth Reaser, and Julia Jones. This photo op thus provided additional publicity for the event and the film itself, even while it invited fans into an ideological position in which their own time was significantly less valuable than the time of industry professionals. Occupying such an ideological position also allowed fans to be rewarded, somewhat paradoxically, with the very value they worked to produce by forming a line and supporting the product in the first place. But instead of remaining with the fans, this value was instantly displaced onto the film's stars as the official industry presence at the event. The work that went into this production of value through waiting was erased by the spectacle of publicity and the naturalization of a hierarchy of labor that places creatives above the line and the labor of fans so far below the line as to become virtually invisible.[100] This kind of public relations maneuver does not simply serve the function of promoting a product or a brand, however; it also helps to build a relationship with fans that situates them in a liminal space that signals proximity to the industry, while ideological and material boundaries establish conditions of distance.[101] In many ways, this is a perfect relationship for the digital age; a simulation of affective proximity that feels more authentic than what we experience out in the world. Comic-Con, of course, is one of those real-world locations where this interplay of proximity and distance happens all at once, illustrating that the powerful ideological hierarchies that divide fans and industry can reinforce that distance even when it is seemingly being undone.

These power imbalances between industry representatives and *Twilight* fans take on additional significance in light of claims that *Twilight* "ruined" Comic-Con and the resultant hostility toward *Twilight* fans at the event, sometimes framed as a rejection of the mainstream, sometimes more overtly misogynistic, but almost always the product of privileged biases about who gets to participate in and define fan culture.[102] Attributing overcrowding and so-called mainstreaming to *Twilight* fans, rather than to Hollywood or the media industries in general, creates a completely false impression of the power of this group, and demonstrates how the same discourses that celebrate "the power of fandom" or, as Henry Jenkins put it, "superpowered fans," can be used to fuel and justify exclusionary attacks.[103] It also distracts from the ways that such divisions can be economically beneficial to the industry, enabling them to "support multiple profit centers by keeping each side of the struggle in tension."[104] Indeed, fans of the *Twilight* franchise might be seen as occupying a liminal space of their own at Comic-Con, as this largely female fan base was ostensibly welcomed via extensive industry promotion but excluded by other fans as too mainstream or, in other words, too feminine.[105]

Conclusion: Between Industry and Fandom

Building on the book's discussion of exclusivity, this chapter proposes a theoretical approach to waiting in line with the aim of locating the place of fans at Comic-Con. I argue that the liminal space and time of waiting in line mirrors the ideological place in which fans frequently find themselves, between leisure and labor. Not only that, but considering lines in an exclusive context like Comic-Con is one way to insert banality back into the conversation in order to interrogate power imbalances between Hollywood and fans. In the process of waiting, Comic-Con fans work in unconventional ways to construct and maintain the order of the line and participate in an economy of waiting that, when paired with the limits of exclusivity, adds value to Hollywood promotions.

My own approach to this topic operates in a similarly liminal space in that it engages with subject matter and practices commonly aligned with fan studies but also draws heavily on critical political economy and media industry studies. The productivity of audiences is a concern that unites these two fields, but scholarship often offers vastly different takes on the topic. While critical political economy argues that even our leisure time is spent working for the media industries, fan studies counters that fan labor and productivity can be a means to other ends, outside of capitalist paradigms.[106] Of course, these two arguments are at odds only when we see them as mutually exclusive.[107] The reason for this incongruity lies in the need to better distinguish between fandom as a discursive construct—a meaning or meanings connected to the activity of fans, but shaped and influenced by institutional powers outside their control—and the passions and investments of individual fans or fan groups. But it is often difficult to know where one stops and the other starts. In the Comic-Con line, much like Comic-Con itself, fans find themselves negotiating power and hierarchies that grow out of material conditions at the same time as Hollywood shapes, constructs, and reconstructs meaning all around them. In the next chapter, I move from the liminal space of the line into a space where Hollywood does much of this discursive work: Hall H.

As this chapter's Camp Breaking Dawn case study suggests, the negotiations that occur between fans and industry in somewhat banal and liminal spaces like the Comic-Con line are productive of ideological meanings that reverberate far beyond the context of a single media event. While the popularity of *Twilight* at Comic-Con, evidenced by the commitment of fans in line and the franchise's promotional presence, seems to suggest that the blockbuster franchise and its fans were welcome at the event, the misogynist backlash (disguised as critiques about mainstream audiences) tells a different story. In this context, scholarship that contends with the complexity of liminality—literal and conceptual—becomes all the more important as it opens up new possibilities for critique—of the insularity of fan cultures, of industry power, and everything in between. With this in mind, I return to the framing question of this chapter: What is the place of fans at Comic-Con, an event that celebrates fandom but is increasingly dominated by Hollywood promotion? We might theorize that fans are both producing and consuming culture at Comic-Con, but we might just as easily argue that the idealized notion of fandom constructed by and through Hollywood's presence at the event doesn't exist at all. Individually, these theories make for tidy conclusions, but if you really want to locate the place of fans at Comic-Con you're more likely to find it in the messy, liminal space of the line.

3

Manufacturing "Hall H Hysteria"

● ● ● ● ● ● ● ● ● ● ● ● ● ● ● ● ● ● ● ●

Hollywood and Comic-Con

> Surrounded by ardent fans, it's easy to
> get sucked into Comic-Con's vortex of
> enthusiasm, forgetting that even with
> 120,000 people descending on the
> convention center, that's still a very,
> very self-selected group.
> —Brian Lowry, *Variety*, 2009

In the spring of 2004, the cover of Comic-Con's *Update* magazine announced "A Mystery Solved."[1] That mystery was how Comic-Con, which had been gradually expanding to fill the entire San Diego Convention Center, would utilize the last of its large, unused halls, Hall H.[2] Located at the southeast end of the convention center, this immense space, bearing a closer resemblance to a warehouse or airplane hangar than a theater, would be filled with 6,500 seats, making it Comic-Con's largest programming room.[3] Not surprisingly, Hall H was earmarked to fill the rising demand of and for

Hollywood programming, and in 2004 every major studio—along with numerous independents—was represented at Comic-Con.[4] That same year, Comic-Con attendance reached almost 100,000.[5] There was also a notable increase in media coverage of the event's importance to Hollywood, with the *New York Times* calling it "a vital promotional tool in movie marketing campaigns" and the *Los Angeles Times* describing, "the multitudes crammed into giant meeting halls to pass judgment on Hollywood's latest works in progress, often setting the tone for how the completed films will be received by the general public."[6] One report even suggested that "studios were . . . spending about $250,000 apiece to rev up the buzz on upcoming projects."[7]

If the opening of this new programming space and the ensuing influx of Hollywood promotion and media attention positioned Hall H as "the white-hot uranium core" to Comic-Con's "nuclear reactor" of film buzz and publicity, this exclusive status was further solidified by the hall's location and spatial configuration.[8] Hall H is situated on the ground floor of the San Diego Convention Center and, at 64,842 square feet, it is the largest of Comic-Con's nineteen programming rooms.[9] While the majority of Comic-Con's programming is located on the second floor of the convention center, Hall H is actually one of an interconnected network of nine halls, the other eight of which make up the 460,859-square-foot Exhibit Hall, a space that I discuss at length in chapter 4. As a subset of the Exhibit Hall separated by "sound absorptive panels" and repurposed with seats, numerous large screens, and a stage, Hall H has a somewhat dark, cavernous appearance as compared to the convention center's carpeted and well-lit meeting rooms and ballrooms on the upper level (figures 3.1 and 3.2).[10] Unlike other programming rooms, the hall can be accessed only from the outside, at the southeast end of the convention center (figure 3.3).[11] Similarly, one cannot access the rest of the convention center directly from Hall H.[12] This distinction facilitates the kind of highly visible queuing that I described at length in chapter 2 and sets Hall H apart, spatially and discursively, even as it remains connected to the rest of the convention.[13] The content presented in Hall H varies but is similarly positioned around exclusivity. For example, in 2011, when the hall's programming expanded to include promotion for numerous popular television shows in addition to feature films, this shift was largely attributed to the increased popularity and legitimacy of genre-based and so-called quality television programs, rather than the erosion of what had been largely a film-centric space.[14] Regardless of their focus,

FIGURE 3.1 Ballroom 20 before an evening panel, Comic-Con 2012. (Photo by the author.)

FIGURE 3.2 Hall H being loaded before a day of panels, Comic-Con 2018. (Photo by the author.)

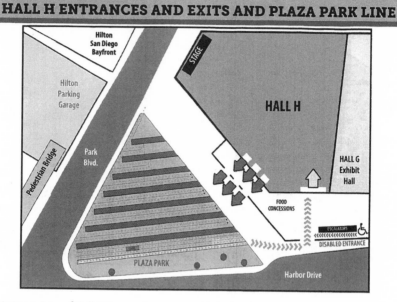

FIGURE 3.3 Map of Hall H lines and entrance published in the Comic-Con International Quick Guide, 2017.

panels always include some combination of the following: a moderator (often a prominent blogger, journalist, or comedian)[15]; the film or television show's director, writer(s), and/or stars; trailers, behind-the-scenes featurettes, or clips[16]; a question and answer session with the audience; free giveaways (swag) or vouchers used to claim giveaways at a later time[17]; surprise announcements[18]; and, of course, a captive audience of up to 6,500 Comic-Con attendees.

Not unlike the "cultivation rituals" John Caldwell describes in *Production Cultures* (2008), presentations in Hall H are ostensibly about drawing insider information out into public or semipublic contexts, ultimately distracting from the fact that Hollywood's "business interactions are highly proprietary and sequestered away from those on 'the outside' by design."[19] Many similar "staged self-disclosures" take place at conferences, trade shows, and film festivals, what Caldwell calls "halfway spaces," where discourses geared toward those in attendance also extend out into the larger community through the trade press.[20] Comic-Con, I argue, represents a very similar context, where Hollywood's mode of address situates fans, alongside members of the press, as "intermediaries for the public."[21] But, as Caldwell argues, the structure of such spaces and events, where the industry controls content and access, also "tend[s] to sanction audience consumption from a specific, regulated vantage point."[22] Hollywood's presence in Hall H is covered by numerous media outlets, and that coverage circulates alongside the buzz produced by attendees. However, the exclusivity of Hall H and its panels is an industry construct, one that works to control the discourses that circulate around its promotions and, if successful, inflate the value of the films and television shows being promoted. Similarly, the mode of address inside the space engages the audience as a generic crowd of fans, while the media coverage surrounding it often treats this crowd as a signifier of fandom, in general, rather than individuals with varied investments. In this way, Hall H provides a key moment where the industry can reassert its cultural and economic power, first, through its ability to situate the audience as fans, often before even they even encounter any promotional paratexts, let alone the text itself, and second, by presenting this group with exclusive experiences inside Hall H, framed as rewards for their fandom or even payment for their promotional labor.[23]

In Hall H, exclusivity is a carefully manufactured experience in need of continuous maintenance; it is simultaneously highly controlled and completely out of control, like the nerve-wracking construction and reconstruction of a wobbly tower of Jenga blocks. This chapter examines a single day in Hall H in order to explain how the industry navigates the seemingly contradictory goals of maintaining the exclusivity of its promotional content, while spreading its promotional message far and wide. While coverage in the press frequently reinforces the notion that at Comic-Con, "actors, directors, producers and marketers [are] expected to show up in person and kiss the ring,"[24] I argue that Hollywood's presence in Hall H is not simply about paying homage to the small segment of its fans attending Comic-Con (and the even smaller segment of fans inside the hall). Instead, the kind of exclusive promotions offered inside Hall H are part of broader efforts on the part of the entertainment industry to decenter fandom as an audience practice and reframe it as an industry construct. Fans, in this context, become part and parcel of the promotional paratext, and their reactions in Hall H are meant to say something—to the industry, to the press, and to a more general audience—about the impact of Hollywood's products.[25] Deployed this way, notions of exclusivity—surrounding the fans in attendance and the content being presented—are the Trojan horse through which Hollywood delivers its marketing messages to a much wider audience. And nowhere are these machinations more evident than in the concept of "Hall H hysteria."

Hall H Hysteria and the Comic-Con False Positive

In 2009, *Variety's* Brian Lowry used the phrase "Hall H hysteria," to describe the fan reaction to promotion in Hall H and the inflated value it produced. "It's easy," Lowry wrote "to get sucked into Comic-Con's vortex of enthusiasm, forgetting that even with 120,000 people descending on the convention center, that's still a very, very, self-selected group."[26] The term "hysteria" is, of course, quite a loaded one. It has long operated, both medically and colloquially, as a way to pathologize and marginalize women in mind and body, making it particularly significant that Lowry coined this phrase just one year after *Twilight's* first Comic-Con panel drew a large contingent of female fans.[27] As a descriptor of "unhealthy emotion or excitement," hysteria has also been deployed to pathologize the behavior of fans more generally and, as Kristina Busse argues, to engage in "boundary policing" by coding "negatively connoted fannish activities" as "specifically female."[28] Hall H hysteria maps onto a similar hierarchy of fan behavior, celebrating "affirmational" fandom that works in step with industry promotion, while also policing responses (even positive ones) that have negative economic outcomes for the industry.[29] But while the unabashed excitement that accompanies a "hysterical" reaction to promotion in Hall H is a desirable source of publicity, the potential unpredictability of this affective response, so the argument goes, also makes Hall H hysteria difficult to anticipate, interpret, and control.

Indeed, Lowry's larger point is that promotion to a "self-selected" group of fans at Comic-Con can lead to what he calls "the Comic-Con false positive," an inflated projection of a film's future success.[30] The notion that Comic-Con fans can, as CNN put it, "help fuel anticipation for a product, or hatch the first cancerous seeds of bad buzz" is a frequent feature in coverage and think pieces about Hollywood's presence at Comic-Con.[31] In a 2008 article in the *Hollywood Reporter*, Steven Zeitchik similarly asks whether Hollywood's new strategy of "marketing to the grassroots" is truly delivering results.[32] "The nerd herd strategy," he argues, may be overvaluing this niche audience as it is not large enough to significantly impact profits, nor are enthusiastic Comic-Con fans a reliable measure of a film's future success.[33] This mix of fascination and incredulity about the influence of Hall

H continued in 2011, when Warner Brothers, Disney, DreamWorks, and The Weinstein Company opted out of Hall H presentations at Comic-Con and the *New York Times* declared that Comic-Con had "turned into a treacherous place" where even the best efforts at publicizing a film could produce unexpected or negative results.[34] And when Fox passed on Hall H in 2016, coverage in the press cited piracy concerns tied to the high-profile leaks of *X-Men: Apocalypse* (Bryan Singer, 2016) and *Deadpool* (Tim Miller, 2016) footage during panels in 2015.[35] These examples reinforce the idea that fans are powerful but unpredictable, necessary but frequently unruly. At the same time, however, they also construct a hierarchy that reinforces Hollywood's economic and cultural power to control when, where, and how fans can access content, even when it is promotional in nature.

In centering Hall H as the hub of Hollywood publicity at Comic-Con, however, these reports glossed over the myriad ways in which these studios—and their parent companies—*were* present at Comic-Con. In 2011, for example, Warner Brothers erected a 3,600-square-foot booth in Comic-Con's exhibit hall, partnered with thirty-six San Diego hotels to distribute forty thousand "limited edition" keycards during the convention, and sponsored Comic-Con's "swag bags," distributed to over 130,000 attendees (figure 3.4).[36] And, as I discuss in the next section, Warner Brothers returned to Hall H in 2012 with a high-profile panel presentation. Similarly, while Twentieth Century Fox withheld film content from Hall H in 2016, Fox TV had a major presence in other programming rooms, a booth in the Exhibit Hall, and a large outdoor installation adjacent to Hall H, which included a *Son of Zorn* (2016–2017) rock wall, a *Rocky Horror Picture Show* (2016) lip painting station, and the "FXHIBITION" promoting shows on the Fox-owned FX network (figure 3.5).[37] Despite ongoing piracy concerns, Fox's absence also wound up being temporary, with the studio returning to Hall H the next year to promote *Kingsman: The Golden Circle* (Matthew Vaughn, 2017). As these examples suggest, cautionary discourses about Hall H hysteria or the dreaded Comic-Con false positive are less the product of unruly or unpredictable fan behavior and, more accurately, the result of the unpredictability of studios, whose cultural and economic heft empowers them to manufacture and exploit exclusivity in Hall H by withholding certain kinds of promotional content, while flooding the convention center and the streets of San Diego with a slew of others.

Although Hall H hysteria emphasizes the activities of audience members *inside* Hall H, studios' anxiety about these reactions are more accurately tied

FIGURE 3.4 Warner Brothers swag bag, Comic-Con 2018. (Photo by the author.)

to what Jenkins et al. call the "spreadability" of their promotional message—and whether the message that emerges is positive, negative, or largely indifferent.[38] While the reactions of 6,500 fans in Hall H are certainly important, it is the ability to reach media consumers outside the Hall that matters most to Hollywood. As Eileen Meehan explains, when it comes to the relationship between fans and the heavily concentrated and integrated media industries, "the logics of a demand-driven market simply do not apply."[39] Because fans represent a reliable revenue stream, particularly when it comes to long-running and expansive media franchises, "the unreliable buyer," Meehan argues, becomes the default "source of revenue growth."[40] Hall H hysteria, then, represents both the spectacle of media promotion for fans inside Hall H and the vehicle through which that promotion travels, with the end goal of generating revenue outside the convention center.

FIGURE 3.5 Fox and FX offsite activation, Comic-Con 2016. (Photo by the author.)

Fox's launch of James Cameron's lucrative *Avatar* (2009) franchise during a 2009 Hall H panel exemplified this approach, incorporating a number of strategies designed to heighten the exclusivity of the experience inside Hall H, while also extending that exclusivity to the rest of the moviegoing public. During the panel, Cameron surprised attendees by screening twenty-five minutes of the film in 3-D, which was largely well received.[41] After the *Avatar* panel, the *Los Angeles Times* declared that, "the approving Internet buzz was instantly deafening."[42] When circulated through blogs and social networks, this buzz worked largely at the level of word-of-mouth marketing. However, the coverage of these responses in major news outlets, like the *Los Angeles Times*, were folded into a campaign designed to build on fan reactions at Comic-Con in order to replicate them with a larger group of consumers.

At the end of the *Avatar* panel, Cameron made a special announcement: "I wanted to do something that was really special in unveiling the film and I think we managed to do that today. But it occurred to me that there's a global audience out there and I wondered if there was a way to capture this kind of magic for people who couldn't get to Comic-Con. And so we have kind of a big announcement here today. Which is we're going to do something really unprecedented."[43] Cameron went on to describe the plan for "*Avatar* day." Several weeks later, on August 21st, Fox would release fifteen minutes of footage to IMAX theaters worldwide. Consumers who went online and secured a ticket would be able to go to the theater and watch this 3-D footage of the film for free. This unique promotional push was scheduled to occur alongside other more conventional marketing strategies, such as the release of trailers to theaters and the launch of a toy line from Mattel, both building on and bolstering the campaign as a whole. This made Cameron's announcement at Comic-Con a kind of advertisement within an advertisement, a marketing mise en abyme that sought to engage a larger audience through the excitement of a special event carrying similar spatio-temporal restrictions, while allowing for significantly greater access. Announcing "*Avatar* Day" at Comic-Con was a way to draw out the exclusivity of the Hall H panel, while also repackaging it as an experience that others could seek out closer to home. As a writer for *Cinema Blend* put it, "This isn't just some cool press event happening in New York or LA, it'll play on that day in IMAX theaters all over the world."[44] While it is difficult to gauge the financial success of this specific strategy, or to determine the kinds of spectators that visited the theater on *Avatar* day, the fact that the tickets to the IMAX screenings were completely sold out indicates that Fox and Cameron were successful in reaching a much larger audience than the 6,500 fans who attended the panel in Hall H.[45] Opening the screening with a special filmed message to viewers, Cameron also attempted to replicate the more intimate setting of Comic-Con with a mediated variation on a Hall H preview panel. With *Avatar* Day, then, the studio built on initial previews at Comic-Con and the growing buzz in the fan community, engaging an even larger group of spectators with a similar special, in-person event, extending Hall H hysteria across the globe. Ultimately *Avatar*'s marketing points to Hollywood's capacity to construct and deconstruct exclusivity, creating limits and boundaries that are designed to be undone, but only in ways that are sanctioned, encouraged, and promoted by the industry.

If the experiences of individual fans at Comic-Con, which can be very real, affective, and emotional, are captured in the unbridled, unpredictable, or uncontrollable reactions frequently denigrated as hysterical, Hall H hysteria, I argue, is something quite different. It is the counterbalance to these possibilities and the product of the industry's continued attempts to control, shape, and capitalize on the exclusivity of Comic-Con's Hall H, a space that exists because of and explicitly *for* Hollywood promotion. Situating fans within a framework that connects their power to Hollywood's success, the notion of Hall H hysteria also sends the message that the industry can and should police this power when it departs from desired outcomes. Ultimately, foregrounding the affective and organic reaction of fans in Hall H distracts from the highly controlled nature of Hollywood promotion at Comic-Con, allowing it to maintain its aura of exclusivity, even as it is repackaged and delivered to a much larger audience. The remainder of this chapter provides a detailed analysis of a day in Hall H in order to explain why it is so "easy to get sucked into Comic-Con's vortex of enthusiasm": it is that way by design.[46]

A Day in Hall H

In June 2012 *Variety* reported on Hollywood's presence at Comic-Con, noting that Warner Brothers had reserved an unusually long three-hour block for Saturday in Hall H.[47] They were expected to present their Winter 2012 and Summer 2013 tentpoles, *The Hobbit: An Unexpected Journey* (Peter Jackson, 2012) and *Man of Steel* (Zach Snyder, 2013), and unconfirmed reports suggested that coproducer Legendary Pictures would join Warner Brothers in presenting their upcoming film *Pacific Rim* (Guillermo del Toro, 2013).[48] When the panel began on Saturday, July 14th, at 2:30 P.M., attendees were already anticipating a spectacular series of presentations, but as the curtains at the front of Hall H pulled back to reveal two massive screens displaying the Warner Brothers logo, the crowd broke into effusive cheers and applause.[49] As a member of that crowd, I spent approximately six hours in line and eight hours in Hall H that day. The schedule of programs was as follows:

11:30–12:30	"Quentin Tarantino's *Django Unchained*"
12:45–1:45	"Open Road Films: *End of Watch* and *Silent Hill: Revelation 3D*"
2:00–2:30	"Trailer Park I"
2:30–5:15	"Warner Bros. Pictures and Legendary Pictures Preview Their Upcoming Lineups"
5:15–6:00	"Trailer Park II"
6:00–7:00	"Marvel Studios: *Iron Man 3*"
7:15–9:15	"Comi-Kev: Q&A with Kevin Smith"[50]

In the subsections that follow, I discuss the daytime portion of this programming, from 11:30 A.M. to 6:00 P.M., capturing the experience of attending a day of panels in Hall H as media coverage and interest in Comic-Con were hitting new heights.[51] In doing so, I explain how studios used the convention space, promotional content, and scheduling of panels to construct highly controlled promotional discourses even as they cultivated seemingly authentic, affective, and unpredictable Hall H hysteria in the crowd. As these strategies and the subsequent media coverage illustrate, the exclusive experiences of fans inside Hall H were meant to spread buzz and publicity beyond the confines of the convention center.

Expanding and Contracting Exclusivity

The first panel of the day, "Quentin Tarantino's *Django Unchained*" took the unusual measure of highlighting the director's name alongside the title of this film. While such naming practices had been used on occasion for directors with a particular cachet among Comic-Con attendees, like James Cameron and Terry Gilliam, this was a clear deviation from the norm for Hall H panels, which was to signal the studio presenting the films or the films themselves. As a result, the panel title conjured up Tarantino's frequent branding as a "fanboy auteur" with an encyclopedic knowledge of cinema, making an implicit argument for the film's presence in Hall H.[52] Though he was part of a panel of stars, which also included Jamie Foxx, Christoph Waltz, Kerry Washington, and Don Johnson, the seemingly organic promotion of exclusivity through Tarantino's authorial presence at Comic-Con also highlighted the ideological problems of the film itself by centering the white male filmmaker's voice, vision, and creativity even as his work relied heavily on the stories and performances of people of color.[53]

In particular, Tarantino took ownership of decisions related to what and how much footage to screen at Comic-Con. In introducing the *Django* footage, he told the crowd that they would watch the same eight-minute industry "sizzle reel" that was screened at Cannes:[54]

> There was a whole talk . . . when we were coming down here about "well, we shouldn't show them that much footage; it might get out; we don't want that to happen; let's just do a four minute reel of this, that, and the other." And I was like NO. The people at Comic-Con have been with us for a long time. They're probably gonna have this hall jam-packed. They've been waiting in

line for a long time. They should see—I'm cool with my footage. I'm cool with the footage. We have much more coming. But I decided that if this is good enough for the industry, it's good enough for the fans.[55]

Tarantino's speech highlights the significance of both time and space as an indicator of exclusivity and value by mentioning the time attendees spent in line and the limited space of the "jam-packed" hall. But it also presents a somewhat simplistic understanding of "the fans," all of whom, he seemed to think, were his own. However, the panel's position early in a day that culminated in previously hyped promotions for *The Hobbit, Man of Steel, Pacific Rim*, and Marvel Studios' Cinematic Universe, paired with the fact that Comic-Con does not clear rooms between panels, meant that *Django Unchained* was virtually guaranteed a "jam-packed" audience. But many of those who lined up overnight and in the early hours of the morning did so in order to attend panels in Hall H *all day*; a detail that Tarantino either ignored or failed to recognize.[56] Such nuances were also lost in *IndieWire's* coverage, which stated that "Hall H was packed with 6000 fans, many of whom stayed up all night to gain a seat, to get a gander at an eight-minute sizzle reel of clips from the first half of Quentin Tarantino's 'Django Unchained.'"[57] Demonstrating how the limits of exclusivity can be expanded to include a large swath of fans and subsequently contracted to fuel industry promotions, when the *Django* panel began, attendees in Hall H were suddenly transformed into Tarantino fans, not only by coverage in the press but also by the director himself.

Expanding and contracting notions of exclusivity were also at play in the presentation of the *Django* "sizzle reel." Though the footage was not produced or assembled *for* Comic-Con, it was still framed as exclusive because of its original presentation at Cannes, which, unlike Comic-Con, is identified as an industry-centered event.[58] Tarantino's assertion that, "if this is good enough for the industry, it's good enough for the fans" was met with raucous applause. This statement encapsulates the way Hollywood appeals to fans at Comic-Con by expanding and contracting the limits of exclusivity, inviting them to feel like industry insiders, even as the material conditions of this relationship betray the power imbalances that actually exist. When the *Django* footage was screened at Cannes, Harvey Weinstein—head of The Weinstein Company until he was exposed as a serial sexual predator and ousted in 2017—presented the reel to "a gathering of journalists," making Tarantino's suggestion that the footage at Cannes was "for the industry" slightly misleading.[59] More accurately, it was presented for a subset of the media industries that produce a large quantity of publicity: critics, reporters, and bloggers.[60]

This Cannes footage was widely reported on, and, notably, many of these reports emerged from the same outlets providing extensive coverage of Comic-Con.[61] The key difference, however, was that the journalists and bloggers in attendance at Cannes reported on and responded to the sizzle reel itself, while articles about the Comic-Con panel also reported on the responses of attendees in Hall H with headlines like, "Quentin Tarantino Wows Hall H," "Tarantino's 'Django Unchained' Shocks, Awes" and "Comic-Con fans give 'Django Unchained' a Standing Ovation."[62] In coverage of the panel, Comic-Con fans who were seeing the footage for the first time took on the same role as the critics at Cannes, whose positive responses helped to produce publicity by telling readers something about the potential quality of the film; but fan responses were also the *content* of the publicity, having been incorporated into critics' reports as they emerged from Comic-Con. In other words, the exclusivity of the panel and footage helped to stir up excitement about the film, while the audience of fans was similarly objectified and repositioned to signify the "sizzle" in the "sizzle reel." Given the overlaps, both in the reporting and in the function of these events, the contrast between Cannes's contracted exclusivity and Comic-Con's expanded exclusivity is glaring: at Cannes, "critics, bloggers and people in suits gathered in a large antechamber, sipping wine"[63] while they waited for Harvey Weinstein to arrive and present the footage, while Comic-Con fans camped out on the hard concrete or lined up for hours to gain access to the same "sizzle reel."

Programming Flow

Open Road Films, a newly formed distribution company, hosted their first Comic-Con panel in the 12:45 P.M. slot following *Django Unchained*. Two major theatrical exhibition chains, AMC Entertainment and Regal Entertainment Group, had formed Open Road in 2011 to "fill a void left by studios now concentrating on tentpoles" by distributing other kinds of films to fill their theaters, especially during the times of year when they weren't profiting on increased traffic from blockbusters.[64] According to then CEO Tom Ortenberg, Open Road's strategy was to "look for films we can acquire at an attractive price and market and distribute in a cost-effective manner to as broad an audience as possible."[65] The distributor's appearance in Comic-Con's Hall H suggests that holding such a panel fit within the company's emphasis on efficiency and frugality. It also says a lot about the major studios that bring their films to Comic-Con. Contrary to discourses in the popular press, such appearances do not necessarily represent a meaningful economic investment in fans as tastemakers. Rather, holding a panel in Hall H requires a relatively low economic investment—particularly in relation to the inflated marketing budgets associated with media franchises and global blockbusters—with the potential for high returns when the promotional message reaches a broader audience.[66] But for a company like Open Road that was not producing its own films, let alone investing in heavily hyped and costly blockbusters, there was even less risk involved. Because of their low profile and position on the schedule, sandwiched between Quentin Tarantino and Warner Brothers' massive panel, Open Road didn't have to live up to any hype or expectations. Even with a lukewarm response in the room (as was the case that day) they could still hope for some goodwill, word of mouth, and media coverage based on their appearance in Hall H. While the reaction to their panel was subdued in comparison to the other presentations that day, Open Road also had an audience that was almost literally captive. With the hall filled to capacity and a line outside that was reportedly 6,496 deep at 1:00 P.M., nearly everyone who was admitted to Hall H in the morning remained in the room during the Open Road panel in order to secure their seat for the rest of the programming that day.[67] The strategic midday scheduling of this panel ensured that the presentation was woven into a kind of Hall H "flow" that, like television programming, kept attendees engaged with advertising content.

Flow, as Raymond Williams describes it, dates back to television's network era, pre–time shifting, when the organization of programming worked to create the sense of a larger, more unified sequence that kept viewers tuned in for long stretches of time and through various commercial interruptions.[68] The sequencing of Hall H panels—which even approximated a prime time slot from the start of the Warner Brothers panel at 2:30 P.M. to the end of the Marvel Studios panel at 7:00 P.M.—replicated this mode of spectatorship and paralleled the liveness of the network television era, as attendees could not pause, stop, rewind, or fast forward the content.[69] Even though all the panels presented in Hall H that day were, at their core, commercials, the programming schedule meant that the content was distributed across a trajectory of exclusivity and value, with lower-profile panels functioning more like traditional commercial breaks, filling time between other portions of the programming and legitimating higher-profile promotions as more exclusive.

In another parallel with network television, Hall H is the only programming space at Comic-Con that is also equipped with bathrooms and a small concession area, which ensures that even if attendees are not actively watching a panel, they are at least able to stay within earshot. Much like a conventional commercial break, the Open Road panel provided a moment for many attendees to dash to the bathroom or grab a bite to eat. But just as such long-standing practices at home did not deter advertisers from buying ad time on television, they did not seem to undermine the upshot of free publicity that surrounds an appearance in Hall H. Instead, the Open Road panel worked to create its own coherence and flow, with David Ayer's gritty police drama, *End of Watch* (2012), building on Tarantino's Comic-Con appearance. The panel also incorporated talking points about the use of body cameras and POV shots in the film, which Ayer directly connected to the aesthetics of video games like *Call of Duty*, in order to situate the film as a fit at Comic-Con.[70] The link to video games also flowed into the company's next presentation for *Silent Hill: Revelation 3D* (Michael J. Basset, 2012), an adaptation of the popular video game franchise.[71]

If the audience treated the Open Road Films panel more like a commercial break than the feature presentation, Comic-Con's two "Trailer Park" presentations, scheduled before the Warner Brothers and Marvel Studios panels, fed this kind of programming flow even more explicitly. The Event Guide's description, which invited attendees to "see the latest in trailers from your upcoming soon-to-be favorite films," could just as easily be describing what many encounter at their local cineplex.[72] But even within the more mundane format of a night out at the cinema, movie trailers are, as Jonathan Gray has argued, geared toward producing excitement by "announcing the wonders of the medium in general" and "bring[ing] to a head the joys of anticipation," while "reinforce[ing] cinemagoing as a repetitive event."[73] It is also worth noting that Trailer Park, which originated with longtime marketing consultant, Jeff Walker, dates back many years and is a remnant of a time when movie trailers were somewhat harder to access and, by extension, more exclusive.[74]

By 2012, however, Trailer Park was less remarkable as an exclusive opportunity and more like the repetitious interlude of a commercial break. In fact, the program, which included trailers for *Dredd* (Pete Travis, 2012),

Finding Nemo 3D (Lee Unkrich and Andrew Stanton, 2012), *Despicable Me 2* (Pierre Coffin and Chris Renaud, 2013), *Hotel Transylvania* (Genndy Tartakovsky, 2012), *Resident Evil: Retribution* (Paul W. S. Anderson, 2012), and *Rise of the Guardians* (Peter Ramsey, 2012), was scheduled to run once on Thursday and twice on Saturday, so any exclusivity that might have been present in the first viewing was undone by the second and third.[75] Some outlets reported on this content, suggesting that programming flow in Hall H may have worked to shift these trailers out of the realm of the everyday and make them part of the show.[76] But most coverage simply omitted descriptions of the Trailer Park program altogether, suggesting an implicit understanding that this was purely commercial content, while simultaneously elevating the rest of the Hall H promotion to more newsworthy and exclusive status. The fact that the trailers screened in 2012 were animated family features and midbudget genre films similarly helped to divert attention to high profile and star-studded promotions for films like *The Hobbit* and *Iron Man 3*. Thus, in the context of programing flow, exclusivity helped to produce a framework or hierarchy through which Comic-Con attendees, as well as those who simply read about Comic-Con online, could make sense of different kinds of promotion at the event. Providing a reminder of what it felt like to simply watch traditional movie trailers also helped to establish, on the industry's terms, what exclusive content looks like.

The Element of Surprise

Technical problems and delays during the first Trailer Park program—likely related to Warner Brothers' immanent multiscreen unveiling—only added to the anticipation surrounding the studio's panel. It is difficult to describe the excitement that filled the room when the Warner Brothers/Legendary panel began, but judging from my own observations and the reports that emerged from the event, Hall H hysteria was in full effect. Alex Billington of *First Showing* described it as "one of the best Hall H panels I have ever attended in my 7 year history at Comic-Con"[77]; MTV declared Warner Brothers the "ultimate winner" at Comic-Con, suggesting that given their Hall H presentation, the competition "wasn't even close"[78]; and *Cinema Blend* simply called it "epic."[79] Producing an authentic surprise in Hall H yields a high return on exclusivity because gossip, speculation, and anticipation leading up to high-profile panels often remove this element, as was the case in 2010, when Marvel's introduction of Joss Whedon as the director of the *Avengers* was undermined by online reports leading up to the Hall H panel.[80]

Given the prevalence of online buzz about who will appear and what will be announced at Comic-Con each year, it is difficult to completely surprise attendees in Hall H. For this reason, part of the pleasure of such surprise announcements or celebrity appearances is in the anticipation and the ability to predict outcomes in advance, thereby increasing not only the exclusivity of the experience but also the sense of exclusivity that accompanies insider knowledge. This means that the surprises in Hall H are as much about delivering on or exceeding a preexisting set of expectations as they are about eliciting an authentic emotional response. For example, when Tim Burton introduced Johnny Depp to attendees in a 2009 panel promoting *Alice in Wonderland* (Tim Burton, 2009), Depp's brief appearance was met with raucous applause and screams from the audience, with news of this celebrity sighting traveling well beyond Hall H. As *E!* reported, "There had been murmurs" that Depp would stop by that day, but there was still a palpable excitement in the crowd.[81] MTV's description of Depp's brief appearance onstage as a "shocking addition" to the panel was both a reflection of his star persona and the result of a careful control of information.[82] While most stars who appear at Comic-Con stay for the duration of the panel, Depp, who had long cultivated the persona of a rebellious outsider, did the bare minimum in order to drum up excitement: he stepped onto the Comic-Con stage and left minutes later, completely avoiding the Q&A portion of the panel. Disney's decision not to announce his appearance in the program and Depp's own elusive star persona made his arrival at Comic-Con somewhat unexpected, but also lowered the expectations of the audience, who may have been predisposed to accept Depp's reticence to participate as part of his particular set of quirks. For Depp, like the stars who visited the Camp Breaking Dawn line in 2011, just showing up was enough to appear generous.[83] Thus a delicate and somewhat counterintuitive balance of anticipation, which builds the sense of exclusivity leading up to the event, and the unexpected, which produces authentic and infectious audience reactions, is what make surprises in Hall H—predictable or not—particularly effective.

Nine years later, Johnny Depp would make another surprise appearance in Hall H, eliciting a somewhat different discursive response. When Depp appeared on stage as his character Grindelwald from *Fantastic Beasts: The Crimes of Grindelwald* (David Yates, 2018), it was a genuine surprise, mostly because of the controversy surrounding his casting in the film and the uncomfortable scheduling of his Hall H appearance, which occurred just an hour after his ex-wife, Amber Heard, appeared on stage to promote her film *Aquaman* (James Wan, 2018).[84] Heard's 2016 divorce filing included allegations of physical abuse, and she subsequently received a seven million dollar settlement from Depp, which she donated to charity. One month before Comic-Con 2018, Depp had also been the subject of a highly critical profile in *Rolling Stone* that suggested his personal life and finances were in shambles.[85] However, I would argue that what seemed like disregard for the negative PR that might surround such an appearance was actually a cynical attempt by Warner Brothers to use the element of surprise to recontextualize and legitimate Depp's casting in the film in light of all these developments. Having him surprise Comic-Con fans *in character* not only avoided the unpredictability of a Q&A session (like his 2009 appearance for Disney), but it also leaned into Depp's problematic star image by fusing it with the fictional *Fantastic Beasts* villain. Fans of the franchise, this appearance seemed to suggest, could feel okay about watching the film because the fictional character Grindelwald (an even more terrible person) had subsumed the real Johnny Depp.

While it is not uncommon for studios to stage surprises—or at least to simulate them—by offering celebrity appearances and special announcements, the Warner Brothers/Legendary technological alteration of Hall H was more unusual and involved significantly more planning and economic investment. In 2009, Hall H had been similarly outfitted with a technological upgrade to 3-D, in order to facilitate a day of panels that culminated in James Cameron's unveiling of footage from *Avatar*. But Warner Brothers' addition of two massive screens on either side of the room had a more palpable impact, altering the actual appearance of the hall. The result was "an immersive atmosphere in a room known for its airplane-hangar feel," and a transformation of the space on a grandiose scale, paralleled only by the 2004 opening of Hall H itself.[86]

In thinking about the impact of this surprise technological transformation, it is worth pausing here to reconsider the geography of Hall H. At 64,842 square feet, the hall is deep and cavernous. A number of aisles divide rows of seats into large horizontal and vertical sections toward the front, middle, and back of the room. One massive screen hangs above the stage (in addition to the screens Warner Brothers added on either side) and three other large screens hang toward the middle and back of the hall. These screens all display a simultaneous video feed of the panels, as well as any additional footage screened by the studios. The *Unofficial SDCC Blog* describes the Hall's configuration and its inherent challenges for attendees:

> You'll be able to see what's happening on stage from any seat in the house, but be prepared and get a set of portable binoculars or use your camera's zoom lens for a natural view of the panel. The seating arrangement inside Hall H isn't the most optimal. First, it's flat, so no auditorium or stadium seating. This means it can be difficult to see the stage when seated behind someone particularly tall. Second, it's wide, meaning if you're in the back and off to the side, you're more likely staring at a panel guest's side profile or looking off to one of the hanging projection screens. And third, about those hanging projection screens. If you have even a moderately decent seat in the middle of the Hall, chances are you'll be sitting directly under one of the screens, or close enough that you'd have to stare directly upward during the entire panel to see anything.[87]

As this description suggests, while there are not technically any "bad" seats in Hall H, there is a hierarchy of seating quality, with the ideal position located in the front and center section of the hall. For this reason, it is important to note that while there is some open seating in this area, there are also numerous rows reserved for studio guests, many of whom are members of the press. Any journalist can apply for a Comic-Con press pass and line up for Hall H with the rest of the attendees, but some—usually those working for high-profile publications or high-traffic websites—will receive formal invitations to cover a studio's Hall H panel in this reserved seating area.[88] However, these hierarchies—among members of the press and among the press and Comic-Con fans—are largely erased in the promotional discourses that circulate inside and around Hall H and identify everyone in the room as fans. In reality, the majority of fans in Hall H rely on the use of one of the Hall's large screens in order to get a more complete view of the events onstage.[89]

Given the audience's reliance on screens during Hall H panels, the appearance of two even larger screens on either side of the stage was a significant change that could be easily viewed from anywhere in the hall. But because these wraparound screens only stretched around the front portion of the hall, they provided a more immersive experience for those seated toward the front, while those in the middle and back portions of the hall got a better

FIGURE 3.6 Hall H wraparound screens, Comic-Con 2013. (Photo by the author.)

view of the overall spectacle (figure 3.6). As a result, one's specific location in the space produced not just exclusivity but *degrees* of exclusivity. Not only did this reinforce the hierarchy that began as fans stood in line overnight to secure their seats (and manifested again in the division between studio-sanctioned journalists and the rest of the audience), but it also positioned those farther back in the hall as spectators of an event happening to audience members at the front.

If we understand exclusivity as something that can be experienced vicariously and in degrees within Hall H, it is possible to see how surprises like this one overcome the limits of exclusivity to travel outside the hall in the form of publicity and buzz, while still maintaining that exclusive aura. The movie blog *Collider* was one of many to describe the unveiling that day, reporting, "The Warner Bros./Legendary panel kicked off in true epic fashion, as curtains to both sides of the main screen opened up to reveal two more gigantic screens. The crowd went wild. Moderator and Comic-Con 2012 MVP Chris Hardwick came out first and introduced the head of Legendary, Thomas Tull. He was in the middle of speaking when the lights went down and gigantic mechanized logos/computer screens came up signaling the entrance of Pacific Rim. Tull quipped, 'Alright, so that's how we do that.'"[90] Other articles described how "fans screamed in excitement as the lights went black and the three screens started displaying graphics simultaneously to introduce the Warner Bros. and Legendary Pictures logos"[91] and suggested that "this feels like what Cinerama was always supposed to be."[92] All these descriptions attempted to capture the experience of being in Hall H that day by referencing the content, the crowd's reaction, and the immersive environment. But what they really did was reproduce an experience akin to sitting in the back of the hall, watching the action unfold. While those reading about the panel at home didn't witness the reveal firsthand, these descriptions offered the chance to experience, vicariously, the excitement that *everyone* inside the hall must have felt. In the process, these reports erased the degrees of exclusivity (and individual experiences) produced by the geography of Hall H, reimagining the surprise as a collective and unified reaction.

Warner Brothers' technological expansion was slightly more unexpected than other Comic-Con "surprises," but it still played on preexisting expectations that Warner Brothers had created in booking an unusually long time slot in Hall H.[93] Indeed, *Variety*, caught up in some Hall H hysteria of its own, suggested that in spite of the ongoing questions about Comic-Con's importance to the industry, Warner Brothers had demonstrated how effective the event could be: "In terms of creating that critical first impression— the likes of which can drive anticipation and the months long fan-sharing of online marketing assets that studios crave—it was Warner Brothers, who managed to leap over the Comic-Con bar in a single bound."[94] Unfortunately for Warner Brothers, the legitimate surprise that they achieved with this technological upgrade would be difficult to repeat. Everyone in the room was witnessing something for the first time and, for better or worse, this extended time slot and technological spectacular had set a high bar for future Comic-Con panels. It is not surprising then, that Warner Brothers repeated this spectacle again in 2013. Not only that, but Sony also added their own multiscreen reveal during an extended panel lasting two hours and ten minutes, screening special footage of *The Amazing Spider-Man 2* (Marc Webb, 2014) in which Spider-Man traversed all three of the screens at the front of the room.[95] Not to be outdone, Warner Brothers upgraded their screens again, from 199 feet in 2013 to 465 feet in 2014, reportedly spending "hundreds of thousands of dollars" to extend the screens around the entire hall.[96] This time, however, the surprise upgrade, like the celebrity appearances I described earlier, was framed by a preexisting set of expectations that Warner Brothers itself had created. On the one hand, this strategy suggests that studios feel compelled to outdo themselves (and each other) with each visit to Hall H. As Warner Brothers' President of Worldwide Marketing Sue Kroll put it, "we go big every year but we had to go bigger."[97] But Hollywood's Hall H surprises don't just reshape the space, as was the case with Warner Brothers' reveal; they also reshape the expectations of their audiences, or at least make these expectations more predictable. If studios and observers have argued that Comic-Con is treacherous because it is difficult to anticipate audience reactions to films or trailers, controlling the context in which this content circulates—controlling the experience—is one way that studios exercise their power inside and outside the convention center.[98]

Plugging the Leaks

Before the Warner Brothers panel began, Eddie Ibrahim, Comic-Con's director of programming, appeared onstage to recite the same speech he had already made multiple times that day: "I'll bet some of you can even say this speech with me," he began, "please don't record any of the footage that you see. Again, the studios have this *exclusively* for you guys who have been in here all day. And I know some of you have been camped out since yesterday waiting for this. So I want to make sure that the studios feel comfortable doing this and they'll keep bringing us this great footage. Let everyone know how cool it was, spread the word, but let's keep the footage in here" (my emphasis).[99] I have witnessed speeches like this one since I began attending Hall H panels in 2009, and the content of these speeches has changed very little from year to year. They always remind attendees of the exclusive content they are about to consume and often connect this to the significant effort they exerted to get into the room. In this way, these speeches suggest that attendees should feel a kind of proprietary right to what they are about to experience, even as they are reminded that, legally speaking, the content belongs solely to the studios. But unlike the 2012 speech, which was more formal and framed as a preemptive strike against piracy, the 2009 speech sounded less practiced, as if Ibrahim was responding to behavior that had been previously happening in the hall:

> It's really, really important that you guys work with us on this. Do not record any of the footage that's being shown. Honestly, the studios are kind of being generous and cutting stuff that's special for you guys and the crowd here. I mean—you can talk about it, blog about it all you want, but please, please do not record it because we don't want to, you know, scare them off and not want

them to bring this kind of footage for us. So I just ask that we don't do that for the rest of the panels. Don't record the footage, okay?[100]

The contrast between the 2009 and 2012 speeches suggests that they have evolved from a punitive to a preventive gesture. The threat of punishment is now recapitulated as a form of behavioral discipline; and the power to discipline, as Foucault reminds us, also means the "power to 'train.'"[101] For this reason, these antipiracy warnings work not only to deter fans from certain behaviors but also to encourage others in their place.

As these warnings clearly illustrate, there is an anxiety on the part of the industry, and by extension, Comic-Con organizers, about controlling how fans approach the material screened in Hall H and what they do with it. On the one hand, fans are encouraged to be attentive to the panels and disseminate hype and buzz about the previews they have seen, but on the other hand, the industry wants to control what kind of publicity gets circulated outside the convention. Antipiracy concerns are so significant, in fact, that in 2013, I was threatened with ejection from the hall as I captured a video of that year's Warner Brothers screen reveal, despite the fact that the only images onscreen at that time were corporate logos belonging to Comic-Con, Warner Brothers, and Legendary Pictures. Whether this was an individual decision made by an overzealous member of the security team or the enforcement of a set of rules handed down from above, it demonstrates how heavily piracy is policed in the space. This fear of piracy—of what are effectively advertisements—is even more baffling in light of the fact that many studios release trailers on the Internet simultaneous to their launch at Comic-Con. For example, footage screened during Open Road Films' *Silent Hill: Revelation 3D* panel was released online the same day, and the trailer for Warner Brothers' *The Campaign* (Jay Roach, 2012) appeared online a few days after it premiered during the studio's Hall H panel that day.[102] More high-profile content, like the *Man of Steel* teaser, was held back by Warner Brothers, though not completely; the following week, the studio released two additional teasers online—sharing much of the same footage screened at Comic-Con.[103]

Despite heavy policing in the space, pirated trailers and footage from the panels make their way online every year too. In 2015, the problem of leaks received significant attention after pirated trailers from Fox's *X-Men: Apocalypse* and *Deadpool*, and Warner Brothers' *Suicide Squad* (David Ayer, 2016), appeared online within hours of their Hall H panels. The reaction—at least from Warner Brothers' Sue Kroll—was pretty definitive: this was "damaging" and a betrayal of "a long-standing trust" between Comic-Con attendees and the studios.[104] Forty-eight hours after the leak, Warner Brothers released their own high-quality version of the *Suicide Squad* trailer online with the accompanying statement from Kroll:

> Warner Bros. Pictures and our *anti-piracy* team have worked tirelessly over the last 48 hours to contain the *Suicide Squad* footage that was *pirated* from Hall H on Saturday. We have been unable to achieve that goal. Today we will release the same footage that has been *illegally* circulating on the web.... We regret this decision as it was our intention to keep the footage as a unique experience for the Comic Con crowd, but we cannot continue to allow the film to be represented by the poor quality of the *pirated* footage *stolen* from our presentation (my emphasis).[105]

Kroll's very frequent and deliberate use of words like "piracy," "illegally," and "stolen" (not to mention the allusions to quality and exclusivity) makes the studio's stance on the leak very clear. However, this emphasis on legality and criminality is particularly interesting given the fact that Warner Brothers' other 2015 Hall H trailer for *Batman v Superman* (Zack Snyder, 2016) was not leaked—at least not in the form of a clandestine bootleg. Instead, the studio posted that trailer online immediately after it premiered at Comic-Con. This distinction is important because Comic-Con's exclusivity suggests that every bit of information emerging from the event might be understood as a leak. In fact, this leakiness is exactly how studios overcome the limits of exclusivity in order to spread publicity outside the convention center. As Paul McDonald explains, "films can only reap economic rewards if they are publicly accessible. At the same time, it is only possible to place economic value against that availability if mechanisms of exclusion are used to create artificial scarcity. Consequently the business of moving images is forever locked into the dialectic of access and exclusion."[106] So what actually marked the *Suicide Squad*, *X-Men: Apocalypse*, and *Deadpool* trailers as leaks were the institutionalized power constructs operating through the legal and regulatory structures of the media industries.

This discourse about piracy and leaks at Comic-Con functions in two ways: First, it is an attempt to instill desirable audience practices. The piracy and circulation of promotional material may not necessarily threaten the economic success of a film, but they take the control of marketing out of the hands of producers and put it in the hands of fans. Antipiracy measures at Comic-Con might also be a way to discourage audiences from engaging in these practices outside the confines of the event, namely by pirating or illegally downloading or streaming entire films and threatening studio profits. At stake for the industry, then, is not so much the circulation of their exclusive footage, rather it is how their marketing strategies are implemented and who, ultimately, retains control of both the discourse and the economic outcomes. The second function of such measures is that they further amplify the excitement and exclusivity of the footage, maintaining the uniqueness of this event. This is especially important when studios *do* finally release Comic-Con footage or trailers online. Controlling the dissemination of this content allows studios to stir up excitement about the properties they are promoting, even before that content is presented to fans or the general public. Much in the same way that the visibility of the line produces a sense of value before the event, antipiracy measures also help to shape the perception that this footage is of significant value to the studios and audiences.

Ultimately, the policing of leaks at Comic-Con presents attendees with examples of bad (piracy) and good (the circulation of publicity) fan behavior. Implicit in these two alternatives, however, is another warning: not only will bad behavior alienate the studios, but failure to conform to the good model of fandom, which works with the industry to produce publicity, might also drive Hollywood away. Thus part of Eddie Ibrahim's antipiracy statement, "I want to make sure that the studios feel comfortable doing this and they'll keep bringing us this great footage," is clarified in the last line of his speech, "Let everyone know how cool it was, spread the word, but lets keep the footage in here."

Synergy

The Warner Brothers and Legendary panels that followed over the next two and a half hours rode the wave of excitement produced when the curtains dropped to reveal the two large screens. While the program listed three films, *Pacific Rim*, *Man of Steel*, and *The Hobbit: An Unexpected Journey*, the panel also included two surprise additions: *Godzilla* (Gareth Edwards, 2014) and *The Campaign*. If the overall arrangement of panels in Hall H creates a kind of programming flow, then the arrangement of films promoted within this particular two and a half hour period was similarly strategic, building toward a crescendo with Peter Jackson's presentation of twelve minutes of footage from *The Hobbit*. This panel was orchestrated not only to promote individual films but also to exploit a synergistic relationship between Warner Brothers and their then partner Legendary Pictures, who had a long-standing cofinancing and distribution deal at the time.[107]

When Legendary Pictures president Thomas Tull stepped onstage to introduce the first part of the program, he thanked Warner Brothers, explicitly tying his company's ability to promote their films on this scale to the conglomerate's financial resources. He also reminded attendees of Legendary's highly successful fan-centered films, *Dark Knight* (Chris Nolan, 2008) and *300* (Zach Snyder, 2006) and located their upcoming film, *Pacific Rim*, within this same tradition by highlighting the subject matter ("giant monsters and giant robots") and connecting the film's director, Guillermo del Toro, to Legendary's other collaborators Chris Nolan and Zach Snyder, all of whom were, much like Tarantino, "fanboy auteurs" specializing in genre films.[108] While Warner Brothers may have been Legendary's collaborator, taking on the financial burden of staging the event, the two and a half hour panel situated all the films, with the exception of *The Hobbit* and *The Campaign*, as Legendary productions, leading the *New York Times* to observe, "Superman was not nearly as super as the big Legendary logo that flashed behind Thomas Tull."[109] Thus, in addition to their shared financial interests through distribution deals with Legendary, Warner Brothers benefited from this pairing because it allowed them to fill a longer time slot, elevate the spectacle, and present themselves, a large conglomerate, alongside the smaller studio, Legendary, as producers of fan-friendly content. In this way, both Warner Brothers and Legendary were able to carve out a powerful position from which to promote a brand identity built on a variety of genre films but united by the enthusiasm and perceived tastes of the Comic-Con audience.

Scale

After the unveiling of the screens and Tull's introduction, Guillermo del Toro appeared onstage to promote his upcoming film *Pacific Rim*, a blockbuster that was also conveniently built around technological spectacle. As del Toro put it, "In a movie like this, when we say twenty-five story robots and twenty-five story monsters, if you don't have a sense of awe and scale, everything is lost."[110] Though he was describing the film itself, del Toro could just as easily have been describing that day's Comic-Con panel, which similarly used scale in an attempt to evoke significant awe from the crowd. But this was not the first time del Toro promoted *Pacific Rim* at Comic-Con. In 2011, the year prior, Legendary Pictures held a much smaller panel in room 6BCF.[111] Unlike the Hall H spectacle, this panel was understated, revealing very little about the film other than its stars and del Toro's repeated description of the subject matter: "giant fucking monsters and giant fucking robots."[112] With very little to *show*, Legendary opted to avoid the scale of Hall H and hold their event in a smaller room with less pomp and circumstance.[113] This confirms something that Comic-Con president John Rogers explained in a 2011 Talk-Back session: while it had become standard practice to seek out large Hollywood films in Hall H and television and smaller media panels in other programming rooms like Ballroom 20 and 6BCF, Rogers insisted, "that is not a convention that we have, it is what the studios are comfortable with."[114] He went on to suggest that because studios often worry that their panel will not fill a large room or will be open to increased critique and exposure in larger venues, like Hall H, they sometimes choose to host their panels in a slightly smaller space (or to skip Comic-Con altogether); even if that means fewer attendees will be able to see their promotions. In another instance, Rogers similarly described removing twenty rows of seats in Hall H in order to appease television studios that were fearful about moving from the smaller Ballroom 20 to the larger venue.[115] Ultimately, Rogers explained this logic by making an implicit statement about Comic-Con's power relative to the studios: it is better that some people get to see the panels, he stressed, than to alienate studios and have no panels at all.[116] This demonstrates the degree to which Comic-Con's organization is shaped by studios' promotional choices and how these choices tend to diverge from the desires of a fan base that is habitually singled out for their importance as tastemakers and loyal consumers. If Comic-Con promotion were truly about the 130,000+ people at the event, then it seems only logical that studios would try to reach as many of those individuals as possible. Instead, a small, exclusive audience guarantees not only a more predictable and controlled response but also one that will make its way out of the space in the form of heightened buzz about the film.

When del Toro screened footage of *Pacific Rim* in Hall H in 2012, he declared that all promotion for the film would go into "radio silence" until the end of the year.[117] This declaration made the footage feel more exclusive in the moment, and it was also mentioned numerous times in coverage of the panel, making it that much more newsworthy.[118] As it turned out, the time between Comic-Con and the end of 2012 was less silent and more accurately a slow, controlled stream of official information mixed with unofficial buzz, building up to the release of the trailer online in December. In August, the movie blog *Collider* posted an interview in which del Toro talked about the film's soundtrack and accompanying collectables, and *Empire Magazine* published location photos from the film, which subsequently made their way online.[119] That September, Warner Brothers announced that they would convert *Pacific Rim* to 3-D, against del Toro's previously stated wishes.[120] Soon after, however, the director backtracked and said he was no longer opposed to the conversion, explaining, "What happened was, in the weeks and months following Comic-Con, what I asked from the studio was to agree to four points that I wanted to do. . . . Now I'm going to be involved in supervising it. What can I tell you? I changed my mind. I'm not running for office. I can do a Romney."[121] Perhaps most interesting was the film's panel during October's New York Comic Con, where del Toro undid his own vow of radio silence, telling the crowd that although the *studio* did not want him to screen the San Diego Comic-Con footage, "the good news is that I don't give a fuck!"[122] The panel also included the unveiling of a new poster and graphic novel prequel to the film.[123] In November, the movie blog *Latino Review* announced, "'Pacific Rim' Viral Marketing Has Begun!" and linked to a short video and a website with a not-so-mysterious clock counting down to what was quickly determined to be the premiere, not of the film, but of its trailer.[124] Finally, on December 12th, Warner Brothers released the trailer, followed soon after by a director's commentary.[125] In light of all this post-Comic-Con promotion, one must question whether radio silence around *Pacific Rim* was ever truly a goal. Instead, IMDb reported 918 separate online articles mentioning the film between July 14, 2012, the date of the Comic-Con panel, and the end of the year, December 31, 2012.[126]

Reframing

The *Pacific Rim* panel was immediately followed by the introduction of surprise guest Gareth Edwards who, along with Legendary Pictures' Thomas Tull, introduced his first feature film, *Godzilla*. It was at this point that the panel's moderator, Chris Hardwick, began to point out an excited fan in the front row and entertained the crowd with jokes that evoked both the positive and the negative connotations of Hall H hysteria.[127] Hardwick's intermittent and condescending jokes, like, "Dude, you just filled your pants," and "I love watching grown men act like tweens at a Taylor Swift concert," mocked the man's reaction as infantile and deployed problematic stereotypes that bring to mind Kristina Busse's observations about the gendered hierarchies of geek culture.[128] At the same time, however, his jokes about the fan's reaction seemed to be reinforcing and celebrating the very excitement the panel was trying to evoke. By the time Zack Snyder came onstage to promote *Man of Steel*, the attendee was overcome with emotion, weeping when he approached the microphone during the Q&A. After complimenting the trailer, he asked, very earnestly, if Snyder would reveal the villain of the film. The request was met with raucous laughter from the crowd and an evasive nonanswer from Snyder, further demonstrating the way in which promotional discourse in Hall H is tightly controlled, despite the air of spontaneity that studios try to produce. Media coverage picked up on this lone fan's response to the preview and used it to promote the film more widely. Headlines read: "'Man of Steel' Footage So Good It Makes Fans Cry," "The Man of Steel Made Fans Cry with Excitement," and "'Superman' Trailer Makes Fans Cry."[129] The fact that these headlines did not accurately reflect the reality of the event demonstrates that reality is not always what matters in such reports. What occurs in the space and time of Comic-Con is, instead, about the ideas and ideologies that grow outward from the materiality of the event. As such, many of the discourses that are produced and reproduced in Hall H have everything to do with studio promotion and very little to do with the real experiences of attendees.

Warner Brothers' presentation for *The Hobbit* concluded the two and a half hour panel, and, despite its popularity, the promotion of this film was already attached to some fairly significant discursive baggage. When Warner Brothers screened ten minutes of footage at CinemaCon, the official convention of the National Association of Theatre Owners, many reports cited a "lukewarm response"[130] to what was supposed to be a groundbreaking technological advance in film production and exhibition: high frame rate or 48 fps.[131] Many compared the footage to a "made for TV movie" or a "soap opera," or called it altogether "non-cinematic."[132] Given this underwhelming response, the *Los Angeles Times Hero Complex* wondered if and how the film could recover from this negative publicity, asking: "Does 'The Hobbit' need a magic moment in Hall H?"[133] Despite its investment in upgrading Comic-Con's screen technology, Warner Brothers and Peter Jackson decided not to show *The Hobbit* footage in 48 fps. One might even speculate that Warner Brothers' other technological upgrade worked as a substitute for the riskier format. While the *New York Times* called this an "unexpectedly timid decision,"[134] Peter Jackson's response was surprisingly nonchalant, especially regarding Comic-Con's relative importance to *The Hobbit*'s ultimate success at the box office.

> I think it's more about protecting the downside, rather than helping the film in any significant way. There is a huge audience waiting to see "The Hobbit," and any positive press from Comic-Con will truthfully have little impact on that. However, as we saw at CinemaCon earlier this year, with our 48 frames per second presentation, negative bloggers are the ones the mainstream press runs with and quotes from. I decided to screen the "Hobbit" reel at Comic-Con in 2-D and 24 frames per second, so the focus stays firmly with the content and not the technical stuff. If people want 3-D and 48fps, that choice will be there for them in December.[135]

Jackson's comments demonstrate several key points that I have discussed throughout this chapter. First, he acknowledges the "huge audience waiting to see 'The Hobbit,'" suggesting that his visit to Comic-Con is more about mitigating any negative press than selling *The Hobbit* to those 6,500 individuals in Hall H. Second, he alludes to the way that extreme reactions, positive or negative, are most frequently those that are seized upon in mainstream coverage. In the case of CinemaCon, he argues, the negative reaction to the technology made for the most compelling story, much in the same way that reporters seized upon the positive response to the *Django* "sizzle reel" or the tearful fan during the *Man of Steel* presentation. Finally, Jackson's comments demonstrate how careful control of content leads to further exclusivity, which can also travel beyond the walls of Comic-Con. While he showed attendees twelve minutes of exclusive footage, he also left something more for opening day, encouraging audiences to pay extra for a special IMAX, 3-D, and/or 48fps ticket.[136] As I have argued throughout this chapter, the limits of exclusivity work, in all of these promotional contexts, as an industry construct that uses Comic-Con, and its attendees, to sell Hollywood's products to a much broader audience.

Conclusion: You Had to Be There

The final panel I attended in Hall H that day was the Marvel Studios panel, which I detailed in the first chapter of this book. About ten minutes in, Robert

Downey Jr. made his dramatic entrance and danced down the aisle to Luther Vandross while wearing an Iron Man glove. But most of what I know about that entrance came from watching footage online after the convention. About ten minutes before the Marvel panel, I moved from my aisle seat to a slightly closer seat that had opened up in the middle of a row on the other side of the hall. So when I heard the familiar cheers of excitement travel through the room, I had no idea what was going on until I looked up at one of the Hall H screens and saw Robert Downey Jr. Alone, and surrounded by much taller people, some of whom were standing on chairs, I spent most of my time looking around the hall and trying to figure out where he was or if he was even in the room at all. I couldn't see a thing. Lest I appear entirely immune from Hall H hysteria myself, I'll admit I was slightly disappointed when I finally realized that his entrance took him down the same aisle I had just left in favor of what seemed, at the time, to be a better seat. By the time he reached the stage, I had spent so much time trying to figure out what was going on that I barely took in his entrance—even on the screens surrounding the room. I wasn't terribly concerned, however, as I knew that video recordings of the panel would be available online in the coming hours and days. When I finally watched the footage, I saw an experience that I was present for, but didn't really witness. But I also knew that if I showed that video to my friends, colleagues, or students—especially those who had never spent a day in Hall H—and told them that I was in the room, the experience they imagined for me would likely be far more meaningful, interesting, and unique than the reality I lived. Attending panels in Hall H is exclusive and exciting by design, but it can also be quite boring, disappointing, or even mundane depending on one's individual experiences and investments. So while Hall H hysteria certainly places great weight on the *experience* of being there, the *fantasy* of being there, I would argue, is much more powerful. The careful control of promotional discourses and cultivation of exclusivity surrounding the space is ultimately what blurs these boundaries between fantasy and reality, between being there and being a vicarious witness, enabling Hall H hysteria to resonate far beyond the convention center. When Hall H opened its doors in 2004, it emerged as an entirely new kind of space at Comic-Con, one that was conceived of exclusively for Hollywood promotion. However, the presence of media industry promotion has long been a part of the Comic-Con experience, illustrating the highly constructed and permeable nature of the limits of exclusivity. In other words, while Hall H's exclusivity is defined by the presence of film and television promotion, such promotion is not limited to Hall H. Not only do promotional messages travel out of the convention center through sanctioned and unsanctioned sharing of footage, video recordings, social media, and professional media coverage, but Hollywood's presence at Comic-Con also extends well beyond Hall H—in offsite activations, massive advertisements that adorn the sides of entire buildings, sponsored rickshaws that shuttle fans around the downtown core, and most notably, in Comic-Con's Exhibit Hall, where studios set up massive trade show–style booths. However, unlike Hall H, the Exhibit Hall is not devoted exclusively to promotion, nor is the industry presence there exclusively rooted in film and television. The Exhibit Hall is also a retail space that was known as the Dealers' Room for Comic-Con's first twenty-five years. If Comic-Con's Hall H provides a promotional context aimed at anticipating future economic transactions, the Exhibit Hall is one of the few spaces at Comic-Con where *actual* economic transactions occur. With this in mind, the final chapter of this book returns to the history of Comic-Con. In doing so, I pivot away from frameworks that privilege fan and industry productivity and promotion in order to examine the role of consumerism and retail at Comic-Con by tracing the evolution of the event's retail space, from Dealers' Room to Exhibit Hall.

4

Ret(ail)con

● ●

From Dealers' Room to
Exhibit Hall

> Be sure to bring plenty of money,
> because at a convention, you'll want
> a lot of it.
> —San Diego's Golden State
> Comic-Con Flyer, 1970

In the first chapter of this book, I outlined Comic-Con's history and suggested that the event's formative early years laid the groundwork for its explosive growth and rise to prominence decades later. Origin stories like this one are a fixture of the superhero genre, revealing the source of a character's power and how they ascended to the status of hero or villain. In the case of the San Diego Comic-Con, the collision of affective and aspirational labor led to the founding of a physical space where fans and industry could come together. And as this space became increasingly inclusive—of industry, of fan cultures, of popular culture—it also became more exclusive; a one of a kind event that is in demand and difficult to access. This pivot solidified

Comic-Con's ascendance to heroic status (or villainous, depending on whom you ask) in popular culture. As I have argued throughout this book, Hollywood production and promotion at Comic-Con are a significant part of this pivot. But I also recognize that in centering these particular sectors of this particular industry, I run the risk of reproducing the same deterministic discourses about the intersection of fandom and industry power at Comic-Con that have enabled Hollywood to construct an aura of exclusivity around its products and capitalize on the free labor of its fans.

With this in mind, this final chapter's examination of Comic-Con's Exhibit Hall returns to the convention's history by drawing on another popular comic book trope: retcon, or retroactive continuity. Andrew Friedenthal defines retconning as "the process whereby creators and/or producers in some way alter the events of the origin, backstory, and/or history of a particular character or story world." These changes, he explains, "create future story potential" even as they hinge on "the influence of the past."[1] So what does it mean to retcon Comic-Con history? While this chapter doesn't alter any historical events, it does alter the lens through which we understand these events by highlighting two underrepresented aspects of fan and media industry studies: consumerism and retail. This chapter explains how the media industries manage to emphasize production and promotion while still centering consumption of all kinds in the exhibit hall. Ultimately I argue that retail and consumption are key parts of, not separate from, exclusivity, promotion, and fan labor at the convention.

While there is plenty of scholarship examining the overlaps, intersections, and convergence of media fans and media industries, this work tends to gravitate toward productivity as the central site of cultural meaning.[2] Consumerism is at once an integral part of fan culture and a structuring absence in fan studies. Perhaps this is because, as Matt Hills once put it, "fans are always already consumers."[3] Historically, fan studies scholarship grappled with this fact either by highlighting other practices that set fans apart from general audiences or by reevaluating fannish consumption as productive and generative in and of itself.[4] Ironically, a very similar obfuscation of consumerism now fuels social media likes, shares, and hashtags that are deployed for promotional purposes.[5] In fact, in *Spreadable Media* (2013), Henry Jenkins et al. draw a direct line between cultural studies approaches that frame "'consumption' as acts of meaning production" and an understanding of social media engagement that "could, in theory, translate into greater economic value (exchange) for media companies and advertisers."[6] This statement is indicative of a continued interest in thinking about fans as *more than* consumers; a strategy that combats reductive understandings of audiences as passive or exploited by the industry. But it also demonstrates how, by situating these activities as exclusive and operating within frameworks of value—economic or cultural—such approaches are always teetering on the edge of being reductive themselves; suggesting that if fans are exclusive because they are *more than* consumers, it must be because they are *more* valuable to the industry.

Similarly the overarching pivot of media industry studies away from the so-called "economic determinism and reductionism" of critical political economy is informed by a desire to foreground "the role of human agents . . . in interpreting, focusing, and redirecting economic forces that provide for complexity and contradiction within media industries."[7] This focus on individual agency seems to both comment on and reproduce the neoliberal structure of work in the creative industries where, as Angela McRobbie explains, "people increasingly have to become their own micro-structures . . . , which in turn requires intensive practices of self-monitoring or 'reflexivity.'"[8] Much in the same way that fan scholarship emphasizes productivity over the everyday practice of media consumption, media industry scholarship rarely examines media retail, which, as Joseph Turow argues, doesn't seem to "signal political or cultural importance" in the same way as other kinds of media industry work.[9] And yet, retail is integral to Hollywood's business models, past and present—from the licensing and merchandizing of media franchises to the rise of home video as an ancillary market.[10] Not only is retail part of the media industries, writ large, but it also provides many of the "day jobs" that aspiring producers or "creatives" must take to support themselves in environments of precarity.[11]

In contrast to these scholarly approaches to fans and industry, Comic-Con seems to be an unabashed celebration of retail and consumerism. As Lincoln Geraghty argues, the San Diego Comic-Con is perhaps "the most iconic site for fan consumption."[12] In print and online, writers have compared the convention's Exhibit Hall to a flea market, a bazaar, a mall, and a garage sale.[13] Capturing the consumerist drive and the numerous retailers that now fill the space, these descriptions all echo Comic-Con International's own branding of the Exhibit Hall as a "shoppers' paradise."[14] And yet, this aspect of the event is often eclipsed by media industry promotion. This is perhaps best captured by Peter Bart's 2004 description of the convention as "an industry trade show masking as a fan show."[15] Indeed, as it entered the twenty-first century, Comic-Con was frequently described as a trade show in the press.[16] In 2005, the *Los Angeles Times* called Comic-Con "the largest, most energetic and most innovative trade show of its kind" and cautioned, "if you've got a comic book, movie, card game, action figure, video game or other entertainment item you hope to sell to the youth market, you'd better be here."[17] Of course, Comic-Con isn't an industry trade show, though it shares many similar attributes.

Timothy Havens's account of the National Association of Television Program Executives (NATPE) Market & Conference's "mammoth billboards advertising new series," "lavish sales 'stands,'" and "giveaways and celebrity photo sessions" that cause word to spread "across the sales floor like wildfire" could just as easily be describing Comic-Con's Exhibit Hall in the twenty-first century.[18] At over 460,000 square feet, Comic-Con's Exhibit Hall covers almost the entire ground floor of the San Diego Convention Center, running over a quarter mile from end to end.[19] Every bit of this space (with the exception of three concession areas) is filled with booths, tables, and pavilions representing a range of businesses from across the popular culture spectrum—from global media conglomerates to comic book dealers—over seven hundred exhibitors in total.[20] Tables and booths are arranged in aisles but are often clustered together based on the size and popularity of the display, the kinds of product being promoted or sold, and companies (or individuals) doing the selling.[21] The result is a concentration of booths devoted to different—or, in the case of the numerous media conglomerates represented, overlapping—sectors of the media industries. Such displays are easily identifiable due to their size (most are several aisles wide or several stories high) and conspicuous corporate branding. The two-story Warner Brothers booth, for example, features the corporate logo surrounded by dozens of screens displaying promotional material and live footage of exclusive signing sessions (figure 4.1). The promotional nature of these displays causes significant congestion in the hall, as they attract large crowds who linger for celebrity appearances and free giveaways. In contrast, the tables rented by smaller retailers and artists tend to blend in with one another in more generic aisles.[22] Because the crowds are much thinner in these areas, it is easier to stop and browse without being pushed or pulled into the tide of thousands of constantly moving bodies (figure 4.2).

Today, retailers in the Exhibit Hall offer a wide range of products, including toys, high-end collectibles, books, clothing, and, of course, comics. But with the influx of industry exhibitors beginning in the late 1970s,

FIGURE 4.1　Warner Brothers booth, Comic-Con 2016. (Photo by the author.)

FIGURE 4.2　Gold and Silver Comics Pavilion, Comic-Con 2017. (Photo by the author.)

the establishment of a comics trade show from 1984 to 2001, and the incorporation of synergy and licensing logics in the twenty-first century, retail and promotion have become increasingly intertwined as the space gradually changed—in name and function—from Dealers' Room to Exhibit Hall. The result is a synergistic space that reconfigures—spatially and ideologically—consumption as a practice aligned with insider access, knowledge, and cultural and economic capital. This process represents the cumulative effects of exclusivity at Comic-Con and in the mainstreaming of fan cultures at large. Even as the lines between fan and industry, insider and outsider, amateur and professional become harder to delineate in discourses about these groups, they are reinforced through socially constructed boundaries and gatekeeping practices that shape and limit our material reality. By connecting the history of the event to larger changes in the media industries, this chapter explains how and why Comic-Con gradually incorporated the promotional tactics and insider rituals of industry trade shows into what was and still is an overwhelmingly retail-centric consumer space.

Collecting, Speculating, and the "Capitalist Spirit" of Comic Fandom

In order to understand Comic-Con's relationship to retailing, it is necessary to return to the prehistory of the event and its roots in the "golden age of comic fandom" during the 1960s.[23] As I outlined in chapter 1, comic publishers were a critical part of the formation of this fandom, as was the notion of aspirational labor, which hinged on the idea that the lines between fandom and industry were so blurry in comic book culture that talented and hardworking fans could eventually make the transition from amateur to professional. Much of this ideological work was happening in and around the realm of production—of comic books, of fan art and writing, even of fan communities—but fan consumption and the retail sector of the industry had an equally important impact on the material practices of comic book fans. Though these early fans participated in a range of creative and social activities, collecting was a central and overarching facet of early comic book culture.[24] Of the over six hundred fanzines published during the 1960s, *Rocket's Blast Comicollector*, an "adzine" where fans could buy, sell, and trade comics by mail, was by far the most popular.[25] And, out of 169 people listed in 1964's *Who's Who in Comic-Fandom*, the "Official Directory of the Academy of Comic-Book Fans and Collectors," 153 identified themselves as "collectors" as opposed to "general fans."[26] Not only did these fans accumulate and appreciate comic books, they also indexed, tracked, bought, sold, and traded them. These practices formed the crux of what Bill Schelly has called "the capitalist spirit" of comic fandom.[27]

But this capitalist spirit was not an inherent attribute of comic book fans everywhere. Rather, collecting and its associated practices arose in response to the industry's mass-market distribution model, commonly referred to as the newsstand model. Like other periodicals at that time, comic books retailed primarily at newsstands; and because they were so inexpensive, many distributors and retailers treated them as interchangeable and disposable. Distributors would deliver "random assortments of titles," and retailers would return unsold comics for credit—sometimes by tearing off the covers and presenting them as a "receipt."[28] And because publishers shouldered the cost of unsold comic books, neither retailers nor distributors had much incentive to keep track of their stock or sales.[29] As a result, readers struggled to follow their favorite new titles, and back issues were difficult to locate.[30] As Pennsylvania fan Raymond Miller put it, "I knew of no one, outside of newsstands and drugstores, who sold comic books, and they only sold new comics. As each year passed, my collection grew and grew with new issues, but never any back issues."[31] As other small businesses that sold comics—local shops and corner stores—were gradually overtaken by large supermarkets, which were even less invested in comics sales, finding and collecting comics became that much more difficult.[32]

Under these conditions, comic collecting became something of a prerequisite for comic fans. On the one hand, we might think of this practice as a bottom-up response to the limits of exclusivity produced by an industry model that failed to respond to the demands of a very small but ravenous market of consumers. Fans of the 1960s fueled the exclusivity of comic books by infusing them with increased affective and economic value. This understanding of fans as *more than* consumers underpins Jonathan David Tankel and Keith Murphy's argument that comic collecting is productive, "a form of capital formation" that "bring[s] pleasure and possibly financial reward to the consumer rather than the producer."[33] But while many collectors of the 1960s certainly reaped these rewards, it wasn't *just* because their "curatorial" approach made them a unique group of consumers.[34]

As scarcity drove up the value of old comics, the absence of reliable retailers left a gap that numerous enterprising fans filled by becoming dealers themselves.[35] The explosion of fanzines in the 1960s provided the perfect forum for burgeoning collectors and dealers to buy and sell comics by mail.[36] And the demand for advertising space for "wants, trades and sales" was so immediate and so great that less than a year after the first issue of *Alter Ego* was published in 1961, editor Jerry Bails created *The ComiCollector*, "an advertising zine devoted to swaps and sales announcements of comics collectors and dealers."[37] One year later, *The Comicollector* had over five hundred subscribers and began publishing bimonthly.[38] By the mid-1960s, this new marketplace for old comic books started gaining mainstream attention as a number of reports sought to understand this increased interest in hanging onto what had been largely viewed as disposable cultural objects. While journalists did not seem especially interested in legitimating comic fandom itself, they used the economic transactions of collectors to legitimate their own coverage and convince readers that this subculture was worthy of their attention.[39] This increased visibility simultaneously reinforced the exclusivity of comics-as-collectibles, especially back issues, while increasing the demand for new issues by encouraging speculation—the purchase of comic books as investments. Part of what made comics, especially those published before the 1960s, so valuable was the fact that so few people had bothered to keep them around.[40] But as this exclusivity fed the demand for new comics, speculators sought to overcome these limits by buying up multiple copies of the same issue and keeping them in pristine condition.[41]

If collectors during the golden age of comic fandom were, as Bart Beaty suggests, rooted in nostalgia and "backward-looking," we might see speculators as future facing and oriented toward economic gain.[42] An early edition of Overstreet's *Comic Book Price Guide* distinguished between collectors and speculators, explaining "the vast majority of panelologists (i.e., comic collectors) want only to enhance their own enjoyment of this popular medium or recapture 'the sense of wonder' that the comics provided in their youth. In addition to these true collectors, there are also those who speculate in comics—i.e., merely buy comics to resell at a profit." But most importantly, the guide noted, "there is a little bit of speculator in all collectors."[43] In many ways, comic book dealers were the figures who bridged this gap between collecting and speculating, as they accumulated old comics and back issues, but also had to predict current and future demand as they acquired new issues from newsstands and independent distributors.[44] For some dealers, selling comics was a hobby, while for others, dealing became a full-fledged business operation.[45] But, not surprisingly, those lines were often blurry. As dealer Bud Plant put it, "basically, we were trying to sell comics so we could get more comics. I would compare being comics fans to being drug addicts. After a while, a lot become dealers to feed their own habit."[46] Not only did buying, selling, trading, and speculation all fall under the general umbrella of collecting, but this hobby, as it arose in comic fandom, also further obscured the line between industry work and fan labor. As dealers and speculators, these individuals were working *in* the comics industry, and as collectors and fans, they helped to feed it.

In addition to the growing number of fans-turned-mail-order dealers, a smattering of used bookstore owners around the country began stockpiling old comics, usually because they were fans of the material.[47] And many fan gatherings doubled as swap meets, like the Los Angeles–based group of teen-aged fans who called themselves SMASH (Society for Magazine Appreciators of Super Heroes) and held lively meetings at their local rec center.[48] If collecting and dealing helped to elevate the commodity status of comic books to a more exclusive context, then these bookstores and swap meets provided a model for how the exclusivity associated with comic books and collectors could extend to physical spaces. And this nascent collectors' and dealers' market, which functioned outside the institutionalized structures of comic distribution and retail, was the context in which the earliest comic conventions, like the Detroit Triple Fan Fair and the New York Comicon, emerged in the mid-1960s.[49] These conventions provided what collectors and dealers so desperately needed: a physical space where they could buy, sell, and trade their old comic books.[50] It comes as little surprise, then, that comic collecting and comic dealers would prove instrumental to the founding of the San Diego Comic-Con in 1970.

Before he moved to San Diego, Comic-Con's founder, Shel Dorf, was part of a thriving fan community in Michigan. In addition to frequent gatherings hosted by Jerry Bails and the Detroit Triple Fan Fair, Detroit area fans had Ableman's Bookstore in Hamtramck. The store's owner, Tom Altschuler, kept a huge assortment of comics and cartoons in his attic, which was closed to the public but open to "serious spenders."[51] When Dorf arrived in San Diego, however, he found that the comic scene there was virtually nonexistent.[52] By some accounts, the only place to get comics in the city was a downtown bookstore that sold coverless comic books.[53] So Dorf turned to several area dealers and collectors who would ultimately join him in organizing the first Comic-Con. While Dorf's investment in community building and the appreciation of comic art has been well documented, the fact that he and his collaborators were heavily involved in collecting, selling, and trading comics suggests that these practices were equally important to Comic-Con's inception. Not only would a convention strengthen San Diego's fan community, it would also give local dealers and collectors a place to buy and sell comics. Though Shel Dorf is widely recognized as Comic-Con's founder, his co-collaborators are quick to point out that it was the group's successful dealers, Richard Alf and Ken Krueger, who kept the event afloat in those early years. Alf's mail-order business enabled him to front crucial funds for the convention, and bookshop owner Ken Krueger drew on his business experience to liaise with the hotel venue, handle contracts, and "keep things rolling along."[54] Scholars have widely identified the importance of comic shops as "cultural spaces" of fandom.[55] But before the emergence of these specialty stores in the 1970s and 1980s, Ken Krueger's bookstore provided a gathering space for San Diego's burgeoning fan community. Similarly, as a mail-order dealer, Richard Alf helped to feed and sustain the collectors' market outside the institutionalized newsstand model of distribution and retail. But ultimately, it was Comic-Con, and other conventions like it, that brought these places, practices, and people together and, in doing so, imagined a new kind of retail space for comic books: The Dealers' Room.

"A Lot of Deals Were Made"

The earliest iteration of the San Diego Comic-Con, the March 21, 1970, "Minicon," built on the template laid out by the first comic conventions in the mid-1960s and included "dealer's tables" that could be rented out for five dollars each and were open throughout the day.[56] The designation of special spaces for the sale of comics and memorabilia at Comic-Con continued that summer and, drawing on the nomenclature of science fiction fandom, the program playfully referred to these spaces as the "Hucksters rooms."[57] An early flyer for the August event encouraged attendees to "come prepared for countless bargains you'll find at the dealers tables. . . . Comics of every description! Artwork! Sci-Fi magazines and pulps! Posters, fanzines, what the heck! . . . But—be sure to bring plenty of money, because at a convention, you'll want a lot of it" (original emphasis).[58] This flyer is notable for two reasons. First, it highlights Comic-Con's eclectic retail environment, which, according to Richard Alf, was a deliberate strategy intended to boost attendance numbers.[59] Second, it foregrounds the importance of retail transactions at the event by encouraging attendees to seek out "bargains" and "bring plenty of money," ultimately connecting consumer practices to the ontology of the comic convention.

As it turned out, shopping in the Dealers' Room was such a popular feature during the first Comic-Con that it threatened to eclipse the rest of the convention. The *San Diego Union* reported that "The 'hustlers rooms'[*sic*] where the dealers tables were set up were so popular they had to be closed during the speeches and lectures" and Shel Dorf added, "We couldn't get the people out of there to listen . . . they just wanted to keep on dealing and buying."[60] The popularity of the Dealers' Room was, no doubt, a direct response to the scarcity of comic books, and back issues in particular, in fans' everyday lives. If being a fan of the material necessitated meticulous collecting, it comes as no surprise that buying and selling would become a driving force at the convention. But the preoccupation with buying and selling material also threatened to eclipse the more intangible, affective practices associated with comics fandom. As this account suggests, many fans may have been more interested in buying and trading comics and collectibles than listening to professional guests (including Ray Bradbury and Jack Kirby) and fans talk about the art form. But paradoxically, the decision to limit access to the Dealers' Room in order to redirect fans to the more educational aspects of the convention's programming may have had the unintended effect of making time spent shopping that much more exclusive.

By 1973, problems with overcrowding in the Dealers' Room would prompt organizers to once again reconfigure the event. This time, in a rapid reversal of their 1970 strategy, they explicitly prioritized retail transactions over the entertainment or educational offerings of the convention's various programs and screenings. The 1973 Wrap-up/1974 Progress Report, provides a detailed explanation of events:

> We're really grateful for the support our many fine dealers gave us this year.
> They had to put up with a lot, but we're sure they think it was worth it,
> considering the business they did! Our original set-up for the dealers' room
> was fine for Wednesday, but quickly proved infeasible on Thursday as more
> and more people arrived and crowded in; the fire marshal became very upset.
> We finally had to expand the dealers' room moving it into what was formerly
> the speakers–films room and reserving one corner of the former dealers' room

for speakers and films! The expanded room was filled to capacity with both dealers and buyers throughout the convention, and, needless to say, a <u>lot</u> of deals were made. (Original emphasis)[61]

From the very beginning, the Dealers' Room was a central part of the Comic-Con experience; and before long, it became so central that organizers were willing to make significant changes and reconfigure the space, midway through the event. Their direct address to dealers in the report, along with their willingness to compromise other programming tracks in order to facilitate buying and selling, lays further groundwork for how the Dealers' Room (and subsequently, the Exhibit Hall) would function in the future—as a space that frequently prioritizes fandom as a business, over the business of being a fan. That contradiction was far less pronounced in 1973, when the lines between fan, collector, and dealer were blurry, if not imperceptible. But that same year also marked a watershed moment in comics history—one that would ultimately make these lines much easier to trace at Comic-Con.

By the early 1970s, the problems with mass-market distribution and newsstand retailers had reached a critical mass. Fans were finding ways and spaces to work around these problems, but the comics industry wasn't reaping the full benefits of the marketplace. To make matters worse for the industry, fan-dealers regularly exploited the mass-market's honor system of returns by buying up popular titles from independent distributors and selling them by mail and at comic conventions for massively inflated prices. Distributors, in turn, would report these copies as unsold and seek refunds from comic book publishers.[62] These scams only exacerbated the comics industry's problem with dwindling sales, and by the early 1970s, even Marvel, the industry leader, was profiting on only three to four out of every ten comics they printed.[63] It was New York–based fan, dealer, convention organizer, and high school teacher Phil Seuling who ultimately developed a solution. In 1973, Seuling approached comic publishers with a plan that would allow them to distribute comics directly to dealers like him. Seuling asked for the same discount offered to newsstand distributors, roughly 60 percent. In exchange, he would do away with the return system, and retailers would sell any leftover comics as back issues.[64] This new direct market distribution system meant shifting the risk from publishers to retailers, but it also meant that comic retailers and their customers would have a more reliable inventory of comics to buy and sell.[65] As Seuling's experience as a convention organizer suggests, the viability of this model had already been proven many times over in the flourishing marketplaces provided by Deal-ers' Rooms around the country.[66]

"Cash Register Receipts and Ledger Columns"

As fan-dealers like Phil Seuling began to work in comic book distribution, a small number of stores specializing in comic books were opening across North America. By the mid-1970s there were approximately thirty comic specialty shops in the United States and Canada. Ten years later, demon-strating the success of the direct market model, the count skyrocketed to upwards of three thousand stores.[67] While there had been plenty of fan-dealers selling comics through mail order and conventions, opening brick and mortar stores required a much greater commitment of time and capi-tal. Selling comics was no longer just a pastime; it was a profession.

The impact of these changes on Comic-Con was twofold. First, the open-ing of comics specialty shops around the country meant that the Dealers' Room was no longer the *only* place and time fans could rifle through old back issues and fill gaps in their collection. And, second, Comic-Con became a place where publishers, distributors, and retailers could connect, not just with fans but also with each other. As the industry and fan culture surround-ing comics changed, so too did the convention's retail space. While retail remained the central feature of the Dealers' Room, by the late 1970s, comic book publishers had also taken an interest in the promotional potentials of the convention. In 1979, Rick Marschall, the editor of Marvel's magazine division, convinced the company to set up a table in the Dealers' Room to promote their comic anthology magazine, *Epic Illustrated* (1980–1986), which, he claimed, may have "helped to start the ball rolling" and opened the door to an increasing number of publishers promoting their books at the event.[68] This strategy grew out of a desire to bring trade show–style promo-tion to the convention floor: "I realized that no American comics-con I had been to had publishers displaying materials in that trade show sense. I con-tacted Shel Dorf who said that to his recollection comic book publishers had never set up at San Diego; pros had attended, but tables were largely fans and collectors and shop owners. My idea was to set up a goodwill table announcing *Epic's* imminent debut, to showcase some of the art in huge reproductions, and to offer promotional materials and solicit opinions."[69] As Marschall's anecdote suggests, the addition of promotional booths to the

Dealers' Room at a time when "comics publishers just didn't do things like set up at comic-cons—and especially without selling products!" marked an early step in broadening and even redefining the purpose of the space.[70]

In 1983, Comic-Con's organizers, recognizing the professional scene that was developing, reached out to the industry and rented "hospitality suites" to "comics companies and other interested parties."[71] That year, thirteen comic companies were represented at Comic-Con, including Marvel, DC, and World Color Press, which printed almost all of the comic books distributed in the United States.[72] This promotional presence extended beyond fan outreach, however, and networking became equally important at Comic-Con. As writer Mark Evanier put it in 1983, "professionals are simply afraid to *not* show for a San Diego Convention because *this* is where it's happening" (original emphasis).[73] In 1984, Comic-Con introduced the Comic Book Expo, a response to the increasing professionalization of fan-dealers as they moved from mail order to specialty shops. Differentiating itself from the fan convention, the Expo was held two days before Comic-Con and offered "a retailer-based schedule of programs including everything from company presentations about new products to detailed information on how to help run a small business, including personal time management, employee and tax advice, technology, marketing, and much more."[74] This trade show arm of Comic-Con engaged far more explicitly with the business side of comics culture and made a direct appeal to retailers by claiming to help "strengthen the direct sales marketplace where it counts, the cash register receipts and the ledger columns!"[75] Comic-Con even situated these goals within the parameters of its nonprofit mission: "Comic-Con and Comic-Book Expo are non-profit entities dedicated to furthering appreciation of popular culture in America. We recognize the specialty retailer as the means by which this exciting and important entertainment will reach a significant portion of the American public. We want to work with the comic book industry to provide an annual event that will strengthen and expand the marketplace, thus furthering our greater goals."[76]

This parallel trade show offered what John Caldwell calls "industrial geography lessons" by reproducing the institutional borders and boundaries that separate different segments of the industry, while simultaneously mapping out ways for professionals to navigate and cross these thresholds.[77] Keeping the trade show "open to bonafide retailers and those affiliated with the industry," but "not the general public," created a spatial and temporal division that allowed Comic-Con and the Comic Book Expo to work symbiotically, while maintaining an ideological gap between them.[78] Fans could mingle with representatives from the comics industry during Comic-Con—dealers, artists, writers, and publishers, all of whom offered tables and booths in the Dealers' Room—but the Comic Expo was "<u>not</u> geared for the general fan" (original emphasis), and would therefore allow business to be conducted "without the interruptions of a large fan convention."[79] Where early comic fandom and the founding of Comic-Con relied on overlaps between dealers, collectors, and fans, the discourse surrounding the Comic Book Expo delineated the differences between these groups by privileging the economic interests of retailers, distributors, and publishers who profited from the activities of fans. However, keeping this trade show separate from Comic-Con itself allowed this to happen in ways that would be nearly imperceptible during the main event. At the same time as fans were being explicitly excluded from this new industry trade show, the retail tables in Comic-Con's Dealers' Room were joined by a steady influx of industry booths, many of whom came for the Expo and stayed for Comic-Con, where they could reach out to consumers as well as retailers.[80]

The differences between the Expo and Comic-Con were also evident in the language used to describe event spaces. While Comic-Con had a Dealers' Room, the Comic Expo had an "exhibition hall."[81] But as the Comic Book Expo, along with Comic-Con's growing attendance numbers, brought a greater industry presence to the fan convention, the gap between a Dealers' Room geared toward retail and an exhibit hall geared toward promotion narrowed significantly. This gradual shift manifested spatially in the convention's move from its longtime home at the El Cortez Hotel to the Convention and Performing Arts Center (CPAC) in the early 1980s.[82] The move to the CPAC meant that the event was now housed in a convention center venue that met the needs of a more professional, industry-oriented trade show.[83] Not only were the facilities able to house Comic-Con's growing schedule of programs, the CPAC also offered extensive exhibiting space, accommodating both the promotional and the retail sectors of the comics industry.[84] Despite these changes, the Dealers' Room retained its name, and a 1984 ad for the convention highlighted a familiar, if somewhat expanded selection of items for sale: "rare old comic books, movie stills and posters, cels, original art, science fiction D&D games, video, t-shirts, buttons, super hero items, new books and magazines, imported toys, etc."[85]

At the same time, however, Comic-Con was inundated with an increased demand for space that accommodated retail alongside industry promotion.

By 1987, the over 250 tables of the 41,000 square foot Dealers' Room housed in CPAC's "giant exhibition hall" were all reserved almost a year in advance.[86] In June 1988, organizers announced a "second dealers room" in CPAC's Golden Hall. However, this multipurpose space would serve as a lounge, house an art show and a "50th anniversary Superman exhibit," and be "filled with booths, primarily representing publishing companies."[87] When Comic-Con arrived in August, the room was referred to as a "Display Room" and, as promised, it was filled with fifty-six exhibitors from the comics publishing and tabletop gaming industries.[88] In 1989, this second space was described as an "exhibitor area" but was still subsumed under the blanket category of "Dealers' Rooms."[89] Finally, in 1990, this second room was renamed the "Exhibitors' Room."[90] For these three years, the convention seemed to be grappling not only with its significant growth in attendance, from eight thousand to almost thirteen thousand, but also with a redefinition of the function of the Dealers' Room itself.[91] With the increasing presence of industry promotion, there was still plenty of selling happening during Comic-Con, but not all of it involved retail transactions. By the time Comic-Con moved to its current home, the San Diego Convention Center, in 1991, the "Dealers' Room" moniker had almost completely disappeared; it was replaced by the "Exhibit Hall", then a 92,000-square-foot space filled with a combination of "exhibitor's booths and dealers tables."[92]

The Comic Book Expo continued during this time and remained a trade-only event, but Comic-Con's gradual shift from Dealers' Room to Exhibit Hall suggests that the line between retail sales and trade show–style exhibition was growing increasingly blurry. In 1991, for example, both Marvel and DC used nearly identical promotional images to advertise in the Comic Book Expo event guide and the Comic-Con program, with minor variations between the ads reinforcing boundaries between the professional trade show and fan convention (figures 4.3 and 4.4). Marvel's Comic Book Expo ad invited attendees to "stop by the booth to meet Marvel Representatives," squarely targeting retailers with a list consisting of members of the company's sales department and vice president of publishing, Mike Hobson. But Hobson and the sales team were notably absent from the Comic-Con ad, which instead invited fans to meet Marvel's "guests," a handful of their writers, editors, artists, "and the rest of the Marvel Gang."[93] DC used the same strategy, but with even subtler variation, inviting Expo attendees to "meet the staff" and Comic-Con fans to "meet the stars."[94] Both ads fit within the logic of the Comic Book Expo in that they appear to treat retailers and fans

WELCOME TO THE
1991 SAN DIEGO
COMIC BOOK EXPO

STOP BY THE BOOTH TO MEET MARVEL REPRESENTATIVES:
MIKE HOBSON CAROL KALISH LOU BANK
SVEN LARSEN BRUCE COSTA SKIP DIETZ MIKE MARTIN

FIGURE 4.3 Ad for Marvel's appearance at the 1991 Comic Book Expo published in the 1991 Comic Book Expo Program.

separately, despite the long-standing overlaps in these areas that date back to the founding of comic fandom and the establishment of the direct market. But even more striking are the similarities between the ads, which seem to suggest that with a few small tweaks to the language or guest list, Marvel and DC could effectively and efficiently pitch to both groups by constructing an aura of exclusivity around in-person events. While reinforcing boundaries between the Comic Book Expo and Comic-Con worked to elevate and professionalize the trade show's attendees, employing trade

FIGURE 4.4 Ad for Marvel's convention booth published in the 1991 San Diego Comic Convention Program Book.

show–style promotion and outreach at Comic-Con similarly situated fans—through their presence at the convention—as an exclusive group of insiders.

The shift from Dealers' Room to Exhibit Hall in the newly constructed and more expansive San Diego Convention Center functioned in much the same way, facilitating a continued and more complete spatial convergence of dealers, industry exhibitors, and fans, with its sprawling and connected halls able to accommodate endless rows of retail tables *and* trade show–style booths. As Comic-Con moved into the 1990s, the Exhibit Hall promised an expanded space for attendees to consume both commodities *and* industry promotion. This period also ushered in a time of significant upheaval in the comics industry and a major wave of consolidation across the media industries that would continue to reshape the form and function of the Exhibit Hall.

It is not surprising then that ten years later, as the convention's attendance numbers and square footage continued to grow, Comic-Con stopped holding its annual comics trade show. Organizers said it had become somewhat redundant as "much of the business that had been taking place at the Expo began to shift to the larger event," which began offering a special "retailers only" space and programming track sponsored by the Comics Professional Retailer Organization.[95] Also significant to this shift was Hollywood's increased professional presence at Comic-Con in the twenty-first century, with the *Hollywood Reporter* noting that in 2002, "a number of Hollywood professionals said they made the trek to San Diego to network with comics industry types or to scout for new properties in hopes of tracking down their next big projects."[96] The Comic Expo, which allowed publishers and distributors to connect with retailers, may have been too insular (and too retail focused) for studios looking to acquire intellectual property. But Comic-Con's ever-broadening, pop-culture focus made it a viable place for studios to connect with comic creators. As the comic book trade show was absorbed into the main event, Comic-Con was increasingly fusing trade-show promotion and retail sales by incorporating synergy and licensing into the geography of the Exhibit Hall. These changes offered a different kind of "industrial geography lesson," which connected consumerism (spending money) and industrial logic (making money) to the pleasure of being a popular culture fan.[97]

Mapping Synergy

The end of the Comic Book Expo in 2001 came after a decade of setbacks for the comics industry. Though the direct market helped to shore up the comics industry in the 1980s and early 1990s, it also made comics culture more insular.[98] And with the books and their fans mostly relegated to specialty shops, storylines and continuity grew increasingly complex, convoluted, and inaccessible to outsiders.[99] At the same time, comic book publishers were eager to capitalize on another boom in the collectors market, and as speculation drove comic sales, publishers fed this demand by spreading their most popular characters across multiple titles, orchestrating publicity stunts, and releasing variant covers and limited editions.[100] If the collector's market of the 1960s was driven by the scarcity of back issues and the "capitalist spirit" of comics fans-turned-dealers, "the speculator boom of the early 1990s resulted," as Bart Beaty put it, "from the deliberate manipulation of the marketplace on the part of the major superhero comic book publishers, who, borrowing from lessons learned by the sport card industry, sought to spur sales on their titles through the creation of artificial scarcities."[101] As comics alienated new readers and the speculation bubble burst, every sector of the industry found itself in dire straits by the mid-1990s. Marvel filed for bankruptcy protection in 1996, and by 1998, countless small distributors had folded along with more than half of the comic shops in North America.[102]

While the comic book industry has undergone a number of boom and bust cycles throughout its history, this particular trajectory included two key pivots—toward synergy and licensing—that not only reshaped the comics industry but also informed the production of media franchises more broadly.[103] The industry leaders, Marvel and DC, both took different paths to recovery but landed roughly in the same place, as "license farms" under the auspices of major media conglomerates that were seeking synergy through the production of media franchises.[104] After the success of 1989's *Batman*, DC leaned in to the synergistic relationship it had already built as a long-time subsidiary of Warner Communications, Inc., and joined the newly formed TimeWarner.[105] Marvel took a more circuitous route, implementing a robust licensing program and acquiring and building relationships with companies that would allow them to extend their IP into other areas, such as trading cards, toys, and film and television production, with the goal of becoming a "mini-Disney."[106] Thanks in large part to its successful foray into media franchising with the launch of the Marvel Cinematic Universe in 2008, the company that once emulated Disney was acquired by the media conglomerate in 2009.[107]

The comic book industry's move from publishing to "license farming" and the increased emphasis on creating and/or capitalizing on synergy through horizontal integration was part of a broader trend of "concentration and conglomeration" that was reshaping the media industries in the 1990s and 2000s.[108] These industrial strategies also illuminate how retail, promotion, and exclusivity became intertwined in the Exhibit Hall, which gradually shifted from a predominantly retail-centric space with an emphasis on comics to a more synergistic space shaped by the same strategies that characterized the media industries at the time, what Tom Schatz described as "'tight diversification' and 'synergy' . . . bringing movie studios into direct play with television production companies, network and cable TV, music and recording companies, and book, magazine, and newspaper publishers and possibly even with games, toys, theme parks, and electronics hardware manufacturers as well."[109]

The shift from Dealers' Room to Exhibit Hall also had the effect of foregrounding the production, distribution, and promotional sectors of the media industries, despite the fact that their representatives were still significantly outnumbered by retailers and small dealers. For example, the 1987 events guide contained a map with an index titled "Dealers Attending the 1987 San Diego Comic-Con," which included a sprinkling of comics publishers and distributors among the slew of small retailers and dealers, and ten years later, the 1997 events guide contained an Exhibitors index, which listed dealers alongside a more robust minority of comic book and book publishers, trading card and collectible companies, film production and video distribution firms, and toy and game manufacturers.[110]

While the event guide indexes represented a vertical and horizontal cross section of the media industries from production to retail, toys to films, the event guide maps marked another noticeable shift in the representation of the Exhibit Hall. The 1994 guide was the first to highlight the centrality of corporate exhibitors by labeling them directly on the map, a practice that has remained in place since that time.[111] The following year, Comic-Con boasted an Exhibit Hall containing "the most comics, games, card, and game companies of any major convention," and the map reflected this statement with large, corporately operated booths situated in the center-right of the room, flanked on either side by tables belonging to smaller distributors, retailers, publishers, and artists.[112] In visualizing this corporate presence, the map depicted them as large blocks of space bearing names such as D.C. Comics, Marvel, Dark Horse, and MCA/Universal, surrounded by comparatively tiny and uniformly sized numbered squares, referring the reader to an index of exhibitors and retailers toward the back of the Events Guide.[113]

While these companies weren't all enveloped under a single corporate umbrella, their integration into the space of the Exhibit Hall illustrates that the logic of synergy extended beyond corporate mergers and acquisitions and into the logic of consumption at Comic-Con, anticipating what is now a much more common mode of transmedia or franchise engagement in digital spaces.[114] Not only that, but this reconfiguring of a retail environment into something more closely resembling a trade show illustrates how this mode of consumption is frequently reframed as exclusive even as it becomes increasingly banal. Because the Exhibit Hall's particular version of synergy wasn't doled out through industry trades and business news covering mergers and acquisitions, but in physical space, the expansion of the Exhibit Hall also meant that the complex relationships and material labor that go into what Derek Johnson calls the "institutionalization of franchise relations," were similarly shaping the Comic-Con experience.[115]

When the San Diego Convention Center completed its expansion in the fall of 2001, Comic-Con's Exhibit Hall also expanded to fill this new space over the next two years, a response to the significant growth in attendance in the 2000s.[116] By 2003, the Exhibit Hall had more than doubled in size and covered 460,859 square feet of the convention center (Halls A–G).[117] In the 2005 Events Guide, the map of the Exhibit Hall featured large areas of space marked off and branded not just with names but with familiar corporate logos, such as Activision, SciFi, Paramount Pictures, Sony Pictures Entertainment, Dreamworks, Mattel, Hasbro, Inc., Disney (featuring segments of the conglomerate: Disney Consumer Products, Disney Publishing Worldwide, and Disneyland), Dark Horse Comics, and DC Comics.[118] Subsequent Exhibit Hall maps—first published as splashy, color inserts in the Events Guide and subsequently as the centerpiece of the Comic-Con Quick Guide—retained this general configuration but reflected an even more pronounced corporate presence, with significantly more space on the map devoted to larger corporate booths, emblazoned with easily recognizable brand logos (figure 4.5).[119]

While the 1995 Exhibit Hall featured mostly comic publishers in its largest booths, the 2000s gave way to an influx of film and television studios and their licensees, as well as an increased visibility for toy and collectibles companies.[120] This increased promotional presence across media industries further replicated the corporate synergy that Lotz and Havens describe as a "kind of conglomerate cross-promotion, in which each new version of a text in a different medium not only makes money, but also drives sales of all other versions of the text."[121] Such a description conjures up a smoothly functioning industrial strategy that produces and reproduces profit. Indeed,

FIGURE 4.5 Portion of Exhibit Hall map published in the 2013 Comic-Con Events Guide.

such industrial logic was and is on display in Comic-Con's Exhibit Hall. In the past, the Dealers' Room was curated around consumer opportunities that appealed to the interests and investments of collectors and sellers, suggesting a kind of unified goal of encouraging the consumption of comics and popular culture, more generally. While this remained a prominent feature of the Exhibit Hall, the newer trade show–style booths, representing the production and distribution arms of the media industries, also promoted consumption by turning corporate synergy into an exclusive experience that extended well beyond the realm of comic books.

Locating Licensing

In 2002, a *Lord of the Rings* Pavilion, which included booths for Sideshow Collectibles, New Line Home Entertainment, Electronic Arts, Houghton Mifflin Company, Games Workshop, and Decipher, was erected in the very center of the Exhibit Hall.[122] In trade show parlance, pavilions are not necessarily structures unto themselves but, rather, pre-constituted areas that bring different exhibitors together around shared content.[123] Pavilions emphasize uniformity and connectivity, and partnering with one or more companies can allow for more cost-effective trade show marketing. However, because pavilions are often sponsored, exhibitors must "only show products that complement [the] sponsor's products and services."[124] In the case of the *Lord of the Rings* Pavilion in 2002, this meant producing a synergistic relationship on the show floor, with participating companies clustering around the film franchise, as opposed to a more broadly, fan-defined notion of Tolkien's fictional universe. While, as Eileen Meehan argues, "the complex structure of interpenetrating cultural industries and the corporate interests of media conglomerates" are "generally invisible to us," upon closer examination, the *Lord of the Rings* Pavilion, which featured displays clustered around a particular set of interconnected texts, also displayed the industrial logic behind this enormously popular franchise.[125]

By early 2002, the *Lord of the Rings: The Fellowship of the Ring* (Peter Jackson, 2001) had earned over $500 million at the box office and spawned a massive amount of merchandise, including Sideshow Collectibles' high-end models and busts and Decipher's trading card game (TCG) and role-playing game (RPG) based on the film.[126] Both of these companies had a licensing deal with the producer of the *Lord of the Rings* trilogy, New Line Cinema, a subsidiary of TimeWarner. Games Workshop signed a similar licensing deal with New Line to manufacture tabletop games based on the films. As a result, the company saw a marked increase in their overall business, as the popularity of their *Lord of the Rings* game tie-ins raised the profile of the company's full line of games.[127] Sideshow Collectibles, Decipher, and Games Workshop were all part of a "two-tiered system" of licensing, "aimed at different age-groups and tastes."[128] While Marvel's Toy Biz would produce action figures and Giant would manufacture clothing for sale in large retail chains aimed at children and a mass-market, companies like Sideshow, Decipher, and Games Workshop produced high-end, collectible products clearly aimed at adult fans of the franchise and "sold in bookstores and similarly dignified outlets."[129] Not only did this concept appeal to fan collectors as an exclusive group of consumers with more distinguished tastes, it also enhanced the exclusivity of the products by limiting their circulation, rather than making them easily accessible at large chain stores. The aesthetic of the Sideshow Comic-Con booth matched this "dignified" approach, with its selection of collectibles on an elaborate display roped off behind museum-style barriers (figure 4.6). Not coincidentally, this more exclusive tier of merchandise was aimed at the similarly exclusive group of *Lord of the Rings* fans, the kind who would likely peruse the pavilion at Comic-Con.[130]

The pavilion also featured a literary presence, but one that was specifically linked to New Line's film franchise. Houghton Mifflin, having published J.R.R. Tolkien's books in the United States since 1954, also acquired the publishing rights to the *Lord of the Rings* films in 2001, releasing new editions of the books as well as film tie-ins, such as *The Fellowship of the Ring Visual Companion* (Jude Fisher, 2001) and *The Art of the Fellowship of the Ring* (Gary Russell, 2002).[131] Houghton Mifflin's presence both acknowledged the significance of the source material to fans at Comic-Con and reinforced the film franchise as a natural extension of Tolkien's literary legacy through the publisher's collaboration with New Line.

Behind the scenes, the rights and licensing associated with the original novels made the franchising of the New Line films significantly more complicated than it appeared at Comic-Con. For example, Electronic Arts (EA) had a contract with New Line to produce video games based on the film franchise, but rival company Vivendi Universal Games owned the rights to the novels and had plans to develop multiple games around the same time.[132] Further confusing this situation was the fact that EA's first installment was a game based on the second film, *Lord of the Rings: The Two Towers*

FIGURE 4.6 Sideshow Collectibles display, Comic-Con 2002. (Image courtesy Raving Toy Maniac www.toymania.com.)

(Jackson, 2002), while Vivendi almost simultaneously released a game based on the first book, *The Fellowship of the Ring* (Tolkien 1954).[133] Not only that, but Vivendi Universal, the parent company of Vivendi Universal Games, also owned *Lord of the Rings* publisher, Houghton Mifflin, having bought the company in 2001.[134] So, while one of Vivendi's subsidiaries (Vivendi Universal Games) held the licensing rights for games based on the original Tolkien novels, the other (Houghton Mifflin) had obtained the publishing rights based on the New Line film franchise. These kinds of overlaps and complexities in the licensing of the franchise extended far beyond video games and were due to "a quirk in the licensing program" for the film series; some of the rights were sold through New Line, while Tolkien Enterprises retained others.[135] While the licensing of *Lord of the Rings* was extremely convoluted and complex, that messiness was somewhat undone when the franchise was reconstituted in the form of a Comic-Con pavilion. Notably excluded from the pavilion were those licensees, like Vivendi Universal, who had purchased the rights to the novels rather than New Line's film franchise.[136] The curation of the *Lord of the Rings* Pavilion, then, was based on a corporate strategy, assembling a group of licensees to promote the consumption of merchandise tied specifically to New Line's investment in the franchise.

The collection of exhibitors also included the presence of a *Lord of the Rings* fan club, with a table set aside for fan site, theonering.net. Another exhibitor, Decipher, was licensed to run the "official" *Lord of the Rings* Fan Club doing double duty as manufacturer of TCGs and RPGs for *Lord of the Rings* and publishers of *The Lord of the Rings Fan Club Official Movie Magazine*.[137] Decipher obtained the licensing rights for the fan club from New Line and ran a website and a magazine that featured regular updates from director Peter Jackson.[138] The inclusion of fans in this pavilion, in both official and unofficial capacities, represents not only the importance of Tolkien fandom to the franchise but also the importance of fandom to the visibility of the franchise. This investment in fan culture was similarly fostered online throughout the production of the films.[139] But as the *Lord of the Rings* Pavilion at Comic-Con indicates, these overlaps between fans and the industry were not just about making fans active participants in the formation of the franchise, they also allowed New Line to effectively license fandom, making it part of the franchise's industrial logic. By inviting fans to participate in this pavilion populated by their licensees, New Line was able to both service and acknowledge the fans, while also situating them, spatially and ideologically, as any other licensee, integrated into a mutually beneficial promotional arrangement that reasserted New Line's position (along with its parent company, Warner Bros.) at the top of the organizational hierarchy. In this way, the pavilion reproduced the kind of "enfranchisement" of consumption that Derek Johnson observed in online spaces, where "the play of consumers within media franchising structures could be described as industrial occupation—both in the sense that consumers take up productive subject positions within the institutions of media industries, and in the sense that as an institutional force those industries increasingly occupy the spaces of collaborative user creation in emerging media environments."[140] Just as these distinctions are easily lost online, it is possible to forget these complexities on the show floor, where companies seem to be unified by the content they produce and promote—*Lord of the Rings* merchandise—rather than by their roles as New Line licensees seeking to profit on the film franchise. Fan clubs, whether officially licensed or simply acknowledged by the films' producers, seemed exclusive but ultimately took their place in this pavilion as another arm of industry promotion.

Attractions like the *Lord of the Rings* Pavilion became increasingly common at Comic-Con as it entered the twenty-first century and the busy Exhibit Hall floor rapidly integrated a variety of media industry interests. In 2004, the Comic-Con event guide announced, "The Lord of the Rings Pavilion [*LoTR*], instituted two years ago, proved to be so hugely popular, serving as an umbrella for a variety of licensees of *LoTR* books, DVDs, and many other items. And now CCI has added a similar area, Lucasfilm Pavilion, in the front of Hall D."[141] Of particular note is the language used in the guide, which describes the *Lord of the Rings* Pavilion not as an "umbrella" for fans, the film, the books, or even merchandise, but for "licensees." Whether this term was deliberately selected to evoke an insider experience being offered to fans or because the terminology was simply seeping into Comic-Con parlance is unclear, but both explanations suggest fans in the Exhibit Hall were being engaged not as *either* consumers *or* aspiring professionals, but as consumers with at least some understanding and interest in the business of popular culture. Indeed, in its inaugural year, the Lucasfilm Pavilion featured a number of trade show–style attractions: fans could pose for pictures with "a 'real sized' X-Wing starfighter and watch *Star Wars* themed footage on the gigantic screen," audition for "the company's upcoming Trivial Pursuit DVD: *Star Wars Edition*," and attend scheduled autograph sessions with stars from the franchise.[142] But accompanying these activities were a variety of opportunities for consumption, described at length in the Comic-Con Events Guide: "Look for Comic-Con specials from a host of Lucasfilm licensees, such as Hasbro's 2004 limited-edition silver-painted sandtrooper action figure, making its debut at Comic-Con. Among the other licensees you'll find in the pavilion with convention-exclusive *Star Wars* merchandise, giveaways, or special events are Gentle Giant, LucasArts, Master Replicas, Code 3 Collectibles, LEGO, CDM LEGO, Pens, Topps, MBNA, *Star Wars Insider* magazine and Hyperspace: The Official *Star Wars* Fan Club, and Anthony Grandio. In addition, the official *Star Wars* shop will stock a variety of *Star Wars Collectibles*."[143] As is clear from this extended description, trade show pitches did not replace retail at Comic-Con during this time. If anything these promotions fueled sales and spending. In fact, two of the above licensees were there to help fans spend money. MBNA was a bank that offered a *Star Wars* MasterCard, and Anthony Grandio was a manufacturer of specialty checks. However, the promise of "convention exclusive *Star Wars* merchandise" demonstrates how the Exhibit Hall of the twenty-first century centered exclusivity as a way to bring merchandise, fans, and industry promotion together by returning to the roots of the Dealers' Room: consumerism and retail.

Comic-Con Exclusives

If there is any doubt that the Exhibit Hall remains rooted in retail and consumerism, one need look no further than the explosion of Comic-Con exclusives—collectibles that are sold or distributed in limited quantities at the convention—in the twenty-first century. Broadly defined, the notion of distributing unique items at the convention dates back to the very first Comic-Con program book in 1970, which featured cover art contributed by popular (and now highly collectible) artist, Jack Kirby. Capturing the nostalgia and collectibility associated with these programs, they are now widely referred to as "souvenir books" and are still distributed for free to attendees each year.[144] The souvenir books feature writing and artwork produced by professionals and fans specifically for the convention, making the books and their contents, by definition, exclusive. The first Comic-Con program, which was distributed for free to three hundred attendees in 1970, has significantly increased in value—in 2018, a copy was listed on eBay for $1,249.50—but the historical significance of the item, the collectibility of Kirby's art, and scarcity likely impacted this dramatic inflation in economic value.[145] Today's souvenir books are polished, two-hundred-page "trade paperbacks" that are mass produced, likely in the hundreds of thousands, so that they can be distributed to all attendees.[146] Marking convention and popular culture milestones, like Comic-Con's fortieth anniversary in 2009 and Superman's seventy-fifth anniversary in 2013, the books are closely tied to the time and space of the convention, and, as such, they operate largely within the framework of nostalgia: meaningful as pieces of ephemera marking the history of the convention or, as the title suggests, a souvenir for those in attendance.[147]

In 1976, The *Star Wars* Corporation sold posters featuring cover art from Marvel's *Star Wars* comic book, another early convention offering in the spirit of the Comic-Con exclusive. According to Lucasfilm's fan relations advisor, Steve Sansweet, "about a thousand had been made, but only a couple hundred were sold." Priced at $1.75 "to try to recover printing costs," these posters were clearly operating largely in a promotional capacity.[148] In 2018, however, original prints of the poster were listed for between $4,600 and $6,500 on eBay, with a slew of reprints ranging in price from $1.00 to around $17.00. Like comic books in the 1960s, both the 1970 Kirby program and this early *Star Wars* tie-in are examples of exclusive items that became collectible as a result of scarcity; they were produced in small quantities, treated as largely disposable, or, in the case of the *Star Wars* poster, were simply undervalued at the time.

Today's Comic-Con exclusives, however, are manufactured with collectibility in mind and more closely resemble the comics industry's top-down approach to exclusivity through the creation of "artificial scarcities" during the speculation boom of the 1980s and '90s.[149] The comics industry extended this strategy to promotion at Comic-Con, enticing fans and collectors to their booths by distributing free comics, like Dark Horse's *San Diego Comic-Con Comics* series, published annually from 1992 to 1995 and produced exclusively for distribution at the convention. Or the 1993 Marvel comics giveaway, *Marvel Live*, produced by the company's Advertising and Promotions Department. However, the influence of synergy and licensing that infused the Exhibit Hall with a trade show atmosphere also significantly impacted the nature of retail sales as retailers, publishers, and media companies were increasingly sharing the space with large toy and collectible manufacturers who embraced both retail and trade show elements by promoting *and* selling their products during Comic-Con.

A smattering of exclusive toys and collectibles appeared for sale at Comic-Con around the turn of the twenty-first century, but the practice of buying and selling exclusives took off with the introduction of Preview Night in 2001. The idea was first proposed by Chuck Rozanski, the longtime comic dealer featured in Morgan Spurlock's *Comic-Con Episode IV* (2011). He thought that allowing a limited number of dealers and artists to mingle on the show floor the night before the convention would bring "back a little of the old personal nature of the convention that made it so unique."[150] But coming as the Comic Book Expo ended, organizers seemed less interested in instituting another exclusive time and space for professional networking and more interested in cultivating exclusivity, in general. While the Expo had separated retailers from "the general fan," Preview Night was open to professionals *and* attendees who purchased a four-day pass to the convention. In this new context, comics and toy companies, many of which were intertwined through licensing deals and media franchising, increasingly began to offer exclusive collectibles that attendees could purchase only from their booths.

According to *ToyFare*, "2001 saw the first exclusive that everyone was clamoring to get: a slight repaint of Mattel's redesigned He-Man figure."[151] This figure, which was produced in a limited run of one thousand, captures the somewhat cynical approach to the production of these products, particularly when it comes to large toy companies who, "tend to offer up slight variations that require different paint or other options, keeping their mass market and big manufacturing scale intact."[152] Taken to this extreme, such exclusives are designed to be even more economically efficient than variant covers and other gimmicks employed by the comics industry, manufacturing scarcity to drive overall sales based on speculation.[153] But for large toy manufacturers, the sale of these items is also a way to promote their toy lines, as was the case with the 2001 He-Man exclusive, which was part of the unveiling of a new line of He-Man toys marking the franchise's twentieth anniversary.[154] However, as the popularity of such products increased, more and more companies began bringing exclusives to Comic-Con. Current suppliers range from manufacturers like Hasbro and Mattel to online specialty retailers like Entertainment Earth and ThinkGeek; even retail chains like Hallmark and Petco sell exclusive items at the convention.[155]

The practice of selling exclusives, however, is not confined to Comic-Con, and such items are commonly offered for sale at larger comic and pop culture conventions across North America as well as in major retail outlets. In fact, the etymology of the term is closely tied to licensing, where the word "exclusive" often refers both to the products and to the license to manufacture and sell them. In many cases, manufacturers sign exclusive licensing agreements with IP holders, but exclusive deals are also forged with mass-market retailers like Target and Wal-Mart in order to entice retailers to highlight particular brands and provide additional publicity, especially in the lead-up to a film's release.[156] However, as Avi Santo notes, the use of exclusive licensing agreements as brand management strategies can be traced back to the late 1800s, well before the establishment of the comic book industry, let alone the first comic convention.[157] In the case of these kinds of licensing agreements, exclusivity works to both promote brands and sell merchandise, making Comic-Con Exclusives right at home in the Exhibit Hall.

Given the close and long-standing ties between comic book retailing and the San Diego Comic-Con, it probably comes as little surprise that the rise of exclusive toys and collectibles at the convention also occurred around the same time that comic specialty shops were diversifying their offerings. Though it was largely a promotional construct, the "batmania" that fueled the sales of Batman merchandise leading up to and after the release of the film in 1989 demonstrated that such items could be a lucrative addition to retailers' inventory.[158] Toys and other merchandise became an even more crucial revenue stream when comic book sales began their decline in 1993.[159] Indeed, Ben Woo notes that the retailers he interviewed between 2009 and 2010 "believed they would not be able to remain profitable or even solvent if they only sold comics."[160] As a result, many comic shops became what Dan Gearino describes as "pop culture stores" or "'all of the above' stores" that, much like Comic-Con itself, highlighted toys and other merchandise as a way to attract "the casual buyer."[161] Notably, this strategic reconfiguration was anticipated by Comic-Con's long-standing practice of highlighting comics alongside a variety of other "popular arts."[162]

However, if stocking toys and other merchandise helped individual comic shops stay afloat as the industry underwent significant shifts, the modern Comic-Con Exhibit Hall captures the ways in which retailers, particularly those "that have interchangeable selections of mainstream comics and related merchandise" must increasingly struggle to compete with larger and more economically powerful players—from mass-market and online retailers who have the heft to negotiate exclusive licensing deals, to distributors and manufacturers selling their products directly to consumers.[163] Though retailers have had to contend with an influx of trade show–style promotion in the Exhibit Hall over the 1990s and 2000s, more disruptive has been the increased presence of large toy and collectible manufacturers like Hasbro, Mattel, and Funko, who have joined the comics industry in promoting *and* selling their products at the event. In 2014, Chuck Rozanski estimated a ten-thousand-dollar loss at the convention and blamed the "seismic changes" brought about by the influx of Comic-Con exclusives offered by publishers and manufacturers in the Exhibit Hall.[164] As Rozanski put it, "the very organizations we most support are those who can cause us the most harm. . . . Not only do they divert revenues into their own pockets, but they also diminish our standing in the fan community by making us appear incomplete."[165] For some time, it was standard practice for dealers to use their Preview Night access to buy as many exclusives as they could, capitalizing on their exclusivity by reselling them at inflated prices. Comic-Con organizers discourage these practices but have largely left it up to individual companies to regulate their sales, as Hasbro and Mattel did in 2013 when they began restricting exhibitor purchases.[166]

This all amounts to a significant shift in Comic-Con's retail environment in that it allows corporate producers to circumvent retailers and sell directly to consumers. By restricting access for independent dealers, companies like Mattel and Hasbro send the message that they are aligned with the interests of the consumer, while the exclusivity of the product guarantees increased demand.[167] Once these sales are made, the exclusives move to a secondary collectors' market where their value is inflated, thus producing greater demand for subsequent exclusives. This same industrial strategy—the creation of false scarcity through the mass production of variants and limited releases—built on the "capitalist spirit" of comics fandom in order to drive speculation and fuel the boom and bust in the comics industry during the 1990s. But while this proved tenuous as a day-to-day business practice, it is right at home in the already exclusive context of the San Diego Comic-Con. In recent years, companies like Mattel, Entertainment Earth, and Factory Entertainment began offering preorders and selling select Comic-Con exclusives online that could either be picked up in person or shipped after the convention—if there was any remaining inventory. If anything, this new development demonstrates how rapidly this strategy of manufactured scarcity has been institutionalized and branded as part of the Comic-Con experience, even as it is deployed to drive sales beyond the convention floor.

In 2016, the *Verge* ran a story on the growing number of collectors who pay for their annual pilgrimage to the convention—and turn a profit—through "toy flipping."[168] But where collectors and speculators in comics fandom tended to treat their acquisitions as long-term investments, Comic-Con exclusives inflate in value almost immediately due to the excitement surrounding the event and the limited availability of the merchandise. These collectors pay for their habit by buying up Comic-Con exclusives and becoming dealers in their own right—through eBay, craigslist, Facebook groups, and message boards.[169] This practice is roundly criticized by many, particularly those who wait for hours or days for a single item, only to see quantities dwindle as they're bought up by flippers. But in many ways, this trend brings the history of Comic-Con's retail space full circle, as it blurs the line between retail as an industrial practice and fandom as consumer activity. When Comic-Con began, fans acted as dealers, driving the market for collectibles. Today, those same dealers are in jeopardy, as producers, distributors, and fans all occupy the role of retailer, capitalizing on the demand for exclusives during and after the convention.

Conclusion: "We're Gonna Go Have a Good Time Now"

When Comic-Con arose from the golden age of comic fandom in the 1960s, collecting was a direct response to conditions of scarcity produced by the comics industry's flawed distribution and retail model. Eager to capitalize on this secondary market, fans became retailers themselves, and dealers' rooms at conventions like Comic-Con were among the first physical spaces that allowed these practices to flourish. However, as the introduction of the direct market opened up new avenues for comic retailing, Comic-Con's space adapted to include an increased industry presence and support the professionalization of fan-dealers and specialty shop owners through the Comic Book Expo. Many of these developments were driven from the bottom up to the extent that fans *and* small retailers held a less privileged economic place in the hierarchy of the media industries, even as they effected the most change. But in recent years, these developments have given way to a top-down model, hinging on manufactured scarcity and driven by media conglomerates, franchises, and licensing deals.

Though retail sales and consumerism are integral to the modern Exhibit Hall experience, the influx of trade show–style promotions—particularly those connected to film and television—ultimately helped to feed the notion that the activities taking place in this space were more affective than economic and fuel discourses about the significance of the convention and fans to the media industries. Indeed, Lincoln Geraghty's observation that "collectibles and souvenirs from a convention can be seen as mementos of that special moment when the fans got close to the actors who inspired them or the television shows or films they cherish" suggests that this interweaving of experiences and objects heightens the exclusivity of the convention.[170] But this same exclusivity is also heavily commodified in the Exhibit Hall as a way to drive sales during and after the event.

The industry's trade show–style booths and pavilions achieve this goal largely by offering free experiences—photo ops, signings, giveaways, or contests—that are tethered to some kind of souvenir—a photo, autographs, swag, or prizes. As promotional materials, these objects are distributed with the goal of channeling nostalgia for a past experience into the promise of future moments of consumption. But when it comes to Comic-Con exclusives, obtaining the item—including the moment of economic exchange—*is* the experience. This process is captured in *Comic-Con Episode IV*, when one of the film's subjects, identified only as "The Collector," travels to Comic-Con to purchase the eighteen-inch Galactus figure, one of Hasbro's 2010 Comic-Con Exclusives.[171] When we join The Collector at Comic-Con, he proudly proclaims that he has waited in line for two days to gain early access and purchase his exclusive toy. He declares, "I will not leave that con. You can pull me out kicking and screaming. I'm not gonna leave until I have those figures." When the line finally begins the slow process of filing into the Exhibit Hall, The Collector braces himself and says, "Here we go." But he is frustrated and dismayed when he sees a flood of attendees coming from another direction, moving him from seventh to thirtieth in line. When he crosses the threshold into the Exhibit Hall, a dramatic score plays, building tension as The Collector runs—for a brief time, in slow motion—toward the Hasbro booth. Upon reaching the booth, he buys his toy and the score swells, marking his victory as he proudly presents Galactus to the camera. He declares, "This is what I came for and I'm done. I'm done! We're gonna go have a good time now." This moment, occurring thirty-eight minutes into the eighty-six-minute film (and a mere five minutes after his first appearance), is the last time we see The Collector on screen.

This brief scene reproduces the thrill associated with the process of collecting Comic-Con exclusives by weaving it into a narrative peppered with well-worn cinematic tropes. The Collector's journey becomes a conquest; he overcomes obstacles, exhibits determination, and ultimately emerges victorious. Not only does this elevate collecting as a more exciting and rewarding pursuit than the mundane consumerism associated with shopping for everyday commodities, but it also encapsulates the system of exchange that exists around exclusivity at Comic-Con, something attendees must *work* to obtain or achieve. This notion of collecting as labor is crystalized when The Collector proclaims, "We're gonna go have a good time now," and subsequently disappears from the film, having completed his work and served his narrative purpose.

Retail and consumerism are at once the most obvious and opaque aspects of Comic-Con. Perhaps this is because, as Spurlock's treatment of The Collector demonstrates, they don't fit neatly into popular narratives about fandom or the convention, which tend to be rooted in the idea that meaningful engagement with popular culture and the media industries has the power to transcend economic concerns and place everyone on an equal footing. But the gradual shift from Dealers' Room to Exhibit Hall, the rise of trade show–style promotion, and the explosion of exclusive merchandise *do* fit neatly into the limits of exclusivity at Comic-Con, where consumerism is reconfigured as labor, and exclusivity is something fans work for and *earn* from the media industries.

Conclusion

• •

From Franchise Wars to Fry
Fans—Comic-Con Anywhere

> Taco Bell was the only restaurant to
> survive the franchise wars . . . now all
> restaurants are Taco Bell.
> —*Demolition Man*, 1993

> Fry Fans rejoice!
> —Today.com, 2018

In 2018, I waited in line for three hours to get into one of the hottest offsite events at the San Diego Comic-Con that year: Taco Bell 2032 (figure C.1).[1] An example of what is known in marketing nomenclature as an "activation" or "experiential marketing," activities like this one, which run in tandem with Comic-Con but are not part of the official event and do not require a badge to gain entry, have grown increasingly popular since I began attending in 2009.[2] Indeed, with "the rise of activation culture" as the *Hollywood Reporter* described it, the promotion happening outside Comic-Con is now as robust as it is inside the convention center, if not *more* prolific.[3] In recent years, I have toured set replicas from the film *Ender's Game* (Gavin Hood, 2013),

FIGURE C.1 Outside the Taco Bell 2032 Activation, Comic-Con 2018. (Photo by the author.)

visited *Suicide Squad*'s Belle Reve Penitentiary, participated in an Adult Swim–themed carnival, watched a sneak preview of ABC's short-lived *Inhumans* (2017) in a pop-up IMAX theater, been immersed in the futuristic setting of *Blade Runner 2049* (Denis Villeneuve, 2017), and died and went to *The Good Place* (NBC, 2016–), all without setting foot inside the San Diego Convention Center.[4] But while these examples all promoted films and television shows, Taco Bell 2032 used a film to promote something else: the fast food chain's new nacho fries.

In doing so, the activation revived Warner Brothers' *Demolition Man* (Marco Brambilla, 1993), a sci-fi action film depicting a dystopia-lite where violence has been all but eradicated, swearing and other "unhealthy" vices are forbidden, advertising jingles replace pop music, and, thanks to the "franchise wars," every restaurant is a Taco Bell.[5] Staged in a downtown San Diego steakhouse over three evenings, Taco Bell 2032 re-created a single scene from the film in which Sylvester Stallone—playing a hardened cop from 1996 who had, until recently, been cryogenically frozen—is invited to an upscale Taco Bell for an evening of fine dining and dancing. The originality of the activation, which resurrected a somewhat idiosyncratic film from the 1990s, the free four-course meal, and, of course, the exclusivity of the experience, which was reportedly limited to around a thousand guests, prompted many websites to include Taco Bell 2032 on their best of Comic-Con 2018 lists.[6]

Despite the activation's positive reception, the idea of promoting a fast food chain at Comic-Con probably seems like a bit of a stretch and yet another piece of evidence to fuel arguments that Comic-Con has strayed from its roots as a fan convention. But the coverage of Taco Bell 2032 was largely positive, embracing the absurdity of the premise and praising the activation's attention to detail.[7] Perhaps this is because Taco Bell 2032 was not actually an official part of the San Diego Comic-Con, it just capitalized on its spatiotemporal proximity to the event. And by tethering itself to Warner Brothers' campy, R-rated blockbuster, the activation seemed like a conceptual fit with Comic-Con's ever-broadening definition of fan culture. By reviving *Demolition Man*'s fictional world and placing Taco Bell at the center of the action, the activation also worked to legitimate the company, promising it was more than just a fast food chain; it was a brand with fans. Most importantly, however, the Taco Bell 2032 activation was part of a much broader integrated marketing campaign that extended this relationship—and ideas about fandom—well beyond the time and space of Comic-Con 2018.[8]

In the introduction to this book, I examined what made Comic-Con unique amidst an increasingly crowded landscape of fan conventions by centering on the relationship forged between the event, fans, and Hollywood, and circumscribed by the limits of exclusivity. Throughout *Only at Comic-Con*, I rooted this analysis in the histories, spaces, and discourses that surround and constitute the event in order to argue that at the San Diego Comic-Con, the limits of exclusivity inflate the value of promotional content, construct an idealized notion of fans as consumers *and* laborers who work in tandem with industry goals, and reinforce the economic and cultural power of Hollywood. However, given that the limits of exclusivity are constructs that are being continually negotiated and redrawn, it seems only fitting to conclude this book by examining how the same notions of exclusivity, fan labor, and industry power that shape promotion *inside* Comic-Con also shape promotion *outside* the event. As a marketing activation constructed around the idea of an exclusive experience, Taco Bell 2032 demonstrates how *Only at Comic-Con* might also illuminate promotional contexts beyond Comic-Con—whether around the corner or in another time and space entirely. Understanding Taco Bell 2032's provenance and placing the activation in the context of Taco Bell's nacho fries marketing campaign extends the applicability of this book's arguments even further. Before examining this final case study, however, this conclusion provides additional context for thinking about experiential marketing and activations outside the time and space of the San Diego Comic-Con.

Activating Promotion, Activating Fans

Though companies have long sought face-to-face interactions with consumers (consider the Pepsi Taste Challenge, for example), it wasn't until the turn of the twenty-first century that "experiential marketing" emerged as a unique discipline in the advertising industry.[9] Kerry Smith and Dan Hanover, the editors of *Event Marketer* magazine, describe experiential marketing in a simple formula: "combine a brand message, elements of interactivity, a targeted audience, and deliver it in a live setting to create a defined outcome."[10] Given how closely this description aligns with many other examples of promotion I describe throughout this book, it probably comes as little surprise that Comic-Con's elevated profile in the twenty-first century roughly coincides with the institutionalization of this marketing approach.

Indeed, the discourses about the marketing activations staged outside Comic-Con look a lot like those surrounding Hall H presentations, which claim that studios are fearful of their fans' reactions and, as a result, must offer increasingly surprising and thrilling presentations in order to have an impact and keep them interested. As the *New York Times* put it, "Comic-Con's epicenter, the San Diego Convention Center, has now grown so chaotic and overcrowded that many movie and television companies complain that it is hard, if not impossible, to stand out. The blinding hubbub, combined with the ever-increasing power of social media, has led many studios and networks to focus more intently on elaborate experiences—'activations' in industry shorthand—in the surrounding hotels and streets."[11] And much like the promotions happening inside Comic-Con, activations are all about "leaning into 'do it for the gram' culture" as one marketing executive put it, in order to present something "that people want to share out as they're experiencing it."[12] But despite this book's title, activations and experiential marketing don't happen *Only at Comic-Con*, they can happen anywhere.

Studios, tech companies, and brands of all kinds regularly stage activations at other large media events and festivals, such as South by Southwest, Sundance, and Coachella.[13] But these high-profile locales aren't the only places you might stumble upon experiential marketing strategies. For example, in promoting its *Gilmore Girls* (WB, 2000–2006; CW, 2006–2007; Netflix, 2016) reboot, Netflix retrofitted coffee shops all over North America to create nearly two hundred "Luke's Diner" pop-ups in the fall of 2016.[14] And in the summer of 2018, Warner Brothers created a VR roadshow to promote *The Meg* (Jon Turteltaub, 2018) at locations like Canada's Wonderland, a theme park outside Toronto, Taste of Lincoln Avenue, a Chicago street festival, and the Vans Warped Tour during the traveling rock concert's stop in Indianapolis.[15] Both of these activations exploited the limits of exclusivity even as they found ways to overcome these limits.

Just as the exclusivity of Comic-Con's Exhibit Hall elevates the experience of retail and shopping, Netflix's *Gilmore Girls* promotion made consuming coffee an exclusive experience by promising to immerse participants in the fictional world of a beloved television show in the confines of their local coffee shop. Even though the large number of pop-ups ensured that people all over North America could access "Luke's Diner," limiting the time of the activation to a single morning created a sense of urgency that ensured the formation of long lines and made the experience feel more exclusive.[16] "*The Meg*: Submersive VR Experience," was a very different kind of activation, one that approximated the visceral experience of a theme park attraction by placing participants in individual booths and incorporating real water into a VR presentation that simulated an encounter with the film's megalodon shark. While Warner Brothers staged a similar activation at Comic-Con to promote their film *It* (Andy Muschietti, 2017) in 2017, *The Meg* activation bypassed the San Diego Comic-Con altogether in order to avoid competing with the slew of other more elaborate activations staged that year.[17] But by bringing "*The Meg* Submersive VR Experience" to local venues like theme parks, festivals, and concerts, Warner Brothers was still able to frame the activation as an exclusive in-person experience, even as it made the actual VR component widely available by way of a free download.[18]

Both activations also relied on the labor of participants, who were encouraged to use social media as a way to spread the promotion more widely. The Warner Brothers activation incorporated a photo op where participants could pose as victims of the giant shark and share a short video online.[19] And the experience also worked in tandem with a campaign that relied largely on social media messaging and word of mouth to reframe the film as a tongue in cheek joyride (much like the VR experience), rather than a serious action film.[20] Like "*The Meg:* Submersive VR Experience," Netflix provided photo ops in their "Luke's Diner" pop-ups. But the company also partnered with Snapchat to extend the exclusivity of the in-person activation to social media. Each coffee cup distributed in "Luke's Diner" included a "snapcode" that gave participants access to a branded *Gilmore Girls* filter for one hour, only.[21] While Netflix distributed only 10,000 coffee cups during the promotion, Snapchat reported that the branded filter reached over 500,000 individuals.[22]

As these examples suggest, experiential marketing and marketing activations are, like Comic-Con, firmly located in the idea of an "experience economy" that extracts additional value (and dollars) by reframing consumption—of promotion, media content, and commodities—as an exclusive experience, while also generating promotion via the unpaid labor of participants.[23] But the use of exclusive experiences as a promotional strategy is not without historical precedent in the media industries. For example, Charles Musser's account of the Vitascope's introduction to American audiences from 1896 to 1897 illustrates how the early film projection technology was also sold using an exclusive context, which was subsequently broadened to reach a much wider audience.[24] According to Musser, Norman Raff and Frank Gammon decided to launch the "screen machine" in New York City, explaining, "we can do much better and make more money for both parties by exhibiting the machine at the start *exclusively* in New York City. The reports through the news-papers go throughout the country, and we shall do a lot of advertising in the shape of news-paper articles which will excite the curiosity of parties interested in such things" (my emphasis).[25] When Edison—who was publicly designated as the inventor of the Vitascope, largely for promotional purposes—presented the technology in New York, the *New York Journal's* coverage played up the exclusivity of the event even more, reading much like the reports that now emerge from Comic-Con's Hall H: "For the first time since Edison has been working on his new invention, the Vitascope, persons other than his trusted employees and assistants were allowed last night to see the workings of the wonderful machine."[26] As Douglas Gomery points out, the goal of this launch was not simply to make money from audiences but to "franchise the technology state by state" by "taking advantage of America's most famous inventor."[27] Thus the Vitascope's New York launch relied on exclusivity to drive word of mouth and ensure the placement of stories in local newspapers around the country. Raff and Gammon also built on the exclusivity of the New York screening, even as they made the technology more widely available. Over the next year, they brought the Vitascope to audiences around the country, attaching screenings to live vaudeville shows, theatrical performances, storefronts, and outdoor venues like parks and resorts; and the technology—like Comic-Con—was deliberately tethered to "a wide range of entertainment forms, cutting across genres."[28] In increasing availability and broadening the audience for Vitascope screenings, Raff and Gammon weren't selling a single show; they were selling a mode of production and consumption in an attempt to ensure profits in perpetuity.[29] For this reason, when reading Musser's account, it is hard to ignore the parallels between the launch of the exhibition technology that precipitated the formation of the U.S. film industry and the launch of the film franchises produced by that same industry over one hundred years later.

In fact, Marvel Studios employed a similar strategy in October 2014 when its president Kevin Feige—along with an entourage of the studio's stars—announced the third phase of Marvel's Cinematic Universe to the press and a gathering of six hundred fans at Disney's El Capitan Theater in Los Angeles.[30] While the announcement was framed as a "fan event" it was really a press conference that had been opened up to fans by way of invitations distributed through social media.[31] This strategy ensured that the press would disseminate the news through official channels, while also positioning the event as an exclusive peek for the very fans that were most likely to share content with their networks. In staging this presentation on its own time and in a venue owned by its parent company, Disney, Marvel Studios was able to create a Comic-Con–style event that was completely under its purview and control.[32] But this ballyhoo was deliberately ephemeral, intended—like the Vitascope launch—to stimulate press coverage and word of mouth. So it hardly mattered when, several years later, Marvel failed to deliver on a number of release dates and titles promised in the presentation.[33] Marvel wasn't just promoting a single film or event; it was selling a franchise. Of course, the launch of the Vitascope and the launch of Phase Three of the Marvel Cinematic Universe are not analogous promotional events, but as this book's examination of Comic-Con's history suggests, considering such parallels is one way to provide nuance and context when discourses make something *feel* new, exciting, and, of course, exclusive.[34]

Indeed, Marvel's reliance on digital technology and social media to blur the lines between press coverage and word of mouth and cultivate an environment that promised insider access to its fans is one of the things that sets its Phase Three announcement apart from Raff and Gammon's 1896 Vitascope launch. In the digital age, experiential marketing is frequently presented as a solution to "the perception of a problematic space of uncertainty at the heart of the relationship between producers and consumers," as Elizabeth Moor puts it.[35] While early fan studies scholarship celebrated the idea that media consumption could act as a site of resistance in our everyday lives, from an industry perspective, experiential marketing represents a break with the everyday in order to present a solution to the "problem" of active audiences, who are interpreting and even ignoring media in ways that seem incongruous and unpredictable.[36] After all, the same digital revolution that promised to transform all of us into an active audience of content producers has also made us into a massive unpaid digital labor force who share, like, tag, and produce content online.[37] As Smith and Hanover put it, consumers can "toss mail, tag e-mails as spam, and unlike a Facebook page. But the face-to-face connection is undeniable, unbreakable—and unblockable."[38] Of course, in making this somewhat ominous statement, Smith and Hanover aren't just talking about a niche audience of fans; they're describing *all* consumers.

Similarly, the discourses that I describe in this book elevate Comic-Con fans as an exclusive audience while simultaneously broadening the definition of fandom to include anyone who, in addition to consuming media and merchandise, actively seeks out and shares promotional content. This broad notion of fandom is also what makes it possible for events like Disney's *Star Wars*–themed product launch, Force Friday, to transform mass-market retailers like Wal-Mart and Target into exclusive environments of promotion and consumption, much like the San Diego Comic-Con.[39] The first Force Friday was held on September 4, 2015, to kick off the explosion of licensed merchandise that flooded stores leading up to the December release of *Star Wars: The Force Awakens* (J. J. Abrams, 2015), the first in Disney's new trilogy of *Star Wars* films.[40] When Disney announced the event in May 2015, their press release made consumption and promotional labor virtually inseparable: "Fans wanting to be the first to get their hands on *Star Wars: The Force Awakens* merchandise can set their hyperspace and social media coordinates now," it read, "they will be able to visit their local retailer starting at midnight on September 4, and are encouraged to document their experience using the hashtags #ForceFriday and #MidnightMadness."[41] Force Friday was also prefaced by a "live, global unboxing event" streaming on the *Star Wars* YouTube channel, where Disney similarly combined the pleasure of consuming and producing promotion by unveiling new products over a period of eighteen hours.[42]

When Force Friday finally arrived, thousands of Wal-Mart, Target, Toys R Us, and Disney Store locations opened their doors at midnight, and media coverage reinforced the idea that those first through the doors to buy the products were the most devoted *Star Wars* fans.[43] While this strategy transformed the product launch into an exclusive fan event, it also mirrored other retail events like Black Friday, for which fandom is not a prerequisite.[44] Indeed, as a 2015 CNN story detailed, Force Friday launched "merch for any taste," including toys (for children and adults), books, games, cosmetics, and food.[45] This made the retail transactions at Force Friday an entry point, not just to the story and characters of the revived *Star Wars* franchise, but also to a broadly defined notion of *Star Wars* fandom that was only accessible via economic capital.[46] But, as the original press release indicated, Force Friday made this consumption even more conspicuous by connecting the event to social media sharing. For example, Target stores also created photo ops that explicitly invited their customers to "#sharetheforce" (figure C.2).[47]

As Force Friday demonstrates, experiential marketing, much like Comic-Con itself, represents a break from the "push" logic of traditional marketing, where advertisers attempt to insert themselves into consumers' everyday routines through content like TV, press, and online advertisements.[48] Similarly, in fusing fast food and fine dining and locating their restaurant in a fictional future envisioned in a campy science fiction film of the 1990s, the Taco Bell 2032 activation reimagined what could be a mundane activity—dining out—as a once in a lifetime experience.[49] This approach isn't all that different from the other spaces I've explored in this book—Comic-Con lines, Hall H, and the Exhibit Hall—all of which take familiar consumer activities—waiting in line, watching ads, and shopping—and elevate them to the status of an exclusive experience by overcoming the "boundary between ordinary and media worlds."[50] At Comic-Con, this happens largely because the convention has been successfully positioned as both an industry and a fan event, with the presence of the media industries signifying the promise to bring Comic-Con fans closer to "media worlds."[51] But while the kinds of insider discourses circulating at and around

FIGURE C.2 Target's 2015 Force Friday promotion, Eugene, Oregon. (Photo by the author.)

Comic-Con frame the event as a way for fans to get closer to the industry, as this book has shown, the media worlds fans encounter at Comic-Con share much in common with experiential marketing, where the exclusive experiences exist to activate a vision of fandom founded on promotional labor and consumption.

Activating Fry Fans and Winning the Franchise Wars

This book's study of Comic-Con has largely centered on how Hollywood's presence—and the presence of media industries more generally—constructs and exploits an aura of exclusivity around the event. Some of the experiential marketing examples I discussed earlier rely on a similar premise. For example, the Marvel Phase Three launch reframed promotion as insider information and Force Friday produced a notion of fandom built on consumption and promotional labor, aligning it with the industry's economic goals. The exclusivity of Taco Bell's Comic-Con activation, while similarly tethered to Hollywood, was more like the promotions for *The Meg* or *Gilmore Girls* in that it situated participants in the middle of a wholly fictional world produced in front of a camera, not behind the scenes.[52] Indeed, while Henry Jenkins has argued that "texts become real" as fans "rework borrowed materials to fit them into the context of lived experience," Taco Bell 2032 activated its brand and made "fry fans" a reality by bringing a fictional text to life.[53] However, as part of a larger integrated marketing campaign, Taco Bell 2032 also makes a compelling case for examining how promotional strategies that rely on the construction of exclusivity, broad generalizations about what constitutes a fan, and the prestige of Hollywood can be found anywhere, even at Taco Bell.[54]

The Taco Bell 2032 activation, which took place from July 19 to 21, 2018, was supposed to celebrate *Demolition Man*'s twenty-fifth anniversary.[55] But the fact that the film's original release date was October 3, 1993, suggests that Taco Bell was much more interested in capitalizing on Comic-Con's timing than on marking the passage of time. Not only that, but the activation's narrow focus on a single scene from the film meant that what Taco Bell 2032 really celebrated was the approximately $12.5 million dollar product placement and tie-in deal that the film's producer, Joel Silver, negotiated with Taco Bell while *Demolition Man* was still in development at Warner Brothers in the early 1990s.[56] As a result of the deal, the fast food chain was inserted into the final version of the script, and Taco Bell reciprocated by featuring *Demolition Man* prominently in their television ads and in-store promotions leading up to the film's release.[57] While a 1993 *Variety* article suggested that these kinds of product placement and tie-in deals were increasingly common as studios worked to offset rising production and marketing costs, the Taco Bell deal still registered as "shameless" promotion at the time.[58] Such product placement deals are more commonplace today, having been normalized through decades of repetition; so much so that with the return of this partnership in 2018, Taco Bell went to great lengths to elevate this promotional strategy from an everyday encounter to a pleasurable, and exclusive, experience.[59]

But the Taco Bell 2032 activation that appeared at Comic-Con in 2018 was not a one-off promotional event. It was actually the culmination of a nearly eight-month-long campaign that fused *Demolition Man*'s passing reference to the "franchise wars" with the introduction of nacho fries, a new Taco Bell menu item to be offered in stores for a limited time.[60] The nacho fries campaign launched in January 2018 with the release of an advertisement masquerading as a movie trailer called "Web of Fries." The ad/trailer featured actor Josh Duhamel uncovering a conspiracy by "the Burger People" and "Big Fries" to keep nacho fries out of the hands of consumers.[61] By March 13, five weeks into the promotion, the fast food chain had reportedly sold 53 million orders of nacho fries, making it the most successful product launch in the company's history.[62] But despite the popularity of this new menu item, Taco Bell kept its promise that nacho fries would only be available for a limited time and removed them from the menu the following month. The launch of the campaign was met with laudatory headlines like "*Fry Fans* Rejoice!" and when nacho fries were pulled from menus, Taco Bell teased that "*fry fans* can find solitude in knowing its all-time best-selling product launch ever won't be gone for long as we already have a return slated for this summer" (my emphasis).[63] Although Taco Bell's Comic-Con activation was still months away, the underlying logic of the "Web of Fries" promotion relied on the same highly constructed (and often contradictory) limits of exclusivity that have made the convention a key site for media industry promotion—complete with a discursively constructed group known as "fry fans".

With its nacho fries launch, Taco Bell managed to take what is, perhaps, the most ubiquitous menu item in North America and infuse it with an aura of exclusivity by making it *even more* ubiquitous. The fast food chain simply restricted access to inflate value and increase demand, and then suggested that anyone who wanted the exclusive menu item must surely be a "fry fan."[64] On the one hand, Taco Bell's use of the phrase "fry fans" demonstrates how diluted the notion of fandom has become in the context of promotional discourses. But, as the editors of *Fandom: Identities and Communities in a Mediated World* point out, "the more being a fan is commonplace and the more it is 'just like being any other media user,' the more it matters."[65] Far from rendering the word meaningless, the idea advanced by the campaign—that Taco Bell's customers are "fry fans"—suggests that the word "fan" is more meaningful than ever.

"Web of Fries" also used the conventions of a movie trailer to elevate its traditional ad campaign.[66] "We wanted to launch Nacho Fries the same way we would an award-winning movie, by borrowing from the best-in-class movie release playbook," explained Taco Bell's senior manager of advertising and brand management.[67] But the trailer was also played for laughs, riffing on the high drama of a Hollywood conspiracy thriller. In so doing, Taco Bell connected the ad to a reputation it had been cultivating—primarily through social media—for several years, as a brand that entertained its "fans" with "a witty and unapologetically sardonic sense of humor."[68] However, like so many of the examples I've described in this book, this identity was also connected to the labor of Taco Bell's so-called "fans", paid and unpaid social media "influencers" who regularly share with and about the fast food chain online.[69] In characterizing the brand, Marisa Thalberg, Taco Bell's chief brand officer, even went so far as to say that she saw the fast food chain as "part of the entertainment business."[70] While this statement elevated the Taco Bell brand by reinforcing the notions of quality that separate promotion from entertainment, it simultaneously advanced and benefited from the idea that the boundaries between texts and paratexts had grown increasingly porous.[71]

These blurry lines between entertainment and promotion are also evident in the contrast between the original product placement deal and its revival in 2018. In 1993, when Taco Bell was featured as a plot point in *Demolition Man*, the product placement and subsequent tie-ins operated as what Jonathan Gray calls "unincorporated paratexts" that added "nothing meaningful to the text or its narrative, storyworld, characters, or style."[72] Though Taco Bell appeared in the film, any fast food chain could have been named the winner of the "franchise wars" with much the same effect. In fact, Warner Brothers famously reedited *Demolition Man* prior to its international release to cut all references to Taco Bell and replace them with Pizza Hut because, at the time, Taco Bell owned only a small number of restaurants outside of North America.[73] However, by June 2018, when Taco Bell began incorporating Warner Brothers' *Demolition Man* into the second phase of its "Web of Fries" campaign, the result looked increasingly like an "incorporated paratext" that "add[ed] to the storyworld and allow[ed] viewers chances to explore that world further" through its cinematic advertisements and the

Taco Bell 2032 activation.[74] But this time, instead of serving as the anchoring text, *Demolition Man* functioned as the paratext, a way of telling us something about a revised storyworld that placed Taco Bell at the center of the action. This might seem like a simple bait and switch if it weren't for the fact that so much of the "Web of Fries" campaign had nothing to do with *Demolition Man* at all.

In retrospect, one can see how the "Web of Fries" trailer's initial talk of conspiracies by franchise giants like "Big Fries" and "Big Burger" might evoke the idea of *Demolition Man*'s franchise wars, but there was no mention of the film anywhere in the original ad, nor was it mentioned in Taco Bell's January press release. This connection wasn't even made in passing in any of the countless media outlets that covered the launch of nacho fries, from *USA Today* to *Bustle*.[75] In fact, it wasn't until Taco Bell's June 28 press release announcing the Comic-Con activation that a clear and deliberate connection was forged between *Demolition Man* and the "Web of Fries" campaign.[76] In addition to stirring up significant buzz about Taco Bell 2032 online, the press release also announced the return of nacho fries to Taco Bell locations—once again for a limited time only—and teased a "sequel" to the "Web of Fries" trailer, both of which were scheduled a week before the activation opened at Comic-Con.[77]

Unlike its predecessor, the "sequel" trailer, "Web of Fries II: Franchise Wars," made overt references to *Demolition Man*, both in its title and through several visual cues, like the ad's futuristic mise-en-scène, an underground resistance not unlike the one featured in the original film, and a fleeting view of a sign reading "San Angeles Hotel," locating the story in the same fictional city as *Demolition Man*.[78] In addition to tying "Web of Fries" to this single film, the campaign continued to play up its conceptual ties to Hollywood marketing to make being a "fry fan" that much more exciting. "When you create a fake trailer for a fake movie for a real product that surpasses all expectations of products (and movie trailers)," Thalberg stated in the June 28 press release, "it seems inevitable that you have to create a sequel. And what better way to tease this sequel, than pay homage to a real movie's 25th anniversary—one that had a very compelling view of a fictional future?"[79]

Calling a dystopian vision of the future—however lightweight and comedic—a "compelling view" is, in my mind, a needle-off-the-record moment. But Taco Bell had tethered its promotion to a very specific kind of text; one that allowed it to shamelessly embrace the idea of a fast food hegemony, while couching this celebration in an ironic wink to its customers. *Demoli-tion Man* didn't spawn a franchise. It didn't even get a sequel. In fact as its 2013 appearance on the popular comedy podcast *How Did This Get Made* suggests, the majority of *Demolition Man* "fans" (if they existed), were likely to approach the film from a distanced, ironic viewpoint.[80] Indeed, these were precisely the kinds of customers Taco Bell had been courting for several years on social media, and through various attempts to rebrand stores and intro-duce menu items with "hipster" appeal.[81] At first glance, this ironic distance might seem to run counter to the notion of fandom constructed in dis-courses about the San Diego Comic-Con, which tend to place high value on literal and figurative proximity to the industry. However, as Mark Andrejevic points out, modes of engagement like "irony, detached cynicism, sarcasm, and, of course, snark" similarly allow audiences to claim insider status, even as they acknowledge that such a position doesn't truly exist.[82] "The goal of self-reflexive knowledge," Andrejevic writes, "is not so much to reshape the media—to imagine how things might be done differently—as it is to take pleasure in identifying with the insiders."[83] If, as Jeffrey Sconce argues, "to speak in an ironic tone is instantly to bifurcate one's audience into those who 'get it' and those who do not," then Taco Bell used this ironic mode of address to invite its customers into what Taco Bell's senior manager of social strategy, Ryan Rimsnider called "the cult of Taco Bell, that fan cul-ture that we've harnessed and we've been cultivating."[84]

The Taco Bell 2032 activation brought this ironic mode of engagement into the real world by serving upscale Taco Bell food in a reproduction of *Demolition Man's* dystopian future. When I entered the activation, I was greeted with the salutation used in the film—"mellow greetings"—and sipped a cocktail of the same name while I waited for my table in the res-taurant's bar area, which also contained futuristic decorations, original props, and a small storefront where patrons could purchase Taco Bell 2032-branded shirts and hats. When my name was called, I was seated, told to "en-joy-joy" (another callback to the film) and given a futuristic (i.e., clear, acrylic) menu outlining a four-course meal consisting of elevated Taco Bell fare like nachos, crunch wraps, fries, and cinnamon twists, all of which I ate while being ser-enaded by a piano player performing retro advertising jingles.[85] Between bites, participants could chuckle at the absurdity of their surroundings, but they might also leave wondering if a future where Taco Bell reigned supreme was really such a bad prospect. While it is tempting to argue that the acti-vation undermined the cultural critique rooted in the film's original concept of the dystopian "franchise wars," the fact of Warner Brothers and Taco Bell's original product placement deal meant that the film was already riddled with the same problematic contradictions. For example, in the future imagined by *Demolition Man*, as Sandra Bullock's character puts it, "it is deemed that anything that is not good for you is bad." The subsequent list she enumerates includes, among other things: alcohol, caffeine, meat, and "anything spicy." Taco Bell 2032, though praised for its attention to detail in re-creating the future imagined in the film, offered all of these forbidden items.[86] While Taco Bell might win the franchise wars in *Demolition Man*, its "fry fans" would be fined, arrested, or forced to join the film's underground rebellion led by Denis Leary, who, in one scene, equates freedom of choice with the freedom to choose between a "T-bone steak" and a "jumbo rack of ribs."

Contradictions like these were similarly absorbed in Taco Bell's identification of its customers as "fry fans" throughout the nacho fries campaign. Not only did the fast food chain erase the significant class-based privilege that makes it possible to be a "fan" of food, but by connecting this group to *Demolition Man* "fans", Taco Bell also advanced the problematic notion that consuming "bad" food could provide the same ironic pleasure as consuming a "bad" movie.[87] Ultimately, this disconnect between the content of the film and the content of Taco Bell's campaign suggests that despite being called a "coup of corporate synergy," "Web of Fries" was never *really* about *Demolition Man*—just like the 1993 film wasn't *really* about Taco Bell.[88] "Web of Fries" was about selling french fries. But in order to make french fries *feel* special, unique, and appealing, the campaign capitalized on connections between Hollywood, exclusivity, and the discursive construction of fandom.

Comic-Con Anywhere

Taco Bell 2032 and the other experiential marketing examples I've discussed throughout this conclusion point to the importance of engaging the concepts I locate *inside* Comic-Con in contexts *outside* the event. But, as this book has argued, the lines dividing inside and outside are often unclear and always ideological. While this book provides a deep examination of the power dynamics that make these lines particularly blurry at Comic-Con, I hope it also makes a compelling case for why they don't stop at the times and spaces I've examined, or even at this single event. When I called this book *Only at Comic-Con*, I did so, in part, to signal the things that make Comic-Con unique: its history, its significance as a space that brings fans and industry together, its importance as a site of both promotion and consumption, and its place in popular discourses about fans and Hollywood. But I also called this book *Only at Comic-Con* because this title captures the contradictions surrounding the limits of exclusivity, which are always expanding and contracting, often at the same time. This book explains how Comic-Con serves as a conduit through which to reinforce the hegemony of the media industries, even as fans are cultivated as an exclusive audience of tastemakers and laborers. But the implications of these arguments reach far beyond Comic-Con. In the same way that the logic of exclusivity—when deployed as a signifier of value—flattens out and reshapes fandom into a demographic, a discourse, a labor force, it also constructs a fictional notion of homogeneity in which culture *is* fandom and fandom *is* the culture. While the limits of exclusivity make it possible to observe that some things happen *Only at Comic-Con*, they also ensure that the discourses, power imbalances, and histories that make Comic-Con exclusive can happen anywhere.

Acknowledgments

A lot of the people I write about in this book—fans, convention organizers, industry professionals, and academics like myself—will sometimes describe what they do as a labor of love. But I've long resisted that idea when it comes to my own work, partly as a way to combat a frequent assumption that many scholars of popular culture and media face—because I'm researching a "fun" topic like the San Diego Comic-Con, the labor is surely less grueling, less rigorous, and less serious—and partly because one of my goals in writing this book is to complicate that very idea. In attempting to reconcile these things, I've learned that for me, the "love" part doesn't grow out of *my* labor at all, but from the generosity, support, and work of the people around me, and the tremendous gratitude I feel to have had them in my corner as I researched and wrote this book.

This project took shape during my time at the University of Michigan, thanks to the guidance, feedback, and support of countless teachers, mentors, colleagues, and friends in the Department of Screen Arts and Cultures (now the Department of Film, Television, and Media), especially those who read early drafts and provided generous feedback. Thank you to Nathan Koob for sharing so many laughs along the way, my pals Katy Peplin and Kayti Lausch for helping me put the "life" in work–life balance, Ben Strassfeld for cheering me on (and for that epic research assist), Dimitri Pavlounis and Josh Morrison for being my Canadian partners in crime, Mike Arnold for countless nights of great conversation and debate, and Richard Mwakasege-Minaya, Feroz Hassan, and Yuki Nakayama for their ongoing encouragement and support. I am so lucky to have been trained alongside this group of brilliant and generous scholars and even luckier to call them my friends.

Richard Abel deserves special thanks, as his classes first inspired me to explore Comic-Con's history through ephemera, archives, and newspapers. And I am so lucky to have worked with Yeidy Rivero, who always asks all the right questions and taught me to be a better scholar and thinker. Thanks also to Aswin Punathambekar for providing incisive feedback that helped to move this project forward. Words cannot describe the gratitude I feel for my advisor and friend Sheila Murphy, not only for her wisdom and willingness to act as both an intellectual and emotional sounding board, but also for the incredible mentorship she's provided over the years. It was Sheila who first encouraged me to travel to Comic-Con in the summer of 2009, and it is safe to say that this book would not exist without her. And my sincere thanks to Daniel Herbert who has been a constant force propelling my intellectual growth and an enthusiastic supporter of my work. His insights and feedback at a number of crucial stages have left an indelible mark on my scholarship and made this book infinitely better.

Thank you also to Derek Johnson who, along with Daniel Herbert, provided invaluable feedback on an earlier and shorter version of chapter 4 of this book, which appears in their edited collection, *Point of Sale: Analyzing Media Retail*. Dan and Derek's impact on my thinking and writing can be felt across *Only at Comic-Con*. I am also grateful to Elizabeth Nielsen for providing feedback on an earlier version of chapter 2, which appears in the *Journal of Fandom Studies* 5, no. 2 (2017). Finally, I am indebted to Matt Hills for his countless sharp insights and generous feedback on my manuscript.

This book, which grew out of seven years of field research at the San Diego Comic-Con, would not have been possible without the financial support I received from the University of Michigan and the University of Oregon. At Michigan, the Department of Screen Arts and Cultures Summer Research Grants, Rackham's Graduate Student Research Grants, and the Sweetland/ Rackham Dissertation Writing Institute enabled me to begin my research. And the University of Oregon's School of Journalism and Communication, College of Arts and Sciences, Oregon Humanities Center, and New Junior Faculty Research Awards Program provided much needed support as I finished this book. This funding also allowed me to seek out and purchase rare Comic-Con ephemera, supplementing the material that I gathered during my visits to two wonderful archives: Michigan State University Library's Comic Arts Collection and the San Diego History Center's Shel Dorf Collection. I appreciate Randy Scott's help in locating Michigan State's diverse assortment of Comic-Con materials, and I am also indebted to Jane Kenealy and the rest of the staff at the San Diego History Center for their help and hospitality during my visits.

Since I arrived at the University of Oregon in 2014, I have had the great fortune to work with a supportive community of colleagues across not one, but two units on campus. Thank you to the faculty and staff in the School of Journalism and Communication, who welcomed me with open arms and provided support and encouragement as I finished this book. I am also very fortunate to have joined an incredible group of scholars and practitioners in the newly formed Department of Cinema Studies. Everyone should have colleagues like Michael Allan, Michael Bray, Sangita Gopal, Dong Hoon Kim, Gabriela Martinez, Kevin May, HyeRyoung Ok, Sergio Rigoletto, Andre Sirois, and Janet Wasko in their corner. And I am especially indebted to Daniel Steinhart and Masami Kawai for cheering me on as I finished this book. I also owe a huge debt of gratitude to the Cinema Studies Staff, Kay Bailey, Tim McGovney, Emily Cornell, Kate Tallman, Michelle Wright, and Veratta Pegram-Floyd, for the many assists they have provided along the way. And, of course, none of this would be possible without the leadership of Michael Aronson and Priscilla Ovalle—I am so grateful for their support, guidance, and encouragement.

Thank you to my undergraduate and graduate students for challenging me, invigorating me, and pushing my thinking in new directions. My graduate research assistant, Kris Wright, was a terrific sounding board, and her willingness to read and talk interminably about Comic-Con lines is much appreciated. The students in my Comic-Con Culture class also deserve special thanks for their unique insights and boundless enthusiasm. Finally, Ann Laudick, Meg Rodgers, and Breanne Schnell may not know it, but watching them navigate and complete their own research projects with such skill and grace was a source of inspiration and light when I needed it most.

I am incredibly grateful and lucky to have met my editor, Lisa Banning. I so appreciate her belief in the project (and her patience with a first-time author!). Her guidance and support have been invaluable, and I'm so glad this book found its home at Rutgers University Press. Thanks, also, to my production editors Cheryl Hirsch and Alissa Zarro for all their help and hard work.

The last and most important part of these acknowledgments is dedicated to the people whom I both leaned on and neglected the most while finishing this book: my family and friends. Thank you to my friends in Canada and the United States, especially my oldest pals, Carolyn Elsner, Melanie Coussens, and Idiko Guylas. Phil Gotfried, Marco Marrocco, and Jarrod Hoogendam also deserve special thanks—the many hours we spent together at Cyber City Comix and at conventions all over the GTA helped to form the foundation on which this book was eventually built. Thanks also to my extended family and stepfamily, far and wide, my in-laws, Jack and Gae Alilunas, and especially to Ken Olive, Robbin Olive, and Ralph Durand, whose love and support mean so much to me.

While I have been incredibly fortunate and gained much over the course of researching and writing this book, the process was also bookended by significant losses. My father, Jim Hanna, was hospitalized in May 2011, just days before I was scheduled to defend my dissertation prospectus, and died three months later, days shy of his 69th birthday. He had an encyclopedic knowledge of film and popular culture, and we spent more weekends than I can count at movie theaters and video stores. These experiences, along with my desire to make him proud, had a significant influence on my decision to pursue a career in this field. In December 2018, my aunt, Peggy Olive, a brilliant scientist, activist, and writer passed away, just as I was finishing this book. While grief fades over time, these losses feel especially acute in moments like this, when I can't help but imagine the pride my father would have felt holding this book in his hands, or the laughs that Peggy and I would have shared as we celebrated with our family.

Of course, these losses make the gratitude and appreciation I feel for my very small and very close-knit family that much stronger. Kelly Hanna is the best sister anyone could ask for. She is also incredibly funny, kind, and wise. She and her amazing partner, Corey Fenster, have sent so much love, encouragement, and most importantly, laughter, my way over the years, and I am so lucky to have them in my life. My mom, Carolyn Olive, is the walking embodiment of unconditional love and support. And her commitment to lifelong learning and growth (and excellent taste in television shows!) has long been a guiding light for me. She is, without a doubt, my role model and hero.

Finally, I can say with certainty that I would not have been able to do any of this without the unwavering support of my partner, colleague, and best friend, Peter Alilunas, who has always been my biggest fan and, in keeping with this book's theme, has done a whole lot of labor as a result. He's read countless drafts, cooked countless meals, waited patiently in countless Comic-Con lines, weathered the ups and downs of this arduous process with me, and somehow came out on the other side just as supportive and loving as ever. I don't know if I will ever be able to adequately express my gratitude for the many things Peter did, big and small, to make this book possible. Alongside Peter's unrelenting support I have also been the recipient of unrelenting snuggles, purrs, and love from my cat, Holmes, who, refreshingly, couldn't care less about Comic-Con—but I thank him just the same. My stepson, Beckett, is just like his dad—loving, thoughtful, kind, and super-smart. He has been so patient and supportive, even on days when I was spending way too much time working or thinking about work. I'm so proud and honored to be his stepmom.

This book is dedicated to my family. The family I lost, the family I found, and the family who has always been there. I'm really proud of this book. A lot of labor *and* love went into it. But I hope they all know that there is no greater love in my life than the love I carry for them in my heart every day.

Notes

Introduction

Epigraph: Marc Graser, "H'w'd Woos Nerd Herd," *Variety*, July 14–20, 2008.

1 Rob Salkowitz, "Jury Decides for San Diego Comic-Con in Trademark Suit," *Forbes*, last modified December 8, 2017, https://www.forbes.com/sites/rob salkowitz/2017/12/08/breaking-jury-decides-for-san-diego-comic-con-in-12m -trademark-suit/.
2 San Diego Comic Convention v. Dan Farr Productions, No. 14-cv-1865 AJB (JMA) (2017).
3 San Diego Comic Convention is the name under which the company was incorporated as a nonprofit in 1975. However, the company and event also frequently use the names San Diego Comic-Con, Comic-Con International, Comic-Con International, Inc., and, most importantly, the shortened title, Comic-Con, interchangeably. "Comic-Con," Trademark Electronic Search System (TESS), last modified 2005, http://tmsearch.uspto.gov/bin/showfield?f=doc&state =4804:98m0d5.2.77; "San Diego Comic Con International," Trademark Electronic Search System (TESS), last modified 2005, http://tmsearch.uspto.gov/bin /showfield?f=doc&state=4805:wgqhhw.3.78; Rob Salkowitz, "'Comic Con' Trademark Battle Escalates as Trial Looms," *Forbes*, last modified June 30, 2017, https://www.forbes.com/sites/robsalkowitz/2017/06/30/comic-con-trademark -battle-escalates-as-trial-looms/.
4 San Diego Comic Convention v. Dan Farr Productions.
5 Michael I. Katz and Rex L. Sears, "Comic Con: A Convention by Any Other Name?" *Orange County Lawyer*, April 2018.
6 William Schelly, *The Golden Age of Comic Fandom*, Limited collectors ed. (Seattle, WA: Hamster Press, 1995), 71; J. Ballmann, *The 1964 New York Comicon: The True Story Behind the World's First Comic Convention* (San Bernardino, CA: Totalmojo Productions, Inc., 2016). The title San Diego's Golden State Comic-Con was in use

until 1972, at which point the convention changed its name to San Diego's West Coast Comic Convention. In 1973 organizers settled on the name San Diego Comic-Con. David Glanzer, Gary Sassaman, and Jackie Estrada, eds., *Comic-Con 40 Souvenir Book* (San Diego: San Diego Comic-Con International, 2009), 60–66.

7 Bill Schelly, a historian and longtime member of comic fandom, uses the term "comicon" to refer to gatherings of comic fans throughout his book on early comics fandom: Schelly, *The Golden Age*, 108–112.

8 The *Oxford English Dictionary* cites a 1940 article in *Astonishing Stories* as the first published use of the term. "Con, N.5," Oxford English Dictionary, last modified 2002, http://www.oed.com/; Katz and Sears, "Comic Con: A Convention by Any Other Name?" For a more detailed discussion of the historical overlaps between comic book and science fiction fandom, see chapter 1 of this book.

9 Katz and Sears, "Comic Con," 34; San Diego Comic Convention v. Dan Farr Productions.

10 San Diego Comic Convention v. Dan Farr Productions.

11 San Diego Comic Convention v. Dan Farr Productions.

12 San Diego Comic Convention v. Dan Farr Productions.

13 Bianca Bruno, "Comic Con Defendant Says He Knew It Was Trademarked," *Courthouse News,* last modified December 7, 2017, https://www.courthousenews.com/comic-con-defendant-says-he-knew-it-was-trademarked/.

14 Lori Weisberg, "Comic-Con Wins $4m in Legal Fees in Trademark Battle with Salt Lake City," *San Diego Union-Tribune*, last modified August 24, 2018, http://www.sandiegouniontribune.com/business/tourism/sd-fi-comiccon-ruling-fees-20180824-story.html.

15 Salkowitz, "Jury Decides for San Diego Comic-Con"; Timothy Geigner, "It Begins: Some Comic Conventions Refusing to Fold after San Diego Comic-Con Gets Its Trademark Win," *Techdirt*, last modified January 4, 2018, https://www.techdirt.com/articles/20180102/07163338907/it-begins-some-comic-conventions-refusing-to-fold-after-san-diego-comic-con-gets-trademark-win.shtml; Weisberg, "Comic-Con Wins $4m."

16 Throughout this book, I use the capitalized, hyphenated "Comic-Con" as shorthand for the San Diego Comic-Con. When referencing comic cons, in general, I use the lower-case, unhyphenated phrase "comic con."

17 Ellen Gamerman, "The Rise of Cons," *Wall Street Journal*, last modified March 3, 2016, https://www.wsj.com/articles/the-rise-of-cons-1457036227. The launch of The Comic Cons Research Project, a government-funded partnership between several Canadian universities and convention organizers, similarly signals the increased prominence and proliferation of comic conventions in recent years. "About," The Comic Cons Research Project, last modified 2018, http://comicconsproject.org/.

18 Despite numerous comments mentioning the error, no correction was issued. Chris Chafin, "San Diego Comic-Con: The Untold History," *Rolling Stone*, last modified July 19, 2017, https://www.rollingstone.com/culture/culture-features/san-diego-comic-con-the-untold-history-194401/.

19 Salkowitz, "'Comic Con' Trademark Battle Escalates."

20 Henry Jenkins, *Convergence Culture: Where Old and New Media Collide* (New York: New York University Press, 2006).

21 See, for example: Matthew Pustz, *Comic Book Culture: Fanboys and True Believers*, Studies in Popular Culture (Jackson: University Press of Mississippi, 1999); Randy Duncan, Matthew J. Smith, and Paul Levitz, *The Power of Comics: History, Form, and Culture*, 2nd ed. (New York: Bloomsbury, 2015); Kristina Busse, "Geek Hierarchies, Boundary Policing, and the Gendering of the Good Fan," *Participations Journal of Audience & Reception Studies* 10, no. 1 (2013); Matt Hills, *Doctor Who: The Unfolding Event—Marketing, Merchandising and Mediatizing a Brand Anniversary*, Palgrave Pivot (New York: Palgrave Macmillan, 2015); Henry Jenkins, Sam Ford, and Joshua Green, *Spreadable Media: Creating Value and Meaning in a Networked Culture*, Postmillennial Pop (New York: New York University Press, 2013).

22 Anne Gilbert, "Live from Hall H: Fan/Producer Symbiosis at San Diego Comic-Con," in *Fandom: Identities and Communities in a Mediated World*, ed. Jonathan Gray, Cornel Sandvoss, and C. Lee Harrington (New York: New York University Press, 2017); Anne Gilbert, "Conspicuous Convention: Industry Interpellation and Fan Consumption at San Diego Comic-Con," in *The Routledge Companion to Media Fandom*, ed. Melissa A. Click and Suzanne Scott (New York: Routledge, 2018); Lincoln Geraghty, *Cult Collectors: Nostalgia, Fandom and Collecting Popular Culture* (London: Routledge, 2014), 93–119.

23 Ben Bolling and Matthew J. Smith, *It Happens at Comic-Con: Ethnographic Essays on a Pop Culture Phenomenon* (Jefferson, NC: McFarland & Company, 2014).

24 Rob Salkowitz, *Comic-Con and the Business of Popular Culture* (New York: McGraw-Hill, 2012); San Diego Comic Convention Inc., *Comic-Con: 40 Years of Artists, Writers, Fans & Friends* (San Francisco: Chronicle Books, 2009).

25 Peter Rowe, "Comic-Con Confidential: Throwing a Pop Culture Blowout with $16 Million, 4,500 Volunteers, 62 Buses, Various Hollywood a-Listers and 'Rock Stars,'" *San Diego Union-Tribune*, last modified July 15, 2018, http://www .sandiegouniontribune.com/entertainment/comic-con/sd-me-comiccon-planning -20180621-story.html; Jackie Estrada, ed. *Comic-Con International 2018 Events Guide* (San Diego: San Diego Comic Convention, 2018); Gary Sassaman, ed. *Comic-Con International 2018 Quick Guide* (San Diego: San Diego Comic Convention, 2018). In 2013, *San Diego Comic-Con Unofficial Blog* produced a useful infographic that provides an overview of the event: Kerry Dixon and Sarah Lacey, "Infographics: How SDCC Compares to Other Conventions," *SDCC Unofficial Blog*, last modified November 4, 2013, http://sdccblog.com/2013/11/how-sdcc -compares-to-other-conventions/.

26 Rowe, "Comic-Con Confidential."

27 Suzanne Scott defines cosplay as "the practice of constructing costumes and props inspired by fictional characters and embodying those characters in real-world spaces such as fan conventions." Suzanne Scott, " 'Cosplay Is Serious Business': Gendering Material Fan Labor on Heroes of Cosplay," *Cinema Journal* 54, no. 3 (2015): 146.
      See, for example, "The Biggest, Best and Most Bonkers Costumes from San Diego's Comic-Con," *NME*, last modified July 23, 2018, https://www.nme.com /blogs/nme-blogs/the-biggest-best-and-most-bonkers-costumes-from-this-weeks -comic-con-2358141; "Comic-Con Attendees Do Not F*ck around When It Comes to Cosplay," *Esquire*, last modified July 23, 2018, https://www.esquire.com /entertainment/movies/g22487173/san-diego-comic-con-2018-photos/; Heather Lake, "Where to Get Last Minute Comic-Con Costumes," Fox 5, last modified

July 17, 2018, https://fox5sandiego.com/2018/07/17/where-to-get-last-minute
-comin-con-costumes/; Lee Moran, "Aaron Paul's Daughter Wore the Cutest
'Breaking Bad' Costume at Comic-Con," Huffington Post, last modified July 20,
2018, https://www.huffingtonpost.com/entry/aaron-paul-daughter-breaking-bad
-costume-comic-con_us_5b51898de4b0de86f48b8829.

28 Some examples of scholarship that engages with cosplay in the context of fan
conventions include Jen Gunnels, "'A Jedi Like My Father Before Me': Social
Identity and the New York Comic Con," *Transformative Works and Cultures* 3
(July 9, 2009), https://journal.transformativeworks.org/index.php/twc/article
/view/161/110; Nicolle Lamerichs, "The Cultural Dynamic of Doujinshi and
Cosplay: Local Anime Fandom in Japan, USA and Europe," *Participations Journal
of Audience & Reception Studies* 10, no. 1 (2013); Scott, "'Cosplay Is Serious
Business'"; Therèsa M. Winge, *Costuming Cosplay: Dressing the Imagination*
(London: Bloomsbury Visual Arts, 2019).

29 I am referring, of course, to Doctor Who.

30 Rowe, "Comic-Con Confidential."

31 I discuss such discourses throughout this book. Examples from 2018 include: Tracy
Brown, "Comic-Con 2018: The Must-See Film, TV and Comic Book Panels," *Los
Angeles Times: Hero Complex,* last modified July 18, 2018, http://www.latimes.com
/entertainment/herocomplex/la-et-hc-sdcc-2018-comic-con-panel-highlights
-20180718-story.html; George Costantino, "Comic-Con Debuts Trailers for
'Fantastic Beasts,' 'Aquaman,' 'Shazam' and More!—ABC News," last modified
July 23, 2018, https://abcnews.go.com/GMA/Culture/comic-con-debuts-trailers
-fantastic-beasts-aquaman-shazam/story?id=56758387; Samantha Tatro, "San
Diego Comic-Con 2018 Announces Full Schedule," 4 New York, last modified
July 10, 2018, http://www.nbcnewyork.com/entertainment/entertainment-news
/San-Diego-Comic-Con-2018-Announces-Full-Schedule-Thursday-Friday
-Saturday-Sunday-Highlights-Panels-Celebrities-Hall-H-487686031.html.

32 As recent discussions about relocating the convention or expanding the San Diego
Convention Center suggest, Comic-Con would most certainly continue to grow if
it could. Jared Aarons, "Mayor Stresses Need for Convention Center Expansion as
Comic-Con 2018 Begins," ABC10 News, last modified July 20, 2018, https://www
.10news.com/entertainment/comic-con/mayor-stresses-need-for-convention
-center-expansion-as-comic-con-2018-begins; Nicholas Eskey, "'San Diego
Comic-Con Staying until 2021' Says Mayor Kevin Faulconer," *The Beat*, last
modified July 1, 2017, http://www.comicsbeat.com/san-diego-comic-con-staying
-until-2021-says-mayor-kevin-faulkner/.

33 Rob Salkowitz, "How ECCC, 2018's First Mega Fan Con, Keeps Getting Bigger
without Going over the Top," *Forbes*, last modified March 1, 2018, https://www
.forbes.com/sites/robsalkowitz/2018/03/01/how-eccc-2018s-first-mega-fan-con
-keeps-getting-bigger-without-going-over-the-top/; John Wenzel, "Denver Comic
Con Reveals Record Attendance, Sets 2017 Dates," *Denver Post*, last modified
July 28, 2016, https://www.denverpost.com/2016/07/28/denver-comic-con-2016
-attendance-2017-dates/; "About Us," Fan Expo Canada, last modified 2018,
https://www.fanexpocanada.com/en/about-us/about-us.html; McKenzie Romero,
"Salt Lake Comic Con Seeks Balance in Its 5-Year Anniversary," Deseret News, last
modified September 29, 2017, https://www.deseretnews.com/article/865689520
/Salt-Lake-Comic-Con-seeks-balance-in-its-5-year-anniversary.html; Jamie Lovett,

"New York Comic Con Was Attended by 151,000 People, Surpasses San Diego," ComicBook.com, last modified October 13, 2014, http://comicbook.com/2014/10 /13/new-york-comic-con-was-attended-by-151-000-people-surpasses-san-/.

The New York Comic-Con was first held in 2006 and is not to be confused with the 1964 New York Comicon described earlier.

34 Crystalyn Hodgkins, "Comic Market 91 Attracts 550,000 Attendees across 3 Days," Anime News Netword, last modified December 31, 2016, http://www .animenewsnetwork.com/daily-briefs/2016-12-31/comic-market-91-attracts-550000 -attendees-across-3-days/.110518; Nick Vivarelli, "Italy's Lucca Comics and Games Festival Celebrates 50 Years," *Variety*, last modified October 28, 2016, https:// variety.com/2016/biz/festivals/italys-lucca-comics-and-games-festival-celebrates -15-years-1201900452/.

35 Rob Salkowitz, "How San Diego Comic-Con Became Fandom's Super-Brand," *Forbes*, last modified July 1, 2016, https://www.forbes.com/sites/robsalkowitz/2016 /07/01/the-business-of-comic-con-sdccs-david-glanzer-on-branding-and -expanding/.

36 Rowe, "Comic-Con Confidential."

37 Hiroaki Tamagawa notes that as an event focusing on fan-produced manga (doujin), Comic Market "is fundamentally different from the typical fan convention organized in the United States and Europe" and is "organized primarily for the distribution of doujin, not for panels, viewing anime, or trafficking in other kinds of merchandise." Hiroaki Tamagawa, "Comic Market as a Space for Self-Expression in Otaku Culture," in *Fandom Unbound: Otaku Culture in a Connected World,* ed. Mizuko Ito, Daisuke Okabe, and Izumi Tsiju (New Haven, CT: Yale University Press, 2012), 107.

While Japanese manga is the most prominent presence at the Lucca convention, Hollywood promotion has also become a feature in recent years. Nick Vivarelli, "Lucca Comics & Games Festival Draws Hollywood Majors to Geek Mecca," *Variety*, last modified October 29, 2015, https://variety.com/2015/scene/festivals /lucca-comics-games-festival-anime-manga-mamoru-oshii-1201628884/.

38 Bolling and Smith, *It Happens at Comic-Con*, 10.

39 "History | Dragoncon," Dragon Con, last modified 2018, http://www.dragoncon .org/?q=history.

40 Italy's Lucca Comics and Games, founded in 1966, predates the San Diego Comic-Con by four years. Vivarelli, "Italy's Lucca Comics and Games Festival."

41 For example, Emerald City Comic Con was founded in 2003, the New York Comic Con began in 2006, and the Denver and Salt Lake City Comic Cons held their first conventions in 2012. Fan Expo Canada dates back earlier than the other conventions in this group, beginning as the Canadian National Comic Book Expo in 1995. Organizers gradually added separate sections, including the Anime Expo (1998), Science Fiction Expo (1999), Horror Expo (2003), and Gaming Expo (2005), until the convention was rebranded in 2006 as Fan Expo, subsuming all these intersecting areas. "About Us."

42 The Denver Comic Con is produced by a nonprofit company called Pop Culture Classroom. Christina Angel, "All Comic Cons Are Not Created Equal: How DCC Is Different," Denver Comic Con, last modified February 14, 2018, https:// denvercomiccon.com/blog/all_comic_cons_are_not_created_equal_how_dcc_is _different/.

43 "Our Shows," ReedPop, last modified 2018, http://www.reedpop.com/Events/. For more on ReedPop, see Rob Salkowitz, "From Rebels to Empire: How Reedpop Is Taking Fan Conventions Global," *Forbes*, last modified April 14, 2017, https://www .forbes.com/sites/robsalkowitz/2017/04/14/in-the-galaxy-of-fan-conventions-the -force-is-strong-with-this-one/.

Other notable companies include Informa and Wizard World. Informa is an events and publishing company, which owns Routledge and Tayor & Francis, among other academic publishers. Their subsidiary, Informa Canada, owns the Fan Expo brand and runs the Toronto convention as well as conventions in Calgary, Edmonton, Vancouver, Boston, Dallas, Tampa, and Orlando, and the Middle East Games Con in Abu Dhabi. Wizard World published fan-oriented magazines like *Wizard* and *Toy World* before shuttering that part of their business and focusing exclusively on fan conventions in 2011. In 2018, Wizard World organized seventeen conventions in cities around the United States. "Informa Exhibitions—Our Events," last modified 2018, https://www.informaexhibitions.com/en/about-us /ourevents.html; Heidi MacDonald, "Wizard World Announces 17 Shows for 2018 While Postponing Five," Comics Beat, last modified September 29, 2017, http:// www.comicsbeat.com/wizard-world-announces-17-shows-for-2018-while -postponing-five/.

44 "Reedpop on the SDCC-SLCC Lawsuit," Comic Con Guide, last modified December 11, 2018, http://www.comicconguide.com/2017/12/nycc-and-other -reedpop-events-will-stay.html.

45 Shel Dorf, "Things I Like to Remember," in *Comic Buyer's Guide 1994 Annual: The Standard Reference for Today's Collector*, ed. Don Thompson and Maggie Thompson (Iola WI: Krause Publications, 1994), 27.

46 San Diego Comic Convention Inc., "Articles of Incorporation of San Diego Comic Convention." August 4, 1975, Series VII: Comic-Con Committee Paperwork, Folder 12, Box 3, Shel Dorf Collection, San Diego History Center.

47 Jeff McDonald, "Comic-Con Is Pretty Profitable, for a Non-Profit," *San Diego Union-Tribune*, last modified July 20, 2016, http://www.sandiegouniontribune.com /news/watchdog/sdut-comic-con-non-profit-2016jul20-story.html.

48 San Diego Comic Convention Inc., *Comic-Con: 40 Years*, 19.

49 "Comic-Con Committee Paperwork." February 6, 1972, Series IV: Comic-Con Committee Paperwork, Folder 12, Box 3, Shel Dorf Collection, San Diego History Center; "San Diego Comic Convention," ProPublica, last modified 2018, https:// projects.propublica.org/nonprofits/.

50 In addition to this labor, the organization pays five independent contracting firms specializing in staffing, security, and convention management between six hundred thousand and over a million dollars each for their services. "San Diego Comic Convention."

In October 2014, Comic-Con's president, John Rogers, quit his telecommunications job to work full time at the nonprofit; however, his weekly hours number twenty-five on Comic-Con's 2015 tax return. Brooks Barnes and Michael Cieply, "A Comic Convention Bursts Its Boundaries," *New York Times*, July 23, 2010; "San Diego Comic Convention."

51 San Diego Comic Convention Inc., *Comic-Con: 40 Years*, 19.

52 John Wilkens, "Comic-Con's Charity Status Draws Questions," *San Diego Union-Tribune*, July 25, 2007; Ken Stone, "Nonprofit Comic-Con Reports Nearly

$10 Million Cash in the Bank," LemonGrovePatch, last modified March 26, 2012, http://lemongrove.patch.com/articles/comic-conwith-net-assets-of-7-millionpays -city-no-business-license-fees; McDonald, "Comic-Con Is Pretty Profitable."

53 McDonald, "Comic-Con Is Pretty Profitable."

54 While APE centered on "small publishing companies, self-publishers, and creators working in the alternative and independent side of the comics industry," Wonder-Con is smaller in size and reach than Comic-Con, but offers similar features, including the presence of Hollywood promotion. In 2012, Comic-Con moved WonderCon from the Bay Area to Anaheim, and the event continues to grow in size and scope. San Diego Comic Convention Inc., *Comic-Con: 40 Years*, 112, 162; "Mini Comic-Con Convention Coming to Anaheim," *Orange County Register*, last modified September 15, 2011, https://www.ocregister.com/2011/09/15/mini-comic -con-convention-coming-to-anaheim/.

55 "#23: Announcing the Comic-Con Museum!" *Toucan: The Official Comic-Con Blog*, last modified July 11, 2018, https://www.comic-con.org/toucan/23 -announcing-comic-con-museum.

56 Josh Spector, "Hollywood Shows Its Stuff, Courts Crowd at Comic-Con," *Hollywood Reporter*, July 21, 2003.

57 While it was and still is standard practice for celebrities (often B-list, or below) to schedule appearances at Comic-Con (and comic conventions, in general) for the purpose of selling autographs or speaking on panels, this kind of presence is more accurately a kind of self-promotion that uses the convention circuit as an additional source of income. For more on this practice, see Lesley Goldberg, "Stars Getting Rich Off Fan Conventions: How to Take Home 'Garbage Bags Full of $20s,'" *Hollywood Reporter*, last modified September 29, 2016, https://www.hollywood reporter.com/live-feed/stars-getting-rich-fan-conventions-933062.

These kinds of appearances are different from the industry promotion identified in the *Hollywood Reporter* article, which suggests all three celebrities were attending to promote upcoming work. This is most evident in Paul Verhoven's case, as the studio, Sony, is even mentioned alongside the note about his preview of *Starship Troopers* (1997). George Johnston, "San Diego Comic Con Draws Hit Hungry H'wood." *Hollywood Reporter*, July 22, 1997.

58 David Glanzer. "Press Release: Comic Con International Enjoys Increased Media Attention." San Diego Comic-Con, Michigan State Library Comic Arts Collection.

59 Thomas J. McLean, "Comics, H'wood Coalesce," *Daily Variety*, July 23, 2001, 18.

60 Gina McIntyre, "H'wood Presence at Comic-Con Book Outing," *Hollywood Reporter*, August 5, 2002.

61 Ben Fritz, "Geek Chic . . . but 'Netsters Wary of Showbiz Wooing." *Variety*, August 2–8, 2004.

62 Scott Bowles, "Comic-Con Illustrates Genre's Rising Influence," *USA Today*, July 26, 2004; Nick Nunziata, "The Birth of Hype," CNN.com, last modified 27 July, 2004, http://www.cnn.com/2004/SHOWBIZ/Movies/07/27/comic.con /index.html.

63 Nunziata, "The Birth of Hype." See also Ben Fritz and Marc Graser, "Drawing H'w'd Interest," *Daily Variety*, July 22, 2004, 19; Borys Kit, "Sith Unveiling Wows Comic-Con Crowd," *Hollywood Reporter*, July 26, 2004; Peter Bart, "Geek Chic: Hollywood Corrals Nerd Herd . . . ," *Variety*, August 2–8, 2004, 1, 3; Laura M.

Holson, "Can Little-Known Heroes Be Hollywood Hits?" *New York Times*, July 26, 2004; John Horn, "Studios Take a Read on Comic Book Gathering; Hollywood Courts a Genre's Enthusiasts, Who Can Raise or Lower Movie's Fortunes," *Los Angeles Times*, July 26, 2004; Johanna Schneller, "Pradas Woo the Pocket Protectors," *Globe and Mail*, August 20, 2004; Susan Wloszczyna and Ann Oldenburg, "Geek Chic; Nerd Is the Word for Popularity in a Wired World," *USA Today*, October 23, 2003; Rebecca Winters Keegan, "Movies: Boys Who Like Toys," *Time*, last modified April 19, 2007, http://www.time.com/time/magazine/article /0,9171,1612687,00.html; Sandro Monetti, "And the Geek Shall Inherit the Earth . . ." *Sunday Express*, July 25, 2010; Lev Grossman, "The Geek Shall Inherit the Earth," Time.com, last modified September 25, 2005, http://www.time.com /time/magazine/article/0,9171,1109317,00.html; Fritz, "Geek Chic . . . but 'Netsters Wary."

64 Bart, "Geek Chic: Hollywood Corrals Nerd Herd . . ."; Fritz, "Geek Chic . . . but 'Netsters Wary."

65 Alex Ben Block and Lucy Autrey Wilson, *George Lucas' Blockbusting* (New York: HarperCollins, 2010), 810–897; Tino Balio, *Hollywood in the New Millennium*, International Screen Industries (London: Palgrave Macmillan on behalf of the British Film Institute, 2013).

66 Balio, 25–26.

67 Graser, "H'w'd Woos Nerd Herd."

68 According to the San Diego Convention Center's website, visitors attended Comic-Con from more than eighty countries around the world. Barbara Moreno, "San Diego Convention Center Welcomes Comic-Con 2018 | San Diego Convention Center," San Diego Convention Center, last modified July 18, 2018, https://visitsandiego.com/2018/07/san-diego-convention-center-welcomes-comic -con-2018.

69 Graser, "H'w'd Woos Nerd Herd."

70 "Swag" is a common term that is used to describe free promotional giveaways, often at conventions and trade shows.

71 Pierre Bourdieu, *Distinction: A Social Critique of the Judgement of Taste* (Cambridge, MA: Harvard University Press, 1984), 471.

72 See, for example, Nadine Hennings, Klaus-Peter Wiedmann, and Christiane Klarmann, "Luxury Brands in the Digital Age—Exclusivity Versus Ubiquity," *Marketing Review St. Gallen* 29, no. 1 (2012); John C. Groth and Stephen W. McDaniel, "The Exclusive Value Principle: The Basis for Prestige Racing," *Journal of Consumer Marketing* 10, no. 1 (1993).

73 Nick Couldry, *Media Rituals: A Critical Approach* (New York: Routledge, 2003), 2.

74 Nick Couldry, *The Place of Media Power: Pilgrims and Witnesses of the Media Age*, Comedia (London; New York: Routledge, 2000), 4–5.

75 Michael Czeiszperger, "Comic-Con Registration Sells 130,000 Tickets in 90 Minutes without a Hitch," PRWeb, last modified June 12, 2014, https://www.prweb .com/releases/2014/06/prweb11931964.htm; Germain Lussier, "The Crazy Lengths People Go to for San Diego Comic Con," io9, last modified July 6, 2015, https://io9 .gizmodo.com/the-crazy-lengths-people-go-to-for-san-diego-comic-con -1715847049.

76 Gilbert, "Live from Hall H," 361. For example, in 2016 and 2017, the SYFY channel produced a show called *SYFY Live From Comic-Con*, which gave home audiences a

glimpse inside the convention. In 2018, much of this coverage shifted to the channel's online news outlet SyFy Wire. "Watch: Here's What We're Doing for San Diego Comic-Con 2018," SYFY Wire, last modified July 15, 2018, http://www.syfy .com/syfywire/watch-heres-what-were-doing-for-san-diego-comic-con-2018.

77 Jenkins, Ford, and Green, *Spreadable Media*.

78 Joseph B. Pine II and James H. Gilmore, *The Experience Economy* (Boston, MA.: Harvard Business Review Press, 2011).

79 Pine and Gilmore, 1–3.

80 I discuss the Exhibit Hall, retail, and Comic-Con Exclusives at length in chapter 4.

81 While Bourdieu's notion of cultural capital operates as the framework through which to describe the accumulation of knowledge, taste, and status, both material and immaterial, in more bourgeois cultural formations, scholars like John Fiske, Matt Hills, and Sarah Thornton point to the ways that cultural capital functions in popular culture, fan, and subcultural formations. Similarly delineated by socially constructed limits, however, we might think of the lines between these cultural spheres as somewhat malleable themselves. Bourdieu, *Distinction*; Bourdieu, "The Forms of Capital," in *Handbook of Theory and Research for the Sociology of Education*, ed. John G. Richardson (Westport, CT: Greenwood Press, 1986); John Fiske, "The Cultural Economy of Fandom," in *The Adoring Audience: Fan Culture and Popular Media*, ed. Lisa A. Lewis (New York: Routledge, 1992); Sarah Thornton, *Club Cultures: Music, Media, and Subcultural Capital*, 1st U.S. ed., Music/Culture (Hanover: University Press of New England, 1996); Matt Hills, *Fan Cultures* (London: Routledge, 2002), 46–64.

82 Karl Marx, *Capital Volume II* (London: Penguin Classics, 1992), 246.

83 Pine II and Gilmore, *The Experience Economy*, 17; Michael Hardt, "Affective Labor," *boundary 2* 26, no. 2 (1999).

84 Mark Jancovich, "Cult Fictions: Cult Movies, Subcultural Capital and the Production and Distribution of Cultural Distinctions," *Cultural Studies* 16, no. 2 (2002): 320.

85 Jenkins, Ford, and Green, *Spreadable Media*, 145.

86 Jenkins, Ford, and Green, 145.

87 Matt Hills uses the launch of *Doctor Who*'s fiftieth anniversary "The Day of the Doctor" trailer at Comic-Con as evidence of tensions between exclusivity and publicity, particularly in the global television landscape. Matt Hills, *Doctor Who: The Unfolding Event—Marketing, Merchandising and Mediatizing a Brand Anniversary* (New York: Palgrave Macmillan, 2015), 30–32.

88 Bourdieu, *Distinction*, 6.

89 As Gray, Sandvoss, and Harrington point out, after the first wave, fan studies' scholars continued to build on Bourdieu's work as a way to emphasize "the replication of social and cultural hierarchies within fan cultures and subcultures." Jonathan Gray, Cornel Sandvoss, and C. Lee Harrington, "Introduction: Why Study Fans?" in *Fandom: Identities and Communities in a Mediated World*, ed. Jonathan Gray, Cornel Sandvoss, and C. Lee Harrington (New York: New York University Press, 2007), 1–7; Gray, Sandvoss, and Harrington, "Introduction: Why Still Study Fans?" in *Fandom: Identities and Communities in a Mediated World*, ed. Jonathan Gray, Cornel Sandvoss, and C. Lee Harrington (New York: New York University Press, 2017), 1–5; Henry Jenkins, *Textual Poachers: Television Fans &*

Participatory Culture (New York: Routledge, 1992), 16–18, 60–62; Fiske, "The Cultural Economy of Fandom."

90 Gray, Sandvoss, and Harrington, "Introduction: Why Still Study Fans?" 3.

91 This status quo, as Quail points out, is rooted in hegemonic constructions of gender, race, and sexuality. Suzanne Scott has similarly identified the hegemonic nature of intersecting discourses about the cultural power of fanboys, while Kristina Busse comments on the gendered hierarchies that circulate in discourses about fan activities. Christine Quail, "Nerds, Geeks, and the Hip/Square Dialectic in Contemporary Television," *Television & New Media* 12, no. 5 (2011): 465–467; Suzanne Scott, "Revenge of the Fanboy: Convergence Culture and the Politics of Incorporation" (PhD diss., University of Southern California, 2011); Busse, "Geek Hierarchies."

92 Borys Kit, "Newly Cool Geeks Rule Comic-Con," *Hollywood Reporter*, July 19, 2006.

93 See also Marc Graser, "Geek Vibe Gives Way to Mainstream Fare," *Daily Variety*, July 24, 2008; Borys Kit, "Mainstream Drowning in Comic-Con's Geek Chic," *Hollywood Reporter*, last modified July 24, 2008, http://www.hollywoodreporter .com/news/mainstream-drowning-comic-cons-geek-116236; Brooks Barnes and Michael Cieply, "A Comic Convention Bursts Its Boundaries," *New York Times*, July 23, 2010.

94 It is worth considering, in fact, whether the idea of mainstream culture has ever been separate from fan culture at all. As Sarah Thornton argues, "the myth of the mainstream" ultimately reduces the notion of mainstream culture to something that subcultural groups subvert or oppose and, in doing so, produce an oversimplified dichotomy that explains little about either group. Thornton, *Club Cultures*, 14, 93–94.

95 As I discuss in chapter 3, discourses about the power of Comic-Con audiences also highlighted the notion that they threaten a film's success by either liking it *too* much and inflating its perceived value or by not liking it enough and damaging its reputation. See, for example, Barnes and Cieply, "Movie Studios Reassess Comic-Con," *New York Times*, June 12, 2011.

96 Eileen Meehan, "Leisure or Labor?: Fan Ethnography and Political Economy," in *Consuming Audiences? Production and Reception in Media Research*, ed. Ingunn Hagen and Janet Wasko (Cresskill, NJ: Hampton Press, Inc., 2000)," 88.

97 William Booth, "At Comic-Con, Nerd Mentality Rules the Day; Hollywood Now Woos Once-Scorned Genre Fans," *Washington Post*, July 19, 2005, C.01.

98 Suzanne Scott, "The Powers That Squee: Orlando Jones and Intersectional Fan Studies," in *Fandom: Identities and Communities in a Mediated World*, ed. Jonathan Gray, Cornel Sandvoss, and C. Lee Harrington (New York: New York University Press, 2017).

99 Kristen J. Warner, *The Cultural Politics of Colorblind TV Casting* (New York: Routledge, 2015), 12.

100 Philip M. Napoli, *Audience Evolution: New Technologies and the Transformation of Media Audiences* (New York: Columbia University Press, 2011), 3.

101 Rebecca Wanzo, "View of African American Acafandom and Other Strangers: New Genealogies of Fan Studies," *Transformative Works and Cultures* 20 (2015), http://journal.transformativeworks.org/index.php/twc/article/view/699/538.; Kristen J. Warner, "ABC's *Scandal* and Black Women's Fandom," in *Copcakes,*

Pinterest, and Ladyporn: Feminized Popular Culture in the Early Twenty-First Century, ed. Elana Levine (Urbana: University of Illinois Press, 2015), 32–50; Scott, "Revenge of the Fanboy"; Mel Stanfill, "View of Doing Fandom, (Mis)Doing Whiteness: Heteronormativity, Racialization, and the Discursive Construction of Fandom | Transformative Works and Cultures," *Transformative Works and Cultures* 8 (2011), http://journal.transformativeworks.org/index.php/twc/article/view/256/243; Busse, "Geek Hierarchies."

102 Derek Johnson, "Fantagonism, Franchising, and Industry Management of Fan Privilege," in *The Routledge Companion to Media Fandom*, ed. Melissa A. Click and Suzanne Scott (New York: Routledge, 2018), 396; Derek Johnson, "From the Ruins: Neomasculinity, Media Franchising, and Struggles over Industrial Reproduction of Culture," *Communication Culture & Critique* 11 (2018): 85–99.

William Proctor and Bridget Kies link "toxic fan practices" to the contradictions within popular culture and fan communities. "On the one hand," they explain, "some see the move toward more inclusive representation as proactive and reflective of genuine social change. Others, however, feel an increasing sense of disempowerment at their loss of privileged status, and social media can . . . serve as a useful tool, allowing them to attempt to overcome a status loss by tweeting, blogging, doxing, and creating niche movements with similarly disempowered fans." Ultimately, they argue, "toxic behaviors" grow out of the same contradictions embedded in the geek chic discourses that I describe in this chapter, "and are often the result of hegemonic elites feeling as though they are marginalized or in the minority." It is important to note, however, that while these attitudes are not new to fan culture, "discourses labeled as toxic are a relatively recent emergence resulting from the particular circumstances of our time." William Proctor and Bridget Kies, "Editors' Introduction: On Toxic Fan Practices and the New Culture Wars," *Participations Journal of Audience & Reception Studies* 15, no. 1 (2018): 130, 135.

For more scholarship on toxic fandom, see Anastasia Salter and Bridget Blodgett, *Toxic Geek Masculinity in Media: Sexism, Trolling, and Identity Policing* (Cham, Switzerland: Springer International Publishing, 2017); Gwendelyn S. Nisbett, "Don't Mess with My Happy Place: Understanding Misogyny in Fandom Communities," in *Mediating Misogyny: Gender, Technology, and Harassment*, ed. Jacqueline Ryan Vickery and Tracy Everbach (Cham, Switzerland: Springer International Publishing, 2018), 171–188; Carrielynn D. Reinhard, *Fractured Fandoms: Contentious Communication in Fan Communities* (London: Rowman & Littlefield, 2018).

103 Todd VanDerWerff, "A Day inside Comic-Con's Hall H: Worshiping in the Ultimate Movie Church," Grantland, last modified July 22, 2013, http://grantland.com/hollywood-prospectus/a-day-inside-comic-cons-hall-h-worshipping-in-the-ultimate-movie-church/; Melanie E. S. Kohnen, "'The Power of Geek': Fandom as Gendered Commodity at Comic-Con," *Creative Industries Journal* 7, no. 1 (2014): 76–77.

104 Johnson, "Fantagonism," 396.

105 As Johnson suggests, this notion of an audience function comparable to Michel Foucault's author function builds on the work of scholars like Ien Ang and Eileen Meehan. Derek Johnson, "Participation Is Magic: Collaboration, Authorial Legitimacy, and the Audience Function," in *A Companion to Media Authorship*, ed. Jonathan Gray and Derek Johnson (Malden, MA: John Wiley & Sons, 2013),

135–157; Ien Ang, *Desperately Seeking the Audience* (New York: Routledge, 1991); Michel Foucault, "What Is an Author?" in *Language, Counter-Memory, Practice: Selected Essays and Interviews*, ed. Donald F. Bouchard (Ithaca, NY: Cornell University Press, 1977), 113–138; Eileen Meehan, "Why We Don't Count," in *Logics of Television: Essays in Cultural Criticism*, ed. Patricia Mellencamp (Bloomington: Indiana University Press, 1990), 378–397.

106 Angela McRobbie, *Be Creative: Making a Living in the New Culture Industries* (Cambridge, UK; Malden, MA: Polity Press, 2015); John Thornton Caldwell, *Production Culture: Industrial Reflexivity and Critical Practice in Film and Television* (Durham, NC: Duke University Press, 2008).

107 Karla Peterson and James Herbert, "Around Here, the Geeks Decide What's Cool." *San Diego Union-Tribune*, July 19, 2006, A1.

108 Caldwell, *Production Culture*, 336.

109 Jonathan Gray, Cornel Sandvoss, and C. Lee Harrington also capture this ethos in their introduction to their 2007 collection *Fandom: Identities and Communities in a Mediated World*, writing, "rather than ridiculed, fan audiences are now wooed and championed by cultural industries, at least as long as their activities do not divert from principles of capitalist exchange and recognize industries' legal ownership of the object of fandom." Busse, "Geek Hierarchies," 77; Gray, Sandvoss, and Harrington, "Introduction: Why Study Fans?" 4.

110 Busse, "Geek Hierarchies."

111 Jenkins, *Convergence Culture*, 3.

112 Jenkins, 22.

113 Marc Graser, "H'wood Learns to Speak Geek," *Daily Variety*, July 24, 2008.

114 Graser, "H'w'd Woos Nerd Herd," 1.

115 Jenkins, *Convergence Culture*, 3; Tiziana Terranova, "Free Labor: Producing Culture for the Digital Economy," *Social Text* 18, no. 2 (2000): 37.

116 Trebor Scholz, *Digital Labor: The Internet as Playground and Factory* (New York: Routledge, 2013); Mel Stanfill and Megan Condis, "Fandom and/as Labor," *Transformative Works and Cultures*, 15 (2014), https://journal.transformativeworks.org/index.php/twc/article/view/593; Abigail De Kosnik, "Fandom as Free Labor," in *Digital Labor: The Internet as Playground and Factory*, ed. Trebor Scholz (New York: Routledge, 2012), 98–111; Vicki Mayer, *Below the Line: Producers and Production Studies in the New Television Economy* (Durham, NC: Duke University Press, 2011); Caldwell, *Production Culture*; Vicki Mayer, Miranda J. Banks, and John Thornton Caldwell, eds., *Production Studies: Cultural Studies of Media Industries* (New York: Routledge, 2009).

As Dallas Smythe famously put it, "the material reality under monopoly capitalism is that all non-sleeping time of most of the population is work time." Dallas W. Smythe, "Communications: Blindspot of Western Marxism," *Canadian Journal of Political and Social Theory* 1, no. 3 (1977): 3.

117 Maureen Ryan, "Only Connect: The Appeal of San Diego Comic-Con—the Watcher," *Chicago Tribune*, last modified July 9, 2009, 2012, http://featuresblogs.chicagotribune.com/entertainment_tv/2009/07/san-diego-comiccon.html.

118 See, for example, Derek Johnson, "After the Industry Turn: Can Production Studies Make an Audience Turn?" *Creative Industries Journal* 7, no. 1 (2014): 50–53; Vicki Mayer, "The Places Where Audience Studies and Production Studies Meet," *Television & New Media* 17, no. 8 (2016): 706–718; Jenkins, *Convergence Culture*;

Jenkins, Ford, and Green, *Spreadable Media*; Paul Booth, *Playing Fans: Negotiating Fandom and Media in the Digital Age* (Iowa City, IA: University of Iowa Press, 2015); Suzanne Scott, "Repackaging Fan Culture: The Regifting Economy of Ancillary Content Models," *Transformative Works and Cultures* 9 (2009). https://journal.transformativeworks.org/index.php/twc/article/view/150.

119 Smythe, "Communications"; Eileen Meehan, "Commodity Audience, Actual Audience: The Blindspot Debate," in *Illuminating the Blindspots: Essays Honoring Dallas W. Smythe*, ed. Janet Wasko, Vincent Mosco, and Manjunath Pendakur (Norwood, NJ: Ablex Publishing Corporation, 1993), 378–397; Eileen R. Meehan, *Why TV Is Not Our Fault: Television Programming, Viewers, and Who's Really in Control*, Critical Media Studies (Lanham, MD: Rowman & Littlefield, 2005).

120 Janet Wasko and Eileen Meehan, "Critical Crossroads or Parallel Routes?" *Cinema Journal* 52, no. 3 (2013), 150–157.

121 Jenkins, *Convergence Culture*, 3; Dallas Walker Smythe, *Dependency Road: Communications, Capitalism, Consciousness, and Canada* (Norwood, NJ: Ablex Pub. Corp., 1981), 23.

Chapter 1   Origin Stories

Epigraph: Mark Evanier, "The Timeless Jack Kirby," *Comic-Con International 2004 Souvenir Book*, 2004, 60–61.

1 As I explain in this chapter, Comic-Con was the product of a collective effort on the part of a number of fans in the San Diego area, which was initiated and spearheaded by Dorf. As one of only two adults involved in the founding of Comic-Con, Dorf signed all the necessary contracts with the first venue, the U.S. Grant Hotel. At the first Comic-Con, he was given the title of "founder and advisor," reflecting his many contributions. While Scott Shaw!, one of the other founding members of Comic-Con's organizing committee, has been critical of what he perceived to be Dorf's appropriation of the founder title in the context of a collective effort, I have not encountered any other significant evidence to suggest that the title was undeserved or heavily contested. Angela Carone and Maureen Cavanaugh, "The First Comic-Con," KPBS Public Media, last modified July 22, 2010, http://www.kpbs.org/news/2010/jul/22/first-comic-con/; Bill Schelly, *Founders of Comic Fandom: Profiles of 90 Publishers, Dealers, Collectors, Writers, Artists and Other Luminaries of the 1950s and 1960s* (Jefferson, NC: McFarland, 2010), 103; Scott Shaw!, "Cartoonist-at-Large #1: The 'Secret Origin' of San Diego's Comic-Con International," Jim Hill Media, last modified July 7, 2005, http://jimhillmedia.com/blogs/scott_shaw/archive/2005/07/07/1717.aspx; San Diego Comic Convention Inc., *Comic-Con: 40 Years of Artists, Writers, Fans & Friends* (San Francisco: Chronicle Books, 2009), 22; Mark Habegger, "Scott Shaw!" Comic-Con Kids, last modified 2013, http://comiccon.sdsu.edu/scott-shaw/.

2 The full recording of this interview is available online: "Recordings of the 1970 San Diego Comic-Con #1: Listen to Them Here!" Comic-Convention Memories, last modified January 8, 2010, http://www.comicconmemories.com/2010/01/08/recordings-of-the-1970-san-diego-comic-con-1-listen-to-them-here/.

3 Actual attendance at the event was closer to three hundred. David Glanzer, Gary Sassaman, and Jackie Estrada, *Comic-Con 40 Souvenir Book* (San Diego: San Diego Comic-Con International, 2009), 60.

4 These photos, taken by Shel Dorf in 1973 and 1974, also appear on the website Comic Convention Memories, which has a collection of hundreds of photos from Comic-Con's early years. "More 1973 San Diego Comic-Con Photos: Can You Identify People in the Pictures?" Comic-Convention Memories, last modified February 28, 2010, http://www.comicconmemories.com/2010/02/28/more-1973 -san-diego-comic-con-photos-can-you-identify-people-in-the-pictures/; "1974 San Diego Comic-Con Photos (Batch 2): Can You Identify People in the Pictures?" Comic-Convention Memories, last modified June 12, 2010, http://www .comicconmemories.com/2010/06/12/1974-san-diego-comic-con-photos-batch-2 -can-you-identify-people-in-the-pictures/; "1974 San Diego Comic-Con Photos (Batch 1): Can You Identify People in the Pictures?" Comic-Convention Memories, last modified May 31, 2010, http://www.comicconmemories.com/2010 /05/31/1974-san-diego-comic-con-photos-batch-1-can-you-identify-people-in-the -pictures/.

5 Rozanski is the owner of Mile High Comics, a large online comic book retailer and retail chain, based in Denver, Colorado.

6 Brian Lowry, "The Early Days of Comic-Con," *Variety*, last modified July 11, 2008, http://variety.com/2008/film/columns/the-early-days-of-comic-con-1117988845/.

7 There is, however, a certain irony to entertainment journalists, whose livelihood is tied to Hollywood promotion and PR, complaining about the prominence of such promotion at Comic-Con. Alexander Abad-Santos, "How the Nerds Lost Comic-Con," The Wire, last modified July 19, 2013, http://www.theatlanticwire .com/entertainment/2013/07/how-nerds-lost-comic-con/67304/.

8 John Rogers was Comic-Con's longest-serving president, having stepped into the role in 1986. Shortly after Comic-Con 2018, Rogers was diagnosed with brain cancer. He passed away on November 10, 2018. Maureen Lee Lenker, "John Rogers, President of Comic-Con International, Dies," *Entertainment Weekly*, last modified November 11, 2018, https://ew.com/comic-con/2018/11/11/john-rogers-president -comic-con-international-dies/.

9 "Comic-Con Talk Back, 2011," Panel, San Diego Comic-Con, San Diego, CA, July 24, 2011.

10 "About Comic-Con International," Comic-Con International: San Diego, last modified 2018, http://www.comic-con.org/about.

11 "John Wilkens, "Comic-Con's Shel Dorf Watches Sadly from the Sidelines as T-Shirts Trump Talent," *San Diego Union-Tribune*, July 16, 2006, E-1.

12 Dorf stopped attending Comic-Con 2001. Mark Evanier, "Comic-Con Founder Shel Dorf Remembered," *Los Angeles Times: Hero Complex*, last modified November 10, 2009, http://herocomplex.latimes.com/uncategorized/shel-dorf -remembered/.

13 Many such letters are housed at the Shel Dorf Collection at the San Diego History Center.

14 In 1992, for example, he sent the committee a photocopy of his message from the 1983 program book. Attached was a letter that read, "I am writing because sometimes it helps to know your early history. This message I wrote in 1983 is a recap of what went before. It reaffirms how I have always felt and continue to feel

about YOU, the volunteer worker." Shel Dorf. "Letter to Committee Members of San Diego Comic-Con, 1992." 1992, Series IX: Shel Dorf Correspondence, Folder 15, Box 3, Shel Dorf Collection, San Diego History Center; Jackie Estrada, ed. *San Diego Comic-Con Souvenir Book 1984* (San Diego: San Diego Comic Convention, Inc., 1984).

15 Also attached to this letter was a copy of the minutes from a directors' meeting in which the board voted to give their general manager a three thousand dollar raise and a three thousand dollar bonus. Several lines below, a motion was passed to reimburse Dorf for twelve dollars and sixty-two cents in postage after he mailed out souvenir books to "Friends of the Con." The money would only be supplied on the condition that he sent them a list of the names. It read, "Know one [*sic*] would care except that we have a Dept. to do mailings, he doesn't have a budget to do mailings or anything and he didn't ask first." Dorf's copy of the minutes also included handwritten notations. Both motions were marked with an exclamation point, punctuated by a note: "P.S. I've gone to my last Comic-Con." Shel Dorf. "Letter to San Diego Comic-Con Board of Directors, May 27, 1994." May 27 1994, Series IX: Shel Dorf Correspondence, Folder 15, Box 3, Shel Dorf Collection, San Diego History Center.

16 While the phrasing is slightly unclear, Dorf's assertion that "my praise far exceeded my criticism" is likely an attempt to clarify his feelings about Rogers and the other organizers, rather than a description of his actual actions. "Letter to John Rogers, August 9, 1999." August 9, 1999, Series IX: Shel Dorf Correspondence, Folder 15, Box 3, Shel Dorf Collection, San Diego History Center.

17 Evanier, "Comic-Con Founder."

18 Dorf struggled with money and wrote the following to a friend in 1994: "My family thinks I'm a real jerk and a failure in life for ending up flat broke while there is money from the con in three banks." Shel Dorf. "Letter to Harlan, October 24, 1996." October 24, 1996, Series IX: Shel Dorf Correspondence, Folder 15, Box 3, Shel Dorf Collection, San Diego History Center.

19 Glanzer, Sassaman, and Estrada, *Comic-Con 40 Souvenir Book*, 82; "San Diego's Golden State Comic-Con Program Book (Minicon)." March 21, 1970, Series I: Programs and Souvenir Books, Folder 1, Box 1, Shel Dorf Collection, San Diego History Center.

20 Karen Hellekson argues this "gift economy" is based on "giving, receiving, and reciprocity" among fans, but outside the realms of commercial value. Karen Hellekson, "A Fannish Field of Value: Online Fan Gift Culture," *Cinema Journal* 48, no. 3 (2009): 114.

21 Malcolm Schwartz and Shel Dorf, "Shel Dorf Q&A" in *1982 San Diego Comic-Con, Inc. Souvenir Book*, ed. Shel Dorf (San Diego: San Diego Comic-Con Inc., 1982); Wilkens, "Comic-Con's Shel Dorf Watches Sadly from the Sidelines as T-Shirts Trump Talent," E-1.

22 Henry Jenkins, *Convergence Culture: Where Old and New Media Collide* (New York: New York University Press, 2006).

23 Patricia Ventura, *Neoliberal Culture: Living with American Neoliberalism* (Burlington, VT: Ashgate Publishing Ltd., 2012), 2.

24 Ventura argues that characteristics of neoliberal culture "were ubiquitously present in the US" by the 1990s and had "reached a kind of maturation point" by the beginning of the twenty-first century. But in tracing the roots of this ideology,

Ventura also cites David Harvey's assertion that the origins of neoliberalism date back to 1978–1980, when key social and economic policy shifts were taking place around the globe. David Harvey, *A Brief History of Neoliberalism* (Oxford: Oxford University Press, 2005), 1; Ventura, *Neoliberal Culture*, 5.

25 Evanier, "The Timeless Jack Kirby," 6.

26 Paul Douglas Lopes, *Demanding Respect: The Evolution of the American Comic Book* (Philadelphia: Temple University Press, 2009), 93.

27 Jenkins, *Convergence Culture*; Mark Andrejevic, "Watching Television without Pity: The Productivity of Online Fans," *Television & New Media* 9, no. 24 (2008): 24–46; Roberta Pearson, "Fandom in the Digital Era," *Popular Communication: The International Journal of Media and Culture* 8, no. 1 (2010): 84–95; Shawna Feldmar Kidman, "Five Lessons for New Media from the History of Comics Culture," *International Journal of Learning and Media* 3, no. 4 (2012): 41–54.

28 Lopes, *Demanding Respect*, 2–3.

29 Matthew Pustz, *Comic Book Culture: Fanboys and True Believers,* Studies in Popular Culture (Jackson: University Press of Mississippi, 1999), 26–43.

30 Robert M. Overstreet, *The Comic Book Price Guide 1976–1977* (New York: Crown Publishers, Inc., 1976), 22; William Schelly, *The Golden Age of Comic Fandom* (Seattle: Hamster Press, 1995), 14.

31 Pustz, *Comic Book Culture*, 39; Schelly, *The Golden Age of Comic Fandom*, 13–14; Lopes, *Demanding Respect*, 51–56.

32 Francesca Coppa, "A Brief History of Media Fandom," in *Fan Fiction and Fan Communities in the Age of the Internet*, ed. Karen Hellekson and Kristina Busse (Jefferson, NC: McFarland), 42–43; Pustz, *Comic Book Culture*, 30.

33 This includes Ken Krueger, one of the founding organizers of the San Diego Comic-Con. San Diego Comic Convention Inc., *Comic-Con: 40 Years of Artists, Writers, Fans & Friends* (San Francisco: Chronicle Books, 2009), 22.

34 Overstreet, *The Comic Book Price Guide 1976–1977*, 22; Schelly, *The Golden Age of Comic Fandom*, 13, 18.

35 Maggie Curtis changed her name when she married Don Thompson in June 1962 and now goes by Maggie Thompson. Maggie Thompson, "June 23, 1962," The Official Website of Maggie Thompson, last modified June 23, 2008, http://www .maggiethompson.com/2008/06/june-23-1962.html; "Fanzine Library: Comic Art #1 (Spring 1961)," The Official Website of Maggie Thompson, last modified August 8, 2010, http://www.maggiethompson.com/1970/01/fanzine-library-comic -art-1-spring-1961.html.

36 Schelly, *The Golden Age of Comic Fandom*, 21; Thompson, "Fanzine Library: Comic Art #1 (Spring 1961)."

37 "Fanzine Library: Comic Art #1 (Spring 1961)."

38 "About Comic-Con International."

39 Scott McCloud, *Understanding Comics: The Invisible Art* (Northampton, MA: Tundra Pub., 1993); Thierry Groensteen, *The System of Comics*, trans. Bart Beaty and Nick Nguyen (Jackson: University Press of Mississippi, 2007).

40 Jenkins, *Convergence Culture*, 2.

41 Kidman, "Five Lessons for New Media," 42.

42 Henry Jenkins, *Textual Poachers: Television Fans & Participatory Culture* (New York: Routledge, 1992); Jonathan Gray, Cornel Sandvoss, and C. Lee Harrington,

Fandom: Identities and Communities in a Mediated World (New York: New York University Press, 2007), 1–4; Kidman, "Five Lessons for New Media," 45–46.

43 "Five Lessons for New Media," 45; Lopes, *Demanding Respect*, 93.

44 Overstreet, *The Comic Book Price Guide 1976–1977*, 22.

45 Pustz, *Comic Book Culture*, 44.

46 *Alter Ego* ran eleven issues between 1961 and 1978 and was revived by Roy Thomas as a magazine (though still describing itself as a fanzine) published by TwoMorrows Publishing in 1997 and was still in circulation as of 2018. Bill Schelly, "A Brief History of Alter Ego (the Magazine)," Bill Schelly, writer, last modified 2014, http://www.billschelly.net/alter-ego/; "Alter Ego," TwoMorrows Publishing, last modified 2016, http://twomorrows.com/index.php?main_page=index&cPath=98_55.

47 Schelly, *The Golden Age of Comic Fandom*, 10.

48 Schelly, *Founders of Comic Fandom*, 202.

49 Schelly, *The Golden Age of Comic Fandom*, 24.

50 Kidman, "Five Lessons for New Media," 45; Schelly, *Founders of Comic Fandom*, 27.

51 Julius Schwartz, "Introduction by Julius Schwartz," in *Alter Ego: The Best of the Legendary Comics Fanzine*, ed. Roy Thomas and Jerry Bails (Raleigh, NC: TwoMorrows Publishing, 2008), 4.

52 Kidman, "Five Lessons for New Media," 45.

53 Jean-Paul Gabilliet, *Of Comics and Men: A Cultural History of American Comic Books* (Jackson: University Press of Mississippi, 2005), 263; Pustz, *Comic Book Culture*, 182.

54 Will Brooker, *Batman Unmasked: Analyzing a Cultural Icon* (New York: Continuum, 2001), 252.

55 Benjamin Woo, "Erasing the Lines between Leisure and Labor: Creative Work in the Comics World," *Spectator* 35, no. 2 (2015): 57–64.

56 Schwartz, "Introduction by Julius Schwartz," 4.

57 Lopes, *Demanding Respect*, 63.

58 Kidman, "Five Lessons for New Media," 46.

59 Melissa Gregg, "Learning to (Love) Labor: Production Cultures and the Affective Turn," *Communication and Critica/Cultural Studies* 6, no. 2 (2009): 209.

60 Michael Hardt, "Affective Labor," *boundary 2* 26, no. 2 (1999): 97–98.

61 Peter Bart, "Advertising: Superman Faces New Hurdles," *New York Times*, September 23, 1962, 166.

62 Though Maggie Thompson (née Curtis) was one of a small number of women who were, as Schelly puts it "central to the founding of comic fandom," their contributions do not seem to garner the same level of recognition in these histories and are in need of more sustained research and attention. Schelly, *Founders of Comic Fandom*, 20, 89; Tom Spurgeon, "Jerry Bails, 1933–2006," *The Comics Reporter*, last modified November 24, 2006, http://www.comicsreporter.com/index.php/jerry_bails_1933_2006/.

63 Bails originally called his organization The Academy of Comic-Book Arts and Sciences, a title that was likely inspired by Hollywood's own award-granting institution, The Academy of Motion Picture Arts and Sciences. But shortly after founding the organization, he changed the name to The Academy of Comic-Book Fans and Collectors, which, according to Bill Schelly, "he felt was less pretentious and more accurate." Schelly, *Founders of Comic Fandom*, 23.

64 Kidman, "Five Lessons for New Media," 45.

65 Schelly, *Founders of Comic Fandom*, 23–24.

66 Dallas W. Smythe, "Communications: Blindspot of Western Marxism," *Canadian Journal of Political and Social Theory* 1, no. 3 (1977); Eileen Meehan, "Leisure or Labor?: Fan Ethnography and Political Economy," in *Consuming Audiences? Production and Reception in Media Research*, ed. Ingunn Hagen and Janet Wasko (Cresskill, NJ: Hampton Press, Inc., 2000); Tiziana Terranova, "Free Labor: Producing Culture for the Digital Economy," *Social Text* 18, no. 2 (2000).

67 Brooker, *Batman Unmasked*, 250–253.

68 Kidman, "Five Lessons for New Media," 46.

69 Schelly, *Founders of Comic Fandom*, 129–130.

70 "February 1966," The Marvel Comics Bullpen Bulletins Index, last modified June 16, 2007, http://bullpenbulletins.blogspot.com/2007/06/february-1966.html.

71 Pustz, *Comic Book Culture*, 46, 54.

72 Schelly, *Founders of Comic Fandom*, 130.

73 Brooke Erin Duffy, "The Romance of Work: Gender and Aspirational Labour in the Digital Culture Industries," *International Journal of Cultural Studies* 19, no. 4 (2015): 1–17.

74 Kathleen Kuehn and Thomas F. Corrigan, "Hope Labor: The Role of Employment Prospects in Online Social Production," *Political Economy of Communication* 1, no. 1 (2013): 10.

75 Kidman, "Five Lessons for New Media," 46.

76 Work-for-hire contracts, in which artists sign over the rights to their creations to their employer, were and are quite common in the comics industry. The United States Copyright Act defines works made for hire as "a work prepared by an employee within the scope of his or her employment" or "a work specially commissioned for use . . . if the parties expressly agree in a written instrument signed by them that work shall be considered a work made for hire." United States Copyright Office, "Works Made for Hire," copyright.gov, last modified September, 2012, http://www.copyright.gov/circs/circ09.pdf.

77 Abigail De Kosnik, "Fandom as Free Labor," in *Digital Labor: The Internet as Playground and Factory*, ed. Trebor Scholz (New York: Routledge, 2012), 110.

78 Gabilliet, *Of Comics and Men*, 117.

79 Lopes, *Demanding Respect*, 88, 94; Schelly, *Founders of Comic Fandom*, 113–117.

80 While multiple scholars and historians cite this event as the earliest known comic convention, the name of the event is unclear. In *The Power of Comics*, Duncan and Smith refer to it as the "Triple Fan Fair"; however, this was the name Shel Dorf gave to the 1965 Detroit convention. For the sake of clarity, I refer to it here as the Hotel Tuller convention. Randy Duncan and Matthew J. Smith, *The Power of Comics: History, Form and Culture* (New York: Continuum, 2009), 183; Pustz, *Comic Book Culture*, 158; Matthew J. Smith, "Comic-Con International," in *Icons of the American Comic Book: From Captain America to Wonder Woman*, ed. Randy Duncan and Matthew J. Smith (Santa Barbara, CA: ABC-CLIO, 2013), 137; Schelly, *The Golden Age of Comic Fandom*, 71, 77.

81 Smith, "Comic-Con International," 137.

82 Schelly, *The Golden Age of Comic Fandom*, 77; Schelly, *Founders of Comic Fandom*, 103.

83 Attracting comic pros to the New York convention was much easier, as the industry's two biggest players, Marvel and DC, were both headquartered in the city. Pustz, *Comic Book Culture*, 158–159; Smith, "Comic-Con International," 137; Schelly, *The Golden Age of Comic Fandom*, 71–74.

84 Schelly, *The Golden Age of Comic Fandom*, 72.

85 Randy Duncan, Matthew J. Smith, and Paul Levitz, *The Power of Comics: History, Form, and Culture*, 2nd ed. (New York: Bloomsbury, 2015), 279.

86 Kidman, "Five Lessons for New Media," 49.

87 Kidman, 49.

88 Jenkins, *Convergence Culture*, 134; Kidman, "Five Lessons for New Media," 45.

89 Richard Butner, "Richard! A Message from the Chairman," in *San Diego Comic-Con Souvenir Book 1975*, ed. Shel Dorf (San Diego: San Diego Comic-Con, 1975).

90 San Diego Comic Convention Inc., *Comic-Con: 40 Years*, 22.

91 San Diego Comic Convention Inc., 22; Shaw!, "Cartoonist-at-Large #1."

92 This group was also unofficially known as the Woodchucks. "San Diego's Golden State Comic-Con Program Book 1970." August, 1970, Series I: Programs & Souvenir Books, Folder 1, Box 1, Shel Dorf Collection, San Diego History Center; San Diego Comic Convention Inc., *Comic-Con: 40 Years*.

93 As Scott Shaw! (one of the original members) recalled, "the group consisted of pros and fans and we were certainly profane at times." Shaw!, "Cartoonist-at-Large #1."

94 Shaw!; "40th-Anniversary Secret Origins of Comic-Con Panel," Shel Dorf Tribute, last modified October 10, 2009, http://www.sheldorftribute.com/2009/10/10/40th-anniversary-secret-origins-of-comic-con-panel/.

95 Mike Towry, "The Birthplace of Comic-Con International," Comic-Convention Memories, last modified February 15, 2010, http://www.comicconmemories.com/2010/02/15/the-birthplace-of-comic-con-international/; Jackie Estrada, ed. *20th Annual San Diego Comic-Con Souvenir Program Book* (San Diego: San Diego Comic Convention Inc., 1989), 71; R. C. Harvey, "Shel Dorf, Founder," in *Comic-Con 40 Souvenir Book*, ed. David Glanzer, Gary Sassaman, and Jackie Estrada (San Diego: San Diego Comic-Con International, 2009), 40–41; Peter Rowe, "From Little Shows Big Cons Grow," *San Diego Union-Tribune*, last modified July 19, 2009, http://www.sandiegouniontribune.com/sdut-lz1a19comicco181351-little-shows-big-cons-grow-2009jul19-htmlstory.html.

96 Harvey, "Shel Dorf, Founder," 41; "San Diego Comic-Con Progress Report No. 1 1973." Series III: Progress Reports and Newsletters, Folder 1, Box 1, Shel Dorf Collection, San Diego History Center.

97 Carone and Cavanaugh, "The First Comic-Con"; Harvey, "Shel Dorf, Founder"; "San Diego's Golden State Comic-Con Program Book 1970." While the 1970 Comic-Con program confirms this narrative, suggesting that plans for the convention were in the works before Dorf's group met the ProFanests, Scott Shaw! says he never heard any mention of a convention at his first few meetings with Dorf. Based on Shaw!'s interview with San Diego State University (filmed after Dorf's death) and evidence from Dorf's correspondence, there was no love lost between these two. Dorf wrote a letter to the *San Diego Tribune* suggesting that Shaw! had repeatedly lied about Comic-Con's true origins by claiming the idea for Comic-Con was formed after he joined and at his parents' home: "Mr. Shaw has used you to get at me with his snide remarks and outright lie. He tried to rewrite

history once before in an interview. I got him to write a retraction." Shel Dorf. "Letter to Mr. John L. Nunes, San Diego Tribune, July 29, 1989." Series IX: Shel Dorf Correspondence, Folder 15, Box 3, Shel Dorf Collection, San Diego History Center; Habegger, "Scott Shaw!"

98 Shaw!, "Cartoonist-at-Large #1."

99 Schelly, *The Golden Age of Comic Fandom*, 122–123.

100 Comic artist, Trina Robbins, designed Vampirella's iconic look. Robbins was a member of science fiction fandom, the underground comix scene, and has written extensively on the history of women in the comics industry. Fredrik Strömberg, "Robbins, Trina," in *Comics through Time: A History of Icons, Idols, and Ideas*, ed. M. Keith Booker (Santa Barbara, CA: ABC-CLIO, 2014), 750–751.

101 In addition to providing funding, Alf's success as a comic book dealer meant that he could promote Comic-Con to his substantial customer base. Schelly, *The Golden Age of Comic Fandom*, 122–123; Rowe, "From Little Shows Big Cons Grow"; Mike Towry, "The Most Important Ads in Comic-Con History," Comic-Convention Memories, last modified April 21, 2010, http://www.comicconmemories.com/2010 /04/21/the-most-important-ads-in-comic-con-history/.

102 San Diego Comic Convention Inc., *Comic-Con: 40 Years*, 20.

103 "San Diego's Golden State Comic-Con Program Book 1970"; Schelly, *The Golden Age of Comic Fandom*, 122; Carone and Cavanaugh, "The First Comic-Con."

104 According to Richard Alf, Dorf and his group of comic fans deliberately sought out and connected with science fiction and film fans because there were so few comic fans in the city. "The First Comic-Con."

105 Shaw!, "Cartoonist-at-Large #1."

106 Barry Alfonso, Richard Alf, Bob Sourk, and Mike Towry were all mail-order dealers. Towry, "The Most Important Ads in Comic-Con History"; Habegger, "Scott Shaw!"

In addition to his Ocean Beach bookstore, Ken Krueger ran two small presses, Shroud Publishers and Dawn Press, and published early works of other founding Comic-Con organizers, Scott Shaw! and Greg Bear. He also worked in comic distribution with Pacific Comics, Capital City, and Diamond Distributors. Glanzer, Sassaman, and Estrada, *Comic-Con 40 Souvenir Book*, 48; Peter Rowe, "Ken Krueger; Ocean Beach Bookstore Was Launching Pad for Comic-Con," last modified November 26, 2009, http://www.utsandiego.com/news/2009/nov/26 /ocean-beach-bookstore-was-launching-pad-comic-con/; Greg Bear, "Biography," Ken Krueger Tribute, http://www.kenkruegertribute.com/biography/. I discuss the importance of retail and comic book dealers to Comic-Con's development in greater depth in chapter 4.

107 For example, Greg Bear went on to a successful career as a science fiction and fantasy writer and Scott Shaw! became a cartoonist and writer who also worked as senior art director for the marketing firm Ogilvy & Mather, overseeing commercials and toy lines. After his time as a teenage comic book dealer, Barry Alfonso went on to work in the music industry, writing songs, press materials, and liner notes. He said his work on Comic-Con "helped [him] to develop invaluable writing and publicity skills." Shaw!, "Cartoonist-at-Large #1"; Glanzer, Sassaman, and Estrada, *Comic-Con 40 Souvenir Book*, 42–51.

108 While R. C. Harvey describes Dorf's employment as a "dream job," Bill Schelly writes that Dorf's eleven-year employment with Milton Caniff was a letdown, at

least initially: "he hated lettering and the pay at first—$35 a week to do six dailies and a Sunday strip—was paltry." However, "later Shel admitted that this assignment had many positive ramifications in his life. For one thing, it allowed him to intensify his relationship with Caniff." In addition to this job, Schelly writes, "In the 1970s, with all the connections he made as chairman of the San Diego Comicon [*sic*], Dorf really came into his own. He became an inveterate interviewer and article-writer for industry fanzines and magazines." Harvey, "Shel Dorf, Founder"; Schelly, *Founders of Comic Fandom*, 103.

109 Dorf et al., "A San Diego Comic-Con Retrospective," in *The 1979 San Diego Comic-Con Tenth Anniversary Souvenir Comic Section* (San Diego: San Diego Comic-Con, 1979), 4. Dorf's use of exclusively male pronouns, in spite of the fact that there were numerous working and aspiring female comic professionals in the 1970s, is indicative of the gendered assumptions that have long plagued comics culture. Here and elsewhere throughout the book, I use "their" or "they" to maintain gender-neutrality.

110 "San Diego Comic-Con Program Book 1973." Series I: Programs & Souvenir Books, Folder 4, Box 1, Shel Dorf Collection, San Diego History Center.

111 Jenkins, *Convergence Culture*, 134.

112 San Diego Comic Convention Inc., *Comic-Con: 40 Years*, 44.

113 Chuck Graham and Barry Alfonso. "San Diego Comic-Con Progress Report No.1 and 1973 Wrap-up Report." Series III: Progress Reports and Newsletters, Folder 40, Box 1, Shel Dorf Collection, San Diego History Center.

114 Graham and Alfonso.

115 Graham and Alfonso.

116 Rik Offenberger, "Comic Book Biography: Pat Broderick," First Comics News, last modified July 1, 2003, http://www.firstcomicsnews.com/pat-broderick-artist-of-the -future/; Bill Schelly, *Sense of Wonder: A Life in Comic Fandom* (Raleigh, NC: TwoMorrows Publishing, 2001), 175–176.

This contest anticipated what would later become a fixture at Comic-Con, beginning in the 1990s: the portfolio review. Each year, Comic-Con provides a dedicated space where aspiring professionals can present portfolios of work to major comic publishers and representatives from other media industries, including, film, animation, video games, and role-playing games. San Diego Comic Convention Inc., *Comic-Con: 40 Years*, 46.

117 Such panels have become even more prominent in recent years. In 2013, for example, over sixty-five panels were devoted to an array of professionalization topics, including "Breaking into Comics the Marvel Way," "Writing for TV: From First Draft to Getting Staffed," "How to Get a Job in the Video Game Industry," and "Creative Techniques for Innovative Creature Design." Shel Dorf and Barry Short, eds., *Progress Report, No. 2*, San Diego Comic-Con (1982), 28–38; Jackie Estrada, ed. *2013 Comic-Con International: Events Guide* (San Diego: Comic-Con International, Inc., 2013).

118 "Recordings of the 1970 San Diego Comic-Con #1: Listen to Them Here!" Comic-Convention Memories. Last modified January 8, 2010. http://www .comicconmemories.com/2010/01/08/recordings-of-the-1970-san-diego-comic -con-1-listen-to-them-here/.

119 Shel Dorf, "Things I Like to Remember," in *Comic Buyer's Guide 1994 Annual: The Standard Reference for Today's Collector*, ed. Don Thompson and Maggie Thompson

(Iola WI: Krause Publications, 1994), 27. Dorf has made this claim on at least two other occasions: "Shel's Message: 'I Did It for Love,'" in *1981 San Diego Comic-Con Souvenir Book*, ed. Mark Stadler (San Diego: San Diego Comic-Con, 1981), 3; Schwartz and Dorf, "Shel Dorf Q&A."

120 Many comic artists, including the creators of Superman, Jerry Siegel and Joe Shuster, signed such contracts and watched the characters they created go on to great success, while they received none of the profits. Shel Dorf was instrumental in helping Siegel and Shuster to seek artistic and economic recompense from DC Comics. Schelly, *Founders of Comic Fandom*, 103.

121 Terranova, "Free Labor," 48.

122 Such labor, Terranova argues, is free both in the sense that it is unpaid and that it is "pleasurable, not imposed." Terranova, 48.

123 "About Comic-Con International."

124 Crawford's inscription read, "for all my friends at the San Diego Comic Convention, with affection" and was followed by an explanation that she was the inspiration for "The Dragon Lady" in the popular comic strip *Terry and the Pirates* by Milton Caniff. "San Diego Comic-Con Program Book 1973."

125 "San Diego Comic-Con 1974 Program Schedule." Series IV: Comic Con Advertising, Folder 1, Box 3, Shel Dorf Collection, San Diego History Center; San Diego Comic Convention Inc., *Comic-Con: 40 Years*, 23.

126 "San Diego Comic-Con 1974 Program Schedule"; *Comic-Con: 40 Years*, 46.

127 *Comic-Con: 40 Years*, 46–47; "San Diego Comic-Con 1974 Program Schedule."

128 "40th-Anniversary Secret Origins of Comic-Con Panel."

129 Schwartz and Dorf, "Shel Dorf Q&A."

130 Mike Towry, "Welcome to Comic-Convention Memories," Comic-Convention Memories, last modified December 10, 2009, http://www.comicconmemories.com /2009/12/10/welcome-to-comic-convention-memories/; "Friday Flashback 006: The History of Comic-Con (and Then-Some!) through Logos," *Toucan: The Official SDCC Blog*, last modified October 18, 2013, http://www.comic-con.org /toucan/friday-flashback-006-history-of-comic-con-and-then-some-through-logos.

131 San Diego Comic Convention Inc., "Articles of Incorporation of San Diego Comic Convention," August 4, 1975, Series VII: Comic-Con Committee Paperwork, Folder 12, Box 3, Shel Dorf Collection, San Diego History Center.

132 Butner, "Richard! A Message from the Chairman."

133 Jenkins, *Convergence Culture*, 2.

134 Thomas Schatz, "The New Hollywood," in *Film Theory Goes to the Movies*, ed. Jim Collins, Hilary Radner, and Ava Collins (New York: Routledge, 1993), 29.

135 The film would eventually be released as *Dracula vs. Frankenstein* in 1971. "San Diego's Golden State Comic-Minicon Flyer." Series IV: Comic-Con Advertising, Folder 1, Box 3, Shel Dorf Collection, San Diego History Center.

136 A write-up on George Pal in the 1980 *Souvenir Book* included a production still from the film, courtesy of Warner Brothers. Mark Stadler, ed. *San Diego Comic-Con Souvenir Book 1980* (San Diego: San Diego Comic Convention, Inc., 1980).

137 1985 coverage in San Diego's weekly paper, the *Reader*, suggested that in the 1970s, Comic-Con was "dominated by hoards of Trekkies who overran the Science Fiction displays." Sue Garson, "Comic Book Characters," *Reader*, August 1, 1985, 11; "1974 San Diego Comic-Con Program" (San Diego: San Diego Comic-Con, 1974).

138 Coppa, "A Brief History of Media Fandom," 43.

139 As Coppa's observation suggests, the notion of "toxic geek masculinity" and its influence on the formation and development of fan cultures long predates the increased visibility of such discourses on social media platforms. Coppa, 45–46; Anastasia Salter and Bridget Blodgett, *Toxic Geek Masculinity in Media: Sexism, Trolling, and Identity Policing* (Cham, Switzerland: Springer International Publishing, 2017).

140 Joan Winston, *The Making of the Trek Conventions* (Chicago: Playboy Press, 1979), 17. Winston's book reprints the following coverage of the 1972 Trek Convention: Frank Beerman, "*Star Trek*: Conclave in NY Looms as Mix of Campy Set and Sci-Fi Buffs," *Variety*, January 19, 1972; Marsano, "Grokking Mr. Spock or May You Never Find a Tribble in Your Chicken Soup," *TV Guide*, March 25, 1972; Anthony Burton, "A Galaxy of Kids Dig Stardust," *Daily News*, January 22, 1972.

141 Glanzer, Sassaman, and Estrada, *Comic-Con 40 Souvenir Book*, 65; Coppa, "A Brief History of Media Fandom," 46.

142 Graham and Alfonso, "San Diego Comic-Con Progress Report No. 1 and 1973 Wrap-up Report."

143 Gerrold is best known for writing the iconic episode, "The Trouble with Tribbles." He has also published several *Star Trek* novelizations and nonfiction books, along with a number of original novels. "San Diego Comic-Con Program Book 1973."

144 StarTrek.com Staff, "Bjo Trimble: The Woman Who Saved Star Trek—Part 1," StarTrek.com, last modified August 31, 2011, http://www.startrek.com/article/bjo-trimble-the-woman-who-saved-star-trek-part-1.

145 "San Diego Comic-Con Program Book 1973." Based on coverage of the event in 1973, this campaign was also discussed in person at the convention, as fans were told to relieve NBC of the notion that a *Star Trek* cartoon was strictly "kid stuff." Ted Burke, "Comics Come Out of the Closet," *Reader*, August 23, 1973.

146 Gerrold would get his wish in 1979, with the release of *Star Trek: The Motion Picture* (Robert Wise). "San Diego Comic-Con Program Book 1973."

147 San Diego Comic Convention Inc., *Comic-Con: 40 Years*, 23, 26; Brian J. Robb, "The Man Who Sold Star Wars," *Star Wars Insider*, January/February 2008, 28–29; Estrada, *San Diego Comic-Con Souvenir Book 1984*; Jeff Jenson, "'Star Wars': Comic-Con '76 Pics," *Entertainment Weekly*, last modified August 2, 2011, http://www.ew.com/gallery/star-wars-comic-con-76-pics?iid=sr-link1.

148 Robb, "The Man Who Sold Star Wars," 29.

149 Paul Cullum, "'Star Wars' 30th Anniversary: How Lucas, ILM Redefined Business-as-Usual," *Variety*, last modified May 4, 2007, https://variety.com/2007/film/news/star-wars-30th-anniversary-1117964328/.

150 He was reportedly asked questions like, "Don't you know that you can't hear explosions in space?" Steve Sansweet, "Which Came First . . . ," in *San Diego Comic-Con International 2007 Souvenir Book*, ed. David Glanzer (San Diego: San Diego Comic-Con 2007), 59.

151 Sansweet, 59. Thomas was also instrumental in convincing Stan Lee to buy the adaptation rights to the film. Roy Thomas, "How I Learned to Stop Worrying & Love 'Star Wars' (within Limits)," *Starlog*, July 1987, 27.

152 Thomas, 26; Cullum, "'Star Wars' 30th Anniversary"; Sansweet, "Which Came First . . . ," 59.

153 Thomas, "How I Learned to Stop Worrying," 28; Cullum, "'Star Wars' 30th Anniversary."

154 Robb, "The Man Who Sold Star Wars," 29. The fact that *Star Wars* was pitched at Comic-Con before the film was released in theaters suggests that the attendees Lippincott described may have been what Bob Rehak calls "design-oriented fans." Such fans, Rehak argues, are "generally less interested in character interaction and psychological relationships than in a fictional universe's contents," most notably, "hardware such as buildings, vehicles, technologies, and weapons." Bob Rehak, *More Than Meets the Eye* (New York: New York University Press, 2018), 28.

155 Glanzer, Sassaman, and Estrada, *Comic-Con 40 Souvenir Book*, 63–64.

156 Attendees from the 1970s often reflect on the strong sense of community and the bonds and friendships they built during the early years of the convention. See, for example: "Comic-Con Memories: The 70s," in *Comic-Con 40 Souvenir Book*, ed. David Glanzer, Gary Sassaman, and Jackie Estrada (San Diego: San Diego Comic-Con International, 2009), 73–76.

157 Schatz, "The New Hollywood."

158 Schatz, 19.

159 Thomas, "How I Learned to Stop Worrying," 28; Jenkins, *Convergence Culture*, 93–130; Jonathan Gray, *Show Sold Separately: Promos, Spoilers, and Other Media Paratexts* (New York: New York University Press, 2010).

160 Thomas, "How I Learned to Stop Worrying," 28.

161 Kal-El is Superman's birth name. Paul Cullum, "Genre Pro Delivers Conventional Wisdom," *Daily Variety*, July 19, 2006, A1.

162 Cullum, A1.

163 allthingsfangirl, "Jeff Walker Awarded Inkpot at Comic-Con 2011," YouTube.com, last modified July 26, 2011, http://www.youtube.com/watch?v=wH404disj7Q; Jeffrey Fleishman, "Blame Those Endless Hall H Lines on Jeff Walker, the Man Who Brought Hollywood to Comic-Con," *Los Angeles Times*, last modified July 20, 2016, http://www.latimes.com/entertainment/movies/la-et-mn-comic-con-jeff -walker-profile-20160713-snap-story.html.

164 Kerry Dixon and Sarah Lacey, "Infographics: How SDCC Compares to Other Conventions," *SDCC Unofficial Blog*. Last modified November 4, 2013. http:// sdccblog.com/2013/11/how-sdcc-compares-to-other-conventions/.

165 Shel Dorf, ed. *San Diego Comic-Con Souvenir Book 1975* (San Diego: San Diego Comic-Con, 1975); Shel Dorf and Jackie Estrada, eds., *1976 San Diego Comic-Con Souvenir Book* (San Diego: San Diego Comic-Con, 1976).

166 While the man and boy depicted are white, the inclusion of an African American woman in this advertisement is significant. This is the only image of a woman of color in the 1980 program (whose cover includes a scantily clad woman with exposed breasts), suggesting that Marvel's ad may have been appealing to a more broad and inclusive vision of comics fandom than what was being reflected by and through the convention at that time. Stadler, *San Diego Comic-Con Souvenir Book 1980*.

167 "About Comic-Con International."

168 "Marvel Entertainment L.L.C," Gale Business Insights: Global, last modified 2014, http://bi.galegroup.com.proxy.lib.umich.edu/global/company/215489?u=lom _umichanna.

169 David Goldman, "Disney to Buy Marvel for $4 Billion," CNN Money, last modified 2009, http://money.cnn.com/2009/08/31/news/companies/disney _marvel/.

170 Marc Graser, "Warner Bros. Creates DC Entertainment," *Variety*, last modified September 9, 2009, http://variety.com/2009/film/news/warner-bros-creates-dc -entertainment-1118008299/.

171 Brigid Alverson, "NYCC: Griepp's White Paper Report Gives Comics Industry a Gold Star," Comic Book Resources, last modified October 10, 2013, http://www .comicbookresources.com/?page=article&id=48400; "Marvel's the Avengers," Box Office Mojo, last modified 2014, http://boxofficemojo.com/movies/?id=avengers11 .htm&adjust_yr=2012&p=.htm.

172 Mark Stadler, ed. *1981 San Diego Comic-Con Souvenir Book* (San Diego: San Diego Comic-Con, Inc., 1981), 3.

173 For footage of this entrance, see Gareth Von Kallenback, "Robert Downey Jr. Iron Man 3 Comic Con Entrance," YouTube, last modified July 14, 2012, https://www .youtube.com/watch?v=c4OHn77YNZI.

174 Marvel repeated this gimmick in 2013, when actor Tom Hiddleston appeared onstage as Loki. The villain demanded that attendees pledge their loyalty to him by screaming his name in exchange for a sneak preview of *Thor: The Dark World* (Alan Taylor, 2013).

175 Dorf, *San Diego Comic-Con Souvenir Book 1975*.

176 Evanier, "The Timeless Jack Kirby."

Chapter 2   The Liminality of the Line and the Place of Fans at Comic-Con

Epigraph: "Comic-Con Talk Back, 2011," Panel, San Diego Comic-Con, San Diego, CA, July 24, 2011.

1 While the constant refreshing is still an important feature of Comic-Con's badge sales, users no longer do so manually. As Comic-Con refined its online sales portal, it implemented a virtual waiting room that refreshes automatically every two minutes to allow randomly selected users to purchase tickets.

2 Michael Czeiszperger, "Comic-Con Registration Sells 130,000 Tickets in 90 Minutes without a Hitch," PRWeb, last modified June 12, 2014, http://www.prweb .com/releases/2014/06/prweb11931964.htm; Tony Maglio, "'Big Bang Theory': The Out-of-This-World TV Ratings," The Wrap, last modified 4 May, 2016, http://www.thewrap.com/big-bang-theory-tv-ratings-season-9-finale-cbs/.

3 Starting in 2006, Comic-Con International began selling tickets online in addition to its mail order and onsite options. In 2007, Comic-Con tickets sold out in advance for the first time. Moving forward, buyers had two options: they could preregister for the following year onsite at Comic-Con or they could purchase tickets online during the general public sale. In 2012, Comic-Con discontinued onsite ticket sales and moved the preregistration online, three weeks after Comic-Con 2012. A host of technical problems plagued Comic-Con's online vending system between 2010 and 2013 as massive demand for tickets led to numerous errors and caused their servers to crash on several occasions. In 2014, organizers shifted to a lottery system, and Comic-Con tickets sold out in ninety minutes. By 2016, Comic-Con tickets sold out in well under an hour. Dave Trumbore, "San Diego Comic-Con 2011 Badges Sell Out in Less Than a Day," Collider, last modified February 6, 2011, http://collider.com/san-diego-comic-con-2011-badges-sell-out /74799/; Joseph M. D. Young, "Virtual Ticket Lines Bring Down Comic-Con

Site," 7 San Diego, last modified February 6, 2011, http://www.nbcsandiego.com /news/local/Comc-Con-Ticket-Sales-115373469.html; Ross Lincoln, "Comic-Con 2013 Sells Out in 93 Minutes but Tech Glitches Frustrate Fans—Again," Deadline, last modified February 16, 2013, http://deadline.com/2013/02/comic-con-2013 -sells-out-in-93-seconds-but-tech-glitches-frustrate-fans-again-432646/; Czeisz-perger, "Comic-Con Registration Sells 130,000 Tickets in 90 Minutes without a Hitch"; Lori Weisberg, "Another Speedy Sellout for Comic-Con Badges," *San Diego Union-Tribune,* last modified February 20, 2016, http://www.sandiego uniontribune.com/news/2016/feb/20/comic-con-badges-sell-out-quickly/.

4 Kristina Busse, "Geek Hierarchies, Boundary Policing, and the Gendering of the Good Fan," *Participations Journal of Audience & Reception Studies* 10, no. 1 (2013): 81; Heather Hendershot, "On Stan Lee, Leonard Nimoy, and Coitus . . . Or, the Fleeting Pleasures of Televisual Nerdom," Antenna: Responses to Media Culture, last modified July 30, 2010, http://blog.commarts.wisc.edu/2010/07/30/on-stan -lee-leonard-nimoy-and-coitus-or-the-fleeting-pleasures-of-televisual-nerdom/.

5 As Suzanne Scott points out in her 2012 interview with Henry Jenkins, "The *Big Bang Theory*'s dual address seems to perfectly encapsulate the industry's conflicted desire to acknowledge fans' growing cultural influence, while still containing them through sitcom conventions." Henry Jenkins and Suzanne Scott, "*Textual Poachers,* Twenty Years Later: A Conversation between Henry Jenkins and Suzanne Scott," in *Textual Poachers* (New York: Taylor & Francis, 2013), xvii.

6 Todd VanDerWerff, "Comic-Con, Day 3: Lines, Lines, Everywhere Lines," A.V. Club, last modified July 24, 2011, http://www.avclub.com/articles/comiccon-day-3 -lines-lines-everywhere-lines,59389/.

7 "Comic-Con Talk Back, 2011."

8 With the exception of the removal of Kinkos from the list of possible lines in 2008, this message appeared unchanged in the Comic-Con Events Guides until 2013, when it disappeared completely. Jackie Estrada, ed. *San Diego Comic-Con International Events Guide 2002* (San Diego: Comic-Con International, 2002); Estrada, *2012 Comic-Con International: San Diego Events Guide* (San Diego: Comic-Con International Inc., 2012), 98; Estrada, *2013 Comic-Con International: Events Guide* (San Diego: Comic-Con International, Inc., 2013), 102.

9 I have experienced this confusion firsthand on several occasions. For example, one year, as I tried to enter the convention center, a staff member directed me to join a line at the far end of the building (almost half a mile away). Upon arriving, another member of the event staff immediately informed me that I was in the wrong place and directed me to return to where I began. This example is far from an isolated incident, however. Problems with incorrect directions from event security and volunteers—particularly with regard to ADA (Americans with Disabilities Act) lines—is a common source of frustration among attendees and often comes up during the event's annual Talk-Back panel.

10 Gary Sassaman and Laura Jones, *Comic-Con International 2017 Quick Guide* (San Diego: Sam Diego Comic Convention, 2017).

11 For a detailed description of this process, see Kerry Dixon, "San Diego Comic-Con Guide: Where Do I Line Up for . . . ," SDCC Unofficial Blog, last modified May 26, 2015, https://sdccblog.com/2015/05/san-diego-comic-con-guide-where -do-i-line-up-for/.

12 Josh Wigler, "'Game of Thrones': A Firsthand Account of the Comic-Con 'Winter Is Here' Activation," The Hollywood Reporter, last modified July 20, 2017, https://www.hollywoodreporter.com/live-feed/game-thrones-at-comic-con-inside -winter-is-activation-1022888; Laura Prudom, "You Too Can Be King in the North with HBO's 'Game of Thrones' Experience at Comic-Con," Mashable, last modified July 20, 2017, https://mashable.com/2017/07/20/game-of-thrones-comic -con-2017-winter-is-here-experience/.

13 Eileen Meehan, "Leisure or Labor?: Fan Ethnography and Political Economy," in *Consuming Audiences? Production and Reception in Media Research*, ed. Ingunn Hagen and Janet Wasko (Cresskill, NJ: Hampton Press, 2000).

14 Alex Stone, "Why Waiting Is Torture," last modified August 18, 2012, http://www .nytimes.com/2012/08/19/opinion/sunday/why-waiting-in-line-is-torture.html.

15 Stone.

16 In the 1950s, for example, some buildings installed mirrors adjacent to their elevators in order to give people something to do while they waited, resulting in a significant reduction in complaints. Richard C. Larson, "There's More to a Line Than Its Wait," *Technology Review* 91, no. 5 (1988): 63–64.

    Joe Moran, a scholar of everyday life, similarly argues that "waiting is frustrating because it is both an unavoidable and marginalized experience: an absolutely essential feature of daily life that is nevertheless associated with wasted time and even shameful indolence." Joe Moran, *Reading the Everyday* (New York: Routledge, 2005), 7.

17 Joe Moran, *Queuing for Beginners: The Story of Daily Life from Breakfast to Bedtime* (London: Profile, 2007), 4–6.

18 Mel Stanfill and Megan Condis, "Fandom and/as Labor," *Transformative Works and Cultures* 15 (2014), https://journal.transformativeworks.org/index.php/twc /article/view/593.

19 Matt Hills, "Always-on Fandom, Waiting and Bingeing: Psychoanalysis as an Engage- ment with Fans' 'Infra-Ordinary' Experiences," in *The Routledge Companion to Media Fandom*, ed. Melissa A. Click and Suzanne Scott (New York: Routledge, 2018), 22.

20 Moran, *Reading the Everyday*, 11.

21 Jeremy Rutz, "I Am Hall H: A Guide to the Biggest Stage at Comic-Con," *SDCC Unofficial Blog*, last modified June 3, 2013, http://sdccblog.com/2013/06/i-am-hall -h-a-guide-to-the-biggest-stage-at-comic-con/.

22 Moran, *Reading the Everyday*, 11; Hills, "Always-on Fandom."

23 Henri Lefebvre, *Everyday Life in the Modern World* (London: Allen Lane, 1971), 53; Moran, *Reading the Everyday*, 8.

24 Victor W. Turner, *The Ritual Process: Structure and Anti-Structure* (Chicago: Aldine Publishing Company, 1966), 95. Billy Ehn and Orvar Löfgren similarly describe waiting as a liminal experience. Billy Ehn and Orvar Löfgren, *The Secret World of Doing Nothing* (Berkeley, CA: University of California Press, 2010), 65.

25 Nick Couldry, *Media Rituals: A Critical Approach* (New York: Routledge, 2003), 22. See also: *The Place of Media Power: Pilgrims and Witnesses of the Media Age* (New York: Routledge, 2000).

26 Other examples include Will Brooker, "A Sort of Homecoming: Fan Viewing and Symbolic Pilgrimage," in *Fandom: Identities and Communities in a Mediated World*, ed. Johnathan Gray, Cornel Sandvoss, and C. Lee Harrington (New York: New

York University Press, 2007), 149–164; Matt Hills, *Fan Cultures* (London: Routledge, 2002); Daniel Dayan and Elihu Katz, *Media Events: The Live Broadcasting of History* (Cambridge, MA: Harvard University Press, 1992); Jennifer E. Porter, "To Boldly Go: *Star Trek* Convention as Pilgrimage," in *Star Trek and Sacred Ground: Explorations of Star Trek, Religion, and American Culture*, ed. Jennifer E. Porter and Darcee L. McLaren (Albany, NY: SUNY Press, 1999).

27 Couldry, *Media Rituals*, 35.

28 Sara Gwenllian-Jones, "Web Wars: Resistance, Online Fandom and Studio Censorship," in *Quality Popular Television: Cult TV, the Industry and Fans*, ed. Mark Jancovich and James Lyons (London: British Film Institute, 2003), 165.

29 For example, Paul Booth argues that *SuperWhoLock* gif fics "hinge on a transition from semantic pastiche to syntactic appropriation and represent a liminal state between fandom and the media industry." Paul Booth, *Playing Fans: Negotiating Fandom and Media in the Digital Age* (Iowa City: University of Iowa Press, 2015), 27.

30 I base this calculation on the maximum number of seats in Hall H, 6,500, and Comic-Con's official, published attendance estimate of roughly 130,000 over four days of the convention (though estimates of actual attendance numbers have been much higher in recent years). "About Comic-Con International."

31 In recent years, for example, the Warner Brothers panel has been scheduled for Saturday morning while the Marvel Studios panel is held Saturday evening. As the introduction's anecdote about the 2013 "Women Who Kick Ass" panel illustrates, guests situated in between these kinds of major promotional events can sometimes find themselves speaking to a distracted or disinterested audience. However, as chapter 3's examination of a day in Hall H also demonstrates, panels that run between larger promotional events can benefit from this placement too.

32 "#21: Hall H and Plaza Park Lines + Toucan Tracker Wristbands!" *Toucan*: The Official Comic-Con Blog, last modified July 9, 2018, https://www.comic-con.org /toucan/21-hall-h-and-plaza-park-lines-toucan-tracker-wristbands.

33 Adam Chitwood, "Comic-Con Implementing New Wristband System for Hall H Line," Collider, last modified July 14, 2014, http://collider.com/comic-con -wristbands-hall-h/.

34 Anthony Breznican, "'Star Wars: The Force Awakens': You Won't Believe the Epic Comic-Con Line to See That Galaxy Far, Far Away," *Entertainment Weekly*, last modified July 10, 2015, http://www.ew.com/article/2015/07/10/star-wars-force -awakens-comic-con-line.

35 Jacob Kastrenakes, "Hall H of Horrors; What Is Comic-Con Doing about the Worst Line in Fandom?" *Verge*, last modified July 12, 2015, http://www.theverge .com/2015/7/12/8937951/comic-con-hall-h-line-horrors.

36 As I discuss in the introduction to this book, Comic-Con's attendance numbers (and their methods for acquiring these numbers) are somewhat opaque. In 2007, Comic-Con reached what organizers called a "self-imposed" attendance limit of approximately 125,000 over the four days of the convention. Geoff Boucher, "Comic-Con Will Stay in San Diego," LA Times: Hero Complex, last modified September 30, 2010, http://herocomplex.latimes.com/comic-con/comic-con -international-san-diego/; David Glanzer, Gary Sassaman, and Jackie Estrada, eds., *Comic-Con 40 Souvenir Book* (San Diego: San Diego Comic-Con International, 2009), 109.

However, overall numbers are frequently reported in excess of this limit, reaching as much as 140,000. Two articles published in the *San Diego Union-Tribune* in July 2012 reported attendance of "more than 130,000" and "around 140,000," while the official website for San Diego's Gaslamp Quarter erroneously claimed Comic-Con attendance was "125,000 PER DAY" (original emphasis). Lori Weisberg and Roger Showley, "Fixing the Con's Cons from Rush to Get Tickets, to Crush in Hall H, Fans Have Plenty of Ideas for Improving Event," *San Diego Union-Tribune*, July 26, 2012, C1; Peter Rowe, "Decoding the Con's Secret Power while Movie and TV Stars Grab Most of the Attention, Fans' Passions Are Served by Narrowly Focused Panels," *San Diego Union-Tribune*, July 11, 2012, A1; "Gaslamp's Comic Con Tips," Gaslamp.org, last modified 2012, http://www.gaslamp.org/comic-con.

By 2014, Comic-Con's own website reported "attendance topping 130,000 in recent years." "About Comic-Con International," Comic-Con.org, last modified 2018, http://www.comic-con.org/about. While that number was still posted to Comic-Con's official website in 2016, other reports from organizers placed attendance numbers at closer to 170,000. Beatriz Valenzuela, "How the Security Team at Comic-Con Works to Keep Fans Safe," *Los Angeles Daily News*, last modified July 16, 2016, http://www.dailynews.com/arts-and-entertainment/20160716/how-the-security-team-at-comic-con-works-to-keep-fans-safe.

In 2016, Comic-Con introduced RFID scanners, which have the potential to yield a more precise head count. However, in 2012 Comic-Con president John Rogers publicly stated that they would never release exact numbers, including a breakdown of attendance for each day of the convention. The reasons for this secrecy were unclear. "Comic-Con Talk Back, 2012," Panel, San Diego Comic-Con, San Diego, CA, July 22, 2012.

37 Rowe, "Decoding the Con's Secret Power," A1.

38 Marc Bernardin, "Even after 15 Years of Braving Crowds at Comic-Con, This Journalist Can Still Find the Love," *Los Angeles Times*, last modified July 24, 2016, http://www.latimes.com/entertainment/movies/la-et-mn-comic-con-finding-the-love-20160724-snap-story.html.

39 Alesandra Dubin, "Strategy Session: How Comic-Con Managed Huge Lines of Attendees," BizBash, last modified July 26, 2012, http://www.bizbash.com/strategy_session_how_comic-con_managed_huge_lines_of_attendees/san-diego/story/23905/; Rowe, "Decoding the Con's Secret Power," A1.

40 Bill Stoddard and Janet Tait, eds., *1991 San Diego Comic-Con Convention Events Guide* (San Diego: San Diego Comic Convention, Inc., 1991), 2.

41 Estrada, *2012 Comic-Con International: San Diego Events Guide*, 2.

42 Dubin, "Strategy Session"; Valenzuela, "How the Security Team at Comic-Con Works to Keep Fans Safe."

43 Michel Foucault, *Discipline and Punish: The Birth of the Prison* (New York: Vintage Books), 136.

44 Foucault, 172–173.

45 Foucault, 206.

46 Foucault, 201. Richard Larson suggests that when companies provide information about the line, wait times, and anticipated delays, customers tend to be more satisfied with the wait. Larson, "There's More to a Line Than Its Wait," 65–66.

47 Comic-Con International, "#22/SDCC 2014: Introducing the Toucan Tracker Wristbands for Hall H's First Panel of the Day!" *Toucan*, last modified July 14, 2014, https://www.comic-con.org/toucan/22sdcc-2014-introducing-toucan -tracker-wristbands-hall-h's-first-panel-of-day.

48 This would not be the first or last time that my questions to security staff at Comic-Con—which were often about seemingly banal aspects of crowd control and lines—provoked confused or slightly suspicious responses.

49 In many cases, attendees enforce these rule themselves and are often as (or more) vigilant about catching line-jumpers than security.

50 David Harvey, *The Condition of Postmodernity* (Cambridge, MA: Blackwell, 1988), 226.

51 Karl Marx, *Grundrisse: Foundations of the Critique of Political Economy*, trans. Martin Nicolaus (London: Penguin Books, 1973), 173.

52 John Fiske, "The Cultural Economy of Fandom," in *The Adoring Audience: Fan Culture and Popular Media*, ed. Lisa A. Lewis (New York: Routledge, 1992), 30.

53 Karen Hellekson, "A Fannish Field of Value: Online Fan Gift Culture," *Cinema Journal* 48, no. 3 (2009): 113–118; Karen Hellekson, "Making Use Of: The Gift, Commerce, and Fans," *Cinema Journal* 54, no. 3 (2015): 125–131.

54 Hellekson, "A Fannish Field of Value," 114.

55 Attendees who are farther back in the room and unable to get a good view of the stage will frequently snap photos of the celebrities on screen. As I elaborate in chapter 3, the excitement of just being in the room makes it worth documenting (even through the mediation of the screen) as a unique, individual, and personal experience.

56 Perhaps the only explicitly (if indirect) economic compensation for waiting occurs in the lines for exclusive collectables or autographs, which can often be sold at a profit immediately after Comic-Con. I discuss this collectors' market at greater length in chapter 4.

57 Suzanne Scott, "Repackaging Fan Culture: The Regifting Economy of Ancillary Content Models," *Transformative Works and Cultures* 3 (2009). https://journal .transformativeworks.org/index.php/twc/article/view/150.

58 Scott.

59 Abigail De Kosnik, "Fandom as Free Labor," in *Digital Labor: The Internet as Playground and Factory*, ed. Trebor Scholz (New York: Routledge, 2012), 99; Alex Lothian, "Living in a Den of Thieves: Fan Video and the Challenges to Owner- ship," *Cinema Journal* 48, no. 4 (2009): 135.

60 Meehan, "Leisure or Labor?"

61 "Commodity Audience, Actual Audience: The Blindspot Debate," in *Illuminating the Blindspots: Essays Honoring Dallas W. Smythe*, ed. Janet Wasko, Vincent Mosco, and Manjunath Pendakur (Norwood, NJ: Ablex Publishing, 1993), 393.

62 Weisberg, "Another Speedy Sellout for Comic-Con Badges."

63 "Hotels," Comic-Con International: San Diego, last modified 2018, https://www .comic-con.org/sites/default/files/forms/cci2018_hotellist_v1.pdf; M. J. Wilke, "Managing Hotel-Apocalypse for SDCC: 2018 Edition," Wayward Nerd, last modified 2018, https://www.waywardnerd.com/hotel-apocalypse-.

64 Pierre Bourdieu, "The Forms of Capital," in *Handbook of Theory and Research for the Sociology of Education*, ed. John G. Richardson (Westport, CT: Greenwood Press, 1986), 252.

65 Barry Schwartz, "Waiting, Exchange, and Power: The Distribution of Time in Social Systems," *American Journal of Sociology* 79, no. 4 (1974): 843.

66 Schwartz, 844.

67 Comic-Con organizers used this phrase in a description of the convention published in the 2003 issue of their *Update* magazine. But the fact that this magazine was sent to registered attendees suggests that this statement was directed at reassuring fans of the exclusivity of their experience, rather than convincing others that they missed out. "2003 Comic-Con Programming: You Had to Be There!" in *Comic-Con International Update 4* (San Diego: Comic-Con International, 2003), 16–35.

68 Jonathan Liebson, "Samsung Experience's 'Suicide Squad' Activation," BizBash, last modified 2016, https://www.bizbash.com/samsung-experiences-suicide-squad -activation-suicide-squad-stars-attended-films/gallery/187713.

69 Marc Graser, "Studios Blitz Comic-Con," *Variety*, last modified July 19, 2010, http://www.variety.com/article/VR1118021897?refcatid=4076&printerfriendly =true.

70 "Comic-Con Talk Back, 2011."

71 Fiske, "The Cultural Economy of Fandom," 42; Hills, *Fan Cultures*, 25.

72 Fiske, 42; Hills, 25.

73 CB's Comic Con Team, "The 6 Best Panels of Comic Con 2012," CinemaBlend .com, last modified July 16, 2013, http://www.cinemablend.com/new/6-Best-Panels -Comic-Con-2012-31960.html.

74 Paige Albiniak, "Comic-Con 2013: Why TV Marketers Brave the Crowds," Promaxbda: International Association for Entertainment Marketing Professionals, last modified July 17, 2013, http://brief.promaxbda.org/content/comic-con-2013 -why-tv-marketers-brave-the-crowds.

75 Peter Huber, "The Economics of Waiting," *Forbes*, December 30, 1996, 150.

76 Todd VanDerWerff, "A Day inside Comic-Con's Hall H: Worshiping in the Ultimate Movie Church." Grantland. Last modified July 22, 2013, http://grantland .com/hollywood-prospectus/a-day-inside-comic-cons-hall-h-worshipping-in-the -ultimate-movie-church/.

77 Alexander Abad-Santos, "How the Nerds Lost Comic-Con." The Wire. Last modified July 19, 2013. http://www.theatlanticwire.com/entertainment/2013/07 /how-nerds-lost-comic-con/67304/; Henry Hanks, "Is This Comic-Con? Fans Debate 'Mainstream' Panels - CNN.com," CNN, last modified July 22, 2010, http://www.cnn.com/2010/SHOWBIZ/07/22/is.this.comicon/index.html.

78 Jessica Sheffield and Elyse Merlo, "Biting Back: Twilight Anti-Fandom and the Rhetoric of Superiority," in *Bitten by Twilight: Youth Culture, Media & the Vampire Franchise*, ed. Melissa A. Click, Jennifer Stevens Aubrey, and Elizabeth Behm-Morawitz (New York: Peter Lang, 2010), 207–222; Melissa Click, "'Rabid,' 'Obsessed,' and 'Frenzied.': Understanding Twilight Fangirls and the Gendered Politics of Fandom," Flow 11, no. 4 (2009), http://www.flowjournal.org/2009/12 /rabid-obsessed-and-frenzied-understanding-twilight-fangirls-and-the-gendered -politics-of-fandom-melissa-click-university-of-missouri/.

79 Liz Ohanesian, "Comic-Con's Twilight Protests: Is There a Gender War Brewing?" last modified July 28, 2009, http://www.laweekly.com/arts/comic-cons-twilight -protests-is-there-a-gender-war-brewing-2373110.

80 Tracy Brown et al., "Every Year of Comic-Con in One Giant Timeline," *Los Angeles Times*, last modified 8 July, 2015, http://www.latimes.com/entertainment /herocomplex/la-et-hc-comic-con-san-diego-timeline-htmlstory.html; Martin and Broeske, "Batmanjuice," K20.

81 Michael Gehlken, "It Begins: Line Forms for Comic-Con," NBC San Diego, last modified July 19, 2011, http://www.nbcsandiego.com/news/local/It-Begins-Line -Forms-for-Comic-Con-125781473.html.

82 Darren Franich, "'Twilight' at Comic-Con 2011: Talking to the Fans at Camp Breaking Dawn," PopWatch, last modified July 20, 2011, http://popwatch.ew.com /2011/07/20/twilight-comic-con-fans-breaking-dawn/.

83 Gehlken, "It Begins."

84 Franich, "'Twilight' at Comic-Con 2011."

85 Franich.

86 Jackie Estrada, *Comic-Con International 2011 Events Guide* (San Diego: Comic-Con International Inc., 2011), 2.

87 Twilight Lexicon, "Tales from the Twilight Comic Con Line: Tuesday Version," Twilight Lexicon, last modified July 20, 2011, http://www.twilightlexicon.com /2011/07/20/tales-from-the-twilight-comic-con-line-tuesday-version/.

88 Franich, "'Twilight' at Comic-Con 2011."

89 Danny Baldwin, "SDCC 2011: The Twilight Saga: Breaking Dawn—Part 1 (Hall H)," Bucket Reviews, last modified July 21, 2011, http://bucketreviews.com/2011 /07/21/sdcc-2011-twilight-breaking-dawn-part-1-hall-h/.

90 Hills, "Always-on Fandom," 23.

91 @Twilight, "The Twilight Saga: 6:56 P.M. 18 Jul 11," Twitter, last modified July 18, 2011, https://twitter.com/Twilight; Jobs Tester, "The Line Has Begun for Breaking Dawn Comic-Con Panel," *TwilightStars-in*, last modified July 19, 2011, http:// twilightstars-in.blogspot.com/2011/07/line-has-begun-for-breaking-dawn-comic .html; Amanda31, "Line for the Breaking Dawn Panel at Comic-Con Has Started!" TwilightMoms.com, last modified July 18, 2011, http://www.twilightmoms.com /2011/07/line-for-the-breaking-dawn-panel-at-comic-con-has-started/; Amanda Bell, "'Twilight' Fans Already Lining up for Thursday's 'Breaking Dawn' Comic-Con Panel," examiner.com, last modified July 18, 2011, http://www.examiner.com /twilight-in-national/twilight-fans-already-lining-up-for-thursday-s-breaking-dawn -comic-con-panel; Hollywood Life Staff, "'Breaking Dawn' at Comic-Con—the Fans Are Already Lining Up!" Hollywood Life, last modified July 19, 2011, http://www.hollywoodlife.com/2011/07/19/breaking-dawn-comic-con-panel -robert-pattinson-kristen-stewart/.

92 @Twilight, "The Twilight Saga: 12:05 P.M.—19 Jul 11," Twitter, last modified July 19, 2011, https://twitter.com/Twilight.

93 "The Twilight Saga: 3:24 P.M.—20 Jul 11," last modified July 20, 2011, https:// twitter.com/Twilight.

94 Twilight Lexicon, "Tales from the Twilight Comic Con Line: Tuesday Version."

95 Melissa Miller, "You Don't Own Me: The Representation of Twilight Fandom," in *It Happens at Comic-Con: Ethnographic Essays on a Pop Culture Phenomenon*, ed. Ben Bolling and Matthew J. Smith (Jefferson, NC: McFarland, 2014), 63–74.

96 Nicole Sperling, "Comic-Con 2011: 'Twilight' Cast Surprises Fans with Breakfast," *Los Angeles Times*: Hero Complex, last modified July 21, 2011, http://herocomplex

.latimes.com/2011/07/21/comic-con-2011-twilight-cast-surprises-fans-with
-breakfast/.

97 For example, one article noted that Nikki Reed "stopped and signed every poster thrown her way, almost bounding over a barrier when a young boy asked for an autograph from across the line." Sperling, "Comic-Con 2011."

98 lostinreviews, "Twilight Breaking Dawn Comic Con Line and Panel," YouTube, last modified July 21, 2011, http://www.youtube.com/watch?v=InJ1EBeKWYg.

99 Such photo ops are an annual occurrence in the Hall H line. Other examples include visits from *The Hobbit* cast members, Zach Snyder and the batmobile, and donuts delivered to *Star Wars* fans on behalf of J. J. Abrams.

100 Vicki Mayer, *Below the Line: Producers and Production Studies in the New Television Economy* (Durham, NC: Duke University Press, 2011), 2–3.

101 Couldry, *The Place of Media Power*, 107–109.

102 Click, "'Rabid,' 'Obsessed,' and 'Frenzied'"; Sheffield and Merlo, "Biting Back."

103 Susan Kresnicka, "Why Understanding Fans Is the New Superpower (Guest Column)," *Variety*, last modified April 2, 2016, http://variety.com/2016/tv /columns/understanding-fans-superpower-troika-1201743513/; Henry Jenkins, "Superpowered Fans: The Many Worlds of San Diego's Comic-Con," *Boom: A Journal of California* 2, no. 2 (2012): 29.

104 Derek Johnson, "Fantagonism, Franchising, and Industry Management of Fan Privilege," in *The Routledge Companion to Media Fandom*, ed. Melissa A. Click and Suzanne Scott (New York: Routledge, 2018), 402.

105 Sheffield and Merlo, "Biting Back," 207; Busse, "Geek Hierarchies."

106 Dallas W. Smythe, "Communications: Blindspot of Western Marxism," *Canadian Journal of Political and Social Theory* 1, no. 3 (1977): 3; Meehan, "Leisure or Labor?"; Hellekson, "A Fannish Field of Value"; Fiske, "The Cultural Economy of Fandom."

107 In fact, as Matt Hills has observed, it is more frequently the case that fans find themselves positioned somewhere between such categories and "cannot be pinned down by singular theoretical approaches or singular definitions." Hills, *Fan Cultures*, xiii.

Chapter 3   Manufacturing "Hall H Hysteria"

Epigraph: Brian Lowry, "Beware the Comic-Con False Positive," *Variety*, last modified July 15, 2009, https://variety.com/2009/scene/columns/beware-the-comic-con-false -positive-1118005970/.

1 Comic-Con International, "The Mystery of Hall H," in *Comic-Con International Update 2* (San Diego Comic-Con International, 2004), 26. *Update* was a magazine mailed to Comic-Con members to provide information about upcoming Comic-Con International events: Comic-Con, Ape, and WonderCon. Prior to the introduction of *Update* in 1995, Comic-Con sent paper or newsprint "Progress Reports." In 2012, organizers replaced their print publication with an official Comic-Con blog, *Toucan*. "Introducing *Toucan*: The Official Blog of Comic-Con International, Wondercon Anaheim, and Ape, the Alternative Press Expo," *Toucan*, last modified December 10, 2012, http://www.comic-con.org/toucan/toucan -official-blog-of-comic-con-international-wondercon-anaheim-and-ape-alternative -press.

2 "The Mystery of Hall H," 26.

3 This hall supplemented the convention's other large programming rooms—
Ballroom 20, which was added in 2001 and seats approximately 4,800; 6CDEF,
which held around 3,000 and was reconfigured as the 2,100-seat 6BCF in 2009;
and the over 1,000-seat 6A. Chris Conaton, "Comic-Con 2008: Bigger Than Ever,
but Does That Mean Better?" Pop Matters, last modified August 6, 2008, https://
www.popmatters.com/comic-con-2008-bigger-than-ever-but-does-that-mean
-better-2496132063.html; Kerry Dixon, "San Diego Comic-Con Room Capacities,"
SDCC Unofficial Blog, last modified June 28, 2015, https://sdccblog.com/2015/06
/san-diego-comic-con-room-capacities/; Jackie Estrada, ed. *2009 Comic-Con
International: San Diego Events Guide* (San Diego: Comic-Con International Inc.,
2009); San Diego Comic Convention Inc., *Comic-Con: 40 Years of Artists, Writers,
Fans & Friends* (San Francisco: Chronicle Books, 2009), 154.

4 *Comic-Con: 40 Years*, 154; David Glanzer, Gary Sassaman, and Jackie Estrada, eds.,
Comic-Con 40 Souvenir Book (San Diego: San Diego Comic-Con International,
2009), 112.

The slate of theatrical releases promoted at Comic-Con in 2004 included
Warner Brothers' *Batman Begins* (Christopher Nolan, 2005) and *Constantine*
(Francis Lawrence, 2005), Paramount's *Sky Captain and the World of Tomorrow*
(Kerry Conran, 2004) and *Team America: World Police* (Trey Parker, 2004),
Disney/Pixar's *The Incredibles* (Brad Bird, 2004), Sony's *The Grudge 2* (Takashi
Shimizu, 2006), Sony/Screen Gems' *Resident Evil: Apocalypse* (Alexander Witt,
2004), 20th Century Fox's *Alien vs. Predator* (Paul W. S. Anderson, 2004) and
Fantastic Four (Tim Story, 2005), and Universal's *Serenity* (Joss Whedon, 2005).
Independents included Rogue Pictures' *Shaun of the Dead* (Edgar Wright, 2004)
and *Seed of Chucky* (Don Mancini, 2004), Dimension Films' *Sin City* (Frank Miller
and Robert Rodriguez, 2005), Lions Gate's *Open Water* (Chris Kentis, 2004) and
Saw (James Wan, 2003), and New Line Cinema's *Blade: Trinity* (David S. Goyer
2004) and *Harold and Kumar Go to White Castle* (Danny Leiner, 2004). John
Horn, "Studios Take a Read on Comic Book Gathering; Hollywood Courts a
Genre's Enthusiasts, Who Can Raise or Lower Movie's Fortunes," *Los Angeles
Times*, July 26, 2004, E1; Jackie Estrada, ed. *Comic-Con International Events Guide
2004* (San Diego, CA: Comic-Con International Inc., 2004).

5 Attendance nearly doubled between 2000, when the convention drew 48,500, and
2004, when an estimated 95,000 attended. Between 2003 and 2004 alone
attendance numbers increased by 25,000. Glanzer, Sassaman, and Estrada,
Comic-Con 40 Souvenir Book, 108–112.

6 Laura M. Holson, "Can Little-Known Heroes Be Hollywood Hits?" *New York Times*,
July 26, 2004, 1; Horn, "Studios Take a Read on Comic Book Gathering," E1.

7 Johanna Schneller, "Pradas Woo the Pocket Protectors," *Globe and Mail*, August 20,
2004, R1.

8 William Booth, "At Comic-Con, Nerd Mentality Rules the Day; Hollywood Now
Woos Once-Scorned Genre Fans," *Washington Post*, July 19, 2005, C1.

9 The San Diego Convention Center has sixty-two rooms and eight Exhibit Halls,
but these rooms are available in at least ninety-six different configurations and can
be separated or merged according to the organizers' needs. See San Diego Convention Center Corporation, "Facility Guide," San Diego Convention Center, last
modified 2018, https://visitsandiego.com/facility/facility-guide.

10 San Diego Convention Center Corporation, "Facility Guide."

11 Gary Sassaman and Laura Jones, *Comic-Con International 2017 Quick Guide* (San Diego: Sam Diego Comic Convention, 2017).

12 When exiting the hall at the end of panels attendees are funneled to an outdoor exit and must reenter the convention center from an adjacent entrance.

13 In recent years, Comic-Con has expanded its programming to several offsite locations, including adjacent hotels, the San Diego Public Library, and the Horton Grand Theater. However, Hall H remains uniquely positioned as a space that is physically attached to, yet separate from, the rest of the convention center.

14 Jen Yamato, "Inside Comic-Con's Hall H, the Most Important Room in Hollywood," *Los Angeles Times*, last modified July 19, 2017, https://www.latimes .com/entertainment/herocomplex/la-et-hc-comic-con-hall-h-20170719-story .html.

15 In recent years, studios have leaned more heavily on celebrities as moderators in Hall H, recruiting comedians like Patton Oswalt, Chris Hardwick, and Conan O'Brien. In 2017, screenwriter, producer, and former *Lost* showrunner Damon Lindelof served as moderator for the *Twin Peaks* panel, and actor and former professional football player Terry Crews moderated Netflix's film panel. Angela Watercutter, "At Comic-Con This Year, the Biggest Stars Were the Moderators," Wired, last modified July 25, 2017, https://www.wired.com/story/comic-con -moderators/.

16 This footage is sometimes assembled specifically for Comic-Con but is always touted as a special, advance look at the film. For example, studios will often premiere movie trailers or footage before they are released to the general public, as was the case when Warner Brothers premiered footage from *Watchmen* (Zach Snyder, 2009) at Comic-Con in July 2008 and subsequently released it on iTunes that December.

17 Instructions about how to use these tickets are projected at regular intervals between panels in Comic-Con's programming rooms. After the panel concludes and any time before the end of the convention, attendees can go to the Programming Premiums Room (previously the more aptly titled Fulfillment Room) to redeem their tickets. Giveaways vary from gift bags full of goodies to T-shirts, hats, posters, or small stickers and buttons. In many cases, attendees do not know what the giveaway is until they arrive at the room, which, in recent years, has been stationed in an adjacent hotel over half a mile away from Hall H.

18 This could include news on a director, casting, or announcements about other films in production. All three of these strategies were present in a 2010 Marvel studios panel launching their film *The Avengers* (Joss Whedon, 2012), an unannounced addition to what, according to the Comic-Con Events Guide, was to be a discussion of *Thor* (Kenneth Brannagh, 2011) and *Captain America: The First Avenger* (Joe Johnston, 2011). While the *Avengers* reveal was a poorly kept secret, the studio presented this as a surprise official announcement about the film. Gregory Ellwood, "Robert Downey, Jr. Introduces 'the Avengers' at San Diego Comic-Con," HitFix, last modified July 24, 2010, http://www.hitfix.com/articles/robert-downey-jr -introduces-the-avengers-at-san-diego-comic-con.

19 John Thornton Caldwell, *Production Culture: Industrial Reflexivity and Critical Practice in Film and Television* (Durham, NC: Duke University Press, 2008), 96–97.

20 Caldwell, 97.

21 Caldwell, 108.

22 Caldwell, 108.

23 Jonathan Gray, *Show Sold Separately: Promos, Spoilers, and Other Media Paratexts* (New York: New York University Press, 2010).

24 Betsy Sharkey, "Have the Geeks Ceded Control?" *Los Angeles Times*, July 18, 2010, D4.

25 Gray, *Show Sold Separately*, 3.

26 Lowry, "Beware the Comic-Con False Positive."

27 For more on the history of this term, see Elaine Showalter, "Hysteria, Feminism, and Gender," in *Hysteria Beyond Freud*, ed. Sander L. Gilman, et al. (Berkeley: University of California Press, 1993), 286–344.

28 "Hysteria, N.," *OED Online*, last modified 2014, http://www.oed.com. Joli Jenson, "Fandom as Pathology," in *The Adoring Audience*, ed. Lisa A. Lewis (London: Routledge, 1992),11; Kristina Busse, "Geek Hierarchies, Boundary Policing, and the Gendering of the Good Fan," *Participations Journal of Audience & Reception Studies* 10, no. 1 (2013): 74.

29 The term "affirmational" originated in an online post by a fan using the moniker, obsession_inc. Busse, "Geek Hierarchies," 77–78, 82; obsession_inc, "Affirmational Fandom vs. Transformational Fandom," Dreamwidth, last modified June 1, 2009, https://obsession-inc.dreamwidth.org/82589.html.

30 Lowry, "Beware the Comic-Con False Positive."

31 Nick Nunziata, "The Birth of Hype," CNN.com, last modified July 27, 2004, http://www.cnn.com/2004/SHOWBIZ/Movies/07/27/comic.con/index.html.

32 Stephen Zeitchik, "The Fan Fantasy," *Hollywood Reporter*, August 1–3, 2008, 20.

33 Zeitchik, 21.

34 Brooks Barnes and Michael Cieply, "Movie Studios Reassess Comic-Con," *New York Times*, June 12, 2011, 7.

35 Matt Donnelly, "20th Century Fox Pulls out of Comic-Con Hall H," The Wrap, last modified April 28, 2016, https://www.thewrap.com/20th-century-fox-pulls-out -of-comic-con-hall-h-presentation-exclusive/.

36 Lesley Goldberg, "Comic-Con 2011: Warner Bros. Booth Will Get a 'Toon Up,'" *Hollywood Reporter*, last modified July 15, 2011, https://www.hollywoodreporter .com/live-feed/comic-con-2011-warner-bros-212083; THR staff, "Comic-Con 2011: Warner Bros. To Create Limited Edition Key Cards for Comic-Con Hotels," *Hollywood Reporter*, last modified June 29, 2011, https://www.hollywoodreporter .com/live-feed/comic-con-2011-warner-bros-206939; Dave Trumbore, "Comic-Con 2011 Collectible Swag Bags Revealed; Will Double as Backpacks," Collider, last modified July 12, 2011, http://collider.com/comic-con-collectible-bags-warner -bros/.

37 "Comic-Con 2016 *Toucan* Tip of the Day #16: There's a Ton of Fun Going on Outside of the Convention Center!" *Toucan*, last modified July 5, 2016, https:// www.comic-con.org/toucan/16-there's-ton-of-fun-going-outside-of-convention -center.

38 Henry Jenkins, Sam Ford, and Joshua Green, *Spreadable Media: Creating Value and Meaning in a Networked Culture*, Postmillennial Pop (New York: New York University Press, 2013), 3.

39 Eileen Meehan, "Leisure or Labor?: Fan Ethnography and Political Economy," in *Consuming Audiences? Production and Reception in Media Research*, ed. Ingunn Hagen and Janet Wasko (Cresskill, NJ: Hampton Press, Inc., 2000), 87.

40 Meehan, 86.

41 For a small sampling of the online response, see Jackie, "Comic-Con 2009: Thursday Roundup," *The Lowdown Blog*, last modified July 27, 2009, http://lowdownblog .com/2009/07/27/comic-con-2009-thursday-roundup/; Rob Keyes, "James Cameron's Avatar Is Epic—Comic-Con 2009," ScreenRant.Com, last modified July 23, 2009, http://screenrant.com/james-camerons-avatar-comiccon-2009-rob -18351/; Associated Press, "James Cameron Wows Comic-Con with 'Avatar,'" Today .com, last modified July 24, 2009, http://www.today.com/id/32126753/ns/today -today_entertainment/t/james-cameron-wows-comic-con-avatar/.

42 John Horn, "Comic-Con's Buzz-Makers," *Los Angeles Times*, July 27, 2009, D1.

43 "20th Century Fox and James Cameron: Avatar," Panel, San Diego Comic-Con, San Diego CA, July 23, 2009.

44 Josh Tyler, "Comic Con: August 21 Is Avatar Day," cinemablend.com, last modified July 23, 2009, http://www.cinemablend.com/new/Comic-Con-August-21-Is -Avatar-Day-14060.html.

45 *Avatar* went on to gross over $2.7 billion worldwide. Julia Boorstin, "Fox's 'Avatar Day' and a 3-D Revolution," CNBC, last modified August 21, 2009, http://www .cnbc.com/id/32510270; "Avatar (2009)," Box Office Mojo, last modified July 10, 2018, http://www.boxofficemojo.com/movies/?id=avatar.htm.

46 Lowry, "Beware the Comic-Con False Positive."

47 Most Hall H panels run between sixty and ninety minutes. A month after this article was published, the Warner Brothers panel appeared on the Comic-Con schedule with a runtime of two and a half hours, the same length as their 2009 panel, where they featured *Where the Wild Things Are* (Spike Jonze, 2009), *The Book of Eli* (The Hughes Brothers, 2010), *A Nightmare on Elm Street* (Samuel Bayer, 2010), *The Box* (Richard Kelly, 2009), *Jonah Hex* (Jimmy Hayward, 2010), and *Sherlock Holmes* (Guy Ritchie, 2009). While slightly shorter than originally planned, this remained an exceptionally long panel; a rarity at that time, even for Warner Brothers, which had skipped Hall H altogether during the previous year. Marc Graser and Josh L. Dickey, "Comic-Con 2012: Who's In and Who's Out," *Variety*, last modified June 12, 2012, http://variety.com/2012/film/news/comic-con -2012-who-s-in-who-s-out-1118055419; Estrada, *2009 Comic-Con International*, 32; Jackie Estrada, *2012 Comic-Con International: San Diego Events Guide* (San Diego: Comic-Con International Inc., 2012), 74; Barnes and Cieply, "Movie Studios Reassess Comic-Con," B1.

48 A few days prior to Comic-Con, reports also emerged that Legendary would present a teaser of their upcoming film *Godzilla* (Gareth Edwards, 2014). Graser and Dickey, "Comic-Con 2012."

Marc Graser and Rachel Abrams, "Legendary Pictures Eyes New Credit Line," last modified April 15, 2011, http://variety.com/2011/film/news/legendary-pictures -eyes-new-credit-line-1118035532/.

49 For video of this reveal, see Steve Younis, "Comic-Con 2012—Hall H Intro #1," YouTube, last modified July 16, 2012, https://www.youtube.com/watch?v =jRtOSwyZNFg.

50 Estrada, *2012 Comic-Con International.*

Having discussed Robert Downey Jr.'s appearance during the Marvel Studios panel in the conclusion to chapter 1, this chapter focuses on the panels that ran between the hours of 11:30 A.M. and 6:00 P.M. Given the extremely long wait prior to the 11:30 A.M. start time (in my case, from approximately 5:00 A.M.), I, along with a large portion of the crowd, left after the Marvel Studios panel and before the Kevin Smith event. This is demonstrative not only of the kinds of panels that attract the most attention in Hall H but also of the impact of scheduling. Kevin Smith's panel is a regular and popular event at Comic-Con, but it is usually staged to close out the day in Hall H. Given the mass exodus that occurs before this panel, it is also seemingly bracketed off from the rest of the programming. Notably, while serving the purpose of self-promotion for Smith's celebrity image, this was the only panel of the day that was not studio sponsored for the explicit purpose of promoting a film or a selection of films.

51 According to Google Trends, for example, searches using the term "Comic-Con" reached an all-time high in July 2012. The movie blog *Slash Film* also included two moments from 2012 in its list of "The best Comic-Con moments of all time." Google Trends, last modified July 12, 2018, https://trends.google.com/; Peter Sciretta, "The Best of Comic-Con: The Coolest and Most Important Moments in Hall H History," Slash Film, last modified July 19, 2017, http://www.slashfilm.com/best-comic-con-moments-of-all-time/3/.

52 Sharon Willis observed that Tarantino has developed a significant fan following because, among other things, his films tend to act as fan texts in and of themselves, full of recycled content and homages. In this way, she argues that Tarantino is evidence of Timothy Corrigan's assertion that authorship can function "as a commercial strategy for organizing audience reception, as a critical concept bound to distribution and marketing aims that identify and address the potential cult status of an auteur." Sharon Willis, "'Style,' Posture, and Idiom," in *Reinventing Film Studies*, ed. Christine Gledhill and Linda Williams (London: Oxford University Press, 2000), 284; Timothy Corrigan, *A Cinema without Walls: Movies and Culture after Vietnam* (Brunswick, NJ: Rutgers University Press, 1991), 103; Suzanne Scott, "Dawn of the Undead Author: Fanboy Auteurism and Zack Snyder's 'Vision,'" in *A Companion to Media Authorship*, ed. Jonathan Gray and Derek Johnson (Malden, MA: Wiley-Blackwell, 2013), 440–462.

53 Roxane Gay described *Django Unchained* as "a white man's slavery revenge fantasy, and one in which white people figure heavily and where black people are, largely, incidental. Django is allowed to regain his dignity because he is freed by a white man. He reunites with his wife, again, with the help of a white man. *Django Unchained* isn't about a black man reclaiming his freedom. It's about a white man working through his own racial demons and white guilt." Roxane Gay, "Surviving 'Django,'" BuzzFeed, last modified January 3, 2013, https://www.buzzfeed.com/roxanegay/surviving-django-80px.

54 In industry terms, a sizzle reel is much like a trailer, in that it is an assembly of footage meant to promote a film. The difference is that a sizzle reel is usually associated with promoting or pitching a film or television show within the industry, rather than to consumers. Dan Abrams, "Sizzle Reels: Produce before You Pitch (Part 1)," Producers Guild of America, last modified 2010, https://www.producersguild.org/?sizzle.

55 Quentin Tarantino, *Quentin Tarantino's Django Unchained, Comic-Con International 2012* (2012), Comic-Con Panel.

56 While I spoke to one person in line who identified the *Django* panel as a highlight, most of the attendees I encountered were more invested in the high-profile Warner Brothers and Marvel panels scheduled later in the day. In this way, the panel appeared to be operating for many as an added bonus or lead-up to an already enticing schedule of panels, rather than the main event.

57 Anne Thompson, "Tarantino and 'Django Unchained' Gang Hit Comic-Con: How Serious Is This Movie," Thompson on Hollywood, last modified July 16, 2012, http://blogs.indiewire.com/thompsononhollywood/tarantino-and-django -unchained-gang-hit-comic-con.

58 Many of my assertions about exclusivity as a marketing tool apply equally to the Cannes film festival. As an event that is covered extensively in the press but is extremely difficult and expensive to attend for the general public, Cannes also holds significant allure as an exclusive space with arguably more limitations to access than Comic-Con. The key difference is that as an industry event, the mode of address at Cannes is not necessarily aimed at fans in attendance, but instead targets members of the media industries, including the press.

59 Gregg Kilday, "Cannes 2012: Quentin Tarantino's 'Django Unchained' Unveiled by Harvey Weinstein," *Hollywood Reporter*, last modified May 21, 2012, http://www .hollywoodreporter.com/news/cannes-2012-quentin-tarantinos-django-327358.

60 *Variety* reported that "The Weinstein Co. invited about 50 journalists" to the presentation, which also included clips from *Silver Linings Playbook* (David O. Russell, 2012) and *The Master* (Paul Thomas Anderson, 2012). Dave McNary, "Weinsteins Preview 'Django,' 'Master' in Cannes," *Variety*, last modified May 21, 2012, http://variety.com/2012/film/news/weinsteins-preview-django-master-in -cannes-1118054431/.

61 For a compilation of this coverage, which included sites like *Ain't It Cool News*, *HitFix*, and *First Showing*, see Matt Singer, "Critics React to 7 Minutes of 'Django Unchained' at Cannes," IndieWire.Com, last modified May 21, 2012, http://blogs .indiewire.com/criticwire/critics-react-to-7-minutes-of-django-unchained-at -cannes.

62 Jeff Otto, "Comic-Con '12: Quentin Tarantino Wows Hall H Faithful with Bombastic Footage from 'Django Unchained' & More from the Presentation," IndieWire.Com, last modified July 15, 2012, http://blogs.indiewire.com/theplaylist /comic-con-quentin-tarantino-wows-hall-h-faithful-with-bombastic-footage-from -django-unchained-more-from-the-presentation-20120715; Nicole Sperling, "Comic-Con 2012: Tarantino's 'Django Unchained' Shocks, Awes," *Los Angeles Times*, last modified July 14, 2012, http://articles.latimes.com/2012/jul/14 /entertainment/la-et-mn-comiccon-2012-quentin-tarantino-shocks-and-awes-with -new-django-unchained-footage-20120714; "Comic-Con Fans Give 'Django Unchained' a Standing Ovation," Starpulse.com, last modified July 16, 2012, http://www.starpulse.com/news/index.php/2012/07/16/comiccon_fans_give _django_unchained_a_. Having been in the room at the time, I question the veracity of this last headline. I have no records in my notes and do not have any memory of a standing ovation after the sizzle reel. It is possible, however, that the ovation may have been centralized in the front section of Hall H but did not spread to the middle/back section, where I was seated.

63 Peter Bradshaw, "Cannes Film Festival Gets Glimpse of Quentin Tarantino's Django Unchained," *Guardian*, last modified May 21, 2012, http://www.guardian .co.uk/film/2012/may/21/cannes-film-festival-quentin-tarantino-django -unchained.

64 Open Road Films was acquired by Tang Media Partners in 2017 and was subsequently rebranded as Global Road Entertainment. Andrew Stewart, "AMC, Regal Hit Open Road," *Variety*, last modified March 7, 2011, http://variety.com/2011/film /news/amc-regal-hit-open-road-1118033459/; Dave McNary, "IM Global, Open Road Owner Tang Media Rebrands as Global Road Entertainment," *Variety*, last modified October 30, 2017, https://variety.com/2017/film/awards/tang-media -partners-rebrands-global-road-entertainment-1202602536/.

65 Mike Flemming, "Theater Chains AMC, Regal Launch Distribution Venture Open Road with Tom Ortenberg at Helm," Deadline, last modified March 7, 2011, https://deadline.com/2011/03/theater-chains-amc-regal-launch-distribution -venture-open-road-with-tom-ortenberg-at-head-111698/.

66 Pamela McClintock, "$200 Million and Rising: Hollywood Struggles with Soaring Marketing Costs," *Hollywood Reporter*, last modified July 31, 2014, https://www .hollywoodreporter.com/news/200-million-rising-hollywood-struggles-721818.

67 It is extremely difficult to get information regarding exact numbers in the various Comic-Con lines, so I was unable to verify the accuracy of the information circulated online. However, a series of tweets, which were collected on the now defunct Storify platform, indicated that the line was very long, stretching behind the convention center and around the waterfront. Regardless of accuracy, the discourses that circulate about Comic-Con lines help to create increased urgency, meaning evidence of the perception of a long line is often just as important as specific numbers. Inscaped, "Comic-Con 2012 Hall H Madness," Storify, last modified July 14, 2012, http://storify.com/Inscaped/comic-con-2012-hall-h -madness.

68 Raymond Williams, *Television: Technology and Cultural Form*, Routledge Classics (London; New York: Routledge, 2003), 86–97.

69 Jane Feuer, "The Concept of Live Television: Ontology as Ideology," in *Regarding Television: Critical Approaches—an Anthology*, ed. E. Ann Kaplan ([Frederick, MD.]: University Publications of America, 1983), 12–22.

70 These talking points, along with a positive review of the panel, also appeared on Collider.com. Adam Chitwood, "Comic-Con: End of Watch Panel Surprises with Exciting Footage and Admirable Characters," Collider, last modified July 14, 2012, http://collider.com/comic-con-end-of-watch/.
   David Ayer would go on to direct the DC comic book adaptation, *Suicide Squad* (2016).

71 The film was a sequel to *Silent Hill* (Christophe Gans, 2006) and an adaptation of the game *Silent Hill 3*.

72 Estrada, *2012 Comic-Con International*, 74.

73 Gray, *Show Sold Separately*, 50.

74 Trailer Park dates back to at least 1997, which was the earliest listing I could locate in available Comic-Con ephemera. However, Walker's involvement in this and other fan conventions, which began in the late 1970s, suggests that what the Comic-Con events guide describes as "A Comic-Con tradition" may have originated even earlier. Janet Tait, ed. *1997 Comic-Con International Events Guide*

(San Diego: Comic-Con International, Inc., 1997), 10; Estrada, *2012 Comic-Con International*.

Demonstrating the potential exclusivity of movie trailers, in November 1998, it was widely reported that *Star Wars* fans bought tickets for *Meet Joe Black* (Martin Brest, 1998) in order to see the trailer for *Star Wars Episode I: Phantom Menace* (George Lucas, 1999). Shortly after this time, movie trailers began to circulate more widely (officially and unofficially) online. Geoff, Williams, "Star Wars: The Phantom Menace; Waiting for the Force," *Cincinnati Post*, February 11, 1999, 1C; Marav Saar, "'Star Wars' Preview Becomes the Main Attraction // Movies: Fans Pay Full Price Just to See a Teaser to the Upcoming Prequel to the Hit Series," *Orange County Register*, November 18, 1998, A01; Keith M. Johnson, "'The Coolest Way to Watch Movie Trailers in the World': Trailers in the Digital Age," *Convergence* 14, no. 2 (2008): 145–160.

75 Based on descriptions of Thursday's trailers and my own experience with the 2:00 and 5:15 P.M. presentations, the programing was identical. Nick Winstead, "Comic-Con Trailer Park Covers a Wide Spectrum of Films," Comicbook.com, last modified July 12, 2012, http://comicbook.com/blog/2012/07/12/comic-con-trailer -park-covers-a-wide-spectrum-of-films/.

76 A 2012 post on comicbook.com, for example, reads "one of the main attractions for many fans is the annual Trailer Park, taking place in the hallowed ground referred to as Hall H." Winstead, "Comic-Con Trailer Park"; Travis Woods, "Comic-Con 2012: Trailer Park Showcases Ads for 'Dredd,' 'Finding Nemo 3d,' and More," last modified July 12, 2012, http://screencrave.com/2012-07-12/comiccon-2012-trailer -park-showcases-ads-dredd-finding-nemo-3d/.

77 Alex Billington, "Comic-Con 2012: 'Man of Steel' + 'Godzilla' + 'Pacific Rim' Video Blog," FirstShowing.Net, last modified July 15, 2012, http://www.firstshowing.net /2012/comic-con-2012-man-of-steel-godzilla-pacific-rim-video-blog/.

78 Kevin P. Sullivan, "San Diego Comic-Con Winners and Losers," MTV, last modified July 16, 2012, http://www.mtv.com/news/articles/1689682/comic-con -2012-recap.jhtml.

79 CB's Comic Con Team, "The 6 Best Panels of Comic Con 2012," CinemaBlend .com. Last modified July 16, 2013, http://www.cinemablend.com/new/6-Best -Panels-Comic-Con-2012-31960.html.

80 For example, two weeks before the panel, Drew McWeeny anticipated almost exactly what would unfold at Comic-Con, writing on *HitFix*, "How much of a reaction do you think there would be if Marvel introduced Joss Whedon as the official director of 'The Avengers,' something they've been refusing to confirm ever since the rumors first broke? And how much of a reaction would there be if he walked out onstage to personally introduce The Avengers?" Drew McWeeny, "Exclusive: Edward Norton Is Not the Hulk in 'the Avengers' . . . but He'd Like to Be," *HitFix*, last modified July 9, 2010, http://www.hitfix.com/blogs/motion -captured/posts/exclusive-edward-norton-is-not-the-hulk-in-the-avengers-but -he-d-like-to-be.

81 I can attest to the surprise element, having been present and among a segment of attendees who had not heard any "murmurs" about Depp's appearance. Natasha Vargas-Cooper, "Johnny Depp Crashes Comic-Con—Then Splits!" E!, last modified July 23, 2009, http://www.eonline.com/news/135572/johnny-depp -crashes-comic-con-then-splits.

Depp made his appearance in a room filled with a large number of fans awaiting an upcoming panel for *Twilight: New Moon* (Chris Weitz, 2009). At that time, Depp was still holding on—however tenuously—to his status as a Hollywood heartthrob and the intersection of Depp fans and *Twilight* fans further amplified the reaction to his unexpected appearance. For this reason, the scheduling of *Alice in Wonderland* and Depp's appearance in this time and place further demonstrates the power of programming flow in Hall H.

82 MTV News Staff, "Johnny Depp, Tim Burton Preview 'Alice in Wonderland' at Comic-Con," MTV News, last modified July 23, 2009, http://www.mtv.com/news/articles/1616846/johnny-depp-tim-burton-preview-alice-wonderland-at-comic-con.jhtml.

83 This was also the case when director Jon Favreau brought Harrison Ford on stage for the *Cowboys and Aliens* (Favreau, 2011) panel in 2011, his first Comic-Con appearance. Ford emerged shackled in handcuffs, a comedic comment on his reluctance to attend the convention. John Young, "Harrison Ford (in Handcuffs!) Makes His First Appearance at Comic-Con for 'Cowboys & Aliens,'" *Entertainment Weekly*, last modified July 24, 2010, http://popwatch.ew.com/2010/07/24/comic-con-harrison-ford-cowboys-aliens/.

84 Alex Stedman and Brent Lang, "Johnny Depp, Amber Heard Appear Moments Apart at Wb's Comic-Con Panel," *Variety*, last modified July 21, 2018, https://variety.com/2018/film/news/johnny-depp-amber-heard-comic-con-1202880368/.

85 Stephen Rodrick, "The Trouble with Johnny Depp," *Rolling Stone*, last modified June 21, 2018, https://www.rollingstone.com/movies/movie-features/the-trouble-with-johnny-depp-666010/.

86 Josh L. Dickey, "Con Still on H'w'd High; 'Man of Steel,' 'Pacific Rim' Draw Fan Buzz WB, Legendary Tout Tentpoles," *Variety*, July 16, 2012, 5.

87 Jeremy Rutz, "I Am Hall H: A Guide to the Biggest Stage at Comic-Con," *SDCC Unofficial Blog*, last modified June 3, 2013, http://sdccblog.com/2013/06/i-am-hall-h-a-guide-to-the-biggest-stage-at-comic-con/.

88 While I was able to glean much about this system over years of research, I finally confirmed my theories about these procedures in a 2018 conversation with a journalist who regularly covers the San Diego Comic-Con.

89 Over seven visits to Comic-Con, I have been seated in various locations throughout Hall H, including the front, center section. My experiences were consistent with this description in that in all but the front and center location, I relied heavily on the screens and my camera's zoom lens to get a closer view of the stage.

90 Adam Chitwood, "Comic-Con: Guillermo Del Toro Wows with Monster vs. Robot Footage at Pacific Rim Panel," Collider, last modified July 15, 2012, http://collider.com/comic-con-pacific-rim/.

91 Derek Lee, "Comic-Con Recap: Warner Bros. and Legendary Pictures Panel," Examiner.com, last modified July 16, 2012, http://www.examiner.com/article/comic-con-recap-warner-bros-and-legendary-pictures-panel.

92 The Deadline Team, "'Pacific Rim,' 'Man of Steel,' 'the Hobbit,' 'Godzilla': What Comic-Con Was Made For," Deadline Hollywood, last modified July 14, 2012, http://www.deadline.com/2012/07/pacific-rim-godzilla-man-of-steel-the-hobbit-what-comic-con-was-made-for/.

93 Alex Billington, "Comic-Con 2012 Live: WB's Panel on 'Hobbit,' 'MOS' + 'Pacific Rim,'" FirstShowing.Net, last modified July 14, 2012, http://www.firstshowing.net

/2012/comic-con-2012-live-wbs-panel-on-hobbit-mos-pacific-rim/; Jacob Hall, "Comic-Con 2012 Saturday Schedule: 'Man of Steel,' 'Iron Man 3' and More," Screen Crush, last modified June 30, 2012, http://screencrush.com/comic-con-2012 -saturday/; Matt Patches, "Comic-Con 2012: The Web's Most Anticipated SDCC Panels," Hollywood.com, last modified July 6, 2012, http://www.hollywood.com /news/movies/32970094/comic-con-2012-the-web-s-most-anticipated-sdcc-panels.

94 Dickey, "Con Still on H'w'd High." *Variety* was not the only publication to make this observation; *HitFix* declared Warner Brothers a Comic-Con "winner": "No studio had a more talked about presentation than Warner Bros. and Legendary Pictures. Stunning the Hall H crowd and their studio peers, the two companies spent a pretty penny to expand the traditional Hall H screen with two side screens tripling the audio visual projection. It was a master display of showmanship and was assisted by the fact the studio partners' films ('The Hobbit,' 'Pacific Rim,' 'Man of Steel,' 'The Campaign,' 'Godzilla') delivered the goods during the panel." Gregory Ellwood, "Comic-Con 2012 Winners and Losers: Robert Downey Jr., Stephenie Meyer, 'Pacific Rim,'" HitFix, last modified July 18, 2012, http://www.hitfix.com /news/comic-con-2012-winners-and-losers-robert-downey-jr-stephenie-meyer -pacific-rim.

95 Jackie Estrada, ed. *2013 Comic-Con International: Events Guide* (San Diego: Comic-Con International, Inc., 2013), 58.

96 Alexandra Cheney, "WB Dazzles Comic-Con, Hall H with Supersized Screens," *Variety*, last modified July 26, 2014, https://variety.com/2014/film/news/warner -bros-screens-comic-con-1201269625/.

97 Cheney.

98 Barnes and Cieply, "Movie Studios Reassess Comic-Con."

99 "Anti-Piracy Warning," Panel, San Diego Comic-Con, San Diego, CA, July 21, 2012.

100 "Anti-Piracy Warning." Panel, San Diego Comic-Con, San Diego, CA, July 23, 2009.

101 Michel Foucault, *Discipline and Punish: The Birth of the Prison* (New York: Vintage Books, 1979), 170.

102 Jacob Hall, "Comic-Con 2012: A New Clip from 'Silent Hill: Revelation 3d,'" Screen Crush, last modified July 14, 2012, http://screencrush.com/comic-con-2012 -clip-from-silent-hill-revelation-3d/; Adam Chitwood, "New Trailer for the Campaign; Plus Watch the Comic-Con Panel with Will Ferrell and Zach Galifi- anakis," Collider, last modified July 19, 2012, http://collider.com/the-campaign -trailer-comic-con-video/.

103 Noelene Clark, "'Man of Steel' Trailers: Superman Lonely at Land, Sea and Air," *Los Angeles Times*: Hero Complex, last modified July 24, 2012, http://herocomplex .latimes.com/movies/man-of-steel-trailer-superman-lonely-at-land-sea-and-air/.

104 Gregg Kilday, "Comic-Con Piracy: 'Suicide Squad,' 'Deadpool' Footage Forces Studios to React," *Hollywood Reporter*, last modified 14 July, 2015, http://www .hollywoodreporter.com/news/comic-con-piracy-suicide-squad-808495.

105 Sue Kroll quoted in Mike Fleming Jr., "Warner Bros Releases 'Suicide Squad' Footage after Being Frustrated by Comic Con Pirates," Deadline Hollywood, last modified July 13, 2015, http://deadline.com/2015/07/suicide-squad-official-movie -footage-exclusive-1201475371/.

106 Paul McDonald, "Piracy and the Shadow History of Hollywood," in *Hollywood and the Law*, ed. Paul McDonald, et al. (London: Palgrave, 2015), 70.

107 Legendary Pictures and Warner Brothers' eight-year co-financing and distribution deal came to an end in June 2013. Marc Graser, "Warner Bros. No Longer in Legendary's Future," *Variety*, last modified June 24, 2013, http://variety.com/2013 /biz/news/warner-bros-no-longer-in-legendarys-future-1200501572/.

    Though Legendary subsequently signed a new deal with Universal, the companies were still entangled through distribution deals on films like *Godzilla* and *300: Rise of an Empire* (Noam Murro, 2014) and once again paired to present an extended Comic-Con panel in 2013. Andrew Wallenstein, "Kevin Tsujihara Breaks Silence on Why Legendary, WB Parted Ways," *Variety*, last modified October 5, 2013, http://variety.com/2013/film/news/kevin-tsujihara-breaks-silence-on-why -legendary-wb-parted-ways-1200697794/.

    I return to this question of corporate synergy in chapter 4's discussion of Comic-Con's Exhibit Hall.

108 Scott, "Dawn of the Undead Author."

109 Brooks Barnes and Michael Cieply, "Hollywood Acts Warily at Comics Convention," *New York Times*, July 16, 2012, B1.

110 "Warner Bros. Pictures and Legendary Pictures Preview Their Upcoming Lineups," Panel, San Diego Comic-Con, San Diego, July 21, 2012.

111 This room seats approximately 2,100 attendees. Dixon, "San Diego Comic-Con Room Capacities."

112 Incidentally, his description of the film changed very little in the following year. "Legendary Pictures Preproduction Preview," San Diego Comic-Con, San Diego, July 22, 2011.

113 As *Hollywood Reporter* suggested, "Legendary Pictures doesn't have a lick of footage to show but it's got the talent to throw its first-ever Comic-Con panel." Borys Kit, "Comic-Con 2011: Guillermo Del Toro and 'Pacific Rim' Cast Set Panel," *Hollywood Reporter*: Heat Vision, last modified July 6, 2011, http://www .hollywoodreporter.com/heat-vision/comic-con-2011-guillermo-del-208442.

114 "Comic-Con Talk Back, 2011," Panel, San Diego Comic-Con, San Diego, CA, July 24, 2011.

115 "Comic-Con Talk Back, 2011."

116 Rogers has made these kinds of statements at various times during the annual Talk Back sessions, particularly when attendees complain about the lines or limited access to particular panels. "Comic-Con Talk Back, 2011."

117 "Warner Bros. Pictures and Legendary Pictures Preview Their Upcoming Lineups."

118 See, for example, Devin Faraci, "Comic-Con 2012: Pacific Rim Tears the Roof Off Hall H," Birth. Movies. Death., last modified July 15, 2012, http://badassdigest.com /2012/07/15/comic-con-2012-pacific-rim-tears-the-roof-off-hall-h/; Jim Vejvoda, "Comic-Con: Pacific Rim Brings Giant Monsters and Robots," IGN.com, last modified July 14, 2012, http://www.ign.com/articles/2012/07/14/comic-con -pacific-rim-brings-giant-monsters-and-robots; Derrick Deanne, "Hall H: Surprises Galore from WB, Which Amazes with Scenes from 'Pacific Rim,' 'the Hobbit,' 'Man of Steel,' and More," *Fandango*, last modified July 15, 2012, http://www .fandango.com/movieblog/hall-h-surprises-galore-from-wb-which-amazes-with -scenes-from-pacific-rim-hobbit-man-of-steel-and-more-718248.html.

119 Steve "Frosty" Weintraub, "Guillermo Del Toro Talks Pacific Rim Soundtrack and Collectables," Collider, last modified August 9, 2012, http://collider.com/guillermo -del-toro-pacific-rim-soundtrack-collectables/187592/; Josh Wilding, "New Images

from Guillermo Del Toro's Pacific Rim," ComicBookMovie.Com, last modified August 30, 2012, http://www.comicbookmovie.com/fansites /JoshWildingNewsAndReviews/news/?a=66529.

120 The reason for the conversion was, no doubt, economically motivated, as Warner Brothers sought to drive up ticket prices and open the door to the lucrative Chinese market. Simon Reynolds, "Guillermo Del Toro 'Strong-Armed' into 'Pacific Rim' 3d Conversion," Digital Spy, last modified September 13, 2012, http://www .digitalspy.com/movies/news/a405796/guillermo-del-toro-strong-armed-into -pacific-rim-3d-conversion.html.

121 Lesnick, "Guillermo Del Toro Talks the Strain and Pacific Rim's 3d Conversion," Shock Till You Drop, last modified September 22, 2012, http://www .shocktillyoudrop.com/news/170043-guillermo-del-toro-talks-the-strain-and -pacific-rims-3d-conversion/.

122 Matt Goldberg, "New York Comic-Con: Guillermo Del Toro Talks Pacific Rim and the Prequel Graphic Novel," Collider, last modified October 13, 2012, http:// collider.com/pacific-rim-recap-new-york-comic-con/.

123 Goldberg.

124 Kellvin Chavez, "'Pacific Rim' Viral Marketing Has Begun!" Latino Review, last modified November 28, 2012, http://latino-review.com/2012/11/pacific-rim-viral -marketing-begun/?utm_source=rss&utm_medium=rss&utm_campaign=pacific -rim-viral-marketing-begun.

125 Brian Gallagher, "'Pacific Rim' Trailer," MovieWeb, last modified December 12, 2012, http://www.movieweb.com/news/pacific-rim-trailer; MTV, "Guillermo Del Toro Provides *Pacific Rim* Trailer Commentary," Comingsoon.net, last modified December 14, 2012, http://www.comingsoon.net/news/movienews.php?id=98032.

126 "News for Pacific Rim (2013)," IMDb, last modified 2019, http://www.imdb.com /title/tt1663662/news?year=2012;start=901.

127 Hardwick, the former CEO of Nerdist Industries and host of AMC's *Talking Dead*, was a frequent and popular panel moderator at Comic-Con until 2018, when his ex-partner published an article detailing three years of emotional and sexual abuse during their relationship. While he was suspended and subsequently reinstated at AMC, his future at Comic-Con was unclear as of early 2019. Ryan Parker, "Nerdist Removes Chris Hardwick References from Site Amid Chloe Dykstra's Abuse Claim," *Hollywood Reporter*, last modified June 15, 2018, https://www .hollywoodreporter.com/news/nerdist-removes-chris-hardwick-references-site -alleged-abuse-claim-1120557.

128 Busse, "Geek Hierarchies"; "Warner Bros. Pictures and Legendary Pictures Preview Their Upcoming Lineups."

129 Borys Kit, "'Man of Steel' Footage So Good It Makes Fans Cry," *Hollywood Reporter*: Heat Vision, last modified July 14, 2012, http://www.hollywoodreporter .com/heat-vision/comic-con-2012-man-steel-super-man-reboot-349325; Ben Arnold, "'Superman' Trailer Makes Fans Cry," Yahoo! Movies UK & Ireland, last modified July 16, 2012, http://uk.movies.yahoo.com/-superman—trailer-makes -fans-cry.html.

130 Pete Hammond, "'The Hobbit' Footage in New Format Draws Lukewarm Response: Cinemacon," Deadline, last modified April 24, 2012, http://www .deadline.com/2012/04/the-hobbit-debuts-at-revolutionary-48-frames-during -warner-bros-exhib-presentation-cinemacon/.

131 This technology involves the filming of high-resolution digital video and its projection at double the usual speed in order to reduce blurring and create a more lifelike image. For more information, see Jamie Lendino, "'The Hobbit' at 48fps: Frame Rates Explained," *PC Magazine*, last modified December 14, 2012, http://www.pcmag.com/article2/0,2817,2403746,00.asp.

132 Amy Kaufman, "Cinemacon: Footage of 'the Hobbit' Draws Mixed Reaction," *Los Angeles Times*, last modified April 24, 2012, http://latimesblogs.latimes.com /movies/2012/04/cinemacon-hobbit-frame-rate-depp-gatsby.html; Mark Hanrahan, "'The Hobbit' 48fps Footage Divides Audiences at Cinemacon," Huff Post Entertainment, last modified April 25, 2012, http://www.huffingtonpost.com /2012/04/25/hobbit-48-fps-footage-divides-audiences_n_1452391.html; Devin Faraci, "Cinemacon2012: The Hobbit Underwhelms at 48 Frames Per Second," Birth. Movies. Death., last modified April 24, 2012, http://badassdigest.com/2012 /04/24/cinemacon-2012-the-hobbit-underwhelms-at-48-frames-per-secon/.

133 Geoff Boucher, "'The Hobbit' at Comic-Con: Peter Jackson's San Diego Plan," *Los Angeles Times*: Hero Complex, last modified July 11, 2012, http://herocomplex .latimes.com/movies/the-hobbit-at-comic-con-peter-jacksons-san-diego-plan/.

134 Barnes and Cieply, "Hollywood Acts Warily at Comics Convention," B1.

135 Boucher, "'The Hobbit' at Comic-Con."

136 These technologies are similarly constructed around exclusivity, as they transform films into media events that can only be experienced in the theater. In fact, exhibition technologies such as these are an example of how the theories I outline in this book might be extended to a wide range of other media events, venues, and experiences.

Chapter 4   Ret(ail)con

Epigraph: "San Diego's Golden State Comic-Con Flyer, 1970." Series IV: Comic-Con Advertising, Folder 1, Box 3, Shel Dorf Collection, San Diego History Center.

1 Andrew J. Friedenthal, *Retcon Game: Retroactive Continuity and the Hyperlinking of America* (Jackson: University Press of Mississippi, 2017), 10–11.

2 Joseph Turow, "The Case for Studying in-Store Media," *Media Industries* 1, no. 1 (2014), 62–63; Matt Hills, *Fan Cultures* (London: Routledge, 2002), 30; Jonathan Gray, Cornel Sandvoss, and C. Lee Harrington, *Fandom: Identities and Communities in a Mediated World* (New York: New York University Press, 2007), 1–16.

3 Hills, *Fan Cultures*, 27.

4 Hills, 27–30; Lincoln Geraghty, *Cult Collectors: Nostalgia, Fandom and Collecting Popular Culture* (London: Routledge, 2014).

5 These practices are at the heart of neo-Marxist critiques of unpaid labor in the digital age. Tiziana Terranova, "Free Labor: Producing Culture for the Digital Economy," *Social Text* 18, no. 2 (Summer 2000): 33–58.

6 Henry Jenkins, Sam Ford, and Joshua Green, *Spreadable Media: Creating Value and Meaning in a Networked Culture*, Postmillennial Pop (New York: New York University Press, 2013), 123.

7 Janet Wasko and Eileen Meehan, "Critical Crossroads or Parallel Routes? Political Economy and New Approaches to Studying Media Industries and Cultural Products," *Cinema Journal* 52, no. 3 (2013), 153; Timothy Havens, Amanda D. Lotz,

and Serra Tinic, "Critical Media Industry Studies: A Research Approach," *Communication, Culture & Critique* 2, no. 2 (2009): 236.

8 Angela McRobbie, *Be Creative: Making a Living in the New Culture Industries* (Cambridge, UK; Malden, MA: Polity Press, 2015), 18.

9 Turow, "The Case for Studying in-Store Media," 64.

The edited collection, *Point of Sale*, in which an earlier version of this chapter was published, represents an important contribution in this regard. Daniel Herbert and Derek Johnson, eds., *Point of Sale: Analyzing Media Retail* (New Brunswick, NJ: Rutgers University Press, 2019).

10 Derek Johnson, *Media Franchising* (New York: New York University Press, 2013); Avi Santo, *Selling the Silver Bullet: The Lone Ranger and Transmedia Brand Licensing* (Austin: University of Texas Press, 2015); Daniel Herbert, *Videoland: Movie Culture at the American Video Store* (Berkeley and Los Angeles: University of California Press, 2014).

11 McRobbie, *Be Creative*, 44.

12 Geraghty, *Cult Collectors*, 7; Anne Gilbert, "Conspicuous Convention: Industry Interpellation and Fan Consumption at San Diego Comic-Con," in *The Routledge Companion to Media Fandom*, ed. Melissa A. Click and Suzanne Scott (New York: Routledge, 2018), 319–328.

13 Liam Burke, "The Pop Culture Petri Dish of Comic-Con," *Irish Times*, July 26, 2011; Geoff Boucher, "Comic-Con 2009; Geek Out," *Los Angeles Times*, July 22, 2009.; Glenn Gaslin, "Superheroes Escape the Page: Comic Book Sales Are Tailing Off, Even as Their Characters Triumph in Other Media," *Vancouver Sun*, July 27, 2002, E3; Eric Tompkins, *The Non-Geeks Guide to Comic-Con* (Lexington, KY: Eric Tompkins, 2012); Tom Spurgeon, "Nerd Vegas; a Guide to Visiting and Enjoying CCI in San Diego, 2008! (Final Version)," *The Comics Reporter*, last modified May 27, 2008, http://www.comicsreporter.com/index.php/briefings/commentary/14163/.

14 San Diego Comic Convention Inc., *Comic-Con: 40 Years of Artists, Writers, Fans & Friends* (San Francisco: Chronicle Books, 2009), 45.

15 Peter Bart, "Geek Chic: Hollywood Corrals Nerd Herd . . ." *Variety*, August 2–8, 2004, 1.

16 A sampling of such publications includes Tanya Rodrigues, "San Diego's Reworked Convention Center Set to Debut," *Orange County Business Journal* 24, no. 34 (2001): 31 31; Marc Graser and Jonathan Bing, "Genre Pix Cultivate Geek Chic," *Variety*, July 28–August 8, 2003, 8; Bart, "Geek Chic," 3; Tony Perry, "It's a Bird. It's Plain: It's Super," *Los Angeles Times*, July 14, 2005, E4; Heidi MacDonald, "Hollywood Cruises Nerd Prom," *Publishers Weekly*, June 20, 2005, 26–27; Tom Carsom, "The Big Shill," *Atlantic Monthly*, May 2005, 127; Scott Collins, "Oh, Boy!" *Chicago Tribune*, January 6, 2006, 3; Jerry Johnston, "Comic Book Fans Have a Blast," *Deseret News*, August 5, 2007, E16; Rory Carroll, "Joss Whedon at Comic-Con: Director Returns Home a God among Geeks," *Guardian*, last modified July 15, 2012, http://www.theguardian.com/culture/2012/jul/15/joss-whedon-comic-con -god; Brooks Barnes, "Seeking Silver-Screen Success," *International Herald Tribune*, July 10, 2012, 16; Rob Salkowitz, *Comic-Con and the Business of Popular Culture* (New York: McGraw-Hill, 2012).

17 Perry, "It's a Bird. It's Plain," E4.

18 Timothy Havens, *Global Television Marketplace* (London: BFI Publishing, 2006), 69–70.

19 Comic-Con International, "Aisles of Smiles!" in *Update*, ed. Dan Vado (San Diego: Comic-Con International, 2005), 24.

20 Christie D'Zurilla, "By the Numbers: San Diego Comic-Con International 2016," *Los Angeles Times*, last modified July 24, 2016, http://www.latimes.com /entertainment/la-et-hc-comic-con-updates-by-the-numbers-san-diego-comic-con -1469118665-htmlstory.html.

21 Artists, small companies, and dealers typically use standard, uniformly sized "tables" while "booths" denote the larger and more costly blocks of space occupied by more high profile exhibitors.

22 Some of these tables are clustered together by theme, most notably the Artists' Alley, a term commonly assigned to spaces at fan conventions where individual artists can reserve small tables (usually at reduced rates) in order to sell sketches and showcase their work. Living up to its title, the Artist's Alley is set apart at one end of the hall and is easy to neglect or miss for those who do not make it a destination.

23 William Schelly, *The Golden Age of Comic Fandom*, Limited collectors ed. (Seattle, WA: Hamster Press, 1995).

24 Paul Douglas Lopes, *Demanding Respect: The Evolution of the American Comic Book* (Philadelphia: Temple University Press, 2009), 98.

25 Jean-Paul Gabilliet, *Of Comics and Men: A Cultural History of American Comic Books* (Jackson: University Press of Mississippi, 2005), 263; Schelly, *The Golden Age of Comic Fandom*, 33, 61; Lopes, *Demanding Respect*, 98.

26 Lattanzi, "Who's Who in Comic Fandom."

27 Schelly, *The Golden Age of Comic Fandom*, 87.

28 Some retailers took advantage of this system and, as Michael Dean points out, "plenty of titleless comic books made their way to flea markets at cut rates." Michael Dean, "Fine Young Cannibals: How Phil Seuling and a Generation of Teenage Entrepreneurs Created the Direct Market and Changed the Face of Comics," *Comics Journal*, no. 277 (2006): 50.

29 Randy Duncan, Matthew J. Smith, and Paul Levitz, *The Power of Comics: History, Form, and Culture*, 2nd ed. (New York: Bloomsbury, 2015), 276.

30 Duncan, Smith, and Levitz, 61.

31 Quoted in Schelly, *The Golden Age of Comic Fandom*, 31.

32 Gabilliet, *Of Comics and Men*, 141.

33 Jonathan David Tankel and Keith Murphy, "Collecting Comic Books: A Study of the Fan and Curatorial Consumption," in *Theorizing Fandom*, ed. Cheryl Harris and Alison Alexander (Cresskill, NJ: Hampton Press, Inc., 1998), 58.

34 Tankel and Murphy, 58–59.

35 Lopes, *Demanding Respect*, 94–96; Matthew Pustz, *Comic Book Culture: Fanboys and True Believers*, Studies in Popular Culture (Jackson: University Press of Mississippi, 1999), 46–47.

36 Bill Schelly, *Founders of Comic Fandom: Profiles of 90 Publishers, Dealers, Collectors, Writers, Artists and Other Luminaries of the 1950s and 1960s* (Jefferson, NC: McFarland, 2010), 41.

37 Schelly, *The Golden Age of Comic Fandom*, 33.

38 *The Comicollector* was such a significant undertaking (in size and circulation) that the publication went through three editors by 1964. That year the *Comicollector* merged with Gordon Love's *The Rocket's Blast* to become *Rocket's Blast Comicollector*, and circulation on the fanzine grew to one thousand by 1966. Schelly, 37, 59–61.

39 In 1965, for example, *Newsweek* opened their article on "comic cultists" by highlighting the hundred-dollar value of the June 1938 issue of *Action Comics*, which featured Superman's first appearance. "Superfans and Batmaniacs," *Newsweek*, February 15, 1965, 89; Pustz, *Comic Book Culture*, 46–47; Gabilliet, *Of Comics and Men*, 137.

40 Robert M. Overstreet, *The Comic Book Price Guide 1976–1977* (New York: Crown Publishers, 1976), 11.

41 This kind of speculation is more commonly identified with the comics industry's boom and bust between the 1980s and 1990s, which I discuss later in this chapter. However, as dealer and historian Robert L. Beerbohm points out, speculation dates back to the origins of comic fandom. Robert L. Beerbohm, "Secret Origins of the Direct Market."

42 Beaty, *Comics versus Art*, 154; Tankel and Murphy, "Collecting Comic Books," 66–67; Duncan, Smith, and Levitz, *The Power of Comics*, 301.

43 As Bart Beaty's research suggests, this notion of a "middle ground, or commonsensical position, separate from both the act of reading and consuming 'Comics'" was still being argued in the publication as late as 1999. Overstreet, *The Comic Book Price Guide 1976–1977*, 11; Beaty, *Comics versus Art*, 155.

44 Beerbohm, "Secret Origins of the Direct Market," *Comic Book Artist*, Fall 1999, 84.

45 Schelly, *Founders of Comic Fandom*, 40–53.

46 Like many comic book dealers, Bud Plant entered the field as a teenaged collector, buying comics from *Rocket's Blast Comic Collector* in the mid-1960s. From there, he and some friends opened Seven Sons Comic Shop in 1968, which was, by some accounts, the first dedicated comics shop in the United States. Over his career, he ran a lucrative mail-order company, traveled to conventions around the country, and opened a number of other retail locations and worked in distribution and publishing. Quoted in Dean, "Fine Young Cannibals," 52; Schelly, *Founders of Comic Fandom*, 46–48.

47 Schelly, 40.

48 The Palms Recreation Center didn't permit monetary transactions on the premises, so the teenaged members of SMASH had to leave the building if they wanted to buy or sell books from one another. "Active Trading Marks Comic Book Collecting," *Los Angeles Times*, October 19 1967, WS2.

49 Schelly, *The Golden Age of Comic Fandom*, 71, 77.

50 Schelly, 65–74.

51 Schelly, *Founders of Comic Fandom*, 102; Shel Dorf, "The Detroit Triple Fan Fair—and How It Came to Be," *Alter Ego*, December 2003, 43.

52 For example, Dealer Steve Schanes reported driving to Los Angeles to buy comics from newsstands and sell them to San Diego collectors. Schelly, *Founders of Comic Fandom*, 102; Dean, "Fine Young Cannibals," 51.

53 It is likely that these books were coverless because they were originally claimed as returns and subsequently resold. Duncan, Smith, and Levitz, *The Power of Comics*, 277; Angela Carone and Maureen Cavanaugh, "The First Comic-Con," KPBS Public Media, last modified July 22, 2010, http://www.kpbs.org/news/2010/jul/22/first-comic-con/.

54 Peter Rowe, "Ken Kruger; Ocean Beach Bookstore Was Launching Pad for Comic-Con," *San Diego Union-Tribune,* last modified November 26, 2009, http://www.utsandiego.com/news/2009/nov/26/ocean-beach-bookstore-was-launching-pad-comic-con/.

55 Pustz, *Comic Book Culture*; Benjamin Woo, "The Android's Dungeon: Comic-Bookstores, Cultural Spaces, and the Social Practices of Audiences," *Journal of Graphic Novels and Comics* 2, no. 2 (2011): 125–136.

56 "San Diego's Golden State Comic-Minicon Flyer." Series IV: Comic-Con Advertising, Folder 1, Box 3, Shel Dorf Collection, San Diego History Center; Schelly, *The Golden Age of Comic Fandom*, 65–74, 77.

57 "San Diego's Golden State Comic-Minicon Flyer"; Donald Franson, "A Key to the Terminology of Science-Fiction Fandom" National Fantasy Fan Federation, 1962.

58 "San Diego's Golden State Comic-Con Flyer, 1970."

59 Carone and Cavanaugh, "The First Comic-Con."

60 Shel Dorf quoted in Andrew Makarushka, "Comics Connoisseurs Here for Golden State Convention," *San Diego Union*, August 2, 1970, B11.

    "Hustlers room" is likely a mistaken reference to the aforementioned "Hucksters rooms."

61 Chuck Graham and Barry Alfonso. "San Diego Comic-Con Progress Report No.1 and 1973 Wrap-up Report." Series III: Progress Reports and Newsletters, Folder 40, Box 1, Shel Dorf Collection, San Diego History Center.

62 Lopes, *Demanding Respect*, 99.

63 Dean, "Fine Young Cannibals," 50.

64 Dean, 51.

65 Dean, 51.

66 Seuling organized a number of high-profile comic conventions in New York beginning in the late 1960s. For more on his contributions to comic fandom, see Schelly, *Founders of Comic Fandom*, 106–108. For more on Seuling's role in creating the direct market, see Dean, "Fine Young Cannibals."

67 Dean, 51, 54.

68 Rick Marschall, "Remembrances of Cons Past," in *1984 San Diego Comic-Con*, ed. Jackie Estrada (San Diego: San Diego Comic Convention, Inc., 1984), np.

69 Marschall.

70 Marschall.

71 Jackie Estrada, "1983 San Diego Comic-Con Progress Report No. 2," May 1983, San Diego Comic-Con, Michigan State University Library Comic Art Collection.

72 Jackie Estrada, "1984 San Diego Comic-Con Progress Report No. 1," December 1983, San Diego Comic-Con, Michigan State University Library Comic Art Collection.

73 Mark Evanier, "Comics: Ny2LA," in *1982 San Diego Comic-Con Inc. Souvenir Book*, ed. Shel Dorf (San Diego: San Diego Comic-Con Inc., 1982), np.

74 San Diego Comic Convention Inc., *Comic-Con: 40 Years*.

75 "Comic Book Expo Flyer, 1986," San Diego Comic-Con, Michigan State University Library Comic Art Collection.

76 "Comic Book Expo Flyer, 1986."

77 John T. Caldwell, "Industrial Geography Lessons: Socio-Professional Rituals and the Boarderlands of Production Culture," in *Mediaspace: Place, Scale and Culture in a Media Age*, ed. Nick Couldry and Anna McCarthy (New York: Routledge, 2004), 163–189.

78 "Comic Book Expo Flyer, 1987," San Diego Comic-Con, Michigan State University Library Comic Art Collection.

79 Mike Pasqua, "Con-Tact #2," San Diego Comic-Con, Michigan State University Library Comic Art Collection; Fay Gates, "Comic Book Expo 84 Letter," March 21, 1984, San Diego Comic-Con, Michigan State University Library Comic Art Collection.

80 San Diego Comic Convention Inc., *Comic-Con: 40 Years*, 60.

81 Gates, "Comic Book Expo 84 Letter."

82 The convention had been previously held at the CPAC in 1979 and 1980 and returned to the El Cortez for a final year in 1981. David Glanzer, Gary Sassaman, and Jackie Estrada, eds., *Comic-Con 40 Souvenir Book* (San Diego: San Diego Comic-Con International, 2009), 72, 78–87, 94–95.

83 Although the CPAC was host to high-profile conventions (American Architects Association in 1977) and performers (Bob Dylan and the Rolling Stones in 1965) in its earlier years, by the 1990s it had fallen into significant disrepair, having been replaced by the newer, larger San Diego Convention Center in 1989. Terry Rodgers, "City's Old Convention Center Has New Owner," *San Diego Union-Tribune*, Sunday, August 1, 1993, B1.

84 San Diego Comic Convention Inc., *Comic-Con: 40 Years*, 60.

85 "Comic-Con Poster, 1984," San Diego Comic-Con, Michigan State University Library Comic Art Collection.

86 Jackie Estrada, "1984 San Diego Comic-Con Progress Report No. 2," April 1984, San Diego Comic-Con, Michigan State University Library Comic Art Collection; Mark Stadler, "San Diego Comic-Con Progress Report No. 1," February, 1987, San Diego Comic-Con, Michigan State University Library Comic Art Collection.

87 Mark Stadler, *San Diego Comic-Con Progress Report No. 2* (San Diego: San Diego Comic Convention, Inc., 1988).

88 Janet Tait, ed., *1988 San Diego Comic-Con Events Guide* (San Diego: San Diego Comic Convention, Inc., 1988), 14.

    While the *1988 San Diego Comic-Con Events Guide* listed only fifty-six, the next year's Progress Report counted "80+ convention-style booths" in the hall. Jackie Estrada, ed., *Progress Report No. 2* (San Diego: San Diego Comic Convention, Inc., 1989), 13.

89 Estrada.

90 Bill Stoddard, ed., *1990 San Diego Comic-Con Events Guide* (San Diego: San Diego Comic Convention, Inc., 1990), 2.

91 Glanzer, Sassaman, and Estrada, *Comic-Con 40 Souvenir Book*, 86–94.

92 While the "What's Changed" section of the *Events Guide* refers to "the Dealers' Room," the space was labeled as the "Exhibit Hall" throughout the remainder of the guide. Bill Stoddard and Janet Tait, eds., *1991 San Diego Comic-Con Convention Events Guide* (San Diego: San Diego Comic Convention, Inc., 1991), 4.

93 While I cannot confirm that they attended Comic-Con and the Expo, it seems likely that Hobson and his sales team participated in both events. Jackie Estrada, ed., *The 1991 San Diego Comic Convention Program Book* (San Diego: San Diego Comic Convention, Inc., 1991); Dave Scroggy, "Comic Book Expo '91," San Diego: San Diego Comic-Con, Inc., 1991.

94 Estrada, *The 1991 San Diego Comic Convention Program Book*; Scroggy, "Comic Book Expo '91."

95 San Diego Comic Convention Inc., *Comic-Con: 40 Years*, 87; "Retailer Programs," Comic-Con.org, last modified July 6, 2017, https://www.comic-con.org/cci /retailer-programs.

96 Gina McIntyre, "H'wood Presence at Comic-Con Book Outing," *Hollywood Reporter*, August 5, 2002, 13.

97 Caldwell, "Industrial Geography Lessons."

98 Dean, "Fine Young Cannibals," 49.

99 Pustz, *Comic Book Culture*, 131.

100 Lopes, *Demanding Respect*, 115–116.

101 Beaty, *Comics versus Art*, 169–170.

102 Lopes, *Demanding Respect*, 117; Matthew P. McAllister, "Ownership Concentration in the U.S. Comic Book Industry," in *Comics and Ideology*, ed. Matthew P. McAllister, Edward H. Sewell Jr., and Ian Gordon (New York Peter Lang, 2001), 24.

103 Mark C. Rogers, "License Farming and the American Comic Book Industry," *International Journal of Comic Arts* (Fall 1999): 132–142; Thomas Schatz, "The New Hollywood," in *Film Theory Goes to the Movies*, ed. Jim Collins, Hilary Radner, and Ava Collins (New York: Routledge, 1993), 8–36; Johnson, *Media Franchising*, 87.

104 Mark Rogers defines license farming as "the use of comics to develop and maintain characters that can be sold for use in other media." Rogers, "License Farming and the American Comic Book Industry," 134.

105 WCI would finalize its historic merger with Time, Inc., less than a year after *Batman*'s release. Eileen Meehan, "'Holy Commodity Fetish, Batman!': The Political Economy of a Commercial Intertext," in *The Many Lives of Batman*, ed. Roberta E. Pearson and William Uricchio (New York: Routledge, 1991), 51; McAllister, "Ownership Concentration in the U.S. Comic Book Industry," 27.

106 Derek Johnson, "Will the Real Wolverine Please Stand Up: Marve's Mutation from Monthlies to Movies," in *Film and Comic Books*, ed. Ian Gordon, Mark Jancovich, and Matthew P. McAllister (Jackson: University Press of Mississippi, 2007), np; Dan Raviv, *Comic Wars* (New York: Broadway Books, 2002), 40; McAllister, "Ownership Concentration in the U.S. Comic Book Industry," 28.

107 For a more detailed account of Marvel's trajectory during this period, see Johnson, *Media Franchising*, 79–105.

108 McAllister, "Ownership Concentration in the U.S. Comic Book Industry."

109 Schatz, "The New Hollywood," 29.

110 Janet Tait, "San Diego Comic-Con Convention Events Guide 1987," 1987, San Diego Comic-Con, Michigan State University Library Comic Art Collection; Janet Tait, *1997 Comic-Con International Events Guide* (San Diego: Comic-Con International, Inc., 1997).

111 Janet Tait, *1994 San Diego Comic-Con Events Guide* (San Diego: Comic-Con International, 1994).

112 Exhibitors included "DC Comics, Marvel Comics, Dark Horse Comics, Tekno*Comix, Wizards of the Coast, Motown, Image Comics, Skybox, Fleer, and many other companies." Janet Tait, *Comic-Con International Update 1* (San Diego: San Diego Comic Convention, 1995), 4; Larry Young, ed., *1995 San Diego Comic Book Convention Events Guide* (San Diego: San Diego Comic Convention Inc., 1995), 5.

113 Tait, *1994 San Diego Comic-Con Events Guide*, 37; Young, *1995 San Diego Comic Book Convention Events Guide*, 5, 53–56.

114 Johnson, *Media Franchising*; Henry Jenkins, *Convergence Culture: Where Old and New Media Collide* (New York: New York University Press, 2006).

115 Johnson, *Media Franchising*, 70.

116 Between 2001 and 2004, attendance grew from 53,000 to 95,000. San Diego Comic Convention Inc., *Comic-Con: 40 Years*, 154; Glanzer, Sassaman, and Estrada, *Comic-Con 40 Souvenir Book*, 109–112.

117 Comic-Con International, "Comic-Con International Celebrates Its 35th Incredible Year!" in *Update* ed. Dan Vado (2004), 11; San Diego Convention Center Corporation, "Facility Guide," San Diego Convention Center, last modified 2018, https://visitsandiego.com/facility/facility-guide.

118 Marvel Comics is notably absent from this collection of corporate logos. In fact, according to the index of exhibitors, the company, which was known at that time as Marvel Enterprises, was stationed at the Activision booth, one of their video game licensees. Jackie Estrada, ed. *San Diego Comic-Con International 2005 Events Guide* (San Diego: Comic-Con International Inc., 2005), map insert; "Activision and Marvel Entertainment Expand Alliance and Extend Interactive Rights for Spider-Man and X-Men Franchises," Marvel.com, last modified November 11, 2005, http://marvel.com/news/story/187/activision_and_marvel_entertainment _expand_alliance_and_extend_interactive_rights_for_spider-man_and_x-men _franchises.

119 Comic-Con introduced color map inserts in 2007. Estrada, *San Diego Comic-Con International 2005 Events Guide*; Jackie Estrada, *2007 Comic-Con International: San Diego Events Guide* (San Diego: Comic-Con International Inc., 2007); Jackie Estrada, *2013 Comic-Con International: Events Guide* (San Diego: Comic-Con International, Inc., 2013), map insert.

120 According to the 1997 Events Guide, HBO, Miramax Films, Playstation, and Sony Computer Entertainment were the only film, television, and video game companies with booths on the show floor. Marvel Entertainment was also a prominent presence and, by this time the company's principal interests rested outside the publishing industry and were more intensely focused on branching out and producing synergy through other media and outlets. Tait, *1997 Comic-Con International Events Guide*, 45–48.

121 Amanda Lotz and Timothy Havens, *Understanding Media Industries* (New York: Oxford University Press, 2012), 21.

122 Jackie Estrada, ed. *San Diego Comic-Con International Events Guide 2002* (San Diego: Comic-Con International, 2002), map insert, 57–61.

Sideshow Collectibles is a company specializing in high-end collectibles, such as busts, figures, and prop replicas; New Line Home Entertainment was the branch of New Line Cinema devoted to home entertainment distribution; Electronic Arts is a producer and distributor of video games; Houghton Mifflin Company is a book publisher; and Games Workshop and Decipher are both manufactures and distributers of board games, card games, and role-playing games.

123 Convention Industry Council, "Apex Industry Glossary—2011 Edition," Pavilion, last modified 2011, http://www.conventionindustry.org/StandardsPractices/APEX /glossary.aspx.

124   Linda Musgrove, *The Complete Idiot's Guide to Trade Shows* (New York: Penguin Group, 2009), 60.

125   Meehan, ""Holy Commodity Fetish, Batman!" 61.

126   "New Line Cinema's 'Lord of the Rings: The Fellowship of the Ring' Ignites Marketplace," *PR Newswire*, www.lexisnexis.com/hottopics/lnacademic.

127   Jonathon Guthrie, "Bilbo Baggins Enters Games Workshop Land Leisure," *Financial Times*, January 31, 2001, 28; Guthrie, "Games Workshop Runs Rings around Its Rivals," *Financial Times*, July 31, 2002, 20.

128   Kristin Thompson, *Frodo Franchise: The Lord of the Rings and Modern Hollywood* (Berkeley, CA: University of California Press, 2007), 194.

129   Marvel merged with Toy Biz in 1998 to become Marvel Enterprises, Inc. Thompson, 194–197; McAllister, "Ownership Concentration in the U.S. Comic Book Industry," 31–32.

130   Confirming the adult-fan orientation of the *Lord of the Rings* Pavilion, New Line Cinema announced a "Become an Orc" contest on the fan site, theonering.net, in which attendees "age 18 and older" could win a session with Weta makeup artists, who would "transform them into an Orc" in front of a crowd of spectators at the *Lord of the Rings* Pavilion. New Line Cinema, "Middle-Earth Invades Comic Con," theonering.net, last modified August 1, 2002, http://archives.theonering.net/perl/newsview/8/1028206742.

131   Houghton Mifflin's deal stipulated two tie-ins for each film. Business/Entertainment Editors, "Houghton Mifflin Acquires U.S. Book Rights to New Line Cinema's 'Lord of the Rings' Movie Trilogy," *Business Wire*, http://search.proquest.com.proxy.lib.umich.edu/docview/446066424?accountid=14667; Karen Raugust, "Lord of Licensing," *Publishers Weekly*, July 2, 2001, 28; Fisher, *Fellowship of the Rings Visual Companion* (Boston: Houghton Mifflin, 2001); Gary Russel, *The Art of the Fellowship of the Ring* (Boston: Houghton Mifflin, 2002).

132   John Gaudiosi, "'Lord of the Rings' Gets Games Deal," *Hollywood Reporter*, July 31, 2001.

133   Thompson, *Frodo Franchise*, 234.

134   Business Editors, "Vivendi Universal Agrees to Acquire Houghton Mifflin in Transaction Valued at $2.2 Billion," *Business Wire*, http://link.galegroup.com.libproxy.uoregon.edu/apps/doc/A75188363/ITOF?u=s8492775&sid=ITOF&xid=03efbb66.

135   Anna Wilde Mathews, "Lord of the Things—Separate Companies Hold Rights to the Products from 'Rings' Books, Films," *Wall Street Journal*, December 17, 2001, B1. For more on the licensing of *Lord of the Rings*, see Thompson, *Frodo Franchise*.

136   Despite their exclusion from New Line's pavilion, Universal Interactive, a subsidiary of Vivendi Universal Games and the studio responsible for publishing the competing *Lord of the Rings* games, was situated directly across the aisle. Estrada, *San Diego Comic-Con International Events Guide 2002*, map insert, 61.
        In the absence of evidence in the form of images or firsthand reports from the Exhibit Hall floor, it is impossible to say with certainty that the company had traveled to Comic-Con to promote their *Fellowship of the Ring* game. However, given that Universal Interactive published only six games in 2002, it is reasonable to believe that *The Lord of the Rings: The Fellowship of the Rings* was among those games promoted in this booth adjacent to, but not a part of, the pavilion. "Univer-

sal Interactive, Inc.," Giant Bomb, last modified 2014, http://www.giantbomb.com
/universal-interactive-inc/3010-124/published/.

137 Thompson, *Frodo Franchise*, 142–143.

138 Thompson, 143.

139 Elana Shefrin, "Lord of the Rings, Star Wars, and Participatory Fandom: Mapping
New Congruencies between the Internet and Media Entertainment Culture,"
Critical Studies in Media Communications 21, no. 3 (2007): 266–267.

140 Johnson, *Media Franchising*, 198–199.

141 The Lucasfilm pavilion has been a regular feature since that time. Jackie Estrada, ed.
Comic-Con International Events Guide 2004 (San Diego, CA: Comic-Con
International Inc., 2004), 5.

142 Estrada, 5.

143 Estrada, 5.

144 This title also distinguishes their function from the more utilitarian Events Guide
and Quick Start Guide.

145 It should also be noted that while an eBay listing may give us some sense of how
the program was valued in 2018, it gives no indication that collectors are willing to
purchase the item at that price.

146 "Souvenir Book," Comic-Con International: San Diego, last modified 2018,
https://www.comic-con.org/cci/souvenir-book.

147 Geraghty, *Cult Collectors*, 1–9.

148 Steve Sansweet, "Which Came First . . ." in *San Diego Comic-Con International 2007
Souvenir Book*, ed. David Glanzer (San Diego: San Diego Comic-Con, 2007), 59.

149 Beaty, *Comics versus Art*, 169.

150 Chuck Rozanski, "San Diego Update—Thursday, July 18, 2001—Mile High
Comics," Mile High Comics, last modified July 18, 2001, http://www
.milehighcomics.com/sdcc071801.html.

151 Jon Gutierrez, "Exclusive Story: A Brief History of San Diego Con Exclusives,"
ToyFare, September 2010.

152 Daniel Rasmus, "Exclusive! The Inside Story of Comic-Con's Most Coveted
Collectibles," GeekWire, last modified August 12, 2017, https://www.geekwire.com
/2017/exclusive-inside-story-comic-cons-coveted-collectibles/.

153 Among the most egregious applications of this strategy is Funko's "Pops!" line of
vinyl figures, which have been, in recent years, extremely popular at Comic-Con.
While the shape and size of figures themselves are relatively standardized, they offer
thousands of variations across popular culture licenses. The company slogan,
perhaps not surprisingly, is "everyone is a fan of something."

154 Bill Jensen, "Eternia Again," *ToyFare*, September 2001, 16.

155 For a sampling of recent exclusives, see "Exclusives," *SDCC Unofficial Blog*, last
modified June 21, 2018, https://sdccblog.com/category/exclusive-news/.

156 Robert Marich, *Marketing to Moviegoers: A Handbook of Strategies and Tactics*,
3rd ed. (Carbondale and Edwardsville: Southern Illinois University Press, 2013),
187–188.

157 Santo, *Selling the Silver Bullet*, 25.

158 Dan Gearino, *Comic Shop: The Retail Mavericks Who Gave Us a New Geek Culture*
(Athens, OH: Swallow Press/Ohio University Press, 2017), 199; Meehan, ""Holy
Commodity Fetish, Batman!"

159 McAllister, "Ownership Concentration in the U.S. Comic Book Industry," 22.

160 Woo, "The Android's Dungeon," 129.

161 How that casual buyer would be received in the store, of course, is another matter, one that is closely tied to the insularity of such spaces. Gearino, *Comic Shop*, 199.

162 As Comic-Con's official history puts it, "That's the way it was planned to be from the very beginning, back in 1970. San Diego Comic Convention Inc., *Comic-Con: 40 Years*, 18.

163 Gearino, *Comic Shop*, 151.

164 Chuck Rozanski, "San Diego Comic Con Report #2," Mile High Comics, last modified July 25, 2014, http://www.milehighcomics.com/newsletter/072514email .html; "San Diego Comic Con Report #3," Mile High Comics, last modified July 26, 2014, http://www.milehighcomics.com/newsletter/072614wemail.html.

165 Rozanski, "San Diego Comic Con Report #2."

166 Rich Johnston, "Hasbro and Mattel Stamp Down on Professional Scalpers at San Diego Comic Con," Bleeding Cool, last modified July 17, 2013, http://www .bleedingcool.com/2013/07/17/hasbro-and-mattel-stamp-down-on-professional -scalpers-at-san-diego-comic-con/.

167 Eileen Meehan, "Leisure or Labor?: Fan Ethnography and Political Economy," in *Consuming Audiences? Production and Reception in Media Research*, ed. Ingunn Hagen and Janet Wasko (Cresskill, NJ: Hampton Press, 2000), 83–84.

168 Jacob Kastrenakes, "Meet the Collectors Who Resell Toys to Pay Off Their Comic-Con Addiction," *Verge*, last modified July 25, 2016, https://www.theverge .com/2016/7/25/12269660/comic-con-2016-resell-toy-flipping-collection.

169 Kastrenakes.

170 Geraghty, *Cult Collectors*, 93–94.

171 Retailing at fifty dollars, this toy was particularly unique as it was "Hasbro's largest single-carded figure ever." Lewis Wallace, "Giant Galactus Is Hasbro's Biggest Comic-Con Exclusive," *Wired*, last modified July 13, 2010, http://www.wired.com /underwire/2010/07/hasbro-comic-con/.

Conclusion

Epigraph: Aly Walansky, "Fry Fans Rejoice! Taco Bell Rolling out Spicy Fries for Just $1," Today, last modified January 3, 2018, https://www.today.com/food/taco-bell-adds -french-fries-menu-1-t120750?cid=sm_npd_td_tw_ma.

1 Caitlin Petrakovitz, "Taco Bell's Comic-Con Pop-up Was Delicious and All Thanks to Demolition Man!" cnet.com, last modified July 20, 2018, https://www.cnet.com /news/taco-bell-comic-con-pop-up-was-delicious-thanks-demolition-man/.

2 Kerry Smith and Dan Hanover, *Experiential Marketing: Secrets, Strategies, and Success Stories from the World's Greatest Brands* (Hoboken, NJ: Wiley, 2016); Jen Yamato, "Why Hollywood Marketing Execs Love Comic-Con Activations, from 'the Good Place' to . . . a Sci-Fi Taco Bell from the Future?" *Los Angeles Times*, last modified July 20, 2018, http://www.latimes.com/entertainment/herocomplex/la -et-hc-comic-con-activations-marketing-20180720-story.html.

3 As the *Hollywood Reporter* notes, like Comic-Con, South by Southwest, a festival and conference that brings together music, film, and interactive media, has also become a popular site for marketing activations. Natalie Jarvey, "How SXSW,

Comic-Con Fueled the Rise of Activation Culture," *Hollywood Reporter*, last modified July 21, 2018, https://www.hollywoodreporter.com/news/how-comic-con -fueled-rise-activation-culture-1128792.

4 Kelly West, "Ender's Game Comic-Con Fan Experience Displays Futuristic Sets, Flash Suits, Weapons and More," CinemaBlend, last modified 2013, https://www .cinemablend.com/new/Ender-Game-Comic-Con-Fan-Experience-Displays -Futuristic-Sets-Flash-Suits-Weapons-More-38558.html; Meagan Damore, "SDCC's Interactive "Suicide Squad" Experience Will Allow Fans to Bust into Belle Reve," CBR.com, last modified June 9, 2016, https://www.cbr.com/sdccs-interactive -suicide-squad-experience-will-allow-fans-to-bust-into-belle-reve/; "Adult Swim at Comic-Con 2016," Adult Swim, last modified 2016, http://www.adultswim.com /presents/sdcc-16/; Jean Bentley, "Comic-Con: Marvel's 'Inhumans' Footage Unveiled in Surprise Imax Sneak Peak," *Hollywood Reporter*, last modified July 21, 2017, https://www.hollywoodreporter.com/live-feed/inhumans-surprise-imax -sneak-peek-comic-con-2017-1022961; Mia Galuppo, "'Blade Runner 2049': Inside the Comic-Con Experience Where You Can Be a Replicant," *Hollywood Reporter*, last modified July 22, 2017, https://www.hollywoodreporter.com/heat-vision/blade -runner-2049-inside-comic-con-2017-experience-1023559; Laura Prudom, "Experience the Good Place in Real Life at Comic-Con with NBC's Interactive Activation—IGN," IGN.com, last modified July 10, 2018, http://www.ign.com /articles/2018/07/10/the-good-place-comic-con-nbc-activation-brooklyn-nine -nine-manifest.

5 In some ways, *Demolition Man*'s view of the future reflects Adorno and Hork-heimer's critique of the culture industries' tendency to produce and reproduce sameness. However, the film's critique also aligns with contemporary conservative ideologies in the United States as it frames political correctness as a threat to free speech and proposes an embrace of anti-intellectualism and a return to so-called traditional American values as the solution. Theodor W. Adorno and Max Horkheimer, "The Culture Industry," in *Dialectic of Enlightenment*, ed. Max Horkheimer and Theodor W. Adorno (New York: Continuum, 2002), 132.

6 Yamato, "Why Hollywood Marketing Execs Love Comic-Con Activations"; "Taco Bell 'Demolition Man' Pop-up Restaurant Wins #SDCC," Brandchannel, last modified July 20, 2018, https://www.brandchannel.com/2018/07/20/taco-bell -demolition-man-popup-san-diego-comic-con/; Devon Maloney, Andrew Liptak, and Dami Lee, "Purge Supplies, Clone Wars Tears, and Shrimp Cocktail Carousels: The Best Things We Saw at San Diego Comic-Con 2018," *Verge*, last modified July 23, 2018, https://www.theverge.com/2018/7/23/17600864/comic-con-sdcc -2018-activations-purge-good-place; Chris Barton and Jen Yamato, "The Best of Comic-Con 2018: 'Doctor Who,' Taco Bell, Celebrity Cosplay and More," *Los Angeles Times*, last modified July 23, 2018, http://www.latimes.com/entertainment /movies/la-et-hc-comic-con-roundup-20180723-story.html.

7 See, for example, Ethan Anderton, "Be Well and Taco Bell: 'Demolition Man' Inspires a Fine Dining Experience from the Future [Comic-Con 2018]," SlashFilm, last modified July 20, 2018, https://www.slashfilm.com/demolition-man-taco-bell -comic-con-2018/.

8 "Integrated marketing" refers to the coordinated management of a campaign to relay a coherent message across a spectrum of platforms and approaches. Charles Doyle, "Integrated Marketing," ed. Charles Doyle, 4th ed., *Oxford Dictionary of*

Marketing (Oxford University Press, 2016), http://www.oxfordreference.com/view /10.1093/acref/9780198736424.001.0001/acref-9780198736424-e-0910.

9 Smith and Hanover, *Experiential Marketing*, 6–11.

10 Smith and Hanover, 2.

11 Brooks Barnes, "Bowie Knives and a Tick Head: Marketing Gets Elaborate at Comic-Con," *New York Times*, last modified July 20, 2017, https://www.nytimes .com/2017/07/20/business/media/comic-con-marketing.html.

12 "Do it for the 'gram" is a reference to the popular social media platform, Instagram. Jarvey, "How SXSW, Comic-Con Fueled the Rise of Activation Culture."

13 Jarvey; Ann-Marie Alcántara, "How 3 Brands Brought Tech to Life at Coachella," *Adweek*, last modified April 19, 2018, https://www.adweek.com/digital/how-3 -brands-brought-tech-to-life-at-coachella/; Priscila Martinez, "Festivals 2.0: How Branded Activations Are Evolving to Survive," *Forbes*, last modified February 16, 2018, https://www.forbes.com/sites/forbesagencycouncil/2018/02/16/festivals-2-0 -how-branded-activations-are-evolving-to-survive/.

14 Dana Hatic, "Drink Free Coffee Like a Gilmore Girl at Hundreds of Luke's Diner Pop-Ups across America," Eater, last modified October 3, 2016, https://www.eater .com/2016/10/3/12929778/gilmore-girls-netflix-lukes-diner-coffee-california-new -york-canada.

15 Anthony D'Alessandro, "How Warner Bros. Tore up B.O. Projections & Auda- ciously Sold 'Meg' as a Horror Comedy for a $44.5m Weekend Win," Deadline, last modified August 12, 2018, https://deadline.com/2018/08/the-meg-box-office -win-marketing-shark-film-1202444293/.

16 Libby Hill, "Fans Get Their 'Gilmore Girls' on at Luke's Diner Pop-up Coffee Shops," *Los Angeles Times*, last modified October 5, 2018, http://www.latimes.com /entertainment/tv/la-et-st-gilmore-girls-anniversary-coffee-shop-20161005-snap -story.html.

17 D'Alessandro, "How Warner Bros. Tore up B.O. Projections."

18 "The Meg: Submersive VR Experience," Warner Bros., last modified July 31, 2018, https://www.warnerbros.com/blogs/2018/07/31/meg-submersive-vr-experience.

19 Jeremy Jones, "The Meg Submersible VR Experience," DestroytheBrain.com, last modified August 6, 2018, http://www.destroythebrai.com/geek-out/the-meg -submersible-vr-experience.

20 D'Alessandro, "How Warner Bros. Tore up B.O. Projections."

21 Lauren Johnson, "Netflix's Gilmore Girls Pop-up Coffee Shops Were a Massive Hit on Snapchat," *Adweek*, last modified October 25, 2016, https://www.adweek.com /digital/netflixs-gilmore-girls-pop-coffee-shops-were-massive-hit-snapchat -174248/.

22 Johnson.

23 Joseph B. Pine II and James H. Gilmore, *The Experience Economy* (Boston, MA: Harvard Business Review Press, 2011); Elizabeth Moor, "Branded Spaces: The Scope of 'New Marketing,'" *Journal of Consumer Culture* 3, no. 1 (2003): 42–43.

24 Charles Musser, "Introducing Cinema to the American Public: The Vitascope in the United States, 1896–7," in *Moviegoing in America*, ed. Gregory A. Waller (Malden, MA: Blackwell 2002), 13–26.

25 Quoted in Musser, 14.

26 Quoted in Musser, 14.

27 Douglas Gomery, *Shared Pleasures: A History of Movie Presentation in the United States*, Wisconsin Studies in Film (Madison: University of Wisconsin Press, 1992), 7.

28 Musser, "Introducing Cinema to the American Public," 17–20.

29 While, as Musser details, the Vitascope was ultimately replaced by other projection technologies, it "effectively launched projected motion pictures as a screen novelty in the United States" and "did much to establish a framework within which subsequent exhibition practices were developed." Musser, 13, 25.

30 Rebecca Ford and Borys Kit, "Marvel Reveals Complete Phase 3 Plans, Dates 'Black Panther,' 'Inhumans,' 'Avengers: Infinity War,'" *Hollywood Reporter*, last modified October 28, 2014, https://www.hollywoodreporter.com/heat-vision/marvel-reveals -complete-phase-3-plans-dates-black-panther-inhumans-avengers-infinity-war -744455.

31 Marc Graser, "5 Things to Expect from Marvel Studios Fan Event," last modified October 28, 2014, https://variety.com/2014/film/news/5-things-to-expect-from -marvel-studios-fan-event-1201341014/.

32 *Variety* even described the presentation as "Comic-Con like." Graser.

33 Mike Mack, "Looking Back at Marvel's Phase 3 Announcement and All the Changes That Have Come Since," Insidethemagic.net, last modified April 30, 2018, https://insidethemagic.net/2018/04/looking-back-at-marvels-phase-3 -announcement-and-all-the-changes-that-have-come-since/.

34 Scholarship questioning and historicizing ideas about "new media" has been especially productive in this regard. See, for example, Wendy Hui Kyong Chun and Thomas Keenan, *New Media, Old Media: A History and Theory Reader* (New York: Routledge, 2006); Lisa Gitelman and Geoffrey B. Pingree, *New Media, 1740–1915*, Media in Transition (Cambridge, MA: MIT Press, 2003); Sheila C. Murphy, *How Television Invented New Media* (New Brunswick, NJ: Rutgers University Press, 2011).

35 Moor, "Branded Spaces," 43.

36 John Fiske, *Television Culture* (New York: Methuen, 1987); Henry Jenkins, *Textual Poachers: Television Fans & Participatory Culture* (New York: Routledge, 1992); Mark Andrejevic, "Watching Television without Pity: The Productivity of Online Fans," *Television & New Media* 9, no. 24 (2008): 25; Moor, "Branded Spaces," 42.

37 Henry Jenkins, *Convergence Culture: Where Old and New Media Collide* (New York: New York University Press, 2006); Tiziana Terranova, "Free Labor," in *Digital Labor: The Internet as Playground and Factory*, ed. Trebor Scholz (New York: Routledge, 2013), 33–57.

38 Smith and Hanover, *Experiential Marketing*, 13.

39 Wal-Mart even connected the event to Comic-Con in a press release, suggesting that "Jedi Knights, rebels and stormtroopers attending San Diego International Comic Con this week can stop by the Topps booth (Booth #2913) and get a first look at a new *Star Wars* collectible initiative," but reminded these potential buyers that the product was "only available at Wal-Mart." "The Force Is Strong at Walmart: Company to Offer a New Generation of Star WarsTM Merchandise at 12:01 A.M. On 'Force Friday,'" Walmart.com, last modified July 9, 2015, https://news.walmart .com/news-archive/2015/07/09/the-force-is-strong-at-walmart-company-to-offer -a-new-generation-of-star-warstm-merchandise-at-12-01-am-on-force-friday.

40 Disney repeated the event in 2016, leading up to *Rogue One: A Star Wars Story* (Gareth Edwards, 2016) and again in 2017 before the release of *Star Wars: The Last Jedi* (Rian Johnson, 2017).

41 "*Star Wars: The Force Awakens* Products to Arrive on 'Force Friday,' September 4," StarWars.com, last modified May 3, 2015, https://www.starwars.com/news/star -wars-the-force-awakens-products-to-arrive-on-force-friday-september-4.

42 Sarah Halzack, "A Guide to 'Force Friday,' the 'Star Wars' Toy Bonanza," *Washington Post*, last modified September 3, 2015, https://www.washingtonpost .com/news/business/wp/2015/09/03/a-guide-to-force-friday-the-star-wars-toy -bonanza/.

For more on "unboxing videos," see David Craig and Stuart Cunningham, "Toy Unboxing: Living in a(n Unregulated) Material World," *Media International Australia* 163, no. 1 (2017): 77–86.

43 Sarah Halzack, "'Star Wars' Fans Pounce on Force Friday, Snap up New Toys," The Washington Post, last modified September 4, 2015, https://www.washingtonpost .com/business/economy/disney-kicks-off-star-wars-bonanza-with-force-friday /2015/09/04/ff3ea6fc-5244-11e5-9812-92d5948a40f8_story.html?utm_term= .bc7545163bce; Halzack, "A Guide to 'Force Friday.'"

44 In describing the event, CNN even called it "Black Friday for 'Star Wars' aficiona- dos." Henry Hanks, "Force Friday: 'Star Wars' Merch for Any Taste," CNN, last modified September 3, 2015, https://www.cnn.com/2015/09/03/living/force-friday -highlights-star-wars-feat/index.html.

45 Hanks.

46 As Suzanne Scott's examination of the #WheresRey hashtag suggests, this imagined notion of a fandom based on the industry's economic bottom line is frequently at odds with the practices and politics of actual fans. Suzanne Scott, "#Wheresrey?: Toys, Spoilers, and the Gender Politics of Franchise Paratexts," *Critical Studies in Media Communication* 34, no. 2 (2017): 138.

47 This hashtag was part of a larger campaign by Target that played on the nostalgia surrounding the franchise's return by asking fans to share their *Star Wars* memories with the goal of creating a "permanent archive." However, Target's "Share the Force" website (https://sharetheforce.target.com/) has since disappeared. Chris Taylor, "Target Wants You to Fill the Internet with Galaxies Full of Star Wars Memories," Mashable, last modified August 25, 2015, https://mashable.com/2015 /08/25/share-the-force/#I2ZyEluDLOq8.

48 Smith and Hanover, *Experiential Marketing*, 13.

49 It is important to note that this activation, like most of the promotions I discuss in this book, was specifically targeting those with the economic means to see dining out as accessible, rather than an already exclusive experience.

50 Nick Couldry, *Media Rituals: A Critical Approach* (New York: Routledge, 2003), 86.

51 Couldry, 86; Lincoln Geraghty, *Cult Collectors: Nostalgia, Fandom and Collecting Popular Culture* (London: Routledge, 2014), 93; Anne Gilbert, "Live from Hall H: Fan/Producer Symbiosis at San Diego Comic-Con," in *Fandom: Identities and Communities in a Mediated World*, ed. Jonathan Gray, Cornel Sandvoss, and C. Lee Harrington (New York: New York University Press, 2017), 355.

52 Though behind-the-scenes disclosures are rooted in reality, they also tell audiences stories that are largely constructed to perpetuate and legitimate Hollywood's power.

As Barbara Klinger argues, "Rather than inciting critical attitudes towards the industry . . . behind-the-scenes 'exposés' vividly confirm Hollywood as a place of marvels brought to the public by talented film professionals." Barbara Klinger, *Beyond the Multiplex: Cinema, New Technologies, and the Home* (Berkeley: University of California Press, 2006), 73; John Thornton Caldwell, *Production Culture: Industrial Reflexivity and Critical Practice in Film and Television* (Durham, N.C., 2008), 283–284.

53 Jenkins, *Textual Poachers*, 51.

54 Not only do such observations illuminate other areas of culture but, as Derek Johnson argues, examining the connections and overlaps between media and fast food franchises is one way to deepen our understanding of "franchising as a business practice" and consider the "economic and cultural assumptions we make about this industrialized reproduction of media culture." Derek Johnson, *Media Franchising* (New York: New York University Press, 2013), 33–34.

55 Hannah Lodge, "SDCC '18: The Year Is 2018 and Taco Bell Has Won the Activation Wars," *The Beat*: The News Blog of Comic Culture, last modified July 21, 2018, http://www.comicsbeat.com/sdcc-18-the-year-is-2018-and-taco-bell-has-won-the -activation-wars/.

56 Product placement is the insertion of brands into a film or television program, while tie-ins describe the placement of film or television content in a company's advertisements and/or in-store promotions. Product placement and tie-ins frequently go hand in hand, as was the case with *Demolition Man*. Robert Marich, *Marketing to Moviegoers: A Handbook of Strategies and Tactics*, 3rd ed. (Carbondale and Edwardsville: Southern Illinois University Press, 2013), 147.

The exact dollar amount of the Taco Bell deal is unclear. While *Brandweek* described it as a $10 million deal, *Hollywood Reporter* suggested Taco Bell had agreed to a $12.5 million deal. Robert Marich, "H'wood Profit Pinch: Is Glass Half Empty . . . ?" *Hollywood Reporter*, November 18 1993, https://advance.lexis.com/api /document?collection=news&id=urn:contentItem:3SJF-CD10-006P-R341 -00000-00&context=1516831; Lisa Marie Petersen, "Demo Derby: Taco Bell, GM Back Sly's New Future Flick," *Brandweek*, October 4, 1993, 1.

57 GM also had a significant product placement and tie-in deal with Warner Brothers, providing producers with sixty-nine million dollars' worth of "concept cars" to feature in the film and creating a television ad featuring a "futuristic dealer set" like the one featured in the film. David Tobenkin, "Promotion 'Man': How Producers Squeezed 99-Cent Burritos and Detroit Wheels into the Futuristic Stallone-Snipes Saga," *Hollywood Reporter*, October 4, 1993, S-6; Petersen, "Demo Derby."

58 Frook and O'steen, "High Volume, Hard Sell Spell Christmas Crunch," 10.

59 Marich, *Marketing to Moviegoers*, 147–180.

60 "Rumors Confirmed: Taco Bell Release Nacho Fries," tacoBell.com, last modified January 3, 2018, https://www.tacobell.com/news/rumors-confirmed-taco-bell-sets -release-date-for-nacho-fries?selectedTag=&selectYear=2018; Yamato, "Why Hollywood Marketing Execs Love Comic-Con Activations."

61 Kristina Monllos, "Taco Bell Made the Perfect Trailer for a Fake Movie about Why They've Never Sold Fries," *Adweek*, last modified January 18, 2018, https://www .adweek.com/brand-marketing/taco-bell-made-the-perfect-trailer-for-a-fake-movie -about-why-theyve-never-sold-fries/.

62 Nancy Luna, "Nacho Fries Become Bestselling Taco Bell Product Launch in Chain History," *Nation's Restaurant News*, last modified March 13, 2018, https://www.nrn.com /food-trends/nacho-fries-become-bestselling-taco-bell-product-launch-chain-history.

63 Brittany Bennett, "Taco Bell's Nacho Fries Are Going Away Soon, but Don't Freak Out," Bustle, last modified March 29, 2018, https://www.bustle.com/p/taco-bells -nacho-fries-are-going-away-soon-but-dont-freak-out-8640990; Walansky, "Fry Fans Rejoice!"

64 "Fry Fans Rejoice! Taco Bell Rolling out Spicy Fries for Just $1," NBC15, last modified January 4, 2018, http://www.nbc15.com/content/news/Fry-fans-rejoice -Taco-Bell-rolling-out-spicy-fries-for-just-1-468027633.html; Bennett, "Taco Bell's Nacho Fries Are Going Away Soon, but Don't Freak Out."

65 Jonathan Gray, Cornel Sandvoss, and C. Lee Harrington, *Fandom: Identities and Communities in a Mediated World*, 2nd ed. (New York: New York University Press, 2017), 23.

66 Brian Steinberg, "Taco Bell Eyes Sequel for Movie-Trailer Ads Touting Nacho Fries," *Variety*, last modified March 29, 2018, https://variety.com/2018/tv/news /taco-bell-nacho-fries-movie-advertising-sequel-1202739155/.

67 Katie Richards, "Ads Go Hollywood: Why Brands Are Faking Out Consumers with Campaigns Disguised as Movie Trailers," *Adweek*, March 5, 2018, 10.

68 Steven Tulman, "How Taco Bell Is Winning at Social Media Marketing," Business 2 Community, last modified July 25, 2017, https://www.business2community.com /social-media/taco-bell-winning-social-media-marketing-01887555; Sarra Boboltz, "Whoever Runs Taco Bell's Twitter Account Deserves a Raise," Huffington Post, last modified December 6, 2017, https://www.huffingtonpost.com/2014/02/28 /taco-bell-tweets_n_4856259.html.

69 Kate Taylor, "Instagram Powers Taco Bell's Innovation Machine—and It's Completely Changing the Fast-Food Menu as We Know It," *Business Insider*, last modified April 26, 2017, https://www.businessinsider.com/instagram-powers-taco -bells-innovation-2017-4.

70 Kirsten Chuba and Christi Carras, "10 Things We Learned at *Variety*'s Massive Summit," *Variety*, last modified March 22, 2018, https://variety.com/2018/biz/news /10-things-learned-variety-massive-summit-1202732600/.

71 Jonathan Gray, *Show Sold Separately: Promos, Spoilers, and Other Media Paratexts* (New York: New York University Press, 2010).

72 Gray, 210.

73 At that time, Pizza Hut and Taco Bell were both owned by PepsiCo, suggesting the two fast food brands were even more interchangeable. The company reportedly paid for the cost of the changes, which was estimated at $250,000. Thomas R. King, "Movies: 'Demolition Man' Trades Tacos for Pizza Abroad," *Wall Street Journal*, December 2, 1993, B1.

74 Gray, *Show Sold Separately*, 210.

75 Alli Hoff Kosik, "Taco Bell's Nacho Fries Are Finally Available & Fans Already Love Them," Bustle, last modified January 25, 2018, https://www.bustle.com/p/taco -bells-nacho-fries-are-finally-available-fans-already-love-them-8013303; Ziati Meyer, "Taco Bell's Nacho Fries Are Rolling Out Nationally," *USA Today*, last modified January 26, 2018, https://www.usatoday.com/story/money/food/2018/01/26/taco -bells-nacho-fries-rolling-out-nationally/1064884001/.

76 "Taco Bell's Nacho Fries Are Coming Back to Reveal the Future Demolition Man Predicted," TacoBell.com, last modified June 28, 2018, https://www.tacobell.com /news/taco-bells-nacho-fries-are-coming-back?selectedTag=&selectYear=2018.

77 "Taco Bell's Nacho Fries Are Coming Back to Reveal the Future Demolition Man Predicted."

   For examples of coverage of the announcement, see Germain Lussier, "A Demolition Man-Style Taco Bell Is Comic to Comic-Con," Gizmodo, last modified June 29, 2018, https://www.gizmodo.com.au/2018/06/a-demolition-man -style-taco-bell-is-coming-to-comic-con/; Ben Pearson, "'Demolition Man 25th Anniversary Pop-up Coming to Comic-Con 2018," SlashFilm, last modified June 28, 2018, https://www.slashfilm.com/demolition-man-comic-con/; Kevin Burwick, "Futuristic Demolition Man Taco Bell Restaurant Is Coming to Comic-Con," Movieweb, last modified July 1, 2018, https://movieweb.com/demolition -man-taco-bell-restaurant-comic-con-2018/; Jenna Anderson, "Taco Bell to Recreate Iconic Restaurant from 'Demolition Man' for SDCC," Comicbook.com, last modified July 1, 2018, https://comicbook.com/movies/2018/07/01/demolition -man-taco-bell-san-diego-comic-con-2018/.

78 A portmanteau of San Diego, Los Angeles, and Santa Barbara, the film explains that San Angeles was established after a catastrophic earthquake in 2010 led the three cities to form a massive metropolis.

79 "Taco Bell's Nacho Fries Are Coming Back to Reveal the Future Demolition Man Predicted."

80 *How Did This Get Made* features three comedians, June Diane Raphael, Paul Scheer, and Jason Mantzoukas, who dissect and discuss, and often celebrate, cinematic failures. For more information about the podcast, see Becca James, "Want to Try Scheer, Raphael, and Mantzoukas's How Did This Get Made? Start Here," Vulture, last modified July 26, 2018, http://www.vulture.com/2018/07/the-best -episode-of-how-did-this-get-made.html.

81 Some examples include Karen Belz, "Um, Taco Bell Is Getting a Hipster Makeover," Hello Giggles, last modified May 23, 2016, https://hellogiggles.com/lifestyle/food -drink/um-taco-bell-getting-hipster-makeover/; Boboltz, "Whoever Runs Taco Bell's Twitter Account Deserves a Raise"; Dale Buss, "Hipster Branding: Taco Bell Woos Cool Kids to Cook Ranch Doritos Locos Tacos," Brandchannel, last modified February 13, 2013, https://www.brandchannel.com/2013/02/13/hipster-branding -taco-bell-woos-cool-kids-to-cool-ranch-doritos-locos-tacos/; Sean O'Neal, "Mcdonald's and Taco Bell Rebrand for a Hip, Upscale Audience That Doesn't Eat at Mcdonald's and Taco Bell," AV Club, last modified April 25, 2014, https://news .avclub.com/mcdonalds-and-taco-bell-rebrand-for-a-hip-upscale-audi-1798268042.

82 Andrejevic, "Watching Television without Pity," 38.

83 Andrejevic, 39–40.

84 Jeffrey Sconce, "Irony, Nihilism, and the New American 'Smart' Film," *Screen* 43, no. 4 (2002): 352; Taylor, "Instagram Powers Taco Bell's Innovation Machine."

85 Mercifully, the pianist did inject some traditional piano bar fare into the mix once in a while.

86 Beth Elderkin and Germain Lussier, "Taco Bell's *Demolition Man* Restaurants Gave Us Nacho Fries, Happy Feelings, and Seashell Butts," 109, last modified July 21, 2018,

https://io9.gizmodo.com/taco-bells-demolition-man-restaurant-gave-us-nacho-frie
-1827665977.

87 Pierre Bourdieu, *Distinction: A Social Critique of the Judgement of Taste* (Cambridge, MA: Harvard University Press, 1984); Caleb Warren and Gina S. Mohr, "Ironic Consumption," *Journal of Consumer Research* (July 27, 2018), https://doi
.org/10.1093/jcr/ucy065.

88 Yamato, "Why Hollywood Marketing Execs Love Comic-Con Activations."

Bibliography

"20th Century Fox and James Cameron: Avatar." Panel, San Diego Comic-Con, San Diego, CA, July 23, 2009.

"#21: Hall H and Plaza Park Lines +Toucan Tracker Wristbands!" Toucan: The Official Comic-Con Blog. Last modified July 9, 2018. https://www.comic-con.org/toucan/21-hall-h-and-plaza-park-lines-toucan-tracker-wristbands.

"#23: Announcing the Comic-Con Museum!" Toucan. Last modified July 11, 2018. https://www.comic-con.org/toucan/23-announcing-comic-con-museum.

"40th-Anniversary Secret Origins of Comic-Con Panel." Shel Dorf Tribute. Last modified October 10, 2009. http://www.sheldorftribute.com/2009/10/10/40th-anniversary-secret-origins-of-comic-con-panel/.

"1974 San Diego Comic-Con Photos (Batch 1): Can You Identify People in the Pictures?" Comic-Convention Memories. Last modified May 31, 2010. http://www.comicconmemories.com/2010/05/31/1974-san-diego-comic-con-photos-batch-1-can-you-identify-people-in-the-pictures/.

"1974 San Diego Comic-Con Photos (Batch 2): Can You Identify People in the Pictures?" Comic-Convention Memories. Last modified June 12, 2010. http://www.comicconmemories.com/2010/06/12/1974-san-diego-comic-con-photos-batch-2-can-you-identify-people-in-the-pictures/.

"1974 San Diego Comic-Con Program." San Diego: San Diego Comic-Con, 1974.

"2003 Comic-Con Programming: You Had to Be There!" In *Comic-Con International Update 4*, San Diego: Comic-Con International, 2003, 16–35.

@Twilight. "The Twilight Saga: 3:24 P.M.—20 Jul 11." Last modified July 20, 2011. https://twitter.com/Twilight.

———. "The Twilight Saga: 6:56 P.M. 18 Jul 11." Twitter. Last modified July 18, 2011. https://twitter.com/Twilight.

———. "The Twilight Saga: 12:05 P.M.—19 Jul 11." Twitter. Last modified July 19, 2011. https://twitter.com/Twilight.

Aarons, Jared. "Mayor Stresses Need for Convention Center Expansion as Comic-Con 2018 Begins." ABC10 News. Last modified July 20, 2018. https://www.10news.com

/entertainment/comic-con/mayor-stresses-need-for-convention-center-expansion
-as-comic-con-2018-begins.

Abad-Santos, Alexander. "How the Nerds Lost Comic-Con." The Wire. Last modified
July 19, 2013. http://www.theatlanticwire.com/entertainment/2013/07/how-nerds
-lost-comic-con/67304/.

"About." The Comic Cons Research Project. Last modified 2018. http://
comicconsproject.org/.

"About Comic-Con International." Comic-Con International: San Diego. Last
modified 2018. http://www.comic-con.org/about.

"About Comic-Con International." Comic-Con.org. Last modified 2018. http://www
.comic-con.org/about.

"About Us." Fan Expo Canada. Last modified 2018. https://www.fanexpocanada.com
/en/about-us/about-us.html.

Abrams, Dan. "Sizzle Reels: Produce before You Pitch (Part 1)." Producers Guild of
America. Last modified 2010. https://www.producersguild.org/?sizzle.

"Active Trading Marks Comic Book Collecting." Los Angeles Times, October 19,
1967, WS2.

"Activision and Marvel Entertainment Expand Alliance and Extend Interactive Rights
for Spider-Man and X-Men Franchises." Marvel.com. Last modified November 11,
2005. http://marvel.com/news/story/187/activision_and_marvel_entertainment
_expand_alliance_and_extend_interactive_rights_for_spider-man_and_x-men
_franchises.

Adorno, Theodor W., and Max Horkheimer. "The Culture Industry: Enlightenment as
Mass Deception." In Dialectic of Enlightenment, edited by Max Horkheimer and
Theodor W. Adorno, 121–167. New York: Continuum, 2002.

"Adult Swim at Comic-Con 2016." Adult Swim. Last modified 2016. http://www
.adultswim.com/presents/sdcc-16/.

Albiniak, Paige. "Comic-Con 2013: Why TV Marketers Brave the Crowds." Promaxbda: International Association for Entertainment Marketing Professionals. Last
modified July 17, 2013. http://brief.promaxbda.org/content/comic-con-2013-why-tv
-marketers-brave-the-crowds.

Alcántara, Ann-Marie. "How 3 Brands Brought Tech to Life at Coachella." Adweek.
Last modified April 19, 2018. https://www.adweek.com/digital/how-3-brands
-brought-tech-to-life-at-coachella/.

allthingsfangirl. "Jeff Walker Awarded Inkpot at Comic-Con 2011." YouTube.com. Last
modified July 26, 2011. http://www.youtube.com/watch?v=wH404disj7Q.

"Alter Ego." TwoMorrows Publishing. Last modified 2016. http://twomorrows.com
/index.php?main_page=index&cPath=98_55.

Alverson, Brigid. "NYCC: Griepp's White Paper Report Gives Comics Industry a Gold
Star." Comic Book Resources. Last modified October 10, 2013. http://www
.comicbookresources.com/?page=article&id=48400.

Amanda31. "Line for the Breaking Dawn Panel at Comic-Con Has Started!" Twilight-
Moms.com. Last modified July 18, 2011. http://www.twilightmoms.com/2011/07
/line-for-the-breaking-dawn-panel-at-comic-con-has-started/.

Anderson, Jenna. "Taco Bell to Recreate Iconic Restaurant from 'Demolition Man' for
SDCC." Comicbook.com. Last modified July 1, 2018. https://comicbook.com
/movies/2018/07/01/demolition-man-taco-bell-san-diego-comic-con-2018/.

Anderton, Ethan. "Be Well and Taco Bell: 'Demolition Man' Inspires a Fine Dining Experience from the Future [Comic-Con 2018]." SlashFilm. Last modified July 20, 2018. https://www.slashfilm.com/demolition-man-taco-bell-comic-con-2018/.

Andrejevic, Mark. "Watching Television without Pity: The Productivity of Online Fans." *Television & New Media* 9, no. 24 (2008): 24–46.

Ang, Ien. *Desperately Seeking the Audience.* New York: Routledge, 1991.

Angel, Christina. "All Comic Cons Are Not Created Equal: How DCC Is Different." Denver Comic Con. Last modified February 14, 2018. https://denvercomiccon.com/blog/all_comic_cons_are_not_created_equal_how_dcc_is_different/.

"Anti-Piracy Warning." Panel, San Diego Comic-Con, San Diego, CA, July 23, 2009.

"Anti-Piracy Warning," Panel, San Diego Comic-Con, San Diego, CA, July 21, 2012.

Arnold, Ben. "'Superman' Trailer Makes Fans Cry." Yahoo! Movies UK & Ireland. Last modified July 16, 2012. http://uk.movies.yahoo.com/-superman—trailer-makes-fans-cry.html.

Associated Press. "James Cameron Wows Comic-Con with 'Avatar.'" *Today.* Last modified July 24, 2009. http://www.today.com/id/32126753/ns/today-today_entertainment/t/james-cameron-wows-comic-con-avatar/.

"Avatar (2009)." Box Office Mojo. Last modified July 10, 2018. http://www.boxofficemojo.com/movies/?id=avatar.htm.

Baldwin, Danny. "SDCC 2011: The Twilight Saga: Breaking Dawn—Part 1 (Hall H)." Bucket Reviews. Last modified July 21, 2011. http://bucketreviews.com/2011/07/21/sdcc-2011-twilight-breaking-dawn-part-1-hall-h/.

Balio, Tino. *Hollywood in the New Millennium.* International Screen Industries. London: Palgrave Macmillan on behalf of the British Film Institute, 2013.

Ballmann, J. *The 1964 New York Comicon: The True Story behind the World's First Comic Convention.* San Bernardino, CA: Totalmojo Productions, 2016.

Barnes, Brooks. "Bowie Knives and a Tick Head: Marketing Gets Elaborate at Comic-Con." *New York Times.* Last modified July 20, 2017. https://www.nytimes.com/2017/07/20/business/media/comic-con-marketing.html.

———. "Seeking Silver-Screen Success of Marvel Proportions; Comics Companies Hope to Turn Obscure Heroes into Hollywood Hits." *International Herald Tribune,* July 10, 2012, 16.

Barnes, Brooks, and Michael Cieply. "A Comic Convention Bursts Its Boundaries." *New York Times,* July 23, 2010, B3.

———. "Hollywood Acts Warily at Comics Convention." *New York Times,* July 16, 2012, B1.

———. "Movie Studios Reassess Comic-Con." *New York Times,* June 12, 2011, 7.

Bart, Peter. "Advertising: Superman Faces New Hurdles." *New York Times,* September 23, 1962, 166.

———. "Geek Chic: Hollywood Corrals Nerd Herd . . ." *Variety,* August 2–8, 2004, 1, 3.

Barton, Chris, and Jen Yamato. "The Best of Comic-Con 2018: 'Doctor Who,' Taco Bell, Celebrity Cosplay and More." *Los Angeles Times.* Last modified July 23, 2018. http://www.latimes.com/entertainment/movies/la-et-hc-comic-con-roundup-20180723-story.html.

Bear, Greg. "Biography." Ken Krueger Tribute. Last modified http://www.kenkruegertribute.com/biography/.

Beaty, Bart. *Comics versus Art.* Toronto: University of Toronto Press, 2012.

Beerbohm, Robert L. "Secret Origins of the Direct Market." *Comic Book Artist*, Fall 1999, 80–91.

Beerman, Frank. "*Star Trek*: Conclave in NY Looms as Mix of Campy Set and Sci-Fi Buffs." *Variety*, January 19, 1972, 1.

Bell, Amanda. "'Twilight' Fans Already Lining Up for Thursday's 'Breaking Dawn' Comic-Con Panel." examiner.com. Last modified July 18, 2011. http://www.examiner.com/twilight-in-national/twilight-fans-already-lining-up-for-thursday-s-breaking-dawn-comic-con-panel.

Belz, Karen. "Um, Taco Bell Is Getting a Hipster Makeover." Hello Giggles. Last modified May 23, 2016. https://hellogiggles.com/lifestyle/food-drink/um-taco-bell-getting-hipster-makeover/.

Bennett, Brittany. "Taco Bell's Nacho Fries Are Going Away Soon, but Don't Freak Out." Bustle. Last modified March 29, 2018. https://www.bustle.com/p/taco-bells-nacho-fries-are-going-away-soon-but-dont-freak-out-8640990.

Bentley, Jean. "Comic-Con: Marvel's 'Inhumans' Footage Unveiled in Surprise IMAX Sneak Peak." *Hollywood Reporter*. Last modified July 21, 2017. https://www.hollywoodreporter.com/live-feed/inhumans-surprise-imax-sneak-peek-comic-con-2017-1022961.

Bernardin, Marc. "Even after 15 Years of Braving Crowds at Comic-Con, This Journalist Can Still Find the Love." *Los Angeles Times*. Last modified July 24, 2016. http://www.latimes.com/entertainment/movies/la-et-mn-comic-con-finding-the-love-20160724-snap-story.html.

Billington, Alex. "Comic-Con 2012 Live: WB's Panel on 'Hobbit,' 'Mos' + 'Pacific Rim.'" FirstShowing.Net. Last modified July 14, 2012. http://www.firstshowing.net/2012/comic-con-2012-live-wbs-panel-on-hobbit-mos-pacific-rim/.

———. "Comic-Con 2012: 'Man of Steel' + 'Godzilla' + 'Pacific Rim' Video Blog." FirstShowing.Net. Last modified July 15, 2012. http://www.firstshowing.net/2012/comic-con-2012-man-of-steel-godzilla-pacific-rim-video-blog/.

Block, Alex Ben, and Lucy Autrey Wilson, eds. *George Lucas' Blockbusting*. New York: HarperCollins, 2010.

Boboltz, Sarra. "Whoever Runs Taco Bell's Twitter Account Deserves a Raise." Huffington Post. Last modified December 6, 2017. https://www.huffingtonpost.com/2014/02/28/taco-bell-tweets_n_4856259.html.

Bolling, Ben, and Matthew J. Smith. *It Happens at Comic-Con: Ethnographic Essays on a Pop Culture Phenomenon*. Jefferson, NC: McFarland, 2014.

Boorstin, Julia. "Fox's 'Avatar Day' and a 3-D Revolution." CNBC. Last modified August 21, 2009. http://www.cnbc.com/id/32510270.

Booth, Paul. *Playing Fans: Negotiating Fandom and Media in the Digital Age*. Iowa City: University of Iowa Press, 2015.

Booth, William. "At Comic-Con, Nerd Mentality Rules the Day; Hollywood Now Woos Once-Scorned Genre Fans." *Washington Post*, July 19, 2005, C.01.

Boucher, Geoff. "Comic-Con 2009; Geek Out." *Los Angeles Times*, July 22, 2009, D1.

———. "Comic-Con Will Stay in San Diego." *Los Angeles Times*: Hero Complex. Last modified September 30, 2010. http://herocomplex.latimes.com/comic-con/comic-con-international-san-diego/.

———. "'The Hobbit' at Comic-Con: Peter Jackson's San Diego Plan." *Los Angeles Times*: Hero Complex. Last modified July 11, 2012. http://herocomplex.latimes.com/movies/the-hobbit-at-comic-con-peter-jacksons-san-diego-plan/.

Bourdieu, Pierre. *Distinction: A Social Critique of the Judgement of Taste*. Cambridge, MA: Harvard University Press, 1984.

———. "The Forms of Capital." In *Handbook of Theory and Research for the Sociology of Education*, edited by John G. Richardson, 241–258. Westport, CT: Greenwood Press, 1986.

Bowles, Scott. "Comic-Con Illustrates Genre's Rising Influence." *USA Today*, July 26, 2004, 4D.

Bradshaw, Peter. "Cannes Film Festival Gets Glimpse of Quentin Tarantino's Django Unchained." *Guardian*. Last modified May 21, 2012. http://www.guardian.co.uk /film/2012/may/21/cannes-film-festival-quentin-tarantino-django-unchained.

brandchannel. "Taco Bell 'Demolition Man' Pop-up Restaurant Wins #SDCC." Brandchannel. Last modified July 20, 2018. https://www.brandchannel.com/2018 /07/20/taco-bell-demolition-man-popup-san-diego-comic-con/.

Breznican, Anthony. "'Star Wars: The Force Awakens': You Won't Believe the Epic Comic-Con Line to See That Galaxy Far, Far Away." *Entertainment Weekly*. Last modified July 10, 2015. http://www.ew.com/article/2015/07/10/star-wars-force -awakens-comic-con-line.

Brooker, Will. *Batman Unmasked: Analyzing a Cultural Icon*. New York: Continuum, 2001.

———. "A Sort of Homecoming: Fan Viewing and Symbolic Pilgrimage." In *Fandom: Identities and Communities in a Mediated World*, edited by Johnathan Gray, Cornel Sandvoss and C. Lee Harrington, 149–164. New York: New York University Press, 2007.

Brown, Tracy. "Comic-Con 2018: The Must-See Film, TV and Comic Book Panels." *Los Angeles Times*: Hero Complex. Last modified July 18, 2018. http://www.latimes .com/entertainment/herocomplex/la-et-hc-sdcc-2018-comic-con-panel-highlights -20180718-story.html.

Brown, Tracy, David Lewis, Jevon Phillips, and Meredith Woerner. "Every Year of Comic-Con in One Giant Timeline." *Los Angeles Times*: Hero Complex. Last modified July 8, 2015. http://www.latimes.com/entertainment/herocomplex/la-et -hc-comic-con-san-diego-timeline-htmlstory.html.

Bruno, Bianca. "Comic Con Defendant Says He Knew It Was Trademarked." Courthouse News. Last modified December 7, 2017. https://www.courthousenews.com /comic-con-defendant-says-he-knew-it-was-trademarked/.

Burke, Liam. "The Pop Culture Petri Dish of Comic-Con." *Irish Times*, July 26, 2011, 12.

Burke, Ted. "Comics Come out of the Closet." *Reader*, August 23, 1973, 1.

Burton, Anthony. "A Galaxy of Kids Dig Stardust." *Daily News*, January 22, 1972.

Burwick, Kevin. "Futuristic Demolition Man Taco Bell Restaurant Is Coming to Comic-Con." Movieweb. Last modified July 1, 2018. https://movieweb.com /demolition-man-taco-bell-restaurant-comic-con-2018/.

Business Editors. "Vivendi Universal Agrees to Acquire Houghton Mifflin in Transaction Valued at $2.2 Billion." *Business Wire*. Published electronically June 1, 2001. http://link.galegroup.com.libproxy.uoregon.edu/apps/doc/A75188363/ITOF?u =s8492775&sid=ITOF&xid=03efbb66.

Business/Entertainment Editors. "Houghton Mifflin Acquires U.S. Book Rights to New Line Cinema's 'Lord of the Rings' Movie Trilogy." *Business Wire*. Published electronically January 16, 2001. http://link.galegroup.com.libproxy.uoregon.edu /apps/doc/A69205665/ITOF?u=s8492775&sid=ITOF&xid=8461147c.

Buss, Dale. "Hipster Branding: Taco Bell Woos Cool Kids to Cook Ranch Doritos Locos Tacos." Brandchannel. Last modified February 13, 2013. https://www .brandchannel.com/2013/02/13/hipster-branding-taco-bell-woos-cool-kids-to-cool -ranch-doritos-locos-tacos/.

Busse, Kristina. "Geek Hierarchies, Boundary Policing, and the Gendering of the Good Fan." *Participations Journal of Audience & Reception Studies* 10, no. 1 (May 2013): 72–91.

Butner, Richard. "Richard! A Message from the Chairman." In *San Diego Comic-Con Souvenir Book 1975*, edited by Shel Dorf, np. San Diego: San Diego Comic-Con, 1975.

Caldwell, John T. "Industrial Geography Lessons: Socio-Professional Rituals and the Boarderlands of Production Culture." In *Mediaspace: Place, Scale and Culture in a Media Age*, edited by Nick Couldry and Anna McCarthy, 163–189. New York: Routledge, 2004.

Caldwell, John Thornton. *Production Culture: Industrial Reflexivity and Critical Practice in Film and Television*. Durham, NC: Duke University Press, 2008.

Carone, Angela, and Maureen Cavanaugh. "The First Comic-Con." KPBS Public Media. Last modified July 22, 2010. http://www.kpbs.org/news/2010/jul/22/first -comic-con/.

Carroll, Rory. "Joss Whedon at Comic-Con: Director Returns Home a God among Geeks." *Guardian*. Last modified July 15, 2012. http://www.theguardian.com /culture/2012/jul/15/joss-whedon-comic-con-god.

Carson, Tom. "The Big Shill." *Atlantic Monthly*, May 2005, 127–128, 130–132.

CB's Comic Con Team. "The 6 Best Panels of Comic Con 2012." CinemaBlend.com. Last modified July 16, 2013. http://www.cinemablend.com/new/6-Best-Panels -Comic-Con-2012-31960.html.

Chafin, Chris. "San Diego Comic-Con: The Untold History." *Rolling Stone*. Last modified July 19, 2017. https://www.rollingstone.com/culture/culture-features/san -diego-comic-con-the-untold-history-194401/.

Chavez, Kellvin. "'Pacific Rim' Viral Marketing Has Begun!" Latino Review. Last modified November 28, 2012. http://latino-review.com/2012/11/pacific-rim-viral -marketing-begun/?utm_source=rss&utm_medium=rss&utm_campaign=pacific -rim-viral-marketing-begun.

Cheney, Alexandra. "WB Dazzles Comic-Con, Hall H with Supersized Screens." *Variety*. Last modified July 26, 2014. https://variety.com/2014/film/news/warner -bros-screens-comic-con-1201269625/.

Chitwood, Adam. "Comic-Con Implementing New Wristband System for Hall H Line." Collider. Last modified 14 July, 2014. http://collider.com/comic-con -wristbands-hall-h/.

———. "Comic-Con: End of Watch Panel Surprises with Exciting Footage and Admirable Characters." Collider. Last modified July 14, 2012. http://collider.com /comic-con-end-of-watch/.

———. "Comic-Con: Guillermo Del Toro Wows with Monster vs. Robot Footage at Pacific Rim Panel." Collider. Last modified July 15, 2012. http://collider.com/comic -con-pacific-rim/.

———. "New Trailer for the Campaign; Plus Watch the Comic-Con Panel with Will Ferrell and Zach Galifianakis." Collider. Last modified July 19, 2012. http://collider .com/the-campaign-trailer-comic-con-video/.

Chuba, Kirsten, and Christi Carras. "10 Things We Learned at *Variety*'s Massive Summit." *Variety*. Last modified March 22, 2018. https://variety.com/2018/biz/news /10-things-learned-variety-massive-summit-1202732600/.

Chun, Wendy Hui Kyong, and Thomas Keenan. *New Media, Old Media: A History and Theory Reader*. New York: Routledge, 2006.

Cieply, Michael, and Brooks Barnes. "Comic-Con, Defending Fantasy Culture as, Now, Itself." *New York Times*, June 29, 2015, B-1.

Cinema, New Line. "Middle-Earth Invades Comic Con." theonering.net. Last modified August 1, 2002. http://archives.theonering.net/perl/newsview/8/1028206742.

Clark, Noelene. "'Man of Steel' Trailers: Superman Lonely at Land, Sea and Air." *Los Angeles Times*: Hero Complex. Last modified July 24, 2012. http://herocomplex .latimes.com/movies/man-of-steel-trailer-superman-lonely-at-land-sea-and-air/.

Click, Melissa. "'Rabid,' 'Obsessed,' and 'Frenzied': Understanding Twilight Fangirls and the Gendered Politics of Fandom." Flow 11, no. 4 (2009). http://www .flowjournal.org/2009/12/rabid-obsessed-and-frenzied-understanding-twilight -fangirls-and-the-gendered-politics-of-fandom-melissa-click-university-of-missouri/.

Collins, Scott. "Oh, Boy! WB Leap a Super Success; Idea to Move 'Smallville' to Thursday Nights Paying Off." *Chicago Tribune*, January 6, 2006, 3.

"Comic Book Expo Flyer, 1986." San Diego Comic-Con, Michigan State University Library Comic Art Collection.

"Comic Book Expo Flyer, 1987." San Diego Comic-Con, Michigan State University Library Comic Art Collection.

"Comic-Con." Trademark Electronic Search System (TESS). Last modified 2005. http://tmsearch.uspto.gov/bin/showfield?f=doc&state=4804:98mod5.2.77.

"Comic-Con 2016 *Toucan* Tip of the Day #16: There's a Ton of Fun Going on Outside of the Convention Center!" *Toucan*. Last modified July 5, 2016. https://www.comic -con.org/toucan/16-there%E2%80%99s-ton-of-fun-going-outside-of-convention -center.

"Comic-Con Committee Paperwork." February 6, 1972, Series IV: Comic-Con Committee Paperwork, Folder 12, Box 3, Shel Dorf Collection, San Diego History Center.

"Comic-Con Fans Give 'Django Unchained' a Standing Ovation." Starpulse.com. Last modified July 16, 2012. http://www.starpulse.com/news/index.php/2012/07/16 /comiccon_fans_give_django_unchained_a_.

Comic-Con International. "#22/SDCC 2014: Introducing the Toucan Tracker Wristbands for Hall H's First Panel of the Day!" Comic-Con *Toucan*. Last modified July 14, 2014. https://www.comic-con.org/toucan/22sdcc-2014-introducing-toucan -tracker-wristbands-hall-h's-first-panel-of-day.

———. "Aisles of Smiles! Comic-Con's Massive Exhibit Hall Rocks!" In *Comic-Con International Update* 3 (2005), 24–25.

———. "Comic-Con International Celebrates Its 35th Incredible Year!" In *Comic-Con International Update* 1 (2004), 10–15.

———. "The Mystery of Hall H." In *Comic-Con International Update* 2, San Diego Comic-Con International, 2004, 26.

"Comic-Con Memories: The 70s." In *Comic-Con 40 Souvenir Book*, edited by David Glanzer, Gary Sassaman, and Jackie Estrada, 73–76. San Diego: San Diego Comic-Con International, 2009.

"Comic-Con Poster, 1984." San Diego Comic-Con, Michigan State University Library Comic Art Collection.

"Comic-Con Talk Back, 2011." Panel, San Diego Comic-Con, San Diego, CA, July 24, 2011. "Comic-Con Talk Back, 2012." Panel, San Diego Comic-Con, San Diego, CA, July 22, 2012.

"Con, N.5." *OED Online*. Last modified 2002. http://www.oed.com/.

Conaton, Chris. "Comic-Con 2008: Bigger Than Ever, but Does That Mean Better?" Pop Matters. Last modified August 6, 2008. https://www.popmatters.com/comic -con-2008-bigger-than-ever-but-does-that-mean-better-2496132063.html.

Convention Industry Council. "Apex Industry Glossary—2011 Edition." Pavilion. Last modified 2011. http://www.conventionindustry.org/StandardsPractices/APEX /glossary.aspx.

Coppa, Francesca. "A Brief History of Media Fandom." In *Fan Fiction and Fan Communities in the Age of the Internet*, edited by Karen Hellekson and Kristina Busse, 41–59. Jefferson, NC: McFarland, 2006.

Corrigan, Timothy. *A Cinema without Walls: Movies and Culture after Vietnam*. New Brunswick, NJ: Rutgers University Press, 1991.

Costantino, George. "Comic-Con Debuts Trailers for 'Fantastic Beasts,' 'Aquaman,' 'Shazam' and More." ABC News. Last modified July 23, 2018. https://abcnews.go .com/GMA/Culture/comic-con-debuts-trailers-fantastic-beasts-aquaman-shazam /story?id=56758387.

Couldry, Nick. *Media Rituals: A Critical Approach*. New York: Routledge, 2003.

———. *The Place of Media Power: Pilgrims and Witnesses of the Media Age*. New York: Routledge, 2000.

Craig, David, and Stuart Cunningham. "Toy Unboxing: Living in a(n Unregulated) Material World." *Media International Australia* 163, no. 1 (2017): 77–86.

Cullum, Paul. "Genre Pro Delivers Conventional Wisdom." *Daily Variety*, July 19, 2006, A1.

———. "'Star Wars' 30th Anniversary: How Lucas, ILM Redefined Business-as-Usual." *Variety*. Last modified May 4, 2007. http://www.variety.com/article/VR1117964328 .html?categoryid=2533&cs=1.

Czeiszperger, Michael. "Comic-Con Registration Sells 130,000 Tickets in 90 Minutes without a Hitch." PRWeb. Last modified June 12, 2014. https://www.prweb.com /releases/2014/06/prweb11931964.htm.

D'Alessandro, Anthony. "How Warner Bros. Tore up B.O. Projections & Audaciously Sold 'Meg' as a Horror Comedy for a $44.5m Weekend Win." Deadline. Last modified August 12, 2018. https://deadline.com/2018/08/the-meg-box-office-win -marketing-shark-film-1202444293/.

D'Zurilla, Christie. "By the Numbers: San Diego Comic-Con International 2016." *Los Angeles Times*. Last modified July 24, 2016. http://www.latimes.com/entertainment /la-et-hc-comic-con-updates-by-the-numbers-san-diego-comic-con-1469118665 -htmlstory.html.

Damore, Meagan. "SDCC's Interactive 'Suicide Squad' Experience Will Allow Fans to Bust into Belle Reve." CBR.com. Last modified June 9, 2016. https://www.cbr.com /sdccs-interactive-suicide-squad-experience-will-allow-fans-to-bust-into-belle-reve/.

Dayan, Daniel, and Elihu Katz. *Media Events: The Live Broadcasting of History*. Cambridge, MA: Harvard University Press, 1992.

The Deadline Team. "'Pacific Rim,' 'Man of Steel,' 'the Hobbit,' 'Godzilla': What Comic-Con Was Made For." Deadline. Last modified July 14, 2012. http://www

.deadline.com/2012/07/pacific-rim-godzilla-man-of-steel-the-hobbit-what-comic
-con-was-made-for/.

De Kosnik, Abigail. "Fandom as Free Labor." In *Digital Labor: The Internet as Playground and Factory*, edited by Trebor Scholz, 98–111. New York: Routledge, 2012.

Dean, Michael. "Fine Young Cannibals: How Phil Seuling and a Generation of Teenage
Entrepreneurs Created the Direct Market and Changed the Face of Comics." *Comics
Journal*, no. 277 (2006): 49–59.

Deanne, Derrick. "Hall H: Surprises Galore from WB, Which Amazes with Scenes
from 'Pacific Rim,' 'the Hobbit,' 'Man of Steel,' and More." *Fandango*. Last modified
July 15, 2012. http://www.fandango.com/movieblog/hall-h-surprises-galore-from
-wb-which-amazes-with-scenes-from-pacific-rim-hobbit-man-of-steel-and-more
-718248.html.

Dickey, Josh L. "Con Still on H'w'd High; 'Man of Steel,' 'Pacific Rim' Draw Fan Buzz
Wb, Legendary Tout Tentpoles." *Variety*, July 16, 2012, 5.

Dixon, Kerry. "San Diego Comic-Con Guide: Where Do I Line up for . . . ." *SDCC
Unofficial Blog*. Last modified May 26, 2015. https://sdccblog.com/2015/05/san
-diego-comic-con-guide-where-do-i-line-up-for/.

Dixon, Kerry, and Sarah Lacey. "Infographics: How SDCC Compares to Other
Conventions." *SDCC Unofficial Blog*. Last modified November 4, 2013. http://
sdccblog.com/2013/11/how-sdcc-compares-to-other-conventions/.

———. "San Diego Comic-Con Room Capacities." *SDCC Unofficial Blog*. Last
modified June 28, 2015. https://sdccblog.com/2015/06/san-diego-comic-con-room
-capacities/.

Donnelly, Matt. "20th Century Fox Pulls out of Comic-Con Hall H." The Wrap. Last
modified April 28, 2016. https://www.thewrap.com/20th-century-fox-pulls-out-of
-comic-con-hall-h-presentation-exclusive/.

Dorf, Shel. "The Detroit Triple Fan Fair—and How It Came to Be." *Alter Ego*,
December 2003, 43–44.

———. "Letter to Committee Members of San Diego Comic-Con, 1992." 1992, Series
IX: Shel Dorf Correspondence, Folder 15, Box 3, Shel Dorf Collection, San Diego
History Center.

———. "Letter to Harlan, October 24, 1996." October 24 1996, Series IX: Shel Dorf
Correspondence, Folder 15, Box 3, Shel Dorf Collection, San Diego History Center.

———. "Letter to John Rogers, August 9, 1999." August 9, 1999, Series IX: Shel Dorf
Correspondence, Folder 15, Box 3, Shel Dorf Collection, San Diego History Center.

———. "Letter to Mr. John L. Nunes, San Diego Tribune, July 29, 1989." Series IX: Shel
Dorf Correspondence, Folder 15, Box 3, Shel Dorf Collection, San Diego History
Center.

———. "Letter to San Diego Comic-Con Board of Directors, May 27, 1994." May 27
1994, Series IX: Shel Dorf Correspondance, Folder 15, Box 3, Shel Dorf Collection,
San Diego History Center.

———, ed. *San Diego Comic-Con Souvenir Book 1975*. San Diego: San Diego Comic-
Con, 1975.

———. "Shel's Message: 'I Did It for Love.'" In *1981 San Diego Comic-Con Souvenir
Book*, edited by Mark Stadler, 3. San Diego: San Diego Comic-Con, 1981.

———. "Things I Like to Remember." In *Comic Buyer's Guide 1994 Annual: The
Standard Reference for Today's Collector*, edited by Don Thompson and Maggie
Thompson, 27. Iola WI: Krause Publications, 1994.

Dorf, Shel, Richard Butner, Steve Garris, and George Valentino Olshevskiy. "A San Diego Comic-Con Retrospective." In *The 1979 San Diego Comic-Con Tenth Anniversary Souvenir Comic Section*, 4. San Diego: San Diego Comic-Con, 1979.

Dorf, Shel, and Jackie Estrada, eds. *1976 San Diego Comic-Con Souvenir Book*. San Diego: San Diego Comic-Con, 1976.

Dorf, Shel, and Barry Short, eds. *Progress Report, No. 2*. San Diego Comic-Con, 1982.

Doyle, Charles. "Integrated Marketing." In *Oxford Dictionary of Marketing*, edited by Charles Doyle. New York: Oxford University Press, 2016. http://www .oxfordreference.com/view/10.1093/acref/9780198736424.001.0001/acref -9780198736424-e-0910.

Dubin, Alesandra. "Strategy Session: How Comic-Con Managed Huge Lines of Attendees." BizBash. Last modified July 26, 2012. http://www.bizbash.com/strategy_session _how_comic-con_managed_huge_lines_of_attendees/san-diego/story/23905/.

Duffy, Brooke Erin. "The Romance of Work: Gender and Aspirational Labour in the Digital Culture Industries." *International Journal of Cultural Studies* 19, no. 4 (2015): 1–17.

Duncan, Randy, and Matthew J. Smith. *The Power of Comics: History, Form and Culture*. New York: Continuum, 2009.

Duncan, Randy, Matthew J. Smith, and Paul Levitz. *The Power of Comics: History, Form, and Culture*. 2nd ed. New York: Bloomsbury, 2015.

Ehn, Billy, and Orvar Löfgren. *The Secret World of Doing Nothing*. Berkeley: University of California Press, 2010.

Elderkin, Beth, and Germain Lussier. "Taco Bell's *Demolition Man* Restaurants Gave Us Nacho Fries, Happy Feelings, and Seashell Butts." io9. Last modified July 21, 2018. https://io9.gizmodo.com/taco-bells-demolition-man-restaurant-gave-us-nacho-frie -1827665977.

Ellwood, Gregory. "Comic-Con 2012 Winners and Losers: Robert Downey Jr., Stephenie Meyer, 'Pacific Rim.'" HitFix. Last modified July 18, 2012. http://www .hitfix.com/news/comic-con-2012-winners-and-losers-robert-downey-jr-stephenie -meyer-pacific-rim.

———. "Robert Downey, Jr. Introduces 'the Avengers' at San Diego Comic-Con." HitFix. Last modified July 24, 2010. http://www.hitfix.com/articles/robert-downey -jr-introduces-the-avengers-at-san-diego-comic-con.

Eskey, Nicholas. "'San Diego Comic-Con Staying until 2021' Says Mayor Kevin Faulconer." *The Beat*: The News Blog of Comic Culture. Last modified July 1, 2017. http://www.comicsbeat.com/san-diego-comic-con-staying-until-2021-says-mayor -kevin-faulkner/.

The Esquire Editors. "Comic-Con Attendees Do Not F*ck around When It Comes to Cosplay." *Esquire*. Last modified July 23, 2018. https://www.esquire.com /entertainment/movies/g22487173/san-diego-comic-con-2018-photos/.

Estrada, Jackie, ed. *20th Annual San Diego Comic-Con Souvenir Program Book*. San Diego: San Diego Comic Convention Inc., 1989.

———, ed. "1983 San Diego Comic-Con Progress Report No. 2." May 1983, San Diego Comic-Con, Michigan State University Library Comic Art Collection.

———, ed. "1984 San Diego Comic-Con Progress Report No. 1." December 1983, San Diego Comic-Con, Michigan State University Library Comic Art Collection.

———, ed. "1984 San Diego Comic-Con Progress Report No. 2." April 1984, San Diego Comic-Con, Michigan State University Library Comic Art Collection.

———, ed. *The 1991 San Diego Comic Convention Program Book*. San Diego: San Deigo Comic Convention, Inc., 1991.

———, ed. *2007 Comic-Con International: San Diego Events Guide*. San Diego: Comic-Con International, Inc., 2007.

———, ed. *2009 Comic-Con International: San Diego Events Guide*. San Diego: Comic-Con International, Inc., 2009.

———, ed. *2012 Comic-Con International: San Diego Events Guide*. San Diego: Comic-Con International, Inc., 2012.

———, ed. *2013 Comic-Con International: Events Guide*. San Diego: Comic-Con International, Inc., 2013.

———, ed. *Comic-Con International 2011 Events Guide*. San Diego: Comic-Con International, Inc., 2011.

———, ed. *Comic-Con International 2018 Events Guide*. San Diego: San Diego Comic Convention, 2018.

———, ed. *Comic-Con International Events Guide 2004*. San Diego, CA: Comic-Con International, Inc., 2004.

———, ed. *Progress Report No. 2*. San Diego: San Diego Comic Convention, Inc., 1989.

———, ed. *San Diego Comic-Con International 2005 Events Guide*. San Diego: Comic-Con International, Inc., 2005.

———, ed. *San Diego Comic-Con International Events Guide 2002*. San Diego: Comic-Con International, Inc., 2002.

———, ed. *San Diego Comic-Con Souvenir Book 1984*. San Diego: San Diego Comic Convention, Inc., 1984.

Evanier, Mark. "Comic-Con Founder Shel Dorf Remembered." *Los Angeles Times*: Hero Complex. Last modified November 10, 2009. http://herocomplex.latimes .com/uncategorized/shel-dorf-remembered/.

———. "Comics: Ny2LA." In *1982 San Diego Comic-Con Inc. Souvenir Book*, edited by Shel Dorf, np. San Diego: San Diego Comic-Con Inc., 1982.

———. "The Timeless Jack Kirby." *Comic-Con International 2004 Souvenir Book*, 2004, 60–61.

"Exclusives." San Diego Comic-Con Unofficial Blog. Last modified June 21, 2018. https://sdccblog.com/category/exclusive-news/.

Faraci, Devin. "Cinemacon2012: The Hobbit Underwhelms at 48 Frames Per Second." Birth. Movies. Death. Last modified April 24, 2012. http://badassdigest.com/2012 /04/24/cinemacon-2012-the-hobbit-underwhelms-at-48-frames-per-secon/.

———. "Comic-Con 2012: Pacific Rim Tears the Roof Off Hall H." Birth. Movies. Death. Last modified July 15, 2012. http://badassdigest.com/2012/07/15/comic-con -2012-pacific-rim-tears-the-roof-off-hall-h/.

"February 1966." The Marvel Comics Bullpen Bulletins Index. Last modified June 16, 2007. http://bullpenbulletins.blogspot.com/2007/06/february-1966.html.

Feuer, Jane. "The Concept of Live Television: Ontology as Ideology." In *Regarding Television: Critical Approaches—an Anthology*, edited by E. Ann Kaplan, 12–22. Frederick, MD: University Publications of America, 1983.

Fisher, Jude. *Fellowship of the Rings Visual Companion*. Boston: Houghton Mifflin, 2001.

Fiske, John. "The Cultural Economy of Fandom." In *The Adoring Audience: Fan Culture and Popular Media*, edited by Lisa A. Lewis, 30–49. New York: Routledge, 1992.

———. *Television Culture*. New York: Methuen, 1987.

Fleishman, Jeffrey. "Blame Those Endless Hall H Lines on Jeff Walker, the Man Who Brought Hollywood to Comic-Con." *Los Angeles Times*. Last modified July 20, 2016. http://www.latimes.com/entertainment/movies/la-et-mn-comic-con-jeff -walker-profile-20160713-snap-story.html.

Fleming Jr., Mike. "Warner Bros Releases 'Suicide Squad' Footage after Being Frustrated by Comic Con Pirates." Deadline. Last modified July 13, 2015. http://deadline.com /2015/07/suicide-squad-official-movie-footage-exclusive-1201475371/.

Flemming, Mike. "Theater Chains AMC, Regal Launch Distribution Venture Open Road with Tom Ortenberg at Helm." Deadline. Last modified March 7, 2011. https://deadline.com/2011/03/theater-chains-amc-regal-launch-distribution -venture-open-road-with-tom-ortenberg-at-head-111698/.

"The Force Is Strong at Walmart: Company to Offer a New Generation of Star WarsTM Merchandise at 12:01 A.M. On 'Force Friday.'" Walmart.com. Last modified July 9, 2015. https://news.walmart.com/news-archive/2015/07/09/the-force-is -strong-at-walmart-company-to-offer-a-new-generation-of-star-warstm-merchandise -at-12-01-am-on-force-friday.

Ford, Rebecca, and Borys Kit. "Marvel Reveals Complete Phase 3 Plans, Dates 'Black Panther,' 'Inhumans,' 'Avengers: Infinity War.'" *Hollywood Reporter*. Last modified October 28, 2014. https://www.hollywoodreporter.com/heat-vision/marvel-reveals -complete-phase-3-plans-dates-black-panther-inhumans-avengers-infinity-war -744455.

Foucault, Michel. *Discipline and Punish: The Birth of the Prison*. New York: Vintage Books, 1979.

———. "What Is an Author?" In *Language, Counter-Memory, Practice: Selected Essays and Interviews*, edited by Donald F. Bouchard, 113–138. Ithaca, NY: Cornell University Press, 1977.

Franich, Darren. "'Twilight' at Comic-Con 2011: Talking to the Fans at Camp Breaking Dawn." PopWatch. Last modified July 20, 2011. http://popwatch.ew.com/2011/07 /20/twilight-comic-con-fans-breaking-dawn/.

Franson, Donald. "A Key to the Terminology of Science-Fiction Fandom." National Fantasy Fan Federation, 1962.

"Friday Flashback 006: The History of Comic-Con (and Then-Some!) through Logos." *Toucan*. Last modified October 18, 2013. http://www.comic-con.org/toucan/friday -flashback-006-history-of-comic-con-and-then-some-through-logos.

Friedenthal, Andrew J. *Retcon Game: Retroactive Continuity and the Hyperlinking of America*. Jackson: University Press of Mississippi, 2017.

Fritz, Ben. "Geek Chic . . . but 'Netsters Wary of Showbiz Wooing." *Variety*, August 2–8, 2004, 1, 41.

Fritz, Ben, and Marc Graser. "Drawing H'w'd Interest." *Daily Variety*, July 22, 2004, 19.

Frook, John Evan, and Kathleen O'steen. "High Volume, Hard Sell Spell Christmas Crunch." *Variety*, November 15, 1993, 9–10.

"Fry Fans Rejoice! Taco Bell Rolling Out Spicy Fries for Just $1." NBC15. Last modified January 4, 2018. http://www.nbc15.com/content/news/Fry-fans-rejoice-Taco-Bell -rolling-out-spicy-fries-for-just-1-468027633.html.

Gabilliet, Jean-Paul. *Of Comics and Men: A Cultural History of American Comic Books*. Jackson: University Press of Mississippi, 2005.

Gallagher, Brian. "'Pacific Rim' Trailer." MovieWeb. Last modified December 12, 2012. http://www.movieweb.com/news/pacific-rim-trailer.

Galuppo, Mia. "'Blade Runner 2049': Inside the Comic-Con Experience Where You Can Be a Replicant." *Hollywood Reporter.* Last modified July 22, 2017. https://www.hollywoodreporter.com/heat-vision/blade-runner-2049-inside-comic-con-2017-experience-1023559.

Gamerman, Ellen. "The Rise of Cons." *Wall Street Journal.* Last modified March 3, 2016. https://www.wsj.com/articles/the-rise-of-cons-1457036227.

Garson, Sue. "Comic Book Characters." *Reader,* August 1, 1985, 1–11.

"Gaslamp's Comic Con Tips." Gaslamp.org. Last modified 2012. http://www.gaslamp.org/comic-con.

Gaslin, Glenn. "Superheroes Escape the Page: Comic Book Sales Are Tailing Off, Even as Their Characters Triumph in Other Media." *Vancouver Sun,* July 27, 2002, E3.

Gates, Fay. "Comic Book Expo 84 Letter." March 21, 1984, San Diego Comic-Con, Michigan State University Library Comic Art Collection.

Gaudiosi, John. "'Lord of the Rings' Gets Games Deal." *Hollywood Reporter,* July 31, 2001, 8.

Gay, Roxane. "Surviving 'Django.'" BuzzFeed. Last modified January 3, 2013. https://www.buzzfeed.com/roxanegay/surviving-django-80px.

Gearino, Dan. *Comic Shop: The Retail Mavericks Who Gave Us a New Geek Culture.* Athens: Swallow Press/Ohio University Press, 2017.

Gehlken, Michael. "It Begins: Line Forms for Comic-Con." NBC San Diego. Last modified July 19, 2011. http://www.nbcsandiego.com/news/local/It-Begins-Line-Forms-for-Comic-Con-125781473.html.

Geigner, Timothy. "It Begins: Some Comic Conventions Refusing to Fold after San Diego Comic-Con Gets Its Trademark Win." Techdirt. Last modified January 4, 2018. https://www.techdirt.com/articles/20180102/07163338907/it-begins-some-comic-conventions-refusing-to-fold-after-san-diego-comic-con-gets-trademark-win.shtml.

Geraghty, Lincoln. *Cult Collectors: Nostalgia, Fandom and Collecting Popular Culture.* London: Routledge, 2014.

Gilbert, Anne. "Conspicuous Convention: Industry Interpellation and Fan Consumption at San Diego Comic-Con." In *The Routledge Companion to Media Fandom,* edited by Melissa A. Click and Suzanne Scott, 319–328. New York: Routledge, 2018.

———. "Live from Hall H: Fan/Producer Symbiosis at San Diego Comic-Con." In *Fandom: Identities and Communities in a Mediated World,* edited by Jonathan Gray, Cornel Sandvoss, and C. Lee Harrington, 354–368. New York: New York University Press, 2017.

Gitelman, Lisa, and Geoffrey B. Pingree, eds. *New Media, 1740–1915.* Media in Transition. Cambridge, MA: MIT Press, 2003.

Glanzer, David. "Press Release: Comic Con International Enjoys Increased Media Attention." San Diego Comic-Con, Michigan State Library Comic Arts Collection.

Glanzer, David, Gary Sassaman, and Jackie Estrada, eds. *Comic-Con 40 Souvenir Book.* San Diego: San Diego Comic-Con International, 2009.

Goldberg, Lesley. "Comic-Con 2011: Warner Bros. Booth Will Get a 'Toon Up.'" *Hollywood Reporter.* Last modified July 15, 2011. https://www.hollywoodreporter.com/live-feed/comic-con-2011-warner-bros-212083.

———. "Stars Getting Rich Off Fan Conventions: How to Take Home 'Garbage Bags Full of $20s.'" *Hollywood Reporter.* Last modified September 29, 2016. https://www.hollywoodreporter.com/live-feed/stars-getting-rich-fan-conventions-933062.

Goldberg, Matt. "New York Comic-Con: Guillermo Del Toro Talks Pacific Rim and the Prequel Graphic Novel." Collider. Last modified October 13, 2012. http://collider.com/pacific-rim-recap-new-york-comic-con/.

Goldman, David. "Disney to Buy Marvel for $4 Billion." CNN Money. Last modified 2009. http://money.cnn.com/2009/08/31/news/companies/disney_marvel/.

Gomery, Douglas. *Shared Pleasures: A History of Movie Presentation in the United States.* Wisconsin Studies in Film. Madison: University of Wisconsin Press, 1992.

Google Trends. Last modified July 12, 2018. https://trends.google.com/.

Graham, Chuck, and Barry Alfonso. "San Diego Comic-Con Progress Report No.1 and 1973 Wrap-up Report." Series III: Progress Reports and Newsletters, Folder 40, Box 1, Shel Dorf Collection, San Diego History Center.

Graser, Marc. "5 Things to Expect from Marvel Studios Fan Event." *Variety.* Last modified October 28, 2014. https://variety.com/2014/film/news/5-things-to-expect-from-marvel-studios-fan-event-1201341014/.

———. "Geek Vibe Gives Way to Mainstream Fare." *Daily Variety,* July 24, 2008, A1.

———. "H'w'd Woos Nerd Herd." *Variety,* July 14–July 20, 2008, 1.

———. "H'wood Learns to Speak Geek." *Daily Variety,* July 28, 2008, 1.

———. "Studios Blitz Comic-Con." *Variety.* Last modified July 19, 2010. http://www.variety.com/article/VR1118021897?refcatid=4076&printerfriendly=true.

———. "Warner Bros. Creates DC Entertainment." *Variety.* Last modified September 9, 2009. http://variety.com/2009/film/news/warner-bros-creates-dc-entertainment-1118008299/.

———. "Warner Bros. No Longer in Legendary's Future." *Variety.* Last modified June 24, 2013. http://variety.com/2013/biz/news/warner-bros-no-longer-in-legendarys-future-1200501572/.

Graser, Marc, and Rachel Abrams. "Legendary Pictures Eyes New Credit Line." *Variety.* Last modified April 15, 2011. http://variety.com/2011/film/news/legendary-pictures-eyes-new-credit-line-1118035532/.

Graser, Marc, and Jonathan Bing. "Genre Pix Cultivate Geek Chic." *Variety,* July 28–August 8, 2003, 8.

Graser, Marc, and Josh L. Dickey. "Comic-Con 2012: Who's In and Who's Out." *Variety.* Last modified June 12, 2012. http://variety.com/2012/film/news/comic-con-2012-who-s-in-who-s-out-1118055419.

Gray, Jonathan. *Show Sold Separately: Promos, Spoilers, and Other Media Paratexts.* New York: New York University Press, 2010.

Gray, Jonathan, Cornel Sandvoss, and C. Lee Harrington, eds. *Fandom: Identities and Communities in a Mediated World.* 2nd ed. New York: New York University Press, 2017.

———. *Fandom: Identities and Communities in a Mediated World.* New York: New York University Press, 2007.

———. "Introduction: Why Still Study Fans?" In *Fandom: Identities and Communities in a Mediated World,* edited by Jonathan Gray, Cornel Sandvoss, and C. Lee Harrington, 1–26. New York: New York University Press, 2017.

———. "Introduction: Why Study Fans?" In *Fandom: Identities and Communities in a Mediated World,* edited by Jonathan Gray, Cornel Sandvoss, and C. Lee Harrington, 1–16. New York: New York University Press, 2007.

Gregg, Melissa. "Learning to (Love) Labor: Production Cultures and the Affective Turn." *Communication and Critical/Cultural Studies* 6, no. 2 (2009): 209–214.

Groensteen, Thierry. *The System of Comics*. Translated by Bart Beaty and Nick Nguyen. Jackson: University Press of Mississippi, 2007.

Grossman, Lev. "The Geek Shall Inherit the Earth." *Time*. Last modified September 25, 2005. http://www.time.com/time/magazine/article/0,9171,1109317,00.html.

Groth, John C., and Stephen W. McDaniel. "The Exclusive Value Principle: The Basis for Prestige Racing." *Journal of Consumer Marketing* 10, no. 1 (1993): 10–16.

Gunnels, Jen. "'A Jedi Like My Father before Me': Social Identity and the New York Comic Con." *Transformative Works and Cultures* 3, July 9, 2009. https://journal .transformativeworks.org/index.php/twc/article/view/161/110.

Guthrie, Jonathon. "Bilbo Baggins Enters Games Workshop Land Leisure." *Financial Times*, January 31, 2001, 28.

———. "Games Workshop Runs Rings around Its Rivals." *Financial Times*, July 31, 2002, 20.

Gutierrez, Jon. "Exclusive Story: A Brief History of San Diego Con Exclusives." *ToyFare*, September 2010, 8.

Gwenllian-Jones, Sara. "Web Wars: Resistance, Online Fandom and Studio Censorship." In *Quality Popular Television: Cult TV, the Industry and Fans*, edited by Mark Jancovich and James Lyons, 163–177. London: British Film Institute, 2003.

Habegger, Mark. "Scott Shaw!" Comic-Con Kids. Last modified 2013. http:// comiccon.sdsu.edu/scott-shaw/.

Hall, Jacob. "Comic-Con 2012 Saturday Schedule: 'Man of Steel,' 'Iron Man 3' and More." Screen Crush. Last modified June 30, 2012. http://screencrush.com/comic -con-2012-saturday/.

———. "Comic-Con 2012: A New Clip from 'Silent Hill: Revelation 3D.'" Screen Crush. Last modified July 14, 2012. http://screencrush.com/comic-con-2012-clip -from-silent-hill-revelation-3d/.

Halzack, Sarah. "A Guide to 'Force Friday,' the 'Star Wars' Toy Bonanza." *Washington Post*. Last modified September 3, 2015. https://www.washingtonpost.com/news /business/wp/2015/09/03/a-guide-to-force-friday-the-star-wars-toy-bonanza/.

———. "'Star Wars' Fans Pounce on Force Friday, Snap up New Toys." *Washington Post*. Last modified September 4, 2015. https://www.washingtonpost.com/business /economy/disney-kicks-off-star-wars-bonanza-with-force-friday/2015/09/04 /ff3ea6fc-5244-11e5-9812-92d5948a40f8_story.html?utm_term=.bc7545163bce.

Hammond, Pete. "'The Hobbit' Footage in New Format Draws Lukewarm Response: Cinemacon." Deadline. Last modified April 24, 2012. http://www.deadline.com /2012/04/the-hobbit-debuts-at-revolutionary-48-frames-during-warner-bros-exhib -presentation-cinemacon/.

Hanks, Henry. "Force Friday: 'Star Wars' Merch for Any Taste." CNN. Last modified September 3, 2015. https://www.cnn.com/2015/09/03/living/force-friday-highlights -star-wars-feat/index.html.

———. "Is This Comic-Con? Fans Debate 'Mainstream' Panels—CNN.com." CNN. Last modified July 22, 2010. http://www.cnn.com/2010/SHOWBIZ/07/22/is.this .comicon/index.html.

Hanrahan, Mark. "'The Hobbit' 48fps Footage Divides Audiences at Cinemacon." Huffington Post Entertainment. Last modified April 25, 2012. http://www .huffingtonpost.com/2012/04/25/hobbit-48-fps-footage-divides-audiences_n _1452391.html.

Hardt, Michael. "Affective Labor." *boundary 2* 26, no. 2 (Summer 1999): 89–100.

Harvey, David. *A Brief History of Neoliberalism*. Oxford: Oxford University Press, 2005.

———. *The Condition of Postmodernity*. Cambridge, MA: Blackwell, 1988.

Harvey, R. C. "Shel Dorf, Founder." In *Comic-Con 40 Souvenir Book*, edited by David Glanzer, Gary Sassaman, and Jackie Estrada, 40–41. San Diego: San Diego Comic-Con International, 2009.

Hatic, Dana. "Drink Free Coffee Like a Gilmore Girl at Hundreds of Luke's Diner Pop-Ups across America." Eater. Last modified October 3, 2016. https://www.eater.com/2016/10/3/12929778/gilmore-girls-netflix-lukes-diner-coffee-california-new-york-canada.

Havens, Timothy. *Global Television Marketplace*. London: BFI Publishing, 2006.

Havens, Timothy, Amanda D. Lotz, and Serra Tinic. "Critical Media Industry Studies: A Research Approach." *Communication, Culture & Critique* 2, no. 2 (June 2009): 234–253.

Hellekson, Karen. "A Fannish Field of Value: Online Fan Gift Culture." *Cinema Journal* 48, no. 3 (2009): 113–118.

———. "Making Use Of: The Gift, Commerce, and Fans." *Cinema Journal* 54, no. 3 (Spring 2015): 125–131.

Hendershot, Heather. "On Stan Lee, Leonard Nimoy, and Coitus . . . Or, the Fleeting Pleasures of Televisual Nerdom." Antenna: Responses to Media Culture. Last modified July 30, 2010. http://blog.commarts.wisc.edu/2010/07/30/on-stan-lee-leonard-nimoy-and-coitus-or-the-fleeting-pleasures-of-televisual-nerdom/.

Hennings, Nadine, Klaus-Peter Wiedmann, and Christiane Klarmann. "Luxury Brands in the Digital Age—Exclusivity Versus Ubiquity." *Marketing Review St. Gallen* 29, no. 1 (2012): 30–35.

Herbert, Daniel. *Videoland: Movie Culture at the American Video Store*. Berkeley and Los Angeles: University of California Press, 2014.

Herbert, Daniel, and Derek Johnson, eds. *Point of Sale: Analyzing Media Retail*. New Brunswick, NJ: Rutgers University Press, 2019.

Hill, Libby. "Fans Get Their 'Gilmore Girls' on at Luke's Diner Pop-up Coffee Shops." *Los Angeles Times*. Last modified October 5, 2018. http://www.latimes.com/entertainment/tv/la-et-st-gilmore-girls-anniversary-coffee-shop-20161005-snap-story.html.

Hills, Matt. "Always-on Fandom, Waiting and Bingeing: Psychoanalysis as an Engagement with Fans' 'Infra-Ordinary' Experiences." In *The Routledge Companion to Media Fandom*, edited by Melissa A. Click and Suzanne Scott, 18–26. New York: Routledge, 2018.

———. *Doctor Who: The Unfolding Event—Marketing, Merchandising and Mediatizing a Brand Anniversary*. Palgrave Pivot. New York: Palgrave Macmillan, 2015.

———. *Fan Cultures*. London: Routledge, 2002.

"History | Dragoncon." Dragon Con. Last modified 2018. http://www.dragoncon.org/?q=history.

Hodgkins, Crystalyn. "Comic Market 91 Attracts 550,000 Attendees across 3 Days." Anime News Network. Last modified December 31, 2016. http://www.animenewsnetwork.com/daily-briefs/2016-12-31/comic-market-91-attracts-550000-attendees-across-3-days/.110518.

Hollywood Life Staff. "'Breaking Dawn' at Comic-Con—the Fans Are Already Lining Up!" Hollywood Life. Last modified July 19, 2011. http://www.hollywoodlife.com/2011/07/19/breaking-dawn-comic-con-panel-robert-pattinson-kristen-stewart/.

Holson, Laura M. "Can Little-Known Heroes Be Hollywood Hits?" *New York Times*, July 26, 2004, 1.

Horn, John. "Comic-Con's Buzz-Makers." *Los Angeles Times*, July 27, 2009, D1.

———. "Studios Take a Read on Comic Book Gathering; Hollywood Courts a Genre's Enthusiasts, Who Can Raise or Lower Movie's Fortunes." *Los Angeles Times*, July 26, 2004, E1.

"Hotels." Comic-Con International: San Diego. Last modified 2018. https://www .comic-con.org/sites/default/files/forms/cci2018_hotellist_v1.pdf.

Huber, Peter. "The Economics of Waiting." *Forbes*, December 30, 1996, 150.

"Hysteria, N." *OED Online*. Last modified, 2014. http://www.oed.com/.

"Informa Exhibitions—Our Events." Last modified 2018. https://www .informaexhibitions.com/en/about-us/ourevents.html.

Inscaped. "Comic-Con 2012 Hall H Madness." Storify. Last modified July 14, 2012. http://storify.com/Inscaped/comic-con-2012-hall-h-madness.

"Introducing *Toucan*: The Official Blog of Comic-Con International, Wondercon Anaheim, and Ape, the Alternative Press Expo." *Toucan*. Last modified December 10, 2012. http://www.comic-con.org/toucan/toucan-official-blog-of-comic-con -international-wondercon-anaheim-and-ape-alternative-press.

Jackie. "Comic-Con 2009: Thursday Roundup." *The Lowdown Blog*. Last modified July 27, 2009. http://lowdownblog.com/2009/07/27/comic-con-2009-thursday -roundup/.

James, Becca. "Want to Try Scheer, Raphael, and Mantzoukas's How Did This Get Made? Start Here." Vulture. Last modified July 26, 2018. http://www.vulture.com /2018/07/the-best-episode-of-how-did-this-get-made.html.

Jancovich, Mark. "Cult Fictions: Cult Movies, Subcultural Capital and the Production and Distribution of Cultural Distinctions." *Cultural Studies* 16, no. 2 (2002): 306–322.

Jarvey, Natalie. "How SXSW, Comic-Con Fueled the Rise of Activation Culture." *Hollywood Reporter*. Last modified July 21, 2018. https://www.hollywoodreporter .com/news/how-comic-con-fueled-rise-activation-culture-1128792.

Jenkins, Henry. *Convergence Culture: Where Old and New Media Collide*. New York: New York University Press, 2006.

———. "Superpowered Fans: The Many Worlds of San Diego's Comic-Con." *Boom: A Journal of California* 2, no. 2 (2012): 22–36.

———. *Textual Poachers: Television Fans & Participatory Culture*. New York: Routledge, 1992.

Jenkins, Henry, Sam Ford, and Joshua Green. *Spreadable Media: Creating Value and Meaning in a Networked Culture*. Postmillennial Pop. New York: New York University Press, 2013.

Jenkins, Henry, and Suzanne Scott. "*Textual Poachers,* Twenty Years Later: A Conversation between Henry Jenkins and Suzanne Scott." In *Textual Poachers*, New York: Taylor & Francis, 2013, vii–l.

Jensen, Bill. "Eternia Again." *ToyFare*, September 2001, 16.

Jenson, Jeff. "'Star Wars': Comic-Con '76 Pics." *Entertainment Weekly*. Last modified August 2, 2011. http://www.ew.com/gallery/star-wars-comic-con-76-pics?iid=sr -link1.

Jenson, Joli. "Fandom as Pathology: The Consequences of Categorization." In *The Adoring Audience*, edited by Lisa A. Lewis, 9–29. London: Routledge, 1992.

Johnson, Derek. "After the Industry Turn: Can Production Studies Make an Audience Turn?" *Creative Industries Journal* 7, no. 1 (2014): 50–53.

———. "Fantagonism, Franchising, and Industry Management of Fan Privilege." In *The Routledge Companion to Media Fandom*, edited by Melissa A. Click and Suzanne Scott, 395–405. New York: Routledge, 2018.

———. "From the Ruins: Neomasculinity, Media Franchising, and Struggles over Industrial Reproduction of Culture." *Communication Culture & Critique* 11 (2018): 85–99.

———. *Media Franchising*. New York: New York University Press, 2013.

———. "Participation Is Magic: Collaboration, Authorial Legitimacy, and the Audience Function." In *A Companion to Media Authorship*, edited by Jonathan Gray and Derek Johnson, 135–157. Malden, MA: John Wiley & Sons, 2013.

———. "Will the Real Wolverine Please Stand Up: Marvel's Mutation from Monthlies to Movies." In *Film and Comic Books*, edited by Ian Gordon, Mark Jancovich, and Matthew P. McAllister, 64–85. Jackson: University Press of Mississippi, 2007.

Johnson, Keith M. "'The Coolest Way to Watch Movie Trailers in the World': Trailers in the Digital Age." *Convergence* 14, no. 2 (2008): 145–160.

Johnson, Lauren. "Netflix's Gilmore Girls Pop-up Coffee Shops Were a Massive Hit on Snapchat." *Adweek*. Last modified October 25, 2016. https://www.adweek.com/digital/netflixs-gilmore-girls-pop-coffee-shops-were-massive-hit-snapchat-174248/.

Johnston, George. "San Diego Comic Con Draws Hit Hungry H'wood." *Hollywood Reporter*, July 22, 1997. https://advance.lexis.com/api/document?collection=news&id=urn:contentItem:3SJF-B3P0-006P-R2MF-00000-00&context=1516831.

Johnston, Jerry. "Comic Book Fans Have a Blast." *Deseret News*, August 5, 2007, E16.

Johnston, Rich. "Hasbro and Mattel Stamp Down on Professional Scalpers at San Diego Comic Con." Bleeding Cool. Last modified July 17, 2013. http://www.bleedingcool.com/2013/07/17/hasbro-and-mattel-stamp-down-on-professional-scalpers-at-san-diego-comic-con/.

Jones, Jeremy. "The Meg Submersible VR Experience." DestroytheBrain.com. Last modified August 6, 2018. http://www.destroythebrain.com/geek-out/the-meg-submersible-vr-experience.

Kallenback, Gareth Von. "Robert Downey Jr. Iron Man 3 Comic Con Entrance." YouTube. Last modified July 14, 2012. https://www.youtube.com/watch?v=c4OHn77YNZI.

Kastrenakes, Jacob. "Hall H of Horrors; What Is Comic-Con Doing about the Worst Line in Fandom?" The Verge. Last modified 12 July, 2015. http://www.theverge.com/2015/7/12/8937951/comic-con-hall-h-line-horrors.

———. "Meet the Collectors Who Resell Toys to Pay Off Their Comic-Con Addiction." The Verge. Last modified July 25, 2016. https://www.theverge.com/2016/7/25/12269660/comic-con-2016-resell-toy-flipping-collection.

Katz, Michael I., and Rex L. Sears. "Comic Con: A Convention by Any Other Name?" *Orange County Lawyer*, April 2018, 32–35.

Kaufman, Amy. "Cinemacon: Footage of 'the Hobbit' Draws Mixed Reaction." *Los Angeles Times*. Last modified April 24, 2012. http://latimesblogs.latimes.com/movies/2012/04/cinemacon-hobbit-frame-rate-depp-gatsby.html.

Keegan, Rebecca Winters. "Movies: Boys Who Like Toys." *Time*. Last modified April 19, 2007. http://www.time.com/time/magazine/article/0,9171,1612687,00.html.

Keyes, Rob. "James Cameron's Avatar Is Epic—Comic-Con 2009." ScreenRant. Last modified July 23, 2009. http://screenrant.com/james-camerons-avatar-comiccon -2009-rob-18351/.

Kidman, Shawna Feldmar. "Five Lessons for New Media from the History of Comics Culture." *International Journal of Learning and Media* 3, no. 4 (2012): 41–54.

Kilday, Gregg. "Cannes 2012: Quentin Tarantino's 'Django Unchained' Unveiled by Harvey Weinstein." *Hollywood Reporter*. Last modified May 21, 2012. http://www .hollywoodreporter.com/news/cannes-2012-quentin-tarantinos-django-327358.

———. "Comic-Con Piracy: 'Suicide Squad,' 'Deadpool' Footage Forces Studios to React." *Hollywood Reporter*. Last modified July 14, 2015. http://www .hollywoodreporter.com/news/comic-con-piracy-suicide-squad-808495.

King, Thomas R. "Movies: 'Demolition Man' Trades Tacos for Pizza Abroad." *Wall Street Journal*, December 2, 1993, B1.

Kit, Borys. "Comic-Con 2011: Guillermo Del Toro and 'Pacific Rim' Cast Set Panel." *Hollywood Reporter*: Heat Vision. Last modified July 6, 2011. http://www .hollywoodreporter.com/heat-vision/comic-con-2011-guillermo-del-208442.

———. "Mainstream Drowning in Comic-Con's Geek Chic." *Hollywood Reporter*. Last modified July 24, 2008. http://www.hollywoodreporter.com/news/mainstream -drowning-comic-cons-geek-116236.

———. "'Man of Steel' Footage So Good It Makes Fans Cry." *Hollywood Reporter*. Last modified July 14, 2012. http://www.hollywoodreporter.com/heat-vision/comic-con -2012-man-steel-super-man-reboot-349325.

———. "Newly Cool Geeks Rule Comic-Con." *Hollywood Reporter*, July 19, 2006, 1.

———. "Sith Unveiling Wows Comic-Con Crowd." *Hollywood Reporter*, July 26, 2004, 1.

Klinger, Barbara. *Beyond the Multiplex: Cinema, New Technologies, and the Home.* Berkeley: University of California Press, 2006.

Kohnen, Melanie E. S. "'The Power of Geek': Fandom as Gendered Commodity at Comic-Con." *Creative Industries Journal* 7, no. 1 (2014): 75–78.

Kosik, Alli Hoff. "Taco Bell's Nacho Fries Are Finally Available & Fans Already Love Them." Bustle. Last modified January 25, 2018. https://www.bustle.com/p/taco-bells -nacho-fries-are-finally-available-fans-already-love-them-8013303.

Kresnicka, Susan. "Why Understanding Fans Is the New Superpower (Guest Column)." *Variety*. Last modified April 2, 2016. http://variety.com/2016/tv/columns /understanding-fans-superpower-troika-1201743513/.

Kuehn, Kathleen, and Thomas F. Corrigan. "Hope Labor: The Role of Employment Prospects in Online Social Production." *The Political Economy of Communication* 1, no. 1 (2013): 9–25.

Lake, Heather. "Where to Get Last Minute Comic-Con Costumes." Fox 5. Last modified July 17, 2018. https://fox5sandiego.com/2018/07/17/where-to-get-last -minute-comin-con-costumes/.

Lamerichs, Nicolle. "The Cultural Dynamic of Doujinshi and Cosplay: Local Anime Fandom in Japan, USA and Europe." *Participations Journal of Audience & Reception Studies* 10, no. 1 (May 2013): 154–176.

Larson, Richard C. "There's More to a Line Than Its Wait." *Technology Review* 91, no. 5 (1988): 60–67.

Lattanzi, Larry. "Who's Who in Comic Fandom." Warren, MI: Academy of Comic-Book Fans and Collectors, 1964.

Lee, Derek. "Comic-Con Recap: Warner Bros. and Legendary Pictures Panel." Examiner.com. Last modified July 16, 2012. http://www.examiner.com/article /comic-con-recap-warner-bros-and-legendary-pictures-panel.

Lefebvre, Henri. *Everyday Life in the Modern World*. London: Allen Lane, 1971.

"Legendary Pictures Preproduction Preview." San Diego Comic-Con, San Diego, July 22, 2011.

Lendino, Jamie. "'The Hobbit' at 48fps: Frame Rates Explained." *PC Magazine*. Last modified December 14, 2012. http://www.pcmag.com/article2/0,2817,2403746,00.asp.

Lenker, Maureen Lee. "John Rogers, President of Comic-Con International, Dies." *Entertainment Weekly*. Last modified November 11, 2018. https://ew.com/comic -con/2018/11/11/john-rogers-president-comic-con-international-dies/.

Lesnick, Silas. "Guillermo Del Toro Talks the Strain and Pacific Rim's 3D Conversion." Shock Till You Drop. Last modified September 22, 2012. http://www .shocktillyoudrop.com/news/170043-guillermo-del-toro-talks-the-strain-and -pacific-rims-3d-conversion/.

Liebson, Jonathan. "Samsung Experience's 'Suicide Squad' Activation." BizBash. Last modified 2016. https://www.bizbash.com/samsung-experiences-suicide-squad -activation-suicide-squad-stars-attended-films/gallery/187713.

Lincoln, Ross. "Comic-Con 2013 Sells out in 93 Minutes but Tech Glitches Frustrate Fans—Again." Deadline. Last modified February 16, 2013. http://deadline.com /2013/02/comic-con-2013-sells-out-in-93-seconds-but-tech-glitches-frustrate-fans -again-432646/.

Lodge, Hannah. "SDCC '18: The Year Is 2018 and Taco Bell Has Won the Activation Wars." *The Beat*. Last modified July 21, 2018. http://www.comicsbeat.com/sdcc-18 -the-year-is-2018-and-taco-bell-has-won-the-activation-wars/.

Lopes, Paul Douglas. *Demanding Respect: The Evolution of the American Comic Book*. Philadelphia: Temple University Press, 2009.

lostinreviews. "Twilight Breaking Dawn Comic Con Line and Panel." YouTube. Last modified July 21, 2011. http://www.youtube.com/watch?v=InJ1EBeKWYg.

Lothian, Alex. "Living in a Den of Thieves: Fan Video and the Challenges to Ownership." *Cinema Journal* 48, no. 4 (2009): 130–136.

Lotz, Amanda, and Timothy Havens. *Understanding Media Industries*. New York: Oxford University Press, 2012.

Lovett, Jamie. "New York Comic Con Was Attended by 151,000 People, Surpasses San Diego." ComicBook.com. Last modified October 13, 2014. http://comicbook.com /2014/10/13/new-york-comic-con-was-attended-by-151-000-people-surpasses-san-/.

Lowry, Brian. "Beware the Comic-Con False Positive." *Variety*. Last modified July 15, 2009. https://variety.com/2009/scene/columns/beware-the-comic-con-false -positive-1118005970/.

———. "The Early Days of Comic-Con." *Variety*. Last modified July 11, 2008. http:// variety.com/2008/film/columns/the-early-days-of-comic-con-1117988845/.

Luna, Nancy. "Nacho Fries Become Bestselling Taco Bell Product Launch in Chain History." *Nation's Restaurant News*. Last modified March 13, 2018. https://www.nrn .com/food-trends/nacho-fries-become-bestselling-taco-bell-product-launch-chain -history.

Lussier, Germain. "The Crazy Lengths People Go to for San Diego Comic Con." io9. Last modified July 6, 2015. https://io9.gizmodo.com/the-crazy-lengths-people-go -to-for-san-diego-comic-con-1715847049.

———. "A Demolition Man-Style Taco Bell Is Comic to Comic-Con." Gizmodo. Last modified June 29, 2018. https://www.gizmodo.com.au/2018/06/a-demolition-man-style-taco-bell-is-coming-to-comic-con/.

MacDonald, Heidi. "Hollywood Cruises Nerd Prom." *Publishers Weekly*, June 20, 2005, 24, 26–27.

———. "Wizard World Announces 17 Shows for 2018 While Postponing Five." *The Beat*. Last modified September 29, 2017. http://www.comicsbeat.com/wizard-world-announces-17-shows-for-2018-while-postponing-five/.

Mack, Mike. "Looking Back at Marvel's Phase 3 Announcement and All the Changes That Have Come Since." Insidethemagic.net. Last modified April 30, 2018. https://insidethemagic.net/2018/04/looking-back-at-marvels-phase-3-announcement-and-all-the-changes-that-have-come-since/.

Maglio, Tony. "'Big Bang Theory': The Out-of-This-World TV Ratings." The Wrap. Last modified May 4, 2016. http://www.thewrap.com/big-bang-theory-tv-ratings-season-9-finale-cbs/.

Makarushka, Andrew. "Comics Connoisseurs Here for Golden State Convention." *San Diego Union*, August 2, 1970, B11.

Maloney, Devon, Andrew Liptak, and Dami Lee. "Purge Supplies, Clone Wars Tears, and Shrimp Cocktail Carousels: The Best Things We Saw at San Diego Comic-Con 2018." The Verge. Last modified July 23, 2018. https://www.theverge.com/2018/7/23/17600864/comic-con-sdcc-2018-activations-purge-good-place.

Marich, Robert. "H'wood Profit Pinch: Is Glass Half Empty . . . ?" *Hollywood Reporter*, November 18, 1993. https://advance.lexis.com/api/document?collection=news&id=urn:contentItem:3SJF-CD10-006P-R341-00000-00&context=1516831.

———. *Marketing to Moviegoers: A Handbook of Strategies and Tactics*. 3rd ed. Carbondale and Edwardsville: Southern Illinois University Press, 2013.

Marsano, William. "Grokking Mr. Spock or May You Never Find a Tribble in Your Chicken Soup." *TV Guide*, March 25, 1972, 16–19.

Marschall, Rick. "Remembrances of Cons Past." In *1984 San Diego Comic-Con*, edited by Jackie Estrada, np. San Diego: San Diego Comic Convention, Inc., 1984.

Martin, Sue, and Pat H. Broeske. "Batmanjuice." *Los Angeles Times*, September 11, 1988, K20.

Martinez, Priscila. "Festivals 2.0: How Branded Activations Are Evolving to Survive." *Forbes*. Last modified February 16, 2018. https://www.forbes.com/sites/forbesagencycouncil/2018/02/16/festivals-2-0-how-branded-activations-are-evolving-to-survive/.

"Marvel Entertainment L.L.C." Gale Business Insights: Global. Last modified 2014. http://bi.galegroup.com.proxy.lib.umich.edu/global/company/215489?u=lom_umichanna.

"Marvel's the Avengers." Box Office Mojo. Last modified 2014. http://boxofficemojo.com/movies/?id=avengers11.htm&adjust_yr=2012&p=.htm.

Marx, Karl. *Capital Volume II*. London: Penguin Classics, 1992.

———. *Grundrisse: Foundations of the Critique of Political Economy*. Translated by Martin Nicolaus. London: Penguin Books, 1973.

Mathews, Anna Wilde. "Lord of the Things—Separate Companies Hold Rights to the Products from 'Rings' Books, Films." *Wall Street Journal*, December 17, 2001, B1.

Mayer, Vicki. *Below the Line: Producers and Production Studies in the New Television Economy*. Durham, NC: Duke University Press, 2011.

———. "The Places Where Audience Studies and Production Studies Meet." *Television & New Media* 17, no. 8 (2016): 706–718.

Mayer, Vicki, Miranda J. Banks, and John Thornton Caldwell, eds. *Production Studies: Cultural Studies of Media Industries*. New York: Routledge, 2009.

McAllister, Matthew P. "Ownership Concentration in the U.S. Comic Book Industry." In *Comics and Ideology*, edited by Matthew P. McAllister, Edward H. Sewell Jr., and Ian Gordon, 15–38. New York: Peter Lang, 2001.

McClintock, Pamela. "$200 Million and Rising: Hollywood Struggles with Soaring Marketing Costs." *Hollywood Reporter*. Last modified July 31, 2014. https://www .hollywoodreporter.com/news/200-million-rising-hollywood-struggles-721818.

McCloud, Scott. *Understanding Comics: The Invisible Art*. Northampton, MA: Tundra Pub., 1993.

McDonald, Jeff. "Comic-Con Is Pretty Profitable, for a Non-Profit." *San Diego Union-Tribune*. Last modified July 20, 2016. http://www.sandiegouniontribune.com /news/watchdog/sdut-comic-con-non-profit-2016jul20-story.html.

McDonald, Paul. "Piracy and the Shadow History of Hollywood." In *Hollywood and the Law*, edited by Paul McDonald, Emily Carman, Eric Hoyt, and Philip Drake, 69–101. London: Palgrave, 2015.

McIntyre, Gina. "Fame by Frame." *Hollywood Reporter*, July 30, 2002, 18.

———. "H'wood Presence at Comic-Con Book Outing." *Hollywood Reporter*, August 5, 2002, 13.

McLean, Thomas J. "Comics, H'wood Coalesce." *Daily Variety*, July 23, 2001, 18.

McNary, Dave. "IM Global, Open Road Owner Tang Media Rebrands as Global Road Entertainment." *Variety*. Last modified October 30, 2017. https://variety.com/2017 /film/awards/tang-media-partners-rebrands-global-road-entertainment-1202602536/.

———. "Weinsteins Preview 'Django,' 'Master' in Cannes." *Variety*. Last modified May 21, 2012. http://variety.com/2012/film/news/weinsteins-preview-django -master-in-cannes-1118054431/.

McRobbie, Angela. *Be Creative: Making a Living in the New Culture Industries*. Malden, MA: Polity Press, 2015.

McWeeny, Drew. "Exclusive: Edward Norton Is Not the Hulk in 'the Avengers' . . . but He'd Like to Be." HitFix. Last modified July 9, 2010. http://www.hitfix.com/blogs /motion-captured/posts/exclusive-edward-norton-is-not-the-hulk-in-the-avengers -but-he-d-like-to-be.

Meehan, Eileen. "Commodity Audience, Actual Audience: The Blindspot Debate." In *Illuminating the Blindspots: Essays Honoring Dallas W. Smythe*, edited by Janet Wasko, Vincent Mosco, and Manjunath Pendakur, 378–397. Norwood, NJ: Ablex Publishing Corporation, 1993.

———. "'Holy Commodity Fetish, Batman!': The Political Economy of a Commercial Intertext." In *The Many Lives of Batman*, edited by Roberta E. Pearson and William Uricchio, 47–65. New York: Routledge, 1991.

———. "Leisure or Labor?: Fan Ethnography and Political Economy." In *Consuming Audiences? Production and Reception in Media Research*, edited by Ingunn Hagen and Janet Wasko, 71–92. Cresskill, NJ: Hampton Press, Inc., 2000.

———. "Why We Don't Count: The Commodity Audience." In *Logics of Television: Essays in Cultural Criticism*, edited by Patricia Mellencamp, 117–132. Bloomington: Indiana University Press, 1990.

———. *Why TV Is Not Our Fault: Television Programming, Viewers, and Who's Really in Control*. Critical Media Studies. Lanham, Md.: Rowman & Littlefield, 2005.

"The Meg: Submersive VR Experience." Warner Bros.com. Last modified July 31, 2018. https://www.warnerbros.com/blogs/2018/07/31/meg-submersive-vr-experience.

Meyer, Ziati. "Taco Bell's Nacho Fries Are Rolling Out Nationally." *USA Today*. Last modified January 26, 2018. https://www.usatoday.com/story/money/food/2018/01/26/taco-bells-nacho-fries-rolling-out-nationally/1064884001/.

Miller, Melissa. "You Don't Own Me: The Representation of Twilight Fandom." In *It Happens at Comic-Con: Ethnographic Essays on a Pop Culture Phenomenon*, edited by Ben Bolling and Matthew J. Smith, 63–74. Jefferson, NC: McFarland, 2014.

Monetti, Sandro. "And the Geek Shall Inherit the Earth . . ." *Sunday Express*, July 25, 2010, 3.

Monllos, Kristina. "Taco Bell Made the Perfect Trailer for a Fake Movie about Why They've Never Sold Fries." Adweek. Last modified January 18, 2018. https://www.adweek.com/brand-marketing/taco-bell-made-the-perfect-trailer-for-a-fake-movie-about-why-theyve-never-sold-fries/.

Moor, Elizabeth. "Branded Spaces: The Scope of 'New Marketing.'" *Journal of Consumer Culture* 3, no. 1 (2003): 39–60.

Moran, Joe. *Queuing for Beginners: The Story of Daily Life from Breakfast to Bedtime*. London: Profile, 2007.

———. *Reading the Everyday*. New York: Routledge, 2005.

Moran, Lee. "Aaron Paul's Daughter Wore the Cutest 'Breaking Bad' Costume at Comic-Con." Huffington Post. Last modified July 20, 2018. https://www.huffingtonpost.com/entry/aaron-paul-daughter-breaking-bad-costume-comic-con_us_5b51898de4b0de86f48b8829.

"More 1973 San Diego Comic-Con Photos: Can You Identify People in the Pictures?" Comic-Convention Memories. Last modified February 28, 2010. http://www.comicconmemories.com/2010/02/28/more-1973-san-diego-comic-con-photos-can-you-identify-people-in-the-pictures/.

Moreno, Barbara. "San Diego Convention Center Welcomes Comic-Con 2018 | San Diego Convention Center." San Diego Convention Center. Last modified July 18, 2018. https://visitsandiego.com/2018/07/san-diego-convention-center-welcomes-comic-con-2018.

MTV. "Guillermo Del Toro Provides *Pacific Rim* Trailer Commentary." Comingsoon.net. Last modified December 14, 2012. http://www.comingsoon.net/news/movienews.php?id=98032.

Murphy, Sheila C. *How Television Invented New Media*. New Brunswick, NJ: Rutgers University Press, 2011.

Musgrove, Linda. *The Complete Idiot's Guide to Trade Shows*. New York: Penguin Group, 2009.

Musser, Charles. "Introducing Cinema to the American Public: The Vitascope in the United States, 1896–7." In *Moviegoing in America*, edited by Gregory A. Waller, 13–26. Malden, MA: Blackwell, 2002.

Napoli, Philip M. *Audience Evolution: New Technologies and the Transformation of Media Audiences*. New York: Columbia University Press, 2011.

"New Line Cinema's 'Lord of the Rings: The Fellowship of the Ring' Ignites Marketplace." *PR Newswire*. Published electronically January 15, 2002. http://www.lexisnexis.com/hottopics/lnacademic.

"News for Pacific Rim (2013)." IMDb. Last modified 2019. http://www.imdb.com/title /tt1663662/news?year=2012;start=901.

Nisbett, Gwendelyn S. "Don't Mess with My Happy Place: Understanding Misogyny in Fandom Communities." In *Mediating Misogyny: Gender, Technology, and Harassment*, edited by Jacqueline Ryan Vickery and Tracy Everbach, 171–188. Cham, Switzerland: Springer International Publishing, 2018.

NME. "The Biggest, Best and Most Bonkers Costumes from San Diego's Comic-Con." *NME*. Last modified July 23, 2018. https://www.nme.com/blogs/nme-blogs/the -biggest-best-and-most-bonkers-costumes-from-this-weeks-comic-con-2358141.

Nunziata, Nick. "The Birth of Hype." CNN. Last modified July 27, 2004. http://www .cnn.com/2004/SHOWBIZ/Movies/07/27/comic.con/index.html.

O'Neal, Sean. "Mcdonald's and Taco Bell Rebrand for a Hip, Upscale Audience That Doesn't Eat at McDonald's and Taco Bell." AV Club. Last modified April 25, 2014. https://news.avclub.com/mcdonalds-and-taco-bell-rebrand-for-a-hip-upscale-audi -1798268042.

obsession_inc. "Affirmational Fandom vs. Transformational Fandom." Dreamwidth. Last modified June 1, 2009. https://obsession-inc.dreamwidth.org/82589.html.

Offenberger, Rik. "Comic Book Biography: Pat Broderick." First Comics News. Last modified July 1, 2003. http://www.firstcomicsnews.com/pat-broderick-artist-of-the -future/.

Ohanesian, Liz. "Comic-Con's Twilight Protests: Is There a Gender War Brewing?" *LA Weekly*. Last modified July 28, 2009. http://www.laweekly.com/arts/comic-cons -twilight-protests-is-there-a-gender-war-brewing-2373110.

Orange County Register. "Mini Comic-Con Convention Coming to Anaheim." *Orange County Register*. Last modified September 15, 2011. https://www.ocregister.com /2011/09/15/mini-comic-con-convention-coming-to-anaheim/.

Otto, Jeff. "Comic-Con '12: Quentin Tarantino Wows Hall H Faithful with Bombastic Footage from 'Django Unchained' & More from the Presentation." IndieWire. Last modified July 15, 2012. http://blogs.indiewire.com/theplaylist/comic-con-quentin -tarantino-wows-hall-h-faithful-with-bombastic-footage-from-django-unchained -more-from-the-presentation-20120715.

"Our Shows." ReedPop. Last modified 2018. http://www.reedpop.com/Events/.

Overstreet, Robert M. *The Comic Book Price Guide 1976–1977*. New York: Crown Publishers, 1976.

Parker, Ryan. "Nerdist Removes Chris Hardwick References from Site Amid Chloe Dykstra's Abuse Claim." *Hollywood Reporter*. Last modified June 15, 2018. https:// www.hollywoodreporter.com/news/nerdist-removes-chris-hardwick-references-site -alleged-abuse-claim-1120557.

Pasqua, Mike. "Con-Tact #2." San Diego Comic-Con, Michigan State University Library Comic Art Collection.

Patches, Matt. "Comic-Con 2012: The Web's Most Anticipated SDCC Panels." Hollywood.com. Last modified July 6, 2012. http://www.hollywood.com/news /movies/32970094/comic-con-2012-the-web-s-most-anticipated-sdcc-panels.

Pearson, Ben. "'Demolition Man' 25th Anniversary Pop-up Coming to Comic-Con 2018." SlashFilm. Last modified June 28, 2018. https://www.slashfilm.com /demolition-man-comic-con/.

Pearson, Roberta. "Fandom in the Digital Era." *Popular Communication: The International Journal of Media and Culture* 8, no. 1 (2010): 84–95.

Perry, Tony. "It's a Bird. It's Plain: It's Super." *Los Angeles Times*, July 14, 2005, E4.

Petersen, Lisa Marie. "Demo Derby: Taco Bell, GM Back Sly's New Future Flick." *Brandweek* October 4, 1993, 1.

Peterson, Karla, and James Herbert. "Around Here, the Geeks Decide What's Cool." *San Diego Union-Tribune* July 19, 2006, A1.

Petrakovitz, Caitlin. "Taco Bell's Comic-Con Pop-up Was Delicious and All Thanks to Demolition Man!" cnet.com. Last modified July 20, 2018. https://www.cnet.com /news/taco-bell-comic-con-pop-up-was-delicious-thanks-demolition-man/.

Pine II, Joseph B., and James H. Gilmore. *The Experience Economy*. Boston, MA: Harvard Business Review Press, 2011.

Porter, Jennifer E. "To Boldly Go: *Star Trek* Convention as Pilgrimage." In *Star Trek and Sacred Ground: Explorations of Star Trek, Religion, and American Culture*, edited by Jennifer E. Porter and Darcee L. McLaren, 245–270. Albany, NY: SUNY Press, 1999.

Proctor, William, and Bridget Kies. "Editors' Introduction: On Toxic Fan Practices and the New Culture Wars." *Participations Journal of Audience & Reception Studies* 15, no. 1 (May 2018): 127–142.

Prudom, Laura. "Experience the Good Place in Real Life at Comic-Con with NBC's Interactive Activation." IGN.com. Last modified July 10, 2018. http://www.ign.com /articles/2018/07/10/the-good-place-comic-con-nbc-activation-brooklyn-nine-nine -manifest.

———. "You Too Can Be King in the North with HBO's 'Game of Thrones' Experience at Comic-Con." Mashable. Last modified July 20, 2017. https://mashable.com/2017 /07/20/game-of-thrones-comic-con-2017-winter-is-here-experience/.

Pustz, Matthew. *Comic Book Culture: Fanboys and True Believers*. Studies in Popular Culture. Jackson: University Press of Mississippi, 1999.

Quail, Christine. "Nerds, Geeks, and the Hip/Square Dialectic in Contemporary Television." *Television & New Media* 12, no. 5 (2011): 460–482.

"Quentin Tarantino's Django Unchained" Panel, San Diego Comic-Con, San Diego, CA, July 21, 2012.

Rasmus, Daniel. "Exclusive! The inside Story of Comic-Con's Most Coveted Collectibles." GeekWire. Last modified August 12, 2017. https://www.geekwire.com/2017 /exclusive-inside-story-comic-cons-coveted-collectibles/.

Raugust, Karen. "Lord of Licensing." *Publishers Weekly*, July 2, 2001, 28.

Raviv, Dan. *Comic Wars*. New York: Broadway Books, 2002.

"Recordings of the 1970 San Diego Comic-Con #1: Listen to Them Here!" Comic-Convention Memories. Last modified January 8, 2010. http://www .comicconmemories.com/2010/01/08/recordings-of-the-1970-san-diego-comic-con -1-listen-to-them-here/.

Rehak, Bob. *More Than Meets the Eye*. New York: New York University Press, 2018.

Reinhard, Carrielynn D. *Fractured Fandoms: Contentious Communication in Fan Communities*. London: Rowman & Littlefield, 2018.

"Retailer Programs." Comic-Con.org. Last modified July 6, 2017. https://www.comic -con.org/cci/retailer-programs.

Reynolds, Simon. "Guillermo Del Toro "Strong-Armed" into 'Pacific Rim' 3D Conversion." Digital Spy. Last modified September 13, 2012. http://www.digitalspy .com/movies/news/a405796/guillermo-del-toro-strong-armed-into-pacific-rim-3d -conversion.html.

Richards, Katie. "Ads Go Hollywood: Why Brands Are Faking Out Consumers with Campaigns Disguised as Movie Trailers." *Adweek*, March 5, 2018, 10.

Robb, Brian J. "The Man Who Sold Star Wars." *Star Wars Insider*, January/February 2008, 28–9.

Rodgers, Terry. "City's Old Convention Center Has New Owner." *San Diego Union-Tribune*, Sunday, August 1, 1993, B1.

Rodrick, Stephen. "The Trouble with Johnny Depp." *Rolling Stone*. Last modified June 21, 2018. https://www.rollingstone.com/movies/movie-features/the-trouble -with-johnny-depp-666010/.

Rodrigues, Tanya. "San Diego's Reworked Convention Center Set to Debut." *Orange County Business Journal* 24, no. 34 (August 20–26, 2001): 31. Rogers, Mark C. "License Farming and the American Comic Book Industry." *International Journal of Comic Arts* (Fall 1999): 132–142.

Romero, McKenzie. "Salt Lake Comic Con Seeks Balance in Its 5-Year Anniversary." *Deseret News*. Last modified September 29, 2017. https://www.deseretnews.com/article /865689520/Salt-Lake-Comic-Con-seeks-balance-in-its-5-year-anniversary.html.

Rowe, Peter. "Comic-Con Confidential: Throwing a Pop Culture Blowout with $16 Million, 4,500 Volunteers, 62 Buses, Various Hollywood A-Listers and 'Rock Stars.'" *San Diego Union-Tribune*. Last modified July 15, 2018. http://www.sandiego uniontribune.com/entertainment/comic-con/sd-me-comiccon-planning-20180621 -story.html.

———. "Decoding the Con's Secret Power While Movie and TV Stars Grab Most of the Attention, Fans' Passions Are Served by Narrowly Focused Panels." *San Diego Union-Tribune*, July 11, 2012, A1.

———. "From Little Shows Big Cons Grow." *San Diego Union-Tribune*. Last modified July 19, 2009. http://www.sandiegouniontribune.com/sdut-lz1a19comicco0181351 -little-shows-big-cons-grow-2009jul19-htmlstory.html.

———. "Ken Krueger; Ocean Beach Bookstore Was Launching Pad for Comic-Con." *San Diego Union-Tribune*. Last modified November 26, 2009. http://www .utsandiego.com/news/2009/nov/26/ocean-beach-bookstore-was-launching-pad -comic-con/.

Rozanski, Chuck. "San Diego Comic Con Report #2." Mile High Comics. Last modified July 25, 2014. http://www.milehighcomics.com/newsletter/072514email.html.

———. "San Diego Comic Con Report #3." Mile High Comics. Last modified July 26, 2014. http://www.milehighcomics.com/newsletter/072614wemail.html.

———. "San Diego Update—Thursday, July 18, 2001—Mile High Comics." Mile High Comics. Last modified July 18, 2001. http://www.milehighcomics.com/sdcc071801 .html.

"Rumors Confirmed: Taco Bell Release Nacho Fries." TacoBell.com. Last modified January 3, 2018. https://www.tacobell.com/news/rumors-confirmed-taco-bell-sets -release-date-for-nacho-fries?selectedTag=&selectYear=2018.

Russel, Gary. *The Art of the Fellowship of the Ring*. Boston: Houghton Mifflin, 2002.

Rutz, Jeremy. "I Am Hall H: A Guide to the Biggest Stage at Comic-Con." SDCC Unofficial Blog. Last modified June 3, 2013. http://sdccblog.com/2013/06/i-am-hall -h-a-guide-to-the-biggest-stage-at-comic-con/.

Ryan, Maureen. "Only Connect: The Appeal of San Diego Comic-Con—the Watcher." *Chicago Tribune*. Last modified 9 July 2009, 2012. http://featuresblogs .chicagotribune.com/entertainment_tv/2009/07/san-diego-comiccon.html.

Saar, Marav. "'Star Wars' Preview Becomes the Main Attraction // Movies: Fans Pay Full Price Just to See a Teaser to the Upcoming Prequel to the Hit Series." *Orange County Register*, November 18, 1998, A01.

Salkowitz, Rob. "'Comic Con' Trademark Battle Escalates as Trial Looms." *Forbes*. Last modified June 30, 2017. https://www.forbes.com/sites/robsalkowitz/2017/06/30 /comic-con-trademark-battle-escalates-as-trial-looms/.

———. *Comic-Con and the Business of Popular Culture*. New York: McGraw-Hill, 2012.

———. "From Rebels to Empire: How Reedpop Is Taking Fan Conventions Global." *Forbes*. Last modified April 14, 2017. https://www.forbes.com/sites/robsalkowitz /2017/04/14/in-the-galaxy-of-fan-conventions-the-force-is-strong-with-this-one/.

———. "How ECCC, 2018's First Mega Fan Con, Keeps Getting Bigger without Going over the Top." *Forbes*. Last modified March 1, 2018. https://www.forbes.com/sites /robsalkowitz/2018/03/01/how-eccc-2018s-first-mega-fan-con-keeps-getting-bigger -without-going-over-the-top/.

———. "How San Diego Comic-Con Became Fandom's Super-Brand." *Forbes*. Last modified July 1, 2016. https://www.forbes.com/sites/robsalkowitz/2016/07/01/the -business-of-comic-con-sdccs-david-glanzer-on-branding-and-expanding/.

———. "Jury Decides for San Diego Comic-Con in Trademark Suit." *Forbes*. Last modified December 8, 2017. https://www.forbes.com/sites/robsalkowitz/2017/12 /08/breaking-jury-decides-for-san-diego-comic-con-in-12m-trademark-suit/.

Salter, Anastasia, and Bridget Blodgett. *Toxic Geek Masculinity in Media: Sexism, Trolling, and Identity Policing*. Cham, Switzerland: Springer International Publishing, 2017.

"San Diego Comic Con International." Trademark Electronic Search System (TESS). Last modified 2005. http://tmsearch.uspto.gov/bin/showfield?f=doc&state =4805:wgqhhw.3.78.

"San Diego Comic Convention." ProPublica. Last modified 2018. https://projects .propublica.org/nonprofits/.

San Diego Comic Convention Inc. "Articles of Incorporation of San Diego Comic Convention." August 4, 1975, Series VII: Comic-Con Committee Paperwork, Folder 12, Box 3, Shel Dorf Collection, San Diego History Center.

———. *Comic-Con: 40 Years of Artists, Writers, Fans & Friends*. San Francisco: Chronicle Books, 2009.

San Diego Comic Convention v Dan Farr Productions, No. 14-cv-1865 AJB (JMA) (2017).

"San Diego Comic-Con 1974 Program Schedule." Series IV: Comic Con Advertising, Folder 1, Box 3, Shel Dorf Collection, San Diego History Center.

"San Diego Comic-Con Program Book 1973." Series I: Programs & Souvenir Books, Folder 4, Box 1, Shel Dorf Collection, San Diego History Center.

"San Diego Comic-Con Progress Report No. 1 1973." Series III: Progress Reports and Newsletters, Folder 1, Box 1, Shel Dorf Collection, San Diego History Center.

San Diego Convention Center Corporation. "Facility Guide." San Diego Convention Center. Last modified 2018. https://visitsandiego.com/facility/facility-guide.

"San Diego's Golden State Comic-Con Flyer, 1970." Series IV: Comic-Con Advertising, Folder 1, Box 3, Shel Dorf Collection, San Diego History Center.

"San Diego's Golden State Comic-Con Program Book 1970." August 1970, Series I: Programs & Souvenir Books, Folder 1, Box 1, Shel Dorf Collection, San Diego History Center.

"San Diego's Golden State Comic-Con Program Book (Minicon)." March 21, 1970, Series I: Programs and Souvenir Books, Folder 1, Box 1, Shel Dorf Collection, San Diego History Center.

"San Diego's Golden State Comic-Minicon Flyer." Series IV: Comic-Con Advertising, Folder 1, Box 3, Shel Dorf Collection, San Diego History Center.

Sansweet, Steve. "Which Came First . . ." In *San Diego Comic-Con International 2007 Souvenir Book*, edited by David Glanzer, 59–60. San Diego: San Diego Comic-Con 2007.

Santo, Avi. *Selling the Silver Bullet: The Lone Ranger and Transmedia Brand Licensing.* Austin: University of Texas Press, 2015.

Sassaman, Gary, ed. *Comic-Con International 2018 Quick Guide*. San Diego: San Diego Comic Convention, 2018.

Sassaman, Gary, and Laura Jones. *Comic-Con International 2017 Quick Guide.* San Diego: San Diego Comic Convention, 2017.

Schatz, Thomas. "The New Hollywood." In *Film Theory Goes to the Movies*, edited by Jim Collins, Hilary Radner, and Ava Collins, 8–36. New York: Routledge, 1993.

Schelly, Bill. "A Brief History of *Alter Ego* (the magazine)." Bill Schelly, Writer. Last modified 2014. http://www.billschelly.net/alter-ego/.

———. *Founders of Comic Fandom: Profiles of 90 Publishers, Dealers, Collectors, Writers, Artists and Other Luminaries of the 1950s and 1960s*. Jefferson, NC: McFarland, 2010.

———. *Sense of Wonder: A Life in Comic Fandom*. Raleigh, NC: TwoMorrows Publishing, 2001.

Schelly, William. *The Golden Age of Comic Fandom*. Seattle: Hamster Press, 1995.

Schneller, Johanna. "Pradas Woo the Pocket Protectors." *Globe and Mail*, August 20, 2004, R1.

Scholz, Trebor, ed. *Digital Labor: The Internet as Playground and Factory*. New York: Routledge, 2013.

Schwartz, Barry. "Waiting, Exchange, and Power: The Distribution of Time in Social Systems." *American Journal of Sociology* 79, no. 4 (1974): 841–870.

Schwartz, Julius. "Introduction by Julius Schwartz." In *Alter Ego: The Best of the Legendary Comics Fanzine*, edited by Roy Thomas and Jerry Bails, 3–4. Raleigh, NC: TwoMorrows Publishing, 2008.

Schwartz, Malcolm, and Shel Dorf. "Shel Dorf Q&A." In *1982 San Diego Comic-Con, Inc. Souvenir Book*, edited by Shel Dorf, np. San Diego: San Diego Comic-Con Inc., 1982.

Sciretta, Peter. "The Best of Comic-Con: The Coolest and Most Important Moments in Hall H History." SlashFilm. Last modified July 19, 2017. http://www.slashfilm.com/best-comic-con-moments-of-all-time/3/.

Sconce, Jeffrey. "Irony, Nihilism, and the New American 'Smart' Film." *Screen* 43, no. 4 (2002): 349–369.

Scott, Suzanne. " 'Cosplay Is Serious Business': Gendering Material Fan Labor on Heroes of Cosplay." *Cinema Journal* 54, no. 3 (2015): 146–154.

———. "Dawn of the Undead Author: Fanboy Auteurism and Zack Snyder's 'Vision.' " In *A Companion to Media Authorship*, edited by Jonathan Gray and Derek Johnson, 440–462. Malden, MA: Wiley-Blackwell, 2013.

———. "The Powers That Squee: Orlando Jones and Intersectional Fan Studies." In *Fandom: Identities and Communities in a Mediated World*, edited by Jonathan Gray, Cornel Sandvoss, and C. Lee Harrington, 387–399. New York: New York University Press, 2017.

——. "Repackaging Fan Culture: The Regifting Economy of Ancillary Content Models." *Transformative Works and Cultures* 3 (2009). https://journal .transformativeworks.org/index.php/twc/article/view/150.

——. "Revenge of the Fanboy: Convergence Culture and the Politics of Incorporation." PhD diss., University of Southern California, 2011.

——. "#Wheresrey?: Toys, Spoilers, and the Gender Politics of Franchise Paratexts." *Critical Studies in Media Communication* 34, no. 2 (2017): 138–147.

Scroggy, Dave. "Comic Book Expo '91." San Diego: San Diego Comic-Con, Inc., 1991.

Sharkey, Betsy. "Have the Geeks Ceded Control?" *Los Angeles Times*, July 18, 2010, D4.

Shaw!, Scott. "Cartoonist-at-Large #1: The "Secret Origin" of San Diego' Comic-Con International." Jim Hill Media. Last modified July 7, 2005. http://jimhillmedia.com /blogs/scott_shaw/archive/2005/07/07/1717.aspx.

Sheffield, Jessica, and Elyse Merlo. "Biting Back: Twilight Anti-Fandom and the Rhetoric of Superiority." In *Bitten by Twilight: Youth Culture, Media & the Vampire Franchise*, edited by Melissa A. Click, Jennifer Stevens Aubrey, and Elizabeth Behm-Morawitz, 207–222. New York: Peter Lang, 2010.

Shefrin, Elana. "Lord of the Rings, Star Wars, and Participatory Fandom: Mapping New Congruencies between the Internet and Media Entertainment Culture." *Critical Studies in Media Communications* 21, no. 3 (2007): 261–281.

Showalter, Elaine. "Hysteria, Feminism, and Gender." In *Hysteria Beyond Freud*, edited by Sander L. Gilman, Helen King, Roy Porter, G. S. Rousseau, and Elaine Showalter, 286–344. Berkeley: University of California Press, 1993.

Singer, Matt. "Critics React to 7 Minutes of 'Django Unchained' at Cannes." IndieWire. Last modified May 21, 2012. http://blogs.indiewire.com/criticwire/critics-react-to-7 -minutes-of-django-unchained-at-cannes.

Smith, Kerry, and Dan Hanover. *Experiential Marketing: Secrets, Strategies, and Success Stories from the World's Greatest Brands*. Hoboken, NJ: Wiley, 2016.

Smith, Matthew J. "Comic-Con International." In *Icons of the American Comic Book: From Captain America to Wonder Woman*, edited by Randy Duncan and Matthew J. Smith, 136–142. Santa Barbara, CA: ABC-CLIO, 2013.

Smythe, Dallas W. "Communications: Blindspot of Western Marxism." *Canadian Journal of Political and Social Theory* 1, no. 3 (1977): 1–27.

——. *Dependency Road: Communications, Capitalism, Consciousness, and Canada*. Norwood, NJ: Ablex, 1981.

"Souvenir Book." Comic-Con International: San Diego. Last modified 2018. https:// www.comic-con.org/cci/souvenir-book.

Spector, Josh. "Hollywood Shows Its Stuff, Courts Crowd at Comic-Con." *Hollywood Reporter*, July 21, 2003, 2.

Sperling, Nicole. "Comic-Con 2011: 'Twilight' Cast Surprises Fans with Breakfast." *Los Angeles Times*: Hero Complex. Last modified July 21, 2011. http://herocomplex .latimes.com/2011/07/21/comic-con-2011-twilight-cast-surprises-fans-with -breakfast/.

——. "Comic-Con 2012: Tarantino's 'Django Unchained' Shocks, Awes." *Los Angeles Times*. Last modified July 14, 2012. http://articles.latimes.com/2012/jul/14 /entertainment/la-et-mn-comiccon-2012-quentin-tarantino-shocks-and-awes-with -new-django-unchained-footage-20120714.

Spurgeon, Tom. "Jerry Bails, 1933–2006." *The Comics Reporter*. Last modified November 24, 2006. http://www.comicsreporter.com/index.php/jerry_bails_1933_2006/.

———. "Nerd Vegas; a Guide to Visiting and Enjoying CCI in San Diego, 2008! (Final Version)." *The Comics Reporter*. Last modified May 27, 2008. http://www .comicsreporter.com/index.php/briefings/commentary/14163/.

Stadler, Mark, ed. *1981 San Diego Comic-Con Souvenir Book*. San Diego: San Diego Comic-Con, Inc., 1981.

———. "San Diego Comic-Con Progress Report No. 1." February, 1987, San Diego Comic-Con, Michigan State University Library Comic Art Collection.

———, ed. *San Diego Comic-Con Progress Report No. 2*. San Diego: San Diego Comic Convention, Inc., 1988.

———, ed. *San Diego Comic-Con Souvenir Book 1980*. San Diego: San Diego Comic Convention, Inc., 1980.

Staff, MTV News. "Johnny Depp, Tim Burton Preview 'Alice in Wonderland' at Comic-Con." MTV News. Last modified July 23, 2009. http://www.mtv.com/news/articles /1616846/johnny-depp-tim-burton-preview-alice-wonderland-at-comic-con.jhtml.

Staff, StarTrek.com. "Bjo Trimble: The Woman Who Saved Star Trek—Part 1." StarTrek .com. Last modified August 31, 2011. http://www.startrek.com/article/bjo-trimble -the-woman-who-saved-star-trek-part-1.

Stanfill, Mel. "View of Doing Fandom, (Mis)Doing Whiteness: Heteronormativity, Racialization, and the Discursive Construction of Fandom." *Transformative Works and Cultures* 8 (2011). http://journal.transformativeworks.org/index.php/twc /article/view/256/243.

Stanfill, Mel, and Megan Condis. "Fandom and/as Labor." *Transformative Works and Cultures* 15 (2014). https://journal.transformativeworks.org/index.php/twc/article /view/593.

"*Star Wars: The Force Awakens* Products to Arrive on 'Force Friday,' September 4." StarWars.com. Last modified May 3, 2015. https://www.starwars.com/news/star -wars-the-force-awakens-products-to-arrive-on-force-friday-september-4.

Stedman, Alex, and Brent Lang. "Johnny Depp, Amber Heard Appear Moments Apart at WB's Comic-Con Panel." *Variety*. Last modified July 21, 2018. https://variety.com /2018/film/news/johnny-depp-amber-heard-comic-con-1202880368/.

Steinberg, Brian. "Taco Bell Eyes Sequel for Movie-Trailer Ads Touting Nacho Fries." *Variety*. Last modified March 29, 2018. https://variety.com/2018/tv/news/taco-bell -nacho-fries-movie-advertising-sequel-1202739155/.

Stewart, Andrew. "AMC, Regal Hit Open Road." *Variety*. Last modified March 7, 2011. http://variety.com/2011/film/news/amc-regal-hit-open-road-1118033459/.

Stoddard, Bill, ed. *1990 San Diego Comic-Con Events Guide*. San Diego: San Diego Comic Convention, Inc., 1990.

Stoddard, Bill, and Janet Tait, eds. *1991 San Diego Comic-Con Convention Events Guide*. San Diego: San Diego Comic Convention, Inc., 1991.

Stone, Alex. "Why Waiting Is Torture." *New York Times*. Last modified August 18, 2012. http://www.nytimes.com/2012/08/19/opinion/sunday/why-waiting-in-line-is -torture.html.

Stone, Ken. "Nonprofit Comic-Con Reports Nearly $10 Million Cash in the Bank." LemonGrovePatch. Last modified March 26, 2012. http://lemongrove.patch.com /articles/comic-conwith-net-assets-of-7-millionpays-city-no-business-license-fees.

Strömberg, Fredrik. "Robbins, Trina." In *Comics through Time: A History of Icons, Idols, and Ideas*, edited by M. Keith Booker, 750–751. Santa Barbara, CA: ABC-CLIO, 2014.

Sullivan, Kevin P. "San Diego Comic-Con Winners and Losers." MTV. Last modified July 16, 2012. http://www.mtv.com/news/articles/1689682/comic-con-2012-recap .jhtml.

"Superfans and Batmaniacs." *Newsweek*, February 15, 1965, 89–90.

SYFY Wire Staff. "Watch: Here's What We're Doing for San Diego Comic-Con 2018." SYFY Wire. Last modified July 15, 2018. http://www.syfy.com/syfywire/watch -heres-what-were-doing-for-san-diego-comic-con-2018.

"Taco Bell's Nacho Fries Are Coming Back to Reveal the Future Demolition Man Predicted." TacoBell.com. Last modified June 28, 2018. https://www.tacobell.com /news/taco-bells-nacho-fries-are-coming-back?selectedTag=&selectYear=2018.

Tait, Janet, ed. *1988 San Diego Comic-Con Events Guide*. San Diego: San Diego Comic Convention, Inc., 1988.

———, ed. *1994 San Diego Comic-Con Events Guide*. San Diego: Comic-Con International, 1994.

———, ed. *1997 Comic-Con International Events Guide*. San Diego: Comic-Con International, Inc., 1997.

———, ed. *Comic-Con International Update 1*. San Diego: San Diego Comic Convention, 1995.

———. "San Diego Comic-Con Convention Events Guide 1987." 1987, San Diego Comic-Con, Michigan State University Library Comic Art Collection.

Tamagawa, Hiroaki. "Comic Market as a Space for Self-Expression in Otaku Culture." In *Fandom Unbound: Otaku Culture in a Connected World*, edited by Mizuko Ito, Daisuke Okabe, and Izumi Tsiju, 107–132. New Haven, CT: Yale University Press, 2012.

Tankel, Jonathan David, and Keith Murphy. "Collecting Comic Books: A Study of the Fan and Curatorial Consumption." In *Theorizing Fandom*, edited by Cheryl Harris and Alison Alexander, 55–68. Cresskill, NJ: Hampton Press, 1998.

Tatro, Samantha. "San Diego Comic-Con '18 Full Schedule: Panels You Can't Miss." 4 New York. Last modified July 10, 2018. http://www.nbcnewyork.com/entertainment /entertainment-news/San-Diego-Comic-Con-2018-Announces-Full-Schedule -Thursday-Friday-Saturday-Sunday-Highlights-Panels-Celebrities-Hall-H -487686031.html.

Taylor, Chris. "Target Wants You to Fill the Internet with Galaxies Full of Star Wars Memories." Mashable. Last modified August 25, 2015. https://mashable.com/2015 /08/25/share-the-force/ - I2ZyEluDLOq8.

Taylor, Kate. "Instagram Powers Taco Bell's Innovation Machine—and It's Completely Changing the Fast-Food Menu as We Know It." *Business Insider*. Last modified April 26, 2017. https://www.businessinsider.com/instagram-powers-taco-bells -innovation-2017-4.

Terranova, Tiziana. "Free Labor." In *Digital Labor: The Internet as Playground and Factory*, edited by Trebor Scholz, 33–57. New York: Routledge, 2013.

———. "Free Labor: Producing Culture for the Digital Economy." *Social Text* 18, no. 2 (Summer 2000): 33–58.

Tester, Jobs. "The Line Has Begun for Breaking Dawn Comic-Con Panel." *Twilight-Stars-in*. Last modified July 19, 2011. http://twilightstars-in.blogspot.com/2011/07 /line-has-begun-for-breaking-dawn-comic.html.

Thomas, Roy. "How I Learned to Stop Worrying & Love 'Star Wars' (within Limits)." *Starlog*, July 1987, 26–29.

Thompson, Anne. "Tarantino and 'Django Unchained' Gang Hit Comic-Con: How Serious Is This Movie." IndieWire. Last modified July 16, 2012. http://blogs .indiewire.com/thompsononhollywood/tarantino-and-django-unchained-gang-hit -comic-con.

Thompson, Kristin. *Frodo Franchise: The Lord of the Rings and Modern Hollywood.* Berkeley: University of California Press, 2007.

Thompson, Maggie. "Fanzine Library: Comic Art #1 (Spring 1961)." The Official Website of Maggie Thompson. Last modified August 8, 2010. http://www .maggiethompson.com/1970/01/fanzine-library-comic-art-1-spring-1961.html.

———. "June 23, 1962." The Official Website of Maggie Thompson. Last modified June 23, 2008. http://www.maggiethompson.com/2008/06/june-23-1962.html.

Thornton, Sarah. *Club Cultures: Music, Media, and Subcultural Capital.* Music/ Culture. 1st U.S. ed. Hanover: University Press of New England, 1996.

THR staff. "Comic-Con 2011: Warner Bros. to Create Limited Edition Key Cards for Comic-Con Hotels." *Hollywood Reporter.* Last modified June 29, 2011. https://www .hollywoodreporter.com/live-feed/comic-con-2011-warner-bros-206939.

Tobenkin, David. "Promotion 'Man': How Producers Squeezed 99-Cent Burritos and Detroit Wheels into the Futuristic Stallone-Snipes Saga." *Hollywood Reporter,* October 4, 1993, S-6.

Tompkins, Eric. *The Non-Geeks Guide to Comic-Con.* Lexington, KY: Eric Tompkins, 2012.

Towry, Mike. "The Birthplace of Comic-Con International." Comic-Convention Memories. Last modified February 15, 2010. http://www.comicconmemories.com /2010/02/15/the-birthplace-of-comic-con-international/.

———. "The Most Important Ads in Comic-Con History." Comic-Convention Memories. Last modified April 21, 2010. http://www.comicconmemories.com/2010 /04/21/the-most-important-ads-in-comic-con-history/.

———. "Welcome to Comic-Convention Memories." Comic-Convention Memories. Last modified December 10, 2009. http://www.comicconmemories.com/2009/12 /10/welcome-to-comic-convention-memories/.

Trumbore, Dave. "Comic-Con 2011 Collectible Swag Bags Revealed; Will Double as Backpacks." Collider. Last modified July 12, 2011. http://collider.com/comic-con -collectible-bags-warner-bros/.

———. "San Diego Comic-Con 2011 Badges Sell out in Less Than a Day." Collider. Last modified February 6, 2011. http://collider.com/san-diego-comic-con-2011 -badges-sell-out/74799/.

Tulman, Steven. "How Taco Bell Is Winning at Social Media Marketing." Business 2 Community. Last modified July 25, 2017. https://www.business2community.com /social-media/taco-bell-winning-social-media-marketing-01887555.

Turner, Victor W. *The Ritual Process: Structure and Anti-Structure.* Chicago: Aldine Publishing Company, 1966.

Turow, Joseph. "The Case for Studying in-Store Media." *Media Industries* 1, no. 1 (January 1, 2014), 62–68.

Twilight Lexicon. "Tales from the Twilight Comic Con Line: Tuesday Version." Twilight Lexicon. Last modified July 20, 2011, 2011. http://www.twilightlexicon .com/2011/07/20/tales-from-the-twilight-comic-con-line-tuesday-version/.

Tyler, Josh. "Comic Con: August 21 Is Avatar Day." cinemablend.com. Last modified July 23, 2009. http://www.cinemablend.com/new/Comic-Con-August-21-Is-Avatar -Day-14060.html.

United States Copyright Office. "Works Made for Hire." copyright.gov. Last modified September, 2012. http://www.copyright.gov/circs/circo9.pdf.

"Universal Interactive, Inc." Giant Bomb. Last modified 2014. http://www.giantbomb .com/universal-interactive-inc/3010-124/published/.

Valenzuela, Beatriz. "How the Security Team at Comic-Con Works to Keep Fans Safe." *Los Angeles Daily News.* Last modified July 16, 2016. http://www.dailynews.com /arts-and-entertainment/20160716/how-the-security-team-at-comic-con-works-to -keep-fans-safe.

Valerie. "Reedpop on the SDCC–SLCC Lawsuit." Comic Con Guide. Last modified December 11, 2018. http://www.comicconguide.com/2017/12/nycc-and-other -reedpop-events-will-stay.html.

VanDerWerff, Todd. "Comic-Con, Day 3: Lines, Lines, Everywhere Lines." A.V. Club. Last modified July 24, 2011. http://www.avclub.com/articles/comiccon-day-3-lines -lines-everywhere-lines,59389/.

———. "A Day inside Comic-Con's Hall H: Worshiping in the Ultimate Movie Church." Grantland. Last modified July 22, 2013. http://grantland.com/hollywood-prospectus /a-day-inside-comic-cons-hall-h-worshipping-in-the-ultimate-movie-church/.

Vargas-Cooper, Natasha. "Johnny Depp Crashes Comic-Con—Then Splits!" E! Last modified July 23, 2009. http://www.eonline.com/news/135572/johnny-depp-crashes -comic-con-then-splits.

Vejvoda, Jim. "Comic-Con: Pacific Rim Brings Giant Monsters and Robots." IGN.com. Last modified July 14, 2012. http://www.ign.com/articles/2012/07/14/comic-con -pacific-rim-brings-giant-monsters-and-robots.

Ventura, Patricia. *Neoliberal Culture: Living with American Neoliberalism.* Burlington, VT: Ashgate Publishing, 2012.

Vivarelli, Nick. "Italy's Lucca Comics and Games Festival Celebrates 50 Years." *Variety.* Last modified October 28, 2016. https://variety.com/2016/biz/festivals/italys-lucca -comics-and-games-festival-celebrates-15-years-1201900452/.

———. "Lucca Comics & Games Festival Draws Hollywood Majors to Geek Mecca." *Variety.* Last modified October 29, 2015. https://variety.com/2015/scene/festivals /lucca-comics-games-festival-anime-manga-mamoru-oshii-1201628884/.

Walansky, Aly. "Fry Fans Rejoice! Taco Bell Rolling Out Spicy Fries for Just $1." *Today.* Last modified January 3, 2018. https://www.today.com/food/taco-bell-adds-french -fries-menu-1-t120750?cid=sm_npd_td_tw_ma.

Wallace, Lewis. "Giant Galactus Is Hasbro's Biggest Comic-Con Exclusive." *Wired.* Last modified July 13, 2010. http://www.wired.com/underwire/2010/07/hasbro -comic-con/.

Wallenstein, Andrew. "Kevin Tsujihara Breaks Silence on Why Legendary, WB Parted Ways." *Variety.* Last modified October 5, 2013. http://variety.com/2013/film/news /kevin-tsujihara-breaks-silence-on-why-legendary-wb-parted-ways-1200697794/.

Wanzo, Rebecca. "View of African American Acafandom and Other Strangers: New Genealogies of Fan Studies." *Transformative Works and Cultures* 20 (2015). http:// journal.transformativeworks.org/index.php/twc/article/view/699/538.

"Warner Bros. Pictures and Legendary Pictures Preview Their Upcoming Lineups." Panel, San Diego Comic-Con, San Diego, July 21, 2012.

Warner, Kristen J. "ABC's Scandal and Black Women's Fandom." In *Cupcakes, Pinterest, and Ladyporn: Feminized Popular Culture in the Early Twenty-First Century,* edited by Elana Levine, 32–50. Urbana, IL: University of Illinois Press, 2015.

———. *The Cultural Politics of Colorblind TV Casting*. New York: Routledge, 2015.

Warren, Caleb, and Gina S. Mohr. "Ironic Consumption." *Journal of Consumer Research* (July 27, 2018). doi:10.1093/jcr/ucy065, https://doi.org/10.1093/jcr/ucy065.

Wasko, Janet, and Eileen Meehan. "Critical Crossroads or Parallel Routes? Political Economy and New Approaches to Studying Media Industries and Cultural Products." *Cinema Journal* 52, no. 3 (2013): 150–157.

Watercutter, Angela. "At Comic-Con This Year, the Biggest Stars Were the Moderators." *Wired*. Last modified July 25, 2017. https://www.wired.com/story/comic-con-moderators/.

Weintraub, Steve 'Frosty'. "Guillermo Del Toro Talks Pacific Rim Soundtrack and Collectables." Collider. Last modified August 9, 2012. http://collider.com/guillermo-del-toro-pacific-rim-soundtrack-collectables/187592/.

Weisberg, Lori. "Another Speedy Sellout for Comic-Con Badges." *San Diego Union-Tribune*. Last modified February 20, 2016. http://www.sandiegouniontribune.com/news/2016/feb/20/comic-con-badges-sell-out-quickly/.

———. "Comic-Con Wins $4m in Legal Fees in Trademark Battle with Salt Lake City." *San Diego Union-Tribune*. Last modified August 24, 2018. http://www.sandiegouniontribune.com/business/tourism/sd-fi-comiccon-ruling-fees-20180824-story.html.

Weisberg, Lori, and Roger Showley. "Fixing the Con's Cons from Rush to Get Tickets, to Crush in Hall H, Fans Have Plenty of Ideas for Improving Event." *San Diego Union-Tribune*, July 26, 2012, C1.

Wenzel, John. "Denver Comic Con Reveals Record Attendance, Sets 2017 Dates." *Denver Post*. Last modified July 28, 2016. https://www.denverpost.com/2016/07/28/denver-comic-con-2016-attendance-2017-dates/.

West, Kelly. "Ender's Game Comic-Con Fan Experience Displays Futuristic Sets, Flash Suits, Weapons and More." CinemaBlend. Last modified 2013. https://www.cinemablend.com/new/Ender-Game-Comic-Con-Fan-Experience-Displays-Futuristic-Sets-Flash-Suits-Weapons-More-38558.html.

Wigler, Josh. "'Game of Thrones': A Firsthand Account of the Comic-Con 'Winter Is Here' Activation." *Hollywood Reporter*. Last modified July 20, 2017. https://www.hollywoodreporter.com/live-feed/game-thrones-at-comic-con-inside-winter-is-activation-1022888.

Wilding, Josh. "New Images from Guillermo Del Toro's Pacific Rim." ComicBookMovie.Com. Last modified August 30, 2012. http://www.comicbookmovie.com/fansites/JoshWildingNewsAndReviews/news/?a=66529.

Wilke, M, J. "Managing Hotel-Apocalypse for SDCC: 2018 Edition." Wayward Nerd. Last modified 2018. https://www.waywardnerd.com/hotel-apocalypse-.

Wilkens, John. "Comic-Con's Charity Status Draws Questions." *San Diego Union-Tribune*, July 25, 2007, A1.

———. "Comic-Con's Shel Dorf Watches Sadly from the Sidelines as T-Shirts Trump Talent." *San Diego Union-Tribune*, July 16, 2006, E-1.

Williams, Geoff. "Star Wars: The Phantom Menace; Waiting for the Force." *Cincinnati Post*, February 11, 1999.

Williams, Raymond. *Television: Technology and Cultural Form*. Routledge Classics. New York: Routledge, 2003.

Willis, Sharon. "'Style,' Posture, and Idiom: Tarantino's Figures of Masculinity." In *Reinventing Film Studies*, edited by Christine Gledhill and Linda Williams, 279–295. London: Oxford University Press, 2000.

Winge, Theresa M. *Costuming Cosplay: Dressing the Imagination*. London: Bloomsbury Visual Arts, 2019.

Winstead, Nick. "Comic-Con Trailer Park Covers a Wide Spectrum of Films." Comicbook.com. Last modified July 12, 2012. http://comicbook.com/blog/2012 /07/12/comic-con-trailer-park-covers-a-wide-spectrum-of-films/.

Winston, Joan. *The Making of the Trek Conventions*. Chicago: Playboy Press, 1979.

Wloszczyna, Susan, and Ann Oldenburg. "Geek Chic; Nerd Is the Word for Popularity in a Wired World." *USA Today*, October 23, 2003, D1.

Woo, Benjamin. "The Android's Dungeon: Comic-Bookstores, Cultural Spaces, and the Social Practices of Audiences." *Journal of Graphic Novels and Comics* 2, no. 2 (2011): 125–136.

———. "Erasing the Lines between Leisure and Labor: Creative Work in the Comics World." *Spectator* 35, no. 2 (Fall 2015): 57–64.

Woods, Travis. "Comic-Con 2012: Trailer Park Showcases Ads for 'Dredd,' 'Finding Nemo 3d,' and More." Last modified July 12, 2012. http://screencrave.com/2012-07 -12/comiccon-2012-trailer-park-showcases-ads-dredd-finding-nemo-3d/.

Yamato, Jen. "Inside Comic-Con's Hall H, the Most Important Room in Hollywood." *Los Angeles Times*. Last modified July 19, 2017. https://www.latimes.com /entertainment/herocomplex/la-et-hc-comic-con-hall-h-20170719-story.html.

———. "Why Hollywood Marketing Execs Love Comic-Con Activations, from 'the Good Place' To . . . a Sci-Fi Taco Bell from the Future?" *Los Angeles Times*. Last modified July 20, 2018. http://www.latimes.com/entertainment/herocomplex/la -et-hc-comic-con-activations-marketing-20180720-story.html.

Young, John. "Harrison Ford (in Handcuffs!) Makes His First Appearance at Comic-Con for 'Cowboys & Aliens.'" *Entertainment Weekly*. Last modified July 24, 2010. http://popwatch.ew.com/2010/07/24/comic-con-harrison-ford-cowboys-aliens/.

Young, Joseph M. D. "Virtual Ticket Lines Bring Down Comic-Con Site." 7 San Diego. Last modified February 6, 2011. http://www.nbcsandiego.com/news/local /Comc-Con-Ticket-Sales-115373469.html.

Young, Larry, ed. *1995 San Diego Comic Book Convention Events Guide*. San Diego: San Diego Comic Convention Inc., 1995.

Younis, Steve. "Comic-Con 2012—Hall H Intro #1." YouTube. Last modified July 16, 2012. https://www.youtube.com/watch?v=jRtOSwyZNFg.

Zeitchik, Steven. "The Fan Fantasy." *Hollywood Reporter*, August 1–3, 2008, 20–21.

Index

About the Author

ERIN HANNA is an assistant professor of cinema studies at the University of Oregon.